T0139307

MOBILE ENTERPRISE TRANSITION AND MANAGEMENT

OTHER AUERBACH PUBLICATIONS

MOBILE ENTERPRISE TRANSITION AND MANAGEMENT

BHUVAN UNHELKAR

CRC Press
Taylor & Francis Group
Boca Raton   London   New York

CRC Press is an imprint of the
Taylor & Francis Group, an **informa** business
AN AUERBACH BOOK

Auerbach Publications
Taylor & Francis Group
6000 Broken Sound Parkway NW, Suite 300
Boca Raton, FL 33487-2742

International Standard Book Number-13: 978-1-4200-7827-5 (Hardcover)

Library of Congress Cataloging-in-Publication Data

Unhelkar, Bhuvan.
   Mobile enterprise transition and management / Bhuvan Unhelkar.
      p. cm. -- (Advanced and emerging communications technologies series)
   Includes bibliographical references and index.
   ISBN 978-1-4200-7827-5 (hardcover : alk. paper)
      1. Mobile commerce. 2. Mobile communication systems. 3. Wireless communication systems. I. Title.

HF5548.34.U54 2009
658.8'72--dc22
                                                        2008039829

Visit the Taylor & Francis Web site at
http://www.taylorandfrancis.com

and the Auerbach Web site at
http://www.auerbach-publications.com

Chinar and Girish

Contents

12   Case Study: Applying METM to a University for a Sustainable Environment

List of Figures

Glossary of Acronyms in Mobile Domain

Acronym	Full form
AMPS	Advanced Mobile Phone System
CDMA	Code Division Multiple Access
CDMA2000	Code Division Multiple Access 2000
EDGE	Enhanced Data Rates for Global Evolution
GPRS	General Packet Radio Service
GSM	Global System for Mobile Communications
HSCSD	High-Speed Circuit-Switched Data
HSDPA	High-Speed Downlink Packet Access
IEEE 802.11a, b, g	IEEE standard for short-range wireless transmissions
IEEE 802.16	IEEE standard for short-range wireless transmissions—new
IS-95	Interim Standard 95
MWS	Mobile Web Services
NMT	Nordisk MobilTelefoni or Nordiska MobilTelefoni-gruppen, Nordic Mobile Telephony
TACS	Total Access Communication System
TDMA	Time Division Multiple Access
TD-SCDMA	Time Division—Synchronous Code Division Multiple Access

TS-CDMA	Time Synchronous—Code Division Multiple Access
UMTS	Universal Mobile Telecommunications System
WAP	Wireless Access Protocol
W-CDMA	Wideband Code Division Multiple Access
Wi-Fi	Wireless Fidelity
WiMax	Worldwide Interoperability for Microwave Access

Defining Mobility

Mobility: Encompasses all aspects of mobile technologies including its network, security, presentation, contents, and applications, and the use of those technologies to connect the organization to its customers, business partners, and workers, independent of location and time, and with personalization. Mobility is considered here specifically outside the constraining realms of the underlying technology. Thus, it is vital to understand that "mobility" is a way of working, not just a way of using mobile technology. Mobility covers services to a wide variety of mobile users, moving inside and outside of the organization, who are seeking value from the organization. The value from mobility is derived from its economic, technical, process, and social dimensions.

Mobility Terms Definitions

Mobility	In view of this background, *mobility* needs to be considered outside the constraining realms of the underlying technology. It is important to understand that "mobility" *is a way of working, not just a way of utilizing available technology*. Among other areas, mobility must cover those working from home, on the road, in hotels, and at airports as well as those moving around within organizational boundaries. A mobile solution must provide not only the technology to provide access, it must also provide the functionality for the user to add value to the company.
Mobile business	The conduct of business and services over portable wireless devices in a business-to-business (B2B) or a business-to-consumer (B2C) market
Mobile commerce	The transactional part of business activities for purchasing goods and services using mobile technology.
Business processes	Those organizational processes that perform business transactions, whether internal or external to the organization.
Mobile business processes	Business processes in which mobile technology has been used to improve the quality of that process.
Mobile enterprise transition	Changing the business processes of an organization by introducing mobile applications and devices to be used as an integral part of the business processes, to gain specific advantages offered by mobility (Marmaridis and Unhelkar 2005). This change in the business processes is a holistic change that involves changes at the customer side also. The employees are also trained to use mobile applications to take full advantage of the benefits of mobility.
Mobile management	Management of the supply and demand of the mobile technology, enhancing the business processes. The impact of mobile technology on restructuring the organization is also an important aspect of mobile management.

Business unit	Identification of the boundary within which the application of models will be done within the research discussed in this book. This unit could be an entire organization or a part of an organization, such as a separate department, or a self-contained business process.
Competitive advantage	The ability of an organization to perform in one or more ways that competitors cannot or will not (Kotler 2003). Sustainable competitive advantage can be obtained by operational effectiveness, that is, by doing the same things the competitors do in a better way, or by strategic positioning, that is, doing things differently from competitors in a way that delivers unique value to customers (Porter 1980, 2001).
Industry	The overall environment of businesses.
Mobile customers	Users of a mobile device who are prepared to pay for the service.
Mobile employees	Employees who are equipped with a mobile gadget and are themselves mobile (i.e., working both in and out of the office).
Mobile business stakeholders	Individuals both inside and outside of the business who have an interest in the business becoming a mobile business.
MET framework	The framework used is from the economic, technical, process, and social factors applied to examine the institution's capability.

Foreword

The debate (tug-of-war) between technology and business is alive and well. Mobile technologies create dramatic changes to business; and business responds with criticisms or accolades, depending on the results achieved. Let us face it—technology is hardly ever to blame if things go wrong! The *way in which* technology is used by the business provides the core value of technology. Mobile technologies, in particular are challenging to business; the mobile devices are perpetually shrinking in size, and the mobile networks are invisible. Yet, the changes to business and society caused by mobile technologies are breathtaking and, at times, surreal. Messages go back and forth over wireless networks through you, me, and the *billion* people who use them and the rest who don't. The success of mobile technologies in business, however, is unlikely to be decided by whatever consumer appeal is added to the upcoming mobile devices, or the trailblazing speed of the ever-widening cellular bandwidths, or the rapidly changing and enriched mobile contents. These factors are all necessary but not sufficient for the success of mobility. The future and the success of mobile technologies will be decided by *how* business *uses* those technologies. So how can a business use mobile technologies?

The answer is judiciously presented in the ensuing pages of this excellent work by Dr. Unhelkar. The title itself, *Mobile Enterprise Transition and Management (METM)*, aptly reflects its theme. This book provides a systematic exposition of the strategic use of mobile technologies in *all* aspects of business.

More than a decade ago, in *Rise and Resurrection of the American Programmer*, I highlighted the key differentiators between successful and unsuccessful software development and deployment projects. These key differentiators are the use of "best practices." The best practice key differentiator is equally true with the METM project, and I can see it being applied astutely throughout this book. Its carefully crafted approach intertwines the wide and varying dimensions of economy, technology, process, and sociology in a comprehensive and cohesive approach, ensuring successful transitions to and management of mobile businesses. The METM framework presented here by Unhelkar fine-tunes and balances the aforementioned four dimensions of a business with step-by-step and meticulously crafted activities that are validated through research. The sequencing of the various activities during enactment of the process in practice is also based on substantial research. The author's analysis of each of the survey data throws light on the relative importance and sequencing of these various factors in METM.

In *Death March,* I had the opportunity to highlight the phenomenal importance of politics in every software project. Needless to say, the importance of politics holds true in *every* project. *Mobile Enterprise Transition and Management* covers this all-important social aspect of the project quite adroitly in Chapters 6 and 7. Chapter 7, in particular, demonstrates the enactment of a project and goes boldly into the sociocultural issues within the project.

Finally, technology has an ongoing responsibility toward society. There is ample demonstration of that approach to responsibility in this book through Chapters 9 and 12 on sustainability and environmental responsibility.

Here, Dr. Unhelkar does not simply espouse theory. The entire approach not only has a solid foundation in research, but case studies demonstrate how his METM framework work is applied.

This book is an invaluable addition to the repertoire of business managers, consultants, project managers, decision makers, technologists, methodologists, sociologists, accountants and researchers, and practitioners. The author is to be highly commended for a work of this quality and comprehensiveness, and readers will have a fruitful journey following the ideas in this book and their application in practice.

Edward Yourdon

Ed Yourdon is a software consultant in his own firm, NODRUOY Inc., as well as co-founder and senior consultant of a software research/analysis firm known as the Cutter Consortium. He has worked in the software field for approximately 40 years, and has published 27 computer-related books and over 550 technical articles. Yourdon has programmed, designed, and tested numerous software applications and programmer-productivity products; has managed numerous projects as a first-level project leader and also as a senior IT executive; and has reviewed numerous software development projects for clients during his consulting career. He is currently focusing on Web 2.0 technologies, and was the guest editor of the October 2006 special issue of the *Cutter IT Journal* on "Creating Business Value with Web 2.0." He has developed an extensive "mind-map" of Web 2.0 concepts, technologies, products, and vendors.

Preface

Mobile Enterprise Transition and Management

Mobile Enterprise Transition and Management (METM) provides a comprehensive, practical, yet research-based methodological framework for transitioning to, and then managing, a mobile businesses. Mobility permeates all aspects of our lives: individual, organizational, and social. Coupled with the Internet, mobility has launched us well and truly into the age of communication of information from the age of information alone. The "Information Age" is a concept of the past. However, as has been true with most technical revolutions, mere introduction of technologies that replicate or automate known and existing business processes hardly ever provides the competitive advantage that businesses strive for. The more advanced and revolutionary a technology is, the more it requires a *strategic* approach to its incorporation in business. Mobile technology is one such technology that needs to be studied, understood, and incorporated by businesses through carefully construed and well-researched strategies. These strategies provide value to the business, its customers, and business partners in introducing and managing the dramatic changes ("disruptions") based on mobile technologies. The discussions undertaken in this book should prove to be invaluable precisely for this reason. This book presents a formal process for transitioning an enterprise to a mobile enterprise. Based on extensive research, literature review, and practical experimentation in mobile enterprise transitions undertaken by the author, the methodological framework for transitions presented in this book encompass significant dimensions influencing enterprises: the economic drivers, the technical edge, the process changes, and the overall social impact of changes to the business. Thus, the METM framework discussed in this book is made up of four pillars or specific dimensions of business: economic, technical, process, and social.

Rationale

This book makes a unique contribution to the literature on mobile technologies and business by providing a detailed understanding of how mobility can be applied to and incorporated by organizations. There is an acute need to consider such a detailed and researched methodological framework that smoothes the path for organizations to transition to a mobile world. This book addresses such a need to understand, configure, enact, and manage the *process* of transitioning to a mobile organization that encompasses wide-ranging sociocultural–managerial–technical viewpoints. Although there is substantial literature on mobility as well as business transitions, this book uniquely aims to bring the two together. The framework for Mobile Enterprise Transition (MET) appearing in this work is bound to be of immense value to both researchers and practitioners in the field of mobility and, hopefully, fill the gap in the areas of mobile transitions and management.

Readers

The content of this book is aimed at the following audience:

Strategic decision makers in the industry. These are the people involved in the process of improving their business operations and services through the adoption and use of mobile technology. This book provides the decision makers with a fairly robust approach to MET that encompasses business as well as technology considerations. The strategies outlined in this book equip the decision makers in the industry to play a *proactive* role in adopting mobile technologies in their business processes. Furthermore, discussions on sociocultural aspects of mobility including customer analysis and demographics, security and privacy concerns, project management, and change management, as well as user training should be of immense interest to consultants and other practitioners from the industry.

Academics responsible for teaching courses related to "mobility." Each chapter in this book is organized in a manner that will correlate with a teaching session in an academic environment. The introduction, detailed discussion, relevant summaries and discussion topics all provide for interesting material for class-based teaching as well as industrial training. The discussion topics can be used for interactive discussions within a seminar or classroom environment enabling participants to consolidate their grasp of the topic. Thus, this book has an appeal for academic teaching courses/subjects in information and communication technologies, mobile information systems, mobile business, advance topics in electronic business, project management, and business process reengineering, to name but a few.

Researchers and higher degree students are involved in understanding, delving deeper, and discovering new bodies of knowledge within their area of interest—in this instance, into the fascinating area of mobility. Master's (honors) and PhD students, as well as academic researchers and teachers, will find the research base of this book quite attractive. Each chapter is based on a significant literature review encompassing a number of books, articles, and Web sites, as well as intensive research conducted by the author.

Contents and Chapter Summaries

This book contains 12 chapters, each laid out in the following form: title, key points, main body of the chapter, summary, and discussion topics. The book has detailed references, a comprehensive index, meaning of acronyms and keywords, figures, tables, and three exhaustive case studies that are invaluable for practitioners. The following table provides a brief overview of each chapter.

Chapter	Description
1. Mobile Business Overview	Provides an update on the contemporary state of mobile business. Discusses the gradually complex ways in which business can utilize mobility. Defines the terms used in the book.
2. Mobile Enterprise Transition Goals and Framework	Outlines the goal of the Mobile Enterprise Transition (MET). Describes the overall MET framework comprising economic, technical, business process, and social dimensions.
3. Mobile Enterprise Transitions: Economic Dimension	Discusses the economic dimension of MET, including the economic drivers and how to handle them.
4. Mobile Enterprise Transitions: Technical Dimension	Discusses the technical dimension of MET. This includes discussion on devices, networks, contents, and applications.
5. Mobile Enterprise Transitions: Process Dimension	Discusses the process dimension of MET. This includes discussion on modeling of processes, applications, and providing value to the context-based user.
6. Mobile Enterprise Transitions: Social Dimension	Discusses the social dimension of MET. This includes discussion on usability, privacy, organizational structures, and change management.
7. Enacting and Managing Mobile Enterprise Transitions	This chapter discusses the practical enactment of the MET methodological framework discussed thus far.
8. Mobile Enterprises: Expansion, Growth, and Management	This chapter focuses on the actual running of a mobile business, including its growth and expansion.
9. Mobile Enterprises: Sustainability and the Environment	This chapter focuses on the ever-increasing opportunities offered by mobility in terms of sustainability and the environment.

Chapter	Description
10. Case Study: Applying METM to a Medium-Sized Pharmaceutical Enterprise	This case study demonstrates the application of METM framework in a practical, medium-sized pharmaceutical enterprise.
11. Case Study: Applying METM to a Small-Sized Travel and Tourism Enterprise	This case study demonstrates the application of METM framework in enabling a small travel and tourism enterprise to successfully adopt mobility.
12. Case Study: Applying METM to a University for Sustainability and Environment	This case study demonstrates the application of METM to enhancing the sustainability and responsibility toward the environment of an education organization.

This book is also supported by three appendices, as summarized in the table below.

Appendix	Description
Appendix A	Research questionnaire used in eliciting survey responses for the MET data and analysis presented in this book
Appendix B	Example use cases from the case studies discussed in this book
Appendix C	CASE tools that can be used for modeling business processes and mobile software systems

Workshop

The material presented in this book has been used in industrial training seminars and workshops. The contents of this book, therefore, effectively form the basis of a one- to two-day workshop. The following table provides a generic outline of a one-day workshop based on this book, which can be extended to a two-day workshop comprising practical discussions and working out a case study in groups. When used in an academic course, each chapter in this book can correspond to a lecture topic, together with practical group work based on the case studies.

		A Mapping of the Chapters in This Book to a One-Day Workshop		
Day	*Session*	*Presentation and Discussion Workshop Topic*	*Relevant Chapters*	*Comments*
1	8:30–10:00	Mobile Business; Mobile Enterprise Transition Process; Economic Dimension of MET	1, 2, 3	Introducing the concept and outlining the MET process. Discussion of the business reasons for MET.
	10:30–12:00	Technical and Process Dimensions of MET	4, 5	Discussing the technical and the methodological drivers of MET.
	1:30–3:00	Social Dimension of MET; Enacting the MET Methodological Framework; Using MET for Sustainability	6, 7	Discussion on the social drivers for MET and explaining how the process is "enacted" in practice.
	3:30–5:00	Understanding the Case Study and Applying MET to a Real-Life Situation	10, 11, 12	Getting a feel for MET—a hands-on approach.

Language

The author firmly believes in gender-neutral language. However, to maintain the simplicity of reading, *she* and *he* have been used freely. Terms like *user* and *manager* represent roles and not people. We may play more than one role at a given time like *consultant, academic,* and *analyst.* As a result, the semantics behind the theory and examples may change, depending on the role you are playing, and should be kept in mind as you peruse this book. *We* throughout the text primarily refers to the reader and the author—you and me. Occasionally, *we* refers to the general business or the Information and Communication Technology (ICT) community, depending on the context.

Critiques

Criticisms of this work are welcome. The author will be grateful to you for your comments, feedback, and criticisms, as they will surely add to the overall knowledge available on mobility and mobile transitions. Here is a big *thank you* to all readers and critiques in advance.

Bhuvan Unhelkar
www.methodscience.com

Acknowledgments

Warren Adkins

Siddharth Bhargav

Dave Curtis

Padmanaabh Desai

Jigisha Gala

Abbass Ghanbary

Priyanka Jain

Kunal Kishnani

Elaine Lawrence

Chinar Mamdapur

San Murugesan

Mohammed Maharmeh

Sargam Parmar

Christopher Payne

Amit Pradhan

Prashant Risbud

Prince Soundararajan

Bharti Trivedi

Asha Unhelkar

Bulbul Vyas

David Wilson

Mindy "Ming-Chien" Wu

Houman Younessi

In addition to the names above, the author is also extremely grateful to students, colleagues, and friends at the University of Western Sydney, University of Technology: Sydney, Gujarat University, NIRMA University (Ahmedabad, India), and Rensselaer Polytechnic Institute (Hartford, Connecticut) for their inputs, research opportunities, comments and criticisms, and practical experiences that have provided invaluable input for this book. Furthermore, members of various discussion forums, including MIRAG, METHODSCIENCE, and HCUBE, have regularly provided comments and feedback, and enabled the survey on mobility across the globe. My heartfelt thanks to all these wonderful people around the world. Also, my thanks to Hemant Unhelkar for his regular phone calls and encouragement throughout the year as I worked on this book. My special thanks also to Dr. Abbass Ghanbary and Mindy "Ming-Chien" Wu who brainstormed with me on various topics of importance; helped me with the investigations, survey, and analysis of the data; drew many of the figures; and edited the text. Finally, thanks to my family—Asha, Sonki, and Keshav—and extended family, Chinar and Girish.

Chapter 1

Mobile Business Overview

We will communicate with each other without the use of technological devices, but through our mind.

Edgar Cayce
On the Millennium

Chapter Key Points

- Provides an overview of contemporary mobile business
- Outlines the strategic importance of Mobile Enterprise Transitions (METs) to mobile business
- Highlights the differences between mobile business and electronic business; also highlights the differences between mobile commerce and mobile business
- Discusses the uniqueness of "location independence" of mobility and its relevance to mobile business
- Discusses the specific business and personal advantages of mobility
- Identifies the specific challenges of mobility, subsequent risks faced by transitioning mobile businesses, and how to ameliorate these risks
- Discusses the increasing complexity of the informative, transactive, operative, and collaborative usage of mobile communication by business

1

Introduction

Mobility is vital in the contemporary business world. This is so because mobility includes the ability of the business to conduct commercial transactions as well as manage itself independent of location and, thereby, also independent of time. The location and time independence of mobility also creates opportunities for businesses to communicate with their customers, users, and other stakeholders, depending on their context. For example, a "mobile" bank customer with a mobile gadget, walking through a shopping center, has a different set of service expectations from her bank than the same customer sitting in the waiting room of a hospital. Whereas she is looking for the available credit from her bank as she strolls through the shopping mall, perhaps to purchase a perfume or a book, the same mobile user is likely to seek the payment status of her medical insurance or the "gap" payment for a medical procedure when she is seated in a hospital's waiting room. These different sets of expectations of a customer from her bank, depending on her changing physical location, the specific time, and the urgency of her need, provide the context (or the backdrop) for a creative and customer-centric bank to tailor its services. Earlier, before the advent of mobility in business, the bank would have still provided the aforementioned information. However, the bank could not have tailored that information and service to the specific context of the customer. Without "mobility" the physical context of the user could not be determined by the service provider. Therefore, the bank was unable to customize and offer its services in a way that would be relevant to the user at a particular point in time. Today, with mobility, businesses are able to dynamically customize products and services that depend on the location of the customer, respond to customer queries round the clock, promote their products in a personalized manner, and provide postsale support to a customer on the move. Numerous such advantages and corresponding challenges stem from the application of mobility to business. These advantages and challenges have been highlighted by many authors, including Unhelkar (2003, 2005a), Arunatileka (2005), Ghanbary (2006), Tsai and Gururajan (2005), and Hawryszkiewycz and Steele (2005). The growing importance of mobility in business is supported by numbers that suggest the global mobile commerce market to be worth $88 billion by 2009 (Glenbrook Partners, LLC 2004). This mobile commerce market has grown in multiples of $3.6 billion, the recorded worth of mobile commerce sales conducted in 2006 (Brad 2006). Pyramid Research estimates that, between 2006 and 2010, total mobile subscribers will increase at a compound annual growth rate of 8.7 percent, reaching 3 billion mobile users by 2008 and topping 3.5 billion or more by year-end 2010.

The unique location independence and time independence of mobility has changed the face of industries such as banking, finance, insurance, education, childcare, distribution, emergency services (fire, police, ambulance), and government services as never before. Leisure and entertainment industries have been affected by the advent of mobility even more than banking, finance, and related commercial industries. This is so because the personalized nature of mobile technology facilitates leisure and entertainment activities, such as watching a video or playing a game, within the private domain of the user. As a result of this popularity of mobility in the entertainment industry, mobile gaming revenues are predicted to reach $430 million in 2009.

Businesses are quick to perceive this growing importance of mobility worldwide. This perception has resulted in an understandable hurry to use mobile technologies in business. However, incorporating mobility in an enterprise in a strategic manner goes far beyond the simple act of providing mobile gadgets to customers, employees, and business partners. The easy availability of and access to mobile gadgets, and the corresponding wireless connectivity undoubtedly provide a significant impetus for "mobilizing an enterprise." The relatively lower costs and abundant availability of mobile gadgets such as mobile phones, personal digital assistants (PDAs), and the latest combination devices such as iPhones* make it much easier for many small and medium organizations, as well as individuals in consulting roles, to bring mobility within the grasp of their business activities. Larger enterprises are keen to capitalize on the abundant availability of mobile technologies and devices in their customer base to reach those customers in innovative ways and provide them with greater value and wider range of services. Nonetheless, enterprises need to be made aware that this abundant availability of a plethora of relatively cheap mobile devices can ensnare organizations. Hurrying to inundate customers, employees, and other stakeholders of the business with mobile devices is a meaningless and risky exercise.

> Ad hoc use of mobility by businesses can result from abundant availability of a plethora of relatively cheap mobile devices. However, organizations need to be made aware of this trap of cheap availability of mobility. Providing all customers, employees, and other stakeholders of the business with mobile devices is a meaningless and risky exercise that should be avoided. Instead, formal mobile transitions need to be embarked upon to derive the full advantage of mobility.

Availability of mobile devices, connectivity, and creation of mobile applications need to be supported by a carefully planned and executed transition process. For example, the sales force needs to be equipped with the easily available handheld devices. However, there is an acute need to formally model the corresponding mobile business processes, study the impact of their mobility on the organizational

---

* Released with much fanfare by Apple in mid-2007.

structure, and understand the security implications of mobile sales. Not undertaking such a formal transition in mobile usage can lead to confusion within the organization and loss of business opportunities in the external world. For example, a pharmaceutical enterprise may equip its medical representatives with high-end, feature-rich mobile PDAs. However, without the benefit of formal mobile transition, the business may not integrate these PDAs with the back-end customer relationship management (CRM) and supply-chain management (SCM) systems. Such "unintegrated" mobile devices may not provide the enterprise with the business advantages that should result from a strategic use of mobile technologies. Availability of mobile gadgets and wireless connectivity are not sufficient to ensure the success of a mobile enterprise. Adoption and utilization of mobility require careful and strategic consideration of the strengths and capabilities, as well as risks and challenges, associated with mobility in the context of the environment in which the business exists (Unhelkar and Agrawal 2007). The myriad mobile devices and applications in the market today provide excellent tools and techniques to the business in terms of reaching out to its customers and partners. The ever-improving wireless connectivity provides the dynamic "bridge" or glue between devices and the business. However, to be successful in mobile business, it is vital that these devices and features are studied, understood, and formally modeled in corresponding business processes. There is also a need to understand the underlying wireless infrastructure, the application enablers, the content and service providers, and the customers. The formal adoption, incorporation, and utilization of mobility in business appear to be in their nascent stages, as observed by Unhelkar (2007), Arunatileka (2006, 2007), and Ghanbary and Unhelkar (2007a, 2007b). Some discussions on mobile transitions are provided by Kalakota and Robinson (2002), Marmaridis and Unhelkar (2005), Tsai and Gururajan (2005), and Basole (2005a, 2005b). However, these discussions do not amount to a specific methodological framework to transition the business to a comprehensive mobile business. Furthermore, studies conducted in early mobile technology adoption also show that there are phenomenal complexities involved in formal mobile adoption by business. Mobile technology adoptions are not a mere technical transition of business applications; they also bring about changes to work practices, organization of the business, and the sociocultural environment in which the business exists (Er and Kay 2005; Unhelkar 2007). Thus, there is an acute need to provide in-depth and strategic consideration of mobility in terms of its adoption by organizations. As mentioned earlier, this strategic consideration of mobility by business requires a comprehensive and carefully thought methodological framework that encompasses all significant dimensions of the business. Strategic application of mobility in business requires the business to be creative and innovative (Murugesan and Unhelkar 2004), have access to a transition framework, organize and carefully plan human resources, handle end-user issues, and consider sociocultural, technical, and environmental aspects in its transition. The framework for strategic adoption of motility should also have a component that facilitates practical enactment

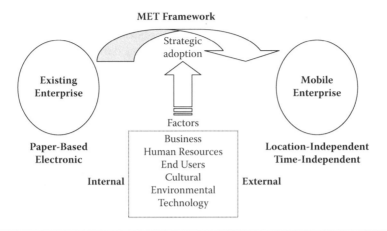

Figure 1.1 Mobile Enterprise Transitions.

(or execution) of the transition process. These requirements of Mobile Enterprise Transitions (METs) and the positioning of MET are illustrated in Figure 1.1, which summarizes the strategic impact of the MET framework on the transitioning of an existing paper-based or electronic enterprise into a mobile enterprise. The enterprise is affected both internally and externally through the transition. The ensuing chapters in this book discuss the comprehensive MET framework and all of the aforementioned requirements for a successful MET.

Figure 1.1 shows how an existing enterprise transitions to a mobile enterprise by the application of the proposed MET framework. The existing enterprise could be paper based or electronic based, and the application of mobile technology widens the reach of these existing enterprises as it makes them location and time independent.

Mobile Change

The dramatic changes resulting from the adoption of mobile technologies by business are akin to the similar radical changes that occurred in the earlier digital revolution of the late 1980s and 1990s. The digital revolution surmounted the need for the physical presence of parties to conduct business transactions. Later, with the growth of the Internet and the World Wide Web (WWW), there has been a significant change in the way in which business, commerce, and industry function (Murugesan et al. 2001). However, the change from electronic to mobile business is happening at a far greater rate than the earlier move from paper-based to electronic business processes.

The strategic consideration of mobility by business requires a comprehensive and carefully thought-out methodological framework that encompasses all significant dimensions of the business. Equipping employees and customers with mobile gadgets is not a strategic adoption of mobility by businesses, as such adoption sidesteps the important issues of network usage, business alliances, mobile applications, content management, and security. Furthermore, strategic adoption of mobility accrues and provides value in time, and is not usually instantaneous, as is expected by mere distribution of mobile gadgets.

The influence of technology on business further influences the fabric of society and the environment in which the business exists. This overall influence of technology on business and, subsequently, on society is exacerbated in the area of mobile communications and technologies. The increasing rate of change and the subsequent influence of this change on society has been aptly described by Toffler in books such as *The Future Shock* (1981) and *The Third Wave* (1980). Mobile technologies, in particular, have had rapid increases in mobile device memory and processing powers, and corresponding rapid falls in costs of these technologies; more importantly, though, the rate at which this is happening is also on the rise. This increasing rate of change brought about by mobile technologies results in an "information and communications overload," which many sections of society are not ready to handle. Later in this book (Chapter 6), the sociocultural implications of MET and mobile business are discussed in greater detail. These accelerating technical changes provide challenges to business when it comes to their transitions. However, at the same time, the increasing rate of change in technology, particularly mobile technology, provides the business with unprecedented new opportunities in global markets and potential for cost savings. Businesses that are prepared to adapt and thrive on these changes are ideally positioned to capitalize on the opportunities offered by mobility. The dynamics of this increasing rate of change is such that more and more organizations are being continuously challenged to adapt to the emerging technologies, requiring them to concentrate on their core competencies and search for competitive advantages and innovations (Adam et al. 2005). For example, although the ubiquity and popularity of the Internet have revolutionized the face of business, with globalization these have also "leveled the playing field" and made competition more intense and immediate (Mackay and Marshall 2004; Porter 2001). This equality in business opportunities means that the size and location of the organization are less relevant in the mobile era. The value, quality, and timeliness of services offered by a mobile organization to its customers and business partners assume greater significance than its size and location.

Users, the devices they use, the network sessions, services and applications, and the content—everything is "on the move" in this mobile era. The wireless connectivity of mobile devices, when studied and applied formally, affords unique opportunities for businesses to expand their reach by seeking new customers and also providing those customers with new types of business transactions. Mobility provides immense personalization in its dealing with customers and provides greater value for the "money and time" spent by the customer with the business. This is so because mobility is able to focus directly on the requirements of customers, and needs to be as generalized as the electronically or physically connected industry. Thus, the change from electronic to mobile business needs to be treated with extra care and consideration than was demanded of the earlier transition from paper-based to electronic business. There are lessons to be learned, however, from the earlier electronic transitions that can be applied to mobile transitions as described by Basole (2005b) and Tsai and Gururajan (2005). Several successful electronic transition methodologies and approaches have been used by businesses in the past to undertake electronic transitions (Arunatileka and Ginige 2003; Kazanis 2004; Sawhney and Zabin 2001). These electronic transition frameworks provide a sound basis for business transitions. Arunatileka (2007) has also described a framework for transition of the business processes of an organization into mobile business processes. That study, however, is restricted to a singular business process. Initial attempts at mobile transitions seem to consider mobile technologies as primarily a tool for better communication rather than part of a comprehensive business strategy. However, practical METs need to expand and use that study as a fully implementable framework that encompasses all dimensions of transitioning. Strategic adoption of mobility in all aspects of a business requires these mobile transitions to be holistic and comprehensive. Thus, the mobile transition framework needs to consider and provide for the economic drivers, technical factors, changes to business processes, and the overall social impact on the business.

The change from electronic to mobile business needs to be considered with extra care and consideration than was demanded of the earlier transition from paper-based to electronic business. This is so because of the extremely rapid changes in the mobile domain, including changes to mobile devices, mobile networks, approaches to mobile content management, and, of course, security across mobile applications and networks. Without a strategic approach to mobile technology adoption by business, the effect of this technology on business and subsequently on society will remain uncontrolled and unmanageable.

Mobile Business Ecosystem

Understanding Mobile Business

The mobile business goes beyond transferring existing business processes onto mobile gadgets. The term business process reengineering (BPR), right from the original discussions by Hammer and Champy (1994), is described as a fundamental rethinking and radical redesign of business processes to achieve dramatic improvements in a critical, contemporary measure of performance, such as cost, quality, services, and speed. Reengineering a company's business processes changes practically all aspects of the company, including people, jobs, management, and the values of the company that are linked together.

Voice communications, sending and receiving text messages (short message services, or SMS), executing applications, and controlling remote machines can all be a part of this strategy for mobile business. The specific "anytime, anywhere" features of mobile technologies and mobile telephony are considered strategically for enhancing the delivery of business services. Mobile technologies, in addition to their ability to communicate, are also coupled with capabilities to process the information that is being wirelessly communicated. These capabilities of mobility have the potential to provide organizations with the means to achieve gains in productivity, efficiency, and other important business performance metrics (Basole 2005b). Thus, it can be observed that a mobile business is not just a reengineering of existing business processes but a complete "new engineering" of the business. This new engineering adopts and integrates mobility in a controlled manner, resulting in a gradually increasing level of confidence for customers and employees, and reduced risks for the business.

Mobile Technology: Influence on Society

As noted earlier, a mobile business continuously aims to make extensive and effective use of the opportunities of location-and-time independence provided by mobile technologies to reach business partners, customers, and other stakeholders. A mobile business incorporates mobility in all aspects of its business processes both internally and externally. Thus, it does far more than merely provide mobile gadgets to its customers and business partners or using the wireless connectivity of mobile networks. There are wide-ranging influences of this emerging technology on business that in turn influence society. This is particularly true of the impact of mobility on business and society as has been discussed by Unhelkar (2005b):

> Mobility has had a significant impact on the quality of life of individuals and the society in which they live. Although the location-aware mobile connectivity has dramatically increased the ability of individuals to communicate, it has also produced

challenges in terms of privacy and new social protocols. The effect of globalization resulting from mobility now needs to be further considered in the context of a global-mobile society.

Some of this wide-ranging impact of mobile technology on business and society are shown in Figure 1.2.

Mobile technology influences business and, in turn, society. Thus, it has a disruptive influence, changing not only the way business operates but also the way we live. Transitioning mobile businesses need to carefully consider this "flow-on" effect of mobility on society. There is also a reverse effect of changes to and needs of society in the way innovations are undertaken and newer technologies are discovered. The boundaries between technology, business, and society need to be studied with utmost care in transitioning to mobile business.

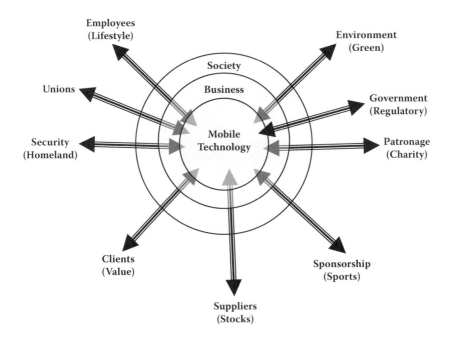

Figure 1.2 Mobile technologies, business, and society: A mobile business "ecosystem."

The influences and impacts of mobile business have far-reaching implications for society by not only providing faster or cheaper ways of functioning for individuals but also becoming a creative cause for a totally different type of society. The boundaries between technology, business, and society are affected by the specific impact of mobility as briefly discussed here:

- Employees (lifestyle): Mobile technology changes the way an employee works, with the potential for an improved working lifestyle.
- Clients (value): Customers derive instantaneous responses from mobile businesses, resulting in higher value to them. Customers are also able to identify and configure the most desired products and indicate that to the business.
- Suppliers (stocks): Inventory calculations and reordering are instantaneous, resulting in improved business.
- Unions (trade): The social networking resulting from mobility is dramatically different from any preceding communications technologies, enabling workers to get together, vote on crucial decisions, and do so in real-time. This social networking has its effect on the way workers organize and unite, using mobility. Mobility, however, is seen in a positive light, with its communications mechanism having the potential within the trade union entities to avoid strikes, inconvenience, and loss of pay as the information can flow faster and more reliably. This is especially important in the new millennium as the workforce is far more literate than before and is aware of its union rights.
- Shareholders: They are the individuals likely to benefit by investments in the mobile businesses. However, these beneficiaries need to keep the dot-com crash at the turn of the millennium in mind when they invest in mobile businesses, as mature mobile business models are still lacking. From a user's viewpoint, however, mobility provides faster and more reliable information for personal shareholding in the various business enterprises. The availability of information independent of location and time allows individuals to hold global business interests and be part of the global business world.
- Environment (green): Mobility provides opportunities for organizations to redesign, recycle, and capitalize on the location independence of mobility to reduce greenhouse emissions.
- Security (homeland): Mobility has provided a big challenge to the security operations of nations. The ubiquitous nature of mobility has enabled antisocial and terrorist elements to abuse it for their purposes, resulting in a great challenge for those responsible for homeland security.
- Sponsorships (sports): Mobile technology supports business in major events (e.g., sports), most notably the sponsorship of '3' mobile of the Australian Test-cricket team and similarly by Vodaphone of the English team.

- Inventory (stocks): Mobile technology provides advantage to the suppliers of raw materials or semifinished goods to business, especially if the suppliers are small businesses that depend on large businesses for the movement of their goods. The business can keep better track of the location of goods around the globe.
- Social activities (charity): Mobile technology supports many businesses that tend to support organizations for the patronage of social activities (e.g., charity)—people can forward money to the bank account of charitable organizations by using their mobile devices while they are participating in social activities away from home or office.

Mobile Commerce

> Mobile business is much more than mobile commerce. Mobile business encompasses strategic use of mobile technologies in all aspects of the business, effectively engineering the internal and external business processes, organizational structure, software applications, customer expectations, and partner collaboration.

Mobile commerce (m-commerce) occasionally gets confused with mobile business. Understanding the difference between the two, however, is helpful in applying the MET framework. Mobile commerce refers to the purchase of products and services using a mobile terminal (Godbole 2006). m-commerce has also been defined as "a layer of applications atop the mobile internet" (Rulke, Iyer, and Chiasson 2003; Schwiderski-Grosche and Knospe 2002) or, explicitly, as "an extension of electronic commerce (E-commerce) in a mobile environment" (Dholakia and Dholakia 2002). However, a mobile business is more than mobile commerce (Kalakota and Robinson 2002). m-commerce deals with only the external or commercial aspect of a business by making use of mobile devices, applications, middleware, and wireless networks (Varshney 2002) to conduct business transactions. It is thus similar to E-commerce as far as its business viewpoint is concerned, and it has indeed emerged from the latter. For example, electronic tracking of courier deliveries or electronic ordering of raw materials are commercial business processes that can now be conducted using mobile devices, resulting in m-commerce. Being external to the business, it is the first and popular application of mobile technologies. However, it is important to keep in mind the difference between these m-commerce transactions and the overall mobile business. A mobile business utilizes mobility in *all* aspects of its business activities, including external and internal business processes, organizational structures, and collaborations with other businesses. Thus, after using mobility in commercial transactions, businesses move to using it in their internal business processes

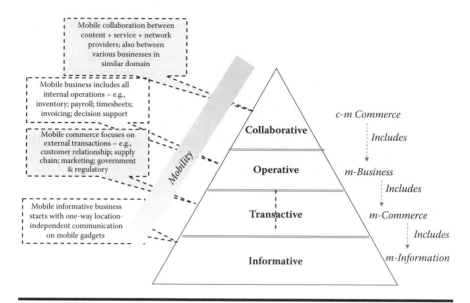

Figure 1.3   Business utilizing the Internet—mobile superimposition.

such as timesheets and inventories. A mobile business results when the internal *and* external business processes are fully integrated with the use of mobile technologies.

Mobile Collaborative Strategy

The strategic vision of comprehensive use of mobile technologies permeates both external and internal aspects of a business and its organizational structure, its relationship with clients and business partners, and its audits and metrics, to name but a few. A mobile business further envisions the use of mobility in collaborating with other businesses to provide value to its customers. Thus, it is not just an extension of an existing (perhaps electronic) business through mobility but a ground-up use of mobility in all aspects of business. A taxonomy of four layers of modern business activities with respect to electronic commerce was put together by Unhelkar (2003). These four layers (of business usage of electronic and Internet opportunities) include information, transaction, operation, and collaboration. This discussion extends and superimposes mobility on the aforementioned four layers of use of communications by a business, resulting in each layer utilizing the location-and-time independence of mobility. The MET framework transitions an organization in an evolutionary and gradual manner wherein it can make use of the four distinct yet related layers in the context of mobile usage (Unhelkar 2005a). These four layers of business usage of mobility are shown in Figure 1.3 as the informative, transactive, operative, and collaborative usages. Mobile business transitions need to consider each layer in Figure 1.3 in the context of mobility.

Informative Mobile Business

The informative usage of mobile communication is to merely provide information. As such, this is a one-way transfer of information requiring minimum security. As shown in Figure 1.3, this is the lowermost layer of the usage triangle. This is also the widest layer of the triangle, indicating that it is the most popular use of mobile communications as it is easier to implement. In the earlier electronic era, this informative use resulted in a static Web site that provided a cost-effective solution to reach wide users (Schneider 2003). Examples of mobile communications for informative usage by business include broadcast of schedules and information on products, services, or places, which capitalizes on the common SMS feature of mobile gadgets. Technical availability of and access to a mobile device is important to enable provision of information. However, the receiving and usage of that information depends on the way in which the individual decides to use the device. For example, a "switched-off" mobile device will not receive information even if it is unconditionally broadcast. Socially, the information layer of mobile Internet usage has the potential for degenerating into mobile spam and other unsolicited messaging that is a part of MET challenges (Unhelkar 2005a).

Transactive Mobile Business

The transactive usage implies "two-way" or "multi-way" communications between the business and the user, resulting in sales of products and services as well as dealing with the third-party credit/debit card organizations that facilitate online payments. As shown in Figure 1.3, this is the next layer of the usage triangle. This transactive usage also includes informative usage, but it is essentially the external or commercial part of the usage of mobility. Technically, devices such as a wireless-enabled PDA or a laptop with necessary security and access to the mobile network are required to conduct these external transactions. More important, though, from a process viewpoint, transactive usage is between parties that are "known" to the business (for example, a registered bank user conducting account transactions), requiring businesses to incorporate upfront registration processes in dealing with their customers. Socially, the convenience of conducting two-way transactions will affect individuals, but so will their confidence in the systems being used for such transactions. The issues of privacy and security start becoming more important in this transactive use of business as compared with the aforementioned informative use. This layer of the triangle is narrower than the informative layer, reflecting the challenge and hence lesser transactive use as compared with informative use.

Operative Mobile Business

The operative layer of mobile business deals with transition of the internal core business processes (that are typically operational in nature) to the mobile Internet.

Common examples of operative business processes that transition to mobility include timesheets and inventory. Thus, mobile technologies may enable a manager using a simple mobile-enabled gadget (phone, pager, or PDA) to keep track of employees, or may enable her to keep a tab on inventory through a combination of PDA and radio frequency identification (RFID) technologies, thereby ensuring a reorder at the right time. As shown in Figure 1.3, this is the third layer of the triangle, which also includes the previous two usages of the triangle. However, this operative usage is primarily focused on the internal operations of the business—which came into the picture much later than the commercial external use of mobility by business. Therefore, the operative layer of the triangle is narrower than the previous transactive layer, as shown in Figure 1.3.

Collaborative Mobile Business

This collaborative layer of mobile usage by business is represented by the tip of the triangle in Figure 1.3. This collaborative usage results in numerous individuals as well as businesses, all cooperating with each other to satisfy the needs and demands of clients and business partners. Groupware and portals are the technical starting points for collaborations. However, the collaborative usage of mobility by business also requires modeling and reengineering the processes of a group of collaborating businesses as against reengineering only the processes of a single business. Creation of collaborating business clusters can be an interesting study on its own, as earlier discussed by Unhelkar (2003, 2005a) and later studied in great detail by Ghanbary (2007).

Unni and Harmon (2005) also have discussed the collaboration as part of mobile usage by business. For example, opportunities exist for businesses to collaborate with each other to analyze and bring together real-time data on location of facilities such as hotels, restaurants, filling stations, retail stores, and weather conditions. This collaborative information provides fast and accurate location services to handsets, depending on the sophistication of the operator's network. Map databases such as Navtech, TeleAtlas, and MapQuest provide maps, routes, and points of interests, whereas positioning services (Nokia, Intrado, Cellpoint) called Gateway Mobile Location Centers (GMLC) provide dynamic real-time information on position of users.

The cluster of collaborating players provides numerous services and solutions that can be combined or packaged together with the wireless operators. The contribution of all collaborating businesses and services is essential for the ability of the business to deploy and support collaborative services. However, this collaborative usage also introduces challenges in terms of ability of business partners to communicate, trust, and work together to satisfy common goals. Sociology, rather than technology, and all the associated sociocultural issues appear to be at the crux of the collaborative use of mobility by business.

Mobile Advantage

Mobile Business Advantage

Realization of the mobile business communications taxonomy can lead to numerous advantages for business. These mobile business advantages eventually translate to prime drivers for a MET. Mobility can help businesses leverage both efficiency and effectiveness. Efficiency implies being able to do more with the same or fewer resources. Effectiveness, however, deals with producing actual results irrespective of costs. Efficiency and effectiveness are both governed by access to real-time information among workers, managers, and business partners who are all mobile. For example, task-driven groups such as service engineers can plan their routes more efficiently and effectively when they have access to real-time information on the calls to be made. Customer expectations can be accurately managed through real-time information on inventories, personnel, and suppliers. Mobility makes the entire organization more responsive, more effective, and therefore more profitable through what can be considered as collective organizational intelligence. It enables dynamic knowledge sharing, utilization, and knowledge management, both internal and external to the organization. Some specific advantages to business resulting from the formal use of mobility are discussed here.

- *Customer service:* Mobility provides immense possibilities for business to enhance it customer service. The acquisition–growth–retention of customers through CRM systems can also be applied in mobile business by enhancing timeliness and the context of service offered to the customers.
- *Access:* Mobility provides enhanced access to the corporate network anywhere and at any time resulting in the ability of the business to reach widely dispersed and moving customers. Mobile access opens doors to engineering new business processes that did not exist in land-based access to the corporate network.
- *Cost savings:* They are realized through more robust mobile devices connected all the time, thus providing better connectivity for internal/operational business processes. Furthermore, as mobile devices enable entry of data or information at the point of collection, mobile businesses reduce duplication of effort and thereby reduce costs. Market forces tend to play a part; in a sluggish market, the cost of setting up full facilities for staff can be prohibitive. The use of home-based workers enables a set of virtualized functions that provide fast response to changing market requirements at minimum cost. Similarly, resources can be optimized through the use of part- or shared-time workers working from home at their convenience. Costs from fixed network solutions are also eliminated by mobile networks.
- *Profit:* Mobility controls variable costs and creates higher margins through the effective sale of goods and services to a wide range of customers. Mobility of workforce provides opportunities for organizations in the digital economy

to create new business processes, reengineer some of the non-value-adding business processes with the aim of creating higher profit margins; and develop new commerce channels within the extended enterprise while controlling implementation, support, and maintenance costs.

■ *Accuracy:* Elimination of transfer of information from paper-based to an electronic medium, wherein mobile devices can be used directly, ensures that errors are reduced. For example, people delivering goods (such as pizzas, groceries) or providing emergency services, looking for timely information, can all give and receive accurate information using mobile gadgets such as tablet PCs.

■ *Productivity:* Numerous business processes such as time sheets, generation of invoices, measuring of inventory, etc., can be improved manyfold through the use of mobility.

■ *Responsiveness:* Corporate systems are accessible at any time, anywhere through mobile devices that provide easier access to customers and employees, thereby improving responsiveness.

■ *Control:* Mobility offers round-the-clock access to business processes for managers who can have better control over processes (Basole 2005a).

■ *Infrastructure:* We also have the opportunity to create a new and flexible mobile infrastructure, which, in turn, lays the foundation for mobile computing operators to gain market share from their competitors.

■ *Single point of contact (SPOC):* Mobility enables business to deal with customers through a single point of contact, which is the mobile device. A single, easy-to-use client interface on the user's mobile device enables easy access to the organization's central networks, databases, and even collaborative functionalities, which the organization may offer to the user on the basis of its associations and alliances with other service providers.

Mobile Personal Advantage

The mobile advantages to the business discussed previously also offer corresponding advantages to individuals. When individuals adopt mobile technologies in subscribing to the services offered by mobile businesses, they reap the benefits of timelines and context. This is so because a mobile gadget, by its very nature, is a personalized device. Some of these mobile advantages to individuals are as follows:

■ *Personalization:* Mobile gadgets provide opportunities for individuals to get *customized services*. Personalization provides a boost to usability of services as they provide the user with the most essential information according to their personal preferences and in a timely context. However, as user preferences change depending on the location, configuring the supporting system for all available locations is a big challenge for both users and system service providers.

- *Voice telephony:* Mobile phones, laptops with mobile phones, PDAs, and car phones are all able to provide the individual with voice telephony.
- *Mobile payments:* Mobility enables individuals to make micropayments through mobile devices for small-time purchases such as from vending machines.
- *Mobile banking services:* Mobile devices can provide personalized updates on balances, credit card transaction approvals, and even transfer of amounts from account to account while the user is on the move.
- *Short messaging services:* These provide the individual with cost-effective national and international messaging facilities that are cheap to use.
- *Mobile music:* Downloading and playing music is a popular personalized application of mobility among young users of mobile devices.
- *Photo sharing*: Enabling instantaneous capture and transmission of photographs and videos with family and friends is an advantage of mobile devices.
- *Content generation:* Active participation of users in information creation, rather than being just passive information consumers, is encouraged in MET. This results in user-generated content (users' opinions and ratings), comprising recommendations that enhance many services. The reason such paradigms became popular is because, among other factors, ordinary users can generate content and provide information to others. However, sometimes it is difficult for users to participate in this activity as they may lack skill and motivation to do so (Vyas and Yoon 2005).

Mobile technologies are highly personalized technologies that are able to reach the customer at the location and time of the customer's choosing. Transitioning mobile businesses need to carefully consider the opportunities offered by this personalization as it enables business to customize its offering according to the dynamically changing personal preferences and needs of the user. The personal nature of mobile technologies, notably mobile devices, is not just restricted to the customer receiving information and services; customers and other users can actively "contribute" to the contents of the business by providing information on their location and inputting the services they would want from the business. User-generated content, including the opinions, ratings, and recommendations of users, are highly unique mobile features that need careful incorporation in mobile business processes.

Mobility Challenges

Mobility, being part of the emerging technologies, has to face the challenges that come with their adoptions. Mobile technology has its own characteristics and limitations, which should be clearly identifiable by business enterprises. These challenges take various forms as mobile devices connect to mobile networks, source content, and provide services to the user. The challenges to mobility arise from the complexity of technologies, the need to deal with multiple access points, movement of users and devices, impact of consumer purchasing patterns on handheld devices, and concerns about corporate security. High-speed mobile telephony, including General Packet Radio Services (GPRS), aided by the growth in Wi-Fi hotspot access points, provides challenges of coverage, timeliness, and privacy. The key to overcoming mobile challenges is to create market differentiation through the use of mobile technologies. A range of challenges are discussed here with the aim of handling them through MET. However, it should be noted that not all challenges need to be handled by all businesses at the same point in time. These challenges are faced by the upcoming mobile business, depending on the demographics of the business and its level of mobile preparedness and maturity.

Business Challenges

A transition path for users is highly valuable in ensuring that they are not disadvantaged while the business undergoes a formal mobile transition. Users need to be carefully transitioned in their use of the business offerings, including services, networks, applications, and content, all of them to be available on their mobile devices, which themselves might change. The need for and importance of business to model the user's mobile devices for use across its networks, applications, and contents cannot be overstressed.

Mobile technologies have technical challenges, and at the same time they also pose challenges to business in terms of their adoption. This is so because mobile technologies bring about dramatic changes (disruptions) to the existing organizational structures, customer interactions, and working styles of employees. The following is a list of some of these business challenges that are faced by organizations transitioning to mobile business.

- *Unwillingness:* Reluctance on the part of a business to formally adopt a new technology and accept the risks associated with its adoption is a major challenge. This unwillingness is mainly due to lack of desire by the business to take risks that a disruptive technology invariably brings with it. However, businesses that have taken the risks of adopting new technologies have also reaped benefits from such adoptions.
- *Resistance to change:* Businesses are reluctant to undergo change, especially if they are doing well in their current situation. However, competition is invariably going to force changes to the business, and therefore there is a case for accepting and preparing for change. The social reason for resistance to change is that, with every new adoption of technology in the past, there have been associated job losses within the organization and also loss of customers external to the organization. However, these losses could be the result of improper or hurried introduction of technologies without the benefits of a process for undertaking such transitions.
- *Cost:* The cost of supporting users and applications at home and on the road is another inhibiting factor. (Users require additional support with mobile devices and accessing the corporate network.) These costs are not just associated with mobile devices but also include the costs of restructuring the teams and the organization that provides services to users.
- *Connectivity:* The need for constant connectivity to the mobile network is a vital issue for mobile network providers. Without such connectivity, the advantage of mobility is not derived to its maximum, but the provision of such connectivity is a challenge especially as the user is roaming continuously.
- *Reliability:* The reliability of mobile connections is a major business challenge as many times wireless calls disconnect while downloading data or Sterling video.
- *Productivity:* Lost work due to a disconnection or flat battery on a mobile device can seriously affect the fortunes of the business.
- *Managing technology:* Consistent maintenance of software and hardware can be an ongoing challenge.
- *Security:* Online payments, user behavior, rules and hassles, mobile virus protection, file encryption, access control, and authentication are the most important security factors in a mobile environment, considering that mobile devices are very personal. In case of loss or theft, an unauthorized person could be accessing corporate or personal data.
- *Integrity:* Integrity of the data and its transmissions over the wireless network ensures that the transmitted data is actually going to the expected individual. The message should be clear and uncorrupted, and promptly received by the intended recipient.
- *Simplicity:* Complication and complexity arising from the use of existing processes together with mobile processes can challenge its adoption by businesses.
- *Safety:* Health hazards possibly associated with mobile devices and mobile transmission towers are negative factors.

- *Privacy:* Mobile users are able to access the corporate database, especially when they contain personal details of customers and employees.
- *Regulations:* Government rules and regulations regarding mobile usage (e.g., FCC911 regulations on auto location) are complex.
- *Standardization:* Technical standards dealing with network interoperability and compatibility of mobile devices (business-to-business, business-to-customer) could be problematic.
- *Control:* Most organizations ensure control and support of their PCs by restricting downloads of images and programs. This control becomes a lot more difficult to apply in a mobile environment.
- *Speed:* Consistent data transmission speed is essential to ensuring commercially viable business processes. However, higher transmission can be very costly.
- *Coverage:* Network coverage in terms of geographical areas is a crucial factor. Coverage in remote areas is an identified and unresolved problem.
- *Convergence:* This includes integration of technologies. Mobile business solutions must integrate into existing enterprise systems and ensure that data can be extracted from corporate systems (e.g., e-mail servers). Hardware, software, and networks must provide the end user with instant and transparent access to information.
- *Adaptation:* The attitude of the people toward adapting to changes is important. Resistance toward new technology is understandable but needs to be overcome for successful transition.
- *Training:* The need for and cost of training could be obstacles to adopting mobile technologies.
- *Management:* The mobile workforce and its activities require control and monitoring.
- *Marketing issues:* Mobility heralds a new era in marketing, with issues such as gender and age being combined with location- and time-specific information to produce a marketing strategy for goods and services.
- *Society:* Mobile technology creates additional pressure in daily lives where perpetual contact, privacy, security, lifestyle, and convenience are issues that change the social landscape. Mobile users communicate with others while driving, or walking on the street, and from public places, creating a need for new etiquettes and manners. For example, commonly, mobile users give priority and attention to the mobile caller even when personal face-to-face conversation is getting disrupted.

Device Challenges

Crucial mobile device challenges include the limited processing power of handsets' microprocessors, memory size, battery life, small screen of handheld devices and their lower resolution, replacement costs of gadgets, personal information residing in a mobile gadget, required ongoing support, network charges, as well as mobile Internet charges. These mobile device challenges include

- *Usability:* Mobile devices are handheld ones with smaller screen size than corresponding wired and desktop devices. Therefore, they suffer from usability issues such as readability, user interactions, etc.
- *Network coverage:* Mobile devices ensure high-fidelity capture of signals. However, at the same time, if the network coverage is not sufficient, they are rendered useless. Therefore, their relevance and value go hand in hand with network coverage.
- *Authentication:* This is essential, particularly multiparty authentication, wherein the identity of the user is confirmed by more than one source.
- *Standards:* Devices need to be able to operate on multiple carrier standards, especially when the user is roaming. Standards for battery chargers, powers, voltages, etc., also come into play when mobile devices are used by global users.
- *Obsolescence:* Mobile devices tend to become obsolete much faster than corresponding desk-based devices. Furthermore, the personalized nature of mobile devices means their obsolescence gets noted much more quickly, reflecting on the individual as well as the organization (in terms of their ability to keep up to date with the technology).
- *Delivery:* Delivery of application and content on mobile devices always require careful planning, modeling, testing, and deployment.
- *Lack of understanding:* Not adequately understanding mobility is a challenge to its widespread use.
- *Social resistance:* Potential stress on the part of the user for being available all the time creates resistance to mobile use.
- *Content generation:* Content is created and provided by the business, but mobility facilitates location-specific generation of content by users.
- *Senior management attitude toward mobility:* A transitioning enterprise needs senior management support to ensure the success of its change processes. Senior management's attitude toward adopting mobility is therefore crucial.
- *Lack of useful business applications:* Both client- and server-side applications that can be of value to users are not available.
- *Theft and loss of gadgets:* What additional policies and tools need to be implemented to safeguard mobile devices such as laptops and PDAs against theft should be considered. The personal data on the mobile device and its ability to access corporate data need to be considered in loss or theft of gadgets.
- *Creation of new business processes:* It is vital that these be done through formal modeling, and the challenges stem from the fact that these business processes need to handle a mobile user whose needs from them change dramatically with change in his or her location.
- *Lack of support for new mobile business processes:* Merely having a new business processes is not sufficient. There is a further need for businesses to be able to

support their processes through employees and call centers. Users need support to use their devices and the business processes that support those devices in the background. Currently, there is no sufficient evidence that users are thus supported. This challenge is further exacerbated by the wide range of devices and their rapid obsolescence mentioned earlier.

■ *Culture shock:* The use of mobile devices and the kind of opportunities it provides to a cross section of different user groups such as elders, adolescents, and carers creates challenges and exposes the cultural gaps between the groups. However, even more challenging is the inappropriate and even illegal use of mobile devices in society (such as using the video features of mobile phones or calling at inappropriate times and creating nuisance).

■ *Lower tolerance of inappropriate services:* As the expectations of mobile customers are already set high due to knowledge and awareness of what mobility can offer them, any shortcomings in providing service are less tolerated.

■ *Uncertainty of service:* Due to potential unreliability of connectivity, there can be disruptions and undependability in service, which in turn can be partially because of the ability of the device to roam.

■ *Intrusion by business:* Customer's private time is encroached upon as the business may not know the state in which the customer is when his or her phone is accessed by another party. This may happen inadvertently too, as the business may be unaware of the actual time zone of the customer owing to global roaming facilities.

■ *Intrusion by business of employee's private time:* Businesses provide handheld devices to their employees with the implicit assumption that the employee will be available to take a call even after normal working hours.

■ *Interference of networks:* As seen in airplanes and hospitals, there are restrictions on the use of mobile devices. The interference caused by use of mobile devices in certain places has both technical and social connotations, and users are required to exercise caution in using such devices. There is also a corresponding health and safety hazard due to misuse of the mobile devices in the aforementioned places.

■ *Lack of ability of certain demographics to use mobile gadgets:* There are many categories of users who are benefited by the availability of mobile gadgets but who are not able to use them. For example, elders in a nursing home may own a mobile device but may not be able to use it; another example is that of very young kids being provided with a device by concerned and caring parents, but the child may not be equipped to use the device. Many users in developing countries such as India and China own the now easily affordable mobile devices. However, these users may not necessarily be very literate (in the traditional sense of the word). These categories of users may not be able to use the full capabilities of mobile devices, including the many different functions, which vary depending on the network and the contract. Businesses that want to interact with such users need to be creative and innovative in the modeling of their business processes to reflect simplicity, fail-safe user interfaces, and social sensitivity and respect toward the needs and nuances of these users.

■ *Reliability of connections:* Mobile connections tend to break off more easily compared to land-based connections. This is because of the movements of the users and mobile coverage being spread out across a wide geographical area compared to land-based connections, which are point to point.

■ *Lack of global system standards:* CDMA, GSM, etc., create a challenge as users have to worry about the standards they are using for their gadgets and services. An ideal option is to merge the current standards and corresponding transmission systems to facilitate interoperability among devices. This increases the usability of the devices and can also improve business collaboration. However, at the same time, it would require certain network players to give up their supposed dominance of the network operations market, and that might be the reason why mobile users and mobile businesses have not yet seen a common mobile network standard.

■ *Narrow network bandwidth:* Occasionally, operations of mobile devices are plagued by lack of supporting bandwidth. Therefore, if the device manufacturer has not considered the possibility of fluctuations in bandwidth, the device will be less usable in practice.

■ *Low memory capacity:* Mobile devices are now expected to be able to execute mobile applications. However, the lower memory capacity of these devices, as compared to desktop machines, can hinder the execution of mobile applications on small handheld devices. Wireless laptops, however, are quite capable of handling these applications provided there is sufficient supporting bandwidth.

■ *Radiation hazard:* This provides an interesting challenge in terms of mobile device usage. For example, a number of studies conducted on the possibilities of radiation hazards on users vary and contradict themselves. They indicate different results, depending on the age group, user types, and even the conductors and sponsors of studies. However, it is considered advisable to keep young children away from prolonged use of mobile phones because of potential health hazards.

Security Challenges

Security of mobile devices provides a bigger challenge than security issues related to wired connectivity. This is so because broadcasts to and from mobile devices in the "open air" are relatively easy to intercept as no physical wires are involved. Mobile security has to take into account viruses that exploit the vulnerability at any point in the network. These vulnerabilities include mobile security appliances that can break down in varying or different physical environments, trust and identity of the mobile user, filtering of unwanted contents, intrusion detection and prevention, and the challenges of encryption over mobile networks. The following are some of the specific security challenges related to mobile devices and networks:

- Broadcast wireless frequencies can be jammed leading to denial-of-service attacks.
- Handheld devices, with limited memory and processing capabilities, are not always able to effectuate encryption and decryption.
- Usually, short-range Wi-Fi-type networks used in the home and office are left open with no firewalls.
- Limited storage on mobile gadgets results in user's private information being stored on a Wireless Access Protocol (WAP) gateway. Therefore, to secure that information, the gateway itself needs to be secured.
- Service providers and network operators are continuously competing with each other for majority share of the business. Such competition prevents the emergence of standards for provision of services. Subsequently, there is a fragmentation of the customer base, and customers are not able to receive a unified and interoperable packaged service.
- Mobility has a unique challenge in comparison with previous technologies due to its nefarious use in illegal and terrorist activity. These activities have been well publicized, and therefore there are numerous restrictions on the use of mobile devices in places such as airlines or other secured areas.
- Mobile devices are more than mobile phones. They are able to capture photographs and videos with ease. Therefore, there are also some social and ethical restrictions on their use (e.g., in a public swimming pool or in an exam hall.) These possibilities of mobile usage need to be considered as a significant challenge by mobile businesses.
- Scalability of the location-aware systems is an important factor that also determines the performance of these systems. Mokbel et al. (2003) defines scalability of location-aware systems as the system's ability to provide real-time responses to a large number of continuous concurrent spatiotemporal queries coming from users to the central system. Mokbel et al. (2003) divided the spatiotemporal queries into snapshot queries and continuous queries. Snapshot queries are those that can be answered using data that is already collected and saved on fixed computing resources. Continuous queries, on the other hand, depend on data progressively accumulating into the fixed resources. They also propose a sharing mechanism for these queries among various entities of the system to achieve optimum scalability of the system (Vyas and Yoon 2005).

■ Unpredictable workload patterns: Mobile infrastructures and solutions need an operating environment that can handle transactions at unpredictable workload patterns and that can also support evolving solutions.

■ Physical security of the device: This is very important as mobile handheld devices can be easily misplaced or lost due to their small size. Mobile devices used by employees give rise to security concerns, especially where the organization uses specialized devices to enable its "roaming" employees, such as road runners for vehicle breakdown services or couriers, access to internal data. A lost mobile device is worth far more than the actual value of the device because of its ability to access organizational data and information.

■ Viruses and spyware: With increasing capabilities, mobile devices are also becoming more susceptible to attacks by viruses, Trojan horses, worms, and spywares. An example of such attacks include flooding of a targeted cell phone with large amount of spam SMS messages that results in constant messaging and paging; resulting in denial of service to the user and associated inconvenience and frustration. Another example is the use of Bluetooth connectivity to infect smart phones that are switched on in a discoverable mode (known as the Cabir worm).

Arguments for Mobile Transition

The discussion thus far provides a detailed understanding of what constitutes a mobile business, and its advantages and challenges. This section discusses and justifies the need for formal mobile transitions by business.

Formal METs consider the critical issues involved in people, processes, and technologies associated with the business. Mobile transitions are further described as the process of subjecting the business processes of an organization to systematic changes to incorporate mobile technologies to gain time and cost saving, and therefore, increase the productivity of those processes (Marmaridis and Unhelkar 2005). The critical success factors for adoption and use of mobile technologies in business have also been discussed by Murugesan (2005). Formal understanding of mobile technology, including devices, networks, standards, and software in the context of mobility, comprises three aspects:

1. The type of devices that are in the market for customers to access mobile technology and the ability of these customers to adapt to such devices
2. The trust and positive perception of customers in the current and impending mobile technology, protocols, and standards (for instance, the third-generation mobiles brought mobile data)
3. The standards and software available so that there is portability irrespective of the network provider, and the investment in technology is not wasted even if the network providers have to be changed

Challenges to Mobile Business

User Transition

Users are likely to carry one or more mobile devices with them. A formal mobile transition ensures that the users are able to make full utilization of the contents, services, and collaborations offered by the business. Thus, successful transitions will not leave it entirely up to users to figure out whether their individual mobile devices are able to accept the new mobile services offered by the business. A transition path for users is highly valuable in ensuring that they are not disadvantaged while the business undergoes a formal transition of its offerings, including services, networks, applications, and contents.

Ensuring Users' Social Compatibility with Usage

User adoption and usage refers to how quickly users get adapted to applications and services offered by the technology and how frequently they use such services to create a demand for them. SMS can be quoted as an example: it began slowly, but has since caught up and surpassed all expectations of mobile network operators, providing users with a simple and very cost-effective way to send messages in real-time and anywhere in the world. SMS usage has also led to the creation of a new, shortened vocabulary in the process.

Business Process Transition

Formal mobile business transitions start with a wide focus, going beyond the technology from the outset. However, the business processes in transition also model on and merge with the mobile enterprise architecture. Changes to business processes need to consider the changes to employee lifestyles and expectations. Neither acceptance of change nor customization of the software is an acceptable solution. To reap cost savings from mobile systems, significant analysis and process reengineering is required, which ensures collaboration and sustained benefits.

Geographical and Environmental Considerations

The nature of mobile systems (especially with multinational corporations) involves transacting across the world—24 hours a day, 7 days a week, globally. Analysts fail to appreciate the geographical, relational, and environmental inhibitors that influence the scope of mobile implementations. Cross-border logistics, culture, language, economics, and regulatory climate are just some considerations that can affect the integration of business processes between regional offices and external organizations, creating communication issues throughout the mobile business processes. Therefore, the performance of all participants in a business process is vital.

Cost and Benefit Considerations

Mobility has potential for not only providing profits to businesses but also increasing these profit margins by producing cost savings in the operational aspects of the business. The initial analysis of cost and benefits needs to consider the investment costs of MET itself, followed by the operational costs. However, given the nature and scope of MET, these are difficult to accurately quantify as mobile business costs can be "fuzzy" and complicated to calculate. In addition, many of the benefits resulting from mobility are intangible, making the cost–benefit calculations more challenging than before.

Capability Assessment

The implementation and support of mobile systems can be rather complex and, therefore, demands experience, resources, and incremental implementations. The planning and analysis phases of MET require appreciation of the level of complexity involved.

Success in METs cannot be achieved without a "guiding" set of well-thought-out activities and tasks, roles, and deliverables. This calls for a systematic study of the existing organization in terms of its current demographics, its current business environment, its technological strengths, the extent and reach of its business processes that would satisfy the needs of its customers, and the sociocultural aspects of the organization itself (including its organization structure, legal impact, and privacy and security issues).

Thus, an important aspect of the evolution and development of mobile business/commerce is the need to keep in mind the evolution of the earlier electronic business as well. This is so because the mobile business and the required mobile transition will have a need to integrate with the electronic transition that the business will have undergone earlier; and there will also be a need to build on the lessons learned from electronic transition of organizations onto the Internet. Understanding electronic transition can benefit mobile transition as it can ensure that the transition being undertaken is not counterproductive to the existing business—particularly the Internet-based electronic business (Marmaridis and Unhelkar 2005).

Implementation and Testing of Mobile Software Applications

Mobile applications and their value should be perceived as beneficial by customers if mobile technologies are to be used as a tool. For example, the most popular applications for teenagers are downloading music and SMS messaging, which is one of the major revenue-earning applications of mobile technology today. A further example is the use of text messages (SMS) for conveying business communications. The study undertaken at Alacrity Technologies (www.alacritytech.com) is a good example of how SMS can be incorporated in business processes to make them more secure and reliable.

Compliance with Regulatory Framework: Legal, Privacy, and Ethical Requirements

A regulatory framework regulates the telecommunications industry and monitors the legal and ethical issues involved. Issues arising from technical, legal, or social aspects of a technology are addressed in the regulatory framework. This addressing of issues involves the introduction of new laws, practices, policies, and procedures in the industry. The regulatory framework also deals with mobile applications and operations, including the fee structure, to ensure that a level playing field is provided for all stakeholders. In Australia, Telstra (the main telecommunications infrastructure provider) has been forced by the regulatory body to reduce the renting costs of links to other service providers, resulting in the discarding of a multimillion dollar broadband expansion project (Nystedt 2006). The legal landscape for dealing with legal issues arising from varied contractual forms is discussed by Neely and Unhelkar (2005).

The aforementioned factors, when considered carefully and strategically, help organizations adopt mobile technologies by spanning across people, processes, and devices globally. This globalization changes the relationship of the organization with its customers and business partners, and also results in changes to its organizational structure. This transition results in changes to and transition of multiple dimensions of the business, and in this book we study all these dimensions and the steps required in undergoing those transitions, so that mobile technologies become a strategic and creative cause for new and expanding global business.

Changes to an organization's business processes resulting from mobile technology adaptation can be external to the organization, such as new technology and applications as well as customers' demands and competitors' activities, and also internal to the organization, such as employees' demands, business practices, and changing attitudes due to the current trends and style prevalent in the business community. Thus, the case for having a robust methodology for changes in business processes due to mobile technologies is established. Consequently, the need to study mobile transition (m-transition) is also established, which forms the cause and basis for this research.

Mobile Transition Risks

The mobile transition rationale also indicates the corresponding risks associated with undertaking mobile transition:

- The lack of a formal methodology to achieve mobile transition can potentially confuse the employees and customers of the organization; it can also prove to be expensive if unsuitable mobile applications and technologies are procured.

■ An ad hoc approach to mobile transition can lead to failure in adopting mobility and, as a result, damage the image of an organization, particularly in the eyes of its stakeholders and customers.

■ Not considering factors such as organizational culture when introducing change can lead to failure in acceptance of new ideas and technologies.

■ The possibility that organization structures, and their goals and objectives, can be affected by a change in the business processes may be a hard sell. Not understanding the business processes that need to be transformed can negatively impact the transition.

■ The lack of planning for coexistence of mobile business processes can inhibit progress. What are the business processes that could be transformed?

■ Not having a steady and phased approach to transition can interrupt its pace.

■ Changes that are happening in the industry to which the organization belongs in terms of business sector could act as a block to implementing mobile technology. (For example, a banking case study identified financial markets as a potential business unit for mobile transition. However, financial markets represent an industry sector by itself within banking that require a separate focus.)

■ Expected impact after the introduction of mobile technology on the selected business units in the organization may not make the transition look attractive.

■ The direct impact on customers once the new technology is fully implemented would be difficult to forecast accurately. What would these be?

■ Anticipated problems during the changeover can magnify the risks of the transition. Would there be any?

Discussion Points

1. How is the mobile business different from electronic or from its preceding paper-based business? Discuss this in the context of people, processes, and technologies.

2. What is the core difference between mobile commerce and mobile business?

3. Why should an organization consider a formal process for transitioning to a mobile business? What are the benefits of such holistic and formal transitions as against an ad hoc use of mobility by business?

4. What are the challenges of mobility in modern business? Discuss from the point of view of people, processes, and technologies.

5. How does a formal mobile transition influence business and society? Discuss, in particular, the social challenges and advantages resulting from the use of mobility by business.

6. Discuss the risks associated with transitioning to a mobile business.

References

Adam, O., Chikova, P., and Hofer, A. 2005. Managing Inter-Organizational Business Processes Using an Architecture for M-Business Scenarios, *Proceedings of the 4th International Conference on Mobile Business*, Sydney, Australia.

Alacrity Technologies (www.alacritytech.com.au).

Arunatileka, D. 2005. Applying Mobile Technologies to Banking Business Processes, *Proceedings of the 2nd Innovation Conference*, University of Western Sydney, Sydney, Australia.

Arunatileka, D. 2006. Applying mobile technologies to banking business processes, in *Handbook of Research in Mobile Business: Technological, Methodological and Social Perspectives*, ed. B. Unhelkar. New York: Idea Group Publishing.

Arunatileka, D. 2007. Mobile Transformation of Business Processes to Enhance Competitive Delivery of Service in Organisations, Ph.D. thesis, School of Computing and Mathematics, University of Western Sydney, Australia.

Arunatileka, S. and Ginige, A. 2003. Application of the Seven E's in eTransformation to the Manufacturing Sector, *Proceedings of the 13th International Conference on eChallenges*, Bologna, Italy.

Basole, R. C. 2005a. Transforming Enterprises through Mobile Applications: A Multi-Phase Framework, *Proceedings of the 11th America's Conference on Information Systems*, Omaha, NE.

Basole, R. C. 2005b. Mobilizing the Enterprise: A Conceptual Model of Transformational Value and Enterprise Readiness, *Proceedings of the 26th ASEM Conference*, Virginia Beach, VA.

Brad, S. 2006. Mobile Commerce Hits the Big Time, retrieved January 1, 2008, from http://www.wirelessweek.com/article.aspx?id=82750

Dholakia, R. R. and Dholakia, N., 2002. Mobility and markets: Emerging outlines of m-commerce, *Journal of Business Research*, article in press.

Er, M. and Kay, R. 2005. Mobile Technology Adoption for Mobile Information Systems: An Activity Theory Perspective, *Proceedings of the 4th International Conference on Mobile Business*, Sydney, Australia.

Ghanbary, A. 2006. Evaluation of mobile technologies in the context of their application, limitation and transformation, in *Handbook of Research in Mobile Business: Technological, Methodological and Social Perspectives,* ed. B. Unhelkar. New York: Idea Group Publishing.

Ghanbary, A. 2007. Collaborative Business Process Engineering (CBPE) across Multiple Organisations, Ph.D. thesis, School of Computing and Mathematics, University of Western Sydney, Sydney, Australia.

Ghanbary, A. and Unhelkar, B. 2007a. Collaborative Business Process Engineering (CBPE) across Multiple Organizations. In a Cluster, *Proceedings of IRMA Conference,* IRMA 2007, Vancouver, Canada, May 19–23.

Ghanbary, A. and Unhelkar, B. 2007b. Technical and Logical Issues Arising from Collaboration across Multiple Organizations, *Proceedings of IRMA Conference,* IRMA 2007, Vancouver, Canada, May 19–23.

Glenbrook Partners, LLC. 2004. Mobile Commerce Market Forecast, retrieved January 1, 2008, from http://www.paymentsnews.com/2004/08/mobile_commerce.html

Godbole, N. 2006, Relating mobile computing to mobile commerce, in *Mobile Business: Technological, Methodological and Social Perspectives,* ed. B. Unhelkar. New York: Idea Group Publishing.

Hammer, M. and Champy, J. 1994. *Reengineering the Corporation*, Australia: Allen and Unwin.

Hawryszkiewycz, I. and Steele, R., 2005. A Framework for Integrating Mobility into Collaborative Business Processes, *Proceedings of the 4th International Conference on Mobile Business*, 2005, ICMB 2005.

Kalakota, R. and Robinson, M. 2002. *M-Business: The Race to Mobility*, New York: McGraw Hill Professional.

Kazanis, P. 2004. Methodologies and Tools for eTransforming Small to Medium size Enterprises, University of Western Sydney, Sydney, Australia.

Mackay, J. and Marshall, P. 2004. *Strategic Management of eBusiness*. Sydney, Australia: John Wiley & Sons.

Marmaridis, I. and Unhelkar, B. 2005. Challenges in Mobile Transformations: A Requirements Modelling Perspective for Small and Medium Enterprises, *Proceedings of the 4th International Conference on Mobile Business, 2005*, ICMB 2005, Sydney, Australia.

Mokbel, M., Aref, W., Hambrusch, S., and Prabhakar, S. 2003. Towards Scalable Location-Aware Services: Requirements and Research Issues. In *Proceedings of 11th ACM International Symposium on Advances in Geographic Information Systems*, New Orleans, LA, 110–117.

Murugesan, S. 2005. Mobile and wireless computing at a crossroads, *Special Cutter IT Journal Issue on Mobility,* 18(6) (June 2005).

Murugesan, S., Deshpande, Y., Hansen, S., and Ginige, A. 2001. Web engineering: A new discipline for development of Web-based systems, in *Web Engineering: Managing Diversity and Complexity of Web Application Development*, eds. S. Murugesan and Y. Deshpande. Berlin, Germany: Springer-Verlag.

Murugesan, S. and Unhelkar, B. 2004. A road map for successful ICT innovation: Turning great ideas into successful implementations, *Cutter IT* 17(11): 5–12.

Neely, M. and Unhelkar, B. 2005. Role of a collaborative commerce legal framework in IT-related litigations, *Cutter IT* 18(11): 11–17.

Nystedt, D. 2006. Telstra Scraps Massive Broadband Plan, retrieved November 4, 2006, from http://www.computerworld.com.au/index.php/id;1934202264

Porter, E. M. 2001. Strategy and the Internet, *Harvard Business Review*, 63–78.

Rulke A., Iyer, A. and Chiasson, G. 2003. The ecology of mobile commerce: Charting a course for success using value chain analysis, in *Mobile Commerce: Technology, Theory and Applications* (114–130), eds. B.E. Mennecke and S. T.J., Hershey, PA: IRM Press (an imprint of Idea Group Inc.).

Sawhney, M. and Zabin, J. 2001. *The Seven Steps to Nirvana—Strategic Insights into eBusiness Transformation.* New York: McGraw Hill.

Schneider, G. P. 2003. *Electronic Commerce*, 4th annual ed. Boston: Thomson Course Technology.

Schwiderski-Grosche, S. and Knospe, H. 2002. Secure mobile commerce, *Electronics and Communication Engineering Journal* 14: 228–238.

Tsai, H. A. B. and Gururajan, R. 2005. Mobile Business: An Exploratory Study to Define a Framework for the Transformation Process, *Proceedings of the 10th Asia Pacific Decision Sciences Institution (APDSI) Conference*, Taipei, Taiwan.

Toffler, A. 1981. *The Future Shock,* London: Pan Books/Collins.

Toffler, A. 1980. *The Third Wave,* London: Pan Books/Collins.

Unhelkar, B., 2003. Understanding Collaborations and Clusters in the e-Business World, We-B Conference (www.we-bcentre.com; with Edith Cowan University), Perth, November 23–24, 2003.

Unhelkar, B. 2005a. Transitioning to a mobile enterprise: A three-dimensional framework, *Cutter IT Journal* 18(8): 5–11.

Unhelkar, B. 2005b. *Practical Object Oriented Analysis*, Melbourne: Thomson Social Science Press.

Unhelkar, B. 2007. Beyond Business Integration—Management Challenges in Collaborative Business Processes, ICFAI Journal of International Business (IJINB), Publication of ICFAI (Institute of Chartered Financial Analysts of India), March 2007.

Unhelkar, B. and Agrawal, S. 2007. Managing mobile enterprise transitions: Outline of an MET framework, ICFAI Journal of International Business (IJINB), Publication of ICFAI (Institute of Chartered Financial Analysts of India), March 2007.

Unni, R. and Harmon, R. 2005. Location-based services: Opportunities and challenges, in *Handbook of Research in Mobile Business: Technological, Methodological and Social Perspectives,* ed. B. Unhelkar. Hershey, PA: IGI Global.

Varshney, U. 2002. Multicast support in mobile commerce applications, *Computer* 35(2): 115–117.

Vyas, A. and Yoon, V. 2005. Information management in mobile environments using location-aware intelligent agent system (Lia). In *Handbook of Research in Mobile Business: Technological, Methodological and Social Perspectives*, ed. B. Unhelkar. New York: Idea Group Publishing.

Chapter 2

Mobile Enterprise Transition Goals and Framework

I keep six honest serving-men
(They taught me all I knew);
Their names are What and Why and When and How and Where
and Who.

Rudyard Kipling
"The Elephant's Child," *Just So Stories*

Chapter Key Points

- Discusses a wide range of goals of MET such as reduced risks in successful transitions, cost reduction, and improved customer service
- Discusses the mobile organizational structure and the effect of MET on the organizational structure
- Discusses and explains the MET phases
- Discusses the unique and personalized nature of mobility
- Discusses the integration of mobility into the existing business processes

Introduction

Mobile technologies contribute uniquely to the communications revolution by eliminating the need for physical land-based connectivity between people, processes, and entities. Adoption by business of this unique wireless connectivity, as discussed in Chapter 1, results in significant impact on business enterprises. This includes changes to the organizational structures; internal and external business processes; and relationships with customers, employees, partners, and stakeholders, and is observed irrespective of the size and geographical location of the organization. However, although the ability of businesses and customers to connect to each other independent of time and location by using mobile technologies drives a significant change in the business, its success depends heavily on a meticulously planned and executed methodological framework. A well-researched, tried-and-tested framework reduces the risk in changing the business and ensures mobile success. This chapter outlines such a methodological framework. Called the Mobile Enterprise Transition (MET) framework, it provides detailed guidance based on the questions of "why, what, how, and who," thereby facilitating the strategic adoption of mobility by business. These generic questions translate to questions related to people, processes, and technologies involved in transitioning to a mobile business. The MET framework, validated by research, provides an orderly approach to mobile business transitions that acknowledges the aforementioned questions, studies them, and incorporates them into four major dimensions of the business in transition. This chapter outlines these four dimensions within the MET framework and how it ensures the successful adoption of mobility by business. The MET framework focuses the goals of the organization on strategic and formal adoption of mobility and, at the same time, ameliorates the risks associated with the transition. Thus, this chapter discusses the goals of MET, managing the expectations of the business, layers and structures of the organizations, the four dimensions, project management considerations, and the overall research framework that forms the basis of the MET framework.

Goals of Mobile Enterprise Transition (MET)

> The strategic use of mobility must incorporate a holistic thinking that considers all significant dimensions of the business. The economic, technical, process, and social dimensions of a business provide the strategic basis for mobile transitions. All internal as well as external factors of a business, the organizational structure of the business, and the customers are studied and modeled in light of their potential for becoming mobile. This study and modeling eventually results in the strategic adoption of mobility by the business.

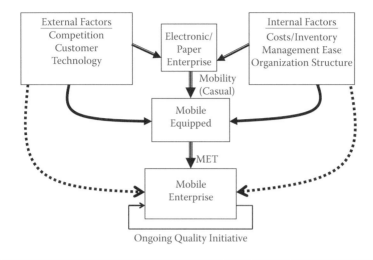

Figure 2.1 Mobile Enterprise Transition (MET) fundamentals—basic.

Significance of MET to Business

MET is a systematic framework helping organizations to strategically adopt mobile technologies in all aspects of their business. The goals of MET are, therefore, discussed within the context of the overall goals of the mobile business. A mobile business primarily wants to engage externally with the customers and business partners in a location-independent and time-independent manner to provide them with services and products. It also wants to exploit the location and time independence of mobility for all its internal business processes. As shown in Figure 2.1, these external and internal business factors such as customer, technology, competition, cost, inventory, management control, and organizational structure undergo radical change when they pressurize an organization to transition to a mobile organization. Figure 2.1 further shows that a casual or ad hoc adoption of mobility by all these aforementioned factors will merely shift the organization to a mobile-equipped one. Complete and successful transformation of a paper-based, land-based, or mobile-equipped enterprise to a comprehensive mobile enterprise occurs only through MET. Thus, extending an earlier definition of mobile transformation given by Marmaridis and Unhelkar (2005), MET can be defined as "evolution of both internal and external business practices through the adoption of suitable mobile technologies and processes resulting in a mobile enterprise."

The mobile business is not just restricted to application of mobility to external and internal business on mobile devices. Strategic use of mobility in all aspects of business requires a "ground up" study and understanding of organizational structures; operational arrangements; customer relationships; and the sociology, physical environment, and ecosystem of the business. The use of mobile gadgets by merely repeating the existing electronic and physical business processes only makes the organization mobile equipped. This usage is not a strategic use of mobility. Such repetition of existing processes on mobile devices leads only to "automation" and "mobilization" and may provide some small-time benefit to the organization, but it does not result in full exploitation of the capabilities of mobile technologies by the business.

The strategic use of mobility must incorporate holistic thinking, a consideration of all internal as well as external factors of the business in the light of their potential for becoming mobile, study of the impact on the environment, and an examination of all the hidden corners of the business that can provide for, and benefit from, mobility. Furthermore, due consideration to the human elements such as usability and privacy of customers and employees are paramount to the success of MET. Thus, one of the primary objectives of MET is to transcend technology and move by providing "value" to all business stakeholders, and exploit the concepts of the location and time independence of mobility. The concept of "value" is discussed in further detail in Chapter 8, where a mature mobile organization is made responsible for "value" metrics rather than profit.

A mobile enterprise also needs to understand the potential offered by mobility in the globalization of business. This is so because wireless networks, satellite communications, and associated gadgets and processes of mobility have a great potential for reaching out globally. Mobile customers and employees are able to "roam" freely around the world with their mobile gadgets without losing connectivity to the business. Thus, business globalization and the society, as discussed by Devereaus and Johansen (1994) and Ranjbar and Unhelkar (2003), are now considered in the context of a global-mobile society by the transitioning business. This global social aspect is discussed in further detail in the social dimension of mobile transitions in Chapter 6.

MET and Business Expectations

The goals of MET need to be in line with the goals of business. Business aims to achieve substantial value for itself, its customer, and its business partners out of its strategic mobile transition. Therefore, these MET goals primarily, and understandably, provide advantages of mobile technologies to business. However, they vary depending on the demographics and mobile maturity of the transitioning organization. In fact, the value from MET to business encompasses a large number of varying factors. The research survey on MET, listed in Appendix A, asked participants to offer descriptive comments on the value, as perceived by them, being provided by mobility to business. These mobile technology values to business can be summarized as follows:

■ *Streamlining of business processes:* MET aims to streamline and organize business processes through engineering and reengineering of those processes. The new and reengineered processes make use of the location and time independence offered by mobility. Both internal and external business processes are studied, modeled, and incorporated with mobility during MET-based transformations, which result in streamlined and optimized business processes. Business Process Modeling Notation (BPMN) and Unified Modeling Language (UML) activity diagrams are being used to achieve this process optimization.

■ *Dynamic customization of products and services:* MET equips the business to dynamically modify and update its offerings to the customer. This depends on the context of the customers, which is dictated by their location, density, urgency, etc. The context of the mobile user is discussed in detail in Chapters 3 and 5.

■ *Organizational structure:* MET brings about changes to the organizational and team structures to ensure they are lean and effective, and not rigid and hierarchical. Flexibility in team structures is positively enhanced by mobile usage.

■ *Cost reduction:* Through MET, a business aims to reduce its cost of operation, marketing, services, and support. Business decision makers are convinced of MET only after they look at their return on investment (ROI) (Younessi 2008).

■ *Profit enhancement:* Results from better customer service, increased number of customers, and improved and optimized external and internal business processes.

■ *Competition:* MET enables the organization to remain competitive by capitalizing on mobile technology before its competing businesses do so.

■ *Personalization of customer service:* Customers are increasingly demanding services that are tailored to their needs. These needs are highly personalized, not only for the customer but also in the context in which the customer is looking for that service. MET provides an opportunity for the business to tailor its offerings to a particular customer at a particular location. Furthermore, such personalization significantly improves the overall experience the customer has with the business.

■ *Value-adding to customer services:* Through MET, employees are able to spend more time with customers at the customer's premises or sites. Employees can also use their mobile devices connected to their enterprise servers to access mobile enterprise applications (e.g., sales), know their internal inventories, and thereby respond immediately to the demands of the customer.

■ *Timely service to customers:* MET ensures that the organization not only provides services but also does so in a timely fashion. Thus, MET enhances the ability of the organization to provide prompt service to its customers, which, in turn, opens up opportunities for newer kinds of services.

■ *Accessibility:* MET improves the ability of the organization to reach out to the customer and also makes it easy for the customer to access the organization's services. Thus, with MET, both the customer and the business are "available" to each other as and when they want. For example, an airline passenger can access flight times while being driven to the airport in a taxi without actually ringing the airline, and a preset parameter can ensure that the relevant information is obtained by the passenger through an SMS on his or her mobile device. Similarly, the accessibility of sports scores, medical information, etc., is increasing with ease. Rapid growth and availability of hot spots is enabling connectivity around airports, hotels, restaurants, schools, and universities.

■ *Reaching wider and dispersed audience:* This goal is significant in MET as it enables the organization to "tap" into audiences (and potential customers) that it would not have access to otherwise. Furthermore, this extension through mobility is at a global level because, through the "roaming" features of modern-day mobile gadgets and networks, a customer need not be in the vicinity of the business to transact business with it. City, country, or regions do not matter, especially when the business wants to access and provide service to the "registered" customer.

■ *Image creation:* Formal use of mobility in all dimensions of business helps to create and promote the image of the organization as a progressive one. This image can potentially lead to improved business.

■ *Environment and sustainability:* This goal of MET enables an organization to launch green initiatives through the use of mobility. Mobility has the opportunity to provide environmentally responsible business strategies, as discussed by Unhelkar and Dickens (2008). Environmental issues with green mobile are further discussed in detail in Chapter 9.

■ *Operational efficiency:* Increased internal business process efficiency can be achieved by applying mobile technologies to those business processes. For example, mobility can assist in human relations (HR), inventory management, time management, and supply-chain management systems by improving information flow within and between these systems. Decisions are taken quickly and accurately by making the necessary information available between people through systems.

■ *Ability to capture data at the source:* With mobility, there is considerable reduction in duplication and errors in sourcing of data for organizational systems. Portable mobile and wireless devices enable critical data to be captured at the time and place of its creation, which, in turn, helps reduce mistakes in capturing data and improves data information quality. For example, an RFID-enabled inventory management system will directly provide stock levels to the system and will not have any translation.

■ *Flexibility in the workplace:* Mobility provides great opportunities for teleworking. Work need not be limited by office space and office hours in the mobile age, and therefore the concept of work itself is evolving with mobility. Mobile technologies enable people with families to balance their work and personal life, as also people who are physically challenged from sickness or past injuries, to find a new avenue for offering their skills and services in the workforce. However, great care needs to be taken to ensure the privacy of mobile employees. The personal quality of life of workers should not suffer as a result of mobile intrusion. A carefully implemented "working away from workspace" plan can help alleviate the challenge of loss of privacy in the workplace, improve employee morale, and also potentially reduce staff turnover.

■ *Increased employee productivity:* MET enables employees and workers in the organization to access various services such as e-mails, personal and corporate calendar, and other groupware enterprise applications while they are on the move, in meetings, participating in conferences, or traveling. Mobility offers the opportunity to productively use otherwise nonutilized time periods by providing employees and managers with direct access to decision support systems.

■ *Improved management understanding and control:* MET enables management at all levels of the business to be involved in the decision-making process. Therefore, there is high potential for integrated decision making by the various stakeholders in the business, leading to a much improved management understanding, structure, operation, and control of the business than before MET.

■ *Facilitating collaboration among various businesses:* Web-enabled portals and corresponding mobile gadgets open the doors not only to "business-to-customer" interaction but also between multiple businesses. Collaboration is the fourth layer of the triangle, as discussed in Chapter 1. Enabling this collaboration through mobility among businesses is a major goal of MET.

■ *Generating content for services:* MET aims to help the business generate timely and relevant content by facilitating user input in the content-generating process. MET ensures sourcing of content, which is a major activity for the mobile business. Transitioning of business is able to generate content through various sources, including user input, regular Web-services-based updates, subscriptions from other service providers, and so on.

■ *Virtual team formation and facilitating team collaboration with no hindrance to team formation:* Mobility opens up enormous opportunities for the creation of virtual teams based on the niche skills of various employees, consultants, and managers. As physical location is not a limitation, these various business players can get together to serve the needs of a particular customer. Further, such virtual teams can also lead to a reduction in staff numbers as it enables the business to tap into the skills of consulting professionals outside the business for shorter and specific durations. The purpose of such reengineering of processes is not focused on staff reduction; however, it does lead to a much leaner team structure (http://www.theleanway.com/).

■ *Outsourcing/smart sourcing:* Globalization has opened the doors to optimizing the utilization of resources. Thus, through online, real-time communication facilities, businesses are able to utilize physically dispersed resources. This giving out of work to areas where there is an abundance of workers is called *outsourcing*. Outsourcing has evolved beyond mere transfer of work for cheap labor. MET creates an environment for collaboration among businesses with data, knowledge, and experience to offer in addition to labor. This collaboration is called *smart sourcing*, as discussed by Hazra (2006).

■ *Improved disaster recovery:* The ability of the business to resume its operations as quickly and efficiently as possible after a disaster occurs is enhanced by MET, mainly because the business is not tied down to a single location in terms of carrying out operations.

MET and Internal Organizational Factors

An organization undergoing MET has an important effect on the organizational structure. As alluded to in the top layer of Figure 2.2, mobility changes it to a "mobile" one. This change results in the flattening of existing hierarchical reporting mechanisms. The mobile organizational structure also provides the customer with easy and direct access to the organization as he or she need not go through a step-by-step bureaucratic process to reach the right person. Through reengineering and new engineering of mobile business processes, customers are able to directly access the relevant employees who can provide them with the service they want. The internal organizational factors, such as internal team structures, reporting hierarchies, number of resources, and their job descriptions are also affected by MET. These internal factors undergoing MET further include the operational processes of the organization, as discussed in Chapter 1, under the business usage triangle

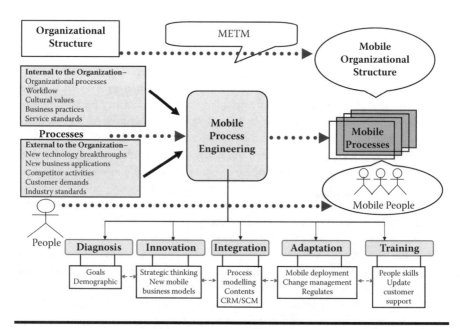

Figure 2.2 Mobile Enterprise Transition (MET) fundamentals—detailed.

(Figure 1.3). The employees and management of a business are usually keen to see mobile-enabled changes to the internal business processes that will improve the quality of their work.

Examples of these internal business processes include time sheets, inventory, payroll, and invoicing. Each of these processes can be performed more efficiently and effectively with the help of mobile gadgets than using the land-based Internet or simple manual processes. Internal accounting practices of the organization are also influenced by changes resulting from adoption of mobility by the business and its effect on the internal business processes. For example, it is easier to meet timelines for sending invoices to customers and closing sales proposals quickly with the help of mobile technologies. Mobility brings about changes to the workflows within the organization, the service standards of the organization, and also its internal work culture. For example, the manner in which time is recorded for the work performed can be made more efficient by providing wireless smartcards to the employees. The expected level of service from an organization, in terms of answering a query or tracking a package, has improved with the introduction of mobility. These changes across all internal business processes are substantial and need to be managed with formal change management.

Formal change management in MET ensures that changes are introduced systematically and in a controlled manner. Most importantly, the sociocultural aspects of changes to the organizational structures due to mobile adoption are anticipated and handled with sensitivity toward the employees. For example, change management has to anticipate changes to the reporting structure of a salesperson who may have been reporting to the sales manager for a few years; mobility enables the bypassing of the need for that formal hierarchy as it allows the salesperson direct access to the information that the manager may have. There is a need for formal change management processes to carefully plan the change and take the employees, such as the salesperson and the sales manager, together into confidence. Change management also deals with formal handling of changes in service standards, wherein employees may have to provide instantaneous service to customers as against a relatively slow service response prior to mobility.

MET and External Organizational Factors

Figure 2.2 also shows factors external to the organization that are affected by MET and need to be considered and managed formally. These external factors form part of the overall demographics of the organization, including the size, type, and the industry cluster to which the organization belongs. Demands from the customer, activities of the competitor, and changes to the way the industry operates all influence an organization from outside its boundaries. MET assesses the impact of mobile technologies on the services that can be provided to customers and the value that can be added to the existing services to customers and business partners, and gives the timelines for its actual enactment.

MET Phases

Figure 2.2 shows in detail the five major phases of MET. These are diagnostics, innovation, integration, adaptation, and training. However, in practice, the adaptation and training phases in mobile adoption get merged into a single phase. The five phases play a significant role during enactment, as discussed in Chapter 7. Here, however, we discuss the air background.

Diagnostics

MET undertakes the diagnostic activity to ascertain the current state of the organization with respect to its mobile maturity. It is based on the demographics of the organization, together with its existing mobile maturity. The details of the demographics of a transitioning organization are discussed in greater detail in the section on MET research later in this chapter. The diagnostics, during enactment, are also discussed in detail in Chapter 7. This important activity can help an organization understand the amount of effort required and the possible timeline for it when it undertakes MET. The four different mobile maturity levels are the preliminary, ad hoc, advanced, and managed states. An organization that merely provides mobile gadgets to its employees and aims at dealing with its clients with very basic processes can be considered to be only at a "preliminary" level of mobile maturity. The next stage is the ad hoc use of mobility across the organization, followed by advanced use in all processes and organizational structures. Finally, there is the most mature state, in which the organization is "mobile managed." These states of mobile maturity are also discussed in greater detail in Chapter 7 on the enactment of MET.

Innovation

The innovative activity of the organization undergoing MET is focused on the strategic thinking and strategy formation aspect of the plan for the transitioning business. Innovation deals with new and creative ways of using mobility in all aspects of business. Therefore, it considers both internal and external process requirements, studies the external environment in which the business exists, and also deals with the departments and similar organizational units in terms of prioritizing the effect of changes on them. These innovative aspects of mobile transitions are shown in Figure 2.2.

Integration

The integration activity of MET brings together internal as well as external business processes that would result in a unified view of the business to its users. The business processes and supporting systems in the current state of the organization are studied carefully to effectuate the necessary changes in those processes and systems due to mobility, as required by stakeholders and as demanded by the industry. Whereas existing processes can be merged together with the help of mobility, there are also completely new processes that need to be engineered. These are integrated internally and externally to achieve process objectives. Process modeling tools and techniques are used here to model new processes as well as anticipate changes to existing ones when mobile technology is introduced. Furthermore, the integration of mobile devices with the processes can be classified as a crucial factor for the success of MET. Changes to business processes are more robust and lasting when the effect of new mobile devices are considered together with them. Agreements with service providers and technology partners, enablers, and network operators need to be finalized during integration. Finally, the content and corresponding content management systems (CMS) also need to be integrated with the processes. The CMS database is also integrated with the existing technologies in the organization, such as software systems and applications, databases, and existing security mechanisms.

Adaptation and Training

The adoption of mobile technology by business needs to be complemented by training for employees and business partners. There may even be an opportunity and a need for training customers, especially when they are engaged in large and complex transactions with the business. The personalized and ubiquitous nature of a mobile device and its small size and weight make imparting any formal training to a day-to-day user very challenging. A computer-disk (CD)- or Internet-based user manual and call center support are ways of helping a user learn how to handle a mobile device. However, the use of mobile business applications, content, and networks require a much more formal training on the part of the transitioning business.

Adaptation and training activities are interlinked with each other, and they usually occur simultaneously during MET. Employees are trained during this activity on new and reengineered mobile business processes. At the same time, some existing, old processes may still be required by the business because of operational reasons, and they can be a part of the transition considerations. Therefore, depending on the complexity of the business processes, there can be a parallel execution of the old as well as new processes. The adaptation of technology and training of employees need to be complemented by potential training for business partners and even customers who have large and complex transactions with the business. The training provided to employees during MET helps them with their customer service and support responsibilities using mobile devices. Employees are trained to provide responses to customer calls for support with high level of personalization (Hsu, Burner, and Kulviwat 2005; Unhelkar 2005). The transitioning organization, with its adaptation and training, creates high levels of service standards, delivery periods, response times, and customer orientation, leading to a new customer-oriented business culture (Unhelkar 2005). Creation of this customer-centric unified business view is one of the significant goals of a mobile business. Table 2.1 maps the goals of a business with corresponding MET implications in achieving those goals.

Mobile Strategic Considerations

MET needs to ensure involvement from all stakeholders of the business so as to understand their perceptions of enterprise goals. The goal of the MET framework, which is a successful transition by a business to mobility, eventually translates into satisfying the goals of the business. Mobile strategic considerations start by an understanding of the goals and demographics of the enterprise, together with its mobile maturity.

A strategic framework for adoption of mobility by an enterprise needs to identify and understand its overall goals. These enterprise goals are based on a number of factors, including its demographics (i.e., size, location, and type of business). The goals must ensure that they align the mobile enterprise with its mission and values. MET aims at generating good "value" for its stakeholders. Strategic considerations in the mobile business start with an assessment of the current status of the enterprise in terms of its current mobile usage and maturity. This leads to the identification and investigation of the various business processes in the organization and an analysis of how MET can be applied to them. The business processes must support the overall goal of the enterprise. MET should also propose a mechanism (metric) to identify and measure the criteria for optimization and improvement that can result from it. Thus, changes to business processes due to mobile technologies must be measured before and after the changes. The speed of response, its relevance to the situation and location, the calculations of dynamicity of mobile groups, and quality of service (QoS) are some examples of such mobile process metrics. These metrics provide a set of measurable criteria rather than an ad hoc understanding of the improvements resulting from MET. MET should ensure the involvement of stakeholders so as to understand their perceptions of the goals in relation to

Table 2.1 Mapping the goals of a mobile business and implications of MET

Factor/viewpoints in mobile business	Goals of mobile business	MET implications
Holistic perspective of the organization	Create and provide a unified view of the business to all stakeholders	Undertake an organizationwide transition of people, processes, and technologies. Do not restrict the transition to only a part of the business
Unit of transition	Each business unit should be the basis of the transition, and it should incorporate mobile technologies in all its functions, processes, and team structures	Understand and decompose the overall transition objectives into small manageable objectives for the business units. Apply the holistic perspective of people, processes, and technologies to a specific business unit. Replicate across the entire organization
Demographics of the organization (including its size, location, etc.)	Understand the maturity of the organization in terms of mobile adoption and ascertain an appropriate starting point for the transition	Analyze the type (product, service, or both) and size (small, medium, large) of the organization. Also ascertain the mobile maturity (ad hoc, preliminary, advanced, managed)
Transition approach	Have a systematic and strategic approach to mobile transition with risk reduction	Provide a well-researched MET framework incorporating economic, technical, process, and social perspectives
Measuring the benefits	Measurement of benefits should be accurate and visible	Return on investments (ROI) calculations; SWOT, balanced scorecard; value generation for customer
Risks and change management	Reduce the risk in transition through formal management of change	Enactment of MET as a project; research and experiment

the mobile enterprise and mobile strategic considerations, including the systems approach to the transition. Furthermore, organizational structures and behaviors need to be understood to strategically apply mobility to them. Enterprises may be abstracted in terms of their structures (what they consist of), their processes and functions (what they do, how they change, and how they bring about change), and the technologies they use. Mobile strategies study the organizational structures; model the processes; and implement and measure the networks, databases, and devices. Understanding and measuring these various organizational factors provide a good perception of how mobility can help improve the performance of such an enterprise. Socially, however, advertisement and customer solicitation need to be carefully and sensitively considered. The offerings of the enterprise in terms of products, services, quality, and sustainability are studied within the context of the MET framework. Strategic mobile considerations need to be more than normal nonstrategic considerations and advantages. As an example, the measurement of strategic advantages is provided in Chapter 3.

Mobile Strategic Partnerships

Mobile strategic partnerships form a significant part of a successful MET. This is so because, in setting up and conducting mobile business, there is substantial interaction between the business, its mobile users, mobile content, application service providers, legal and regulatory agencies dealing with mobile compliance, and mobile network operators (Unni and Harmon 2005). Mobile businesses create and provide content and services to customers, and mobile network operators enable transmission of that content over their networks. Thus, as shown in Figure 2.3, mobile network operators together with suppliers and clients exercise considerable influence over the mobile business. This is so because these network operators are in an excellent position to leverage the location data generated in their networks, its authentication information, user preferences, and billing relationships with their

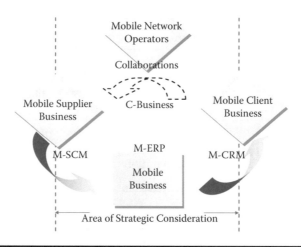

Figure 2.3   Mobile business is closely linked to clients' and suppliers' business.

customers (Prem 2002). Therefore, as shown in Figure 2.3, the area of strategic consideration for the transitioning mobile business includes a part of the business of its suppliers and clients as a result of their significant interdependence on each other due to mobility. Table 2.2 further summarizes and highlights the importance of and the issues involved in forming a strategic relationship between the mobile business, suppliers, clients, and corresponding network operators early on in MET. An understanding of these relationships ensures that the partners are well prepared to collaborate with each other both technically and socially. Due considerations of these strategic issues by the mobile business lays the foundation for specific approaches to mobile adoptions.

Mobile Organizational Structures

Mobility changes the way in which an organization structures itself in terms of its people, their roles, responsibilities, and reporting hierarchy. Emerging organizational structures resulting from mobility are of immense importance in the mobile transition process. These structures are flat and loose, as compared to the hierarchical and rigid structures of the premobile era. This is so because of the numerous crisscrossing of communication channels due to mobility. Mobile processes ensure that the focus of the organizational structure changes from an organization- or department-centric view to a customer-centric one. Organizational and team structures are affected by the way mobility changes the management of human resources and by sociocultural issues in managing MET. Direct access to management and the employee responsible for providing the service means that there is less need for a hierarchical structure in the organization wherein customer requests go through departmental circles to reach the right person.

Mobile Content and Services

Mobile content and services provide significant input in the formation of strategic alliances sought by mobile businesses. For example, although mobile operators are able to capture location data, they need to combine it with the data and information available from content providers to be able to tailor their services to customers' needs. This combination of location-specific services together with mobile content provides excellent opportunities to transitioning businesses to create market differentiation. The incentive to content providers to pair up with network operators is the opportunity to brand the service offered by the latter. During the early stages of MET, it is vital that the business studies and formulates its strategy in terms of how it combines the offerings of the operators and the corresponding content providers. Alternatively, the business itself might be providing content, and in such cases the content provider must work out a win–win strategy together with the network operator as it undertakes MET. For example, consider the scenario in which a network operator and a content provider can together offer services such as a sports

Table 2.2 Mobile strategic partnership issues to be considered in MET

Stakeholders in mobile business	Strategic issues to be considered in becoming mobile
Mobile network operator	Carrier versus partner for the contents and services to be provided by the business
	Pricing model for partnership
	Ability to ascertain and use location information on customers to promote business
	Mobile network technologies for transmission and quality of service
	Ownership issues in terms of mobile content
	Privacy and security issues, particularly from customer viewpoint, in terms of who has and uses customer data
Mobile business	Develop high-value location-based services
	Organize collaborations and partnerships with location-based service providers
	Develop and manage content for mobile services
	Manage changes to organizational structures of the business, and possibility of clients and suppliers
	Develop mobile applications that will create value for customers
	Forge alliances and partnerships with carriers/network operators and other content and application providers
	Create new and successful pricing structures for customers and suppliers
	Integrate online and offline services and business processes to provide uniform view to users
	Handle privacy and security issues related to use of customer data
Mobile client business	Changes to customer relationship management systems due to mobility and processes
	Use extranets and intranets to enable the client to relate to the transitioning business
	Accommodate the client in decision-making process

Table 2.2 *(continued)* **Mobile strategic partnership issues to be considered in MET**

Mobile supplier business	Changes to supply-chain management system
	Application of lean management approach to mobile SCM
	Impact of the individual employee's decision making due to mobile access on the supply chain

score or a traffic update. At times, the operators have a high degree of control over the distribution of mobile contents. This control over the mobile network allows their operators to create greater profit margins for themselves. Therefore, they can brand or cobrand the service, depending on the brand image of the service provider. In the sports score example, network operators can provide the sports score as their own, or if the service provider is a well-known sports association, then the operator can cobrand the score with the sports association. Privacy and security concerns of customers need to be considered in the branding of services in MET as it requires sharing of location and related context information by network operators with trusted partners (Akcayli et al. 2001). The network operators are usually keen not to reduce their role to mere providers of infrastructure for the content sought by customers and users of services. Therefore, they are usually reluctant to participate in a business model wherein content developers have direct access to location- and context-specific data that allows them to deal directly with customers. Network operators can participate in a shared-revenue model with their partners, wherein they retain the right to bill the customer and, thereby, maintain some sort of ownership of the customer for the entire package of services being offered to the customer. Although content developers are free to set prices for their services and attract customers, they end up with a slice of the overall revenue obtained from the customer in this shared-business model.

Service providers need to make appropriate choices from a range of mobile technologies that are available to them to provide their services. For example, the selection of a mobile technology to ascertain the location and context of the customer can provide great opportunities for service providers to customize their services. This is also the difference between a successful mobile content and service provider organization and one that is merely partnering with a network operator. Location- and context-specific data can be obtained from global positioning systems (GPSs), Bluetooth, RFID, and even local WLANs. When a service provider accesses, stores, analyzes, and uses such location- and context-based information of existing and potential customers, it also has the opportunity to bypass the need to partner with a mobile network operator. However, at the same time, such a service provider business may then be limited to the specific locations where there is an opportunity for interfacing with willing customers through WLANs or Bluetooth technologies.

The advantage of going alone, and not partnering with a network operator to provide the service, with a possible time lag before the customer base for the service provider is large enough for the business to be cost effective. Therefore, in terms of strategic decision making during the early stages of MET, it is vital that the business undergoing MET gives due consideration to the network operators, the content, and service providers.

Mobile Business Application Considerations

The transitioning mobile has to consider various business applications and the changes to these applications and packages resulting from mobile technology adoptions. These are

- *Customer relationship management (CRM):* Mobile customer relationship management (m-CRM) must create close relationships with their customers by providing "value." Customers want reliable and fast service, and CRM provides those services to enable the business to gain more customers. CRM is crucial in a mobile business as it is the system that provides it with the ability to directly contact customers and users. Furthermore, personalization of the customer's interaction (such as automated voice interaction that takes into account ethnic diversity and vocabulary) is of great value in an m-CRM. Customers are not interested in the internal functioning of the company. Technology, software, people, and reengineered business processes are brought together in a synergy to provide "value" through CRM.
- *Supply-chain management (SCM):* Mobile SCM provides systems support and value to suppliers who are the business partners of the transitioning mobile business. Direct interaction of the business with the suppliers through mobile applications potentially eliminates the middleman or retailer. A mobile-enabled and streamlined purchase order process reduces the price of the product by eliminating the process overheads by saving time and money. SCM attempts to deliver materials to customers at the best cost it can and as quickly as possible. The information about delivery of products is of equal importance and is provided by SCM using mobility. Similarly, financial matters as well as purchase order transmissions are provided with ease using mobile gadgets. Mobile SCM provides greater flexibility in monitoring and controlling the many documents and their delivery statuses (e.g., order status).
- *Enterprise resource planning (ERP):* Organizations realize the importance of having knowledge of back-office systems that help them improve their customer order and integration of their clusters and provide them with timely information on their day-to-day activities. This is further enhanced by mobility, but the changes to ERP systems for mobility need to be carefully carried out following a process.

- *Procurement systems:* Procurement has a broader meaning, and includes purchasing, transportation, warehousing, and inbound receiving of goods ordered. Mobile procurement systems provide the organization with the opportunity to have better control of their inventory and purchasing processes with the help of up-to-date and relevant information on the internal movement of goods.
- *Human resource (HR) systems:* In the mobile business, these provide opportunities for improved internal HR management by means of personalization of time sheets and payrolls. Enterprise Bargaining Agreements online and other responsibilities of HR are also modified by the use of mobile devices. Further changes in HR systems by mobility include changes in job roles and definitions, shift management, security of goods and premises, and delivery of services. These HR functions are enhanced by the use of mobility.
- *Payroll:* Payroll systems are part of HR, and mobile technologies can be put to creative use in applications to save time and enhance value to employees. As HR systems change and manage rosters, they are linked to payroll to automatically generate a pay list based on the automated roster instead of using a human supervisor.
- *System integration:* Mobile business applications need to integrate all the disparate systems running organizations. Such system integration means more than the mere provision of interfaces (typically XML-based or WML interfaces) for the systems. Formal system integration brings together content, applications, security, and transmission networks.
- *Knowledge management (KM):* Knowledge management can be enhanced with mobility by making it more reliable and accessible to the entire organization anywhere and anytime. Knowledge is created by correlating information on the available services and products of the organization and industry. This correlation requires the system to have excellent search capabilities that also make use of mobile inputs. Specifically, mobility facilitates this linking of and correlation between silos of information in a dynamic manner as access to them is no longer restricted to a physical location. Mobility also provides an excellent opportunity for business to improve their environmental responsibilities by recycling products and streamlining movement of goods. Environmentally intelligent systems have an opportunity to incorporate mobility in them, which will help the organizations using such systems to improve their environment-related performance (such as carbon emissions, which is discussed in Chapter 9).

Interoperability Layers

Location-based businesses deliver services at the specific locations of the users. These services vary depending on the technologies being used by different service providers. However they need to be supported at various layers, as shown in Figure 2.4. The base layer is the transmission network layer, which is where mobile network

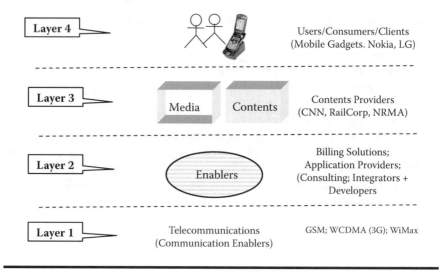

Layer 4	Users/Consumers/Clients (Mobile Gadgets. Nokia, LG)
Layer 3	Contents Providers (CNN, RailCorp, NRMA)
Layer 2	Billing Solutions; Application Providers; (Consulting; Integrators + Developers
Layer 1	GSM; WCDMA (3G); WiMax

Figure 2.4 Layers and players in mobile business.

operators are providing their part of the services. Next is layer 2, the layer of the enablers of mobile services, which include application developers, billing solutions providers, and integrators. The enablers themselves provide the basis for the use of media and content, which are accessed by mobile gadgets for the mobile user. The services are thus provided by a business entity that makes use of the common network transmission technologies provided by another business entity—mobile network operators. Therefore, there is an ongoing need for interoperability between wireless network platforms and location-aware content providers. The 3G (third generation) network has a direct impact on market growth because it affects software, device, and content development. The challenge for such integration also impacts customer growth and retention as it has a bearing on costs, inconsistency of user interfaces, privacy and security concerns, and possibly learning challenges by users of new services. The need for interoperability is coupled with the need to have a standardized mobile payment infrastructure.

Pricing

Pricing of products and services is a significant strategic component of the transition in undertaking MET. Newly created and offered mobile service (and related products) needs to consider not only the setup and operational costs but also price differentials with other business partners and network operators. A successful pricing strategy can facilitate market growth for the mobile business. However, it is not based merely on the value of the content but, equally if not more, on the perceived value of the overall benefit derived from a service (Harmon and Laird 1997). The offerings of a mobile business are in terms of personalized, context-specific, timely, and easy-to-use services. When the customer perceives the services as such, he or she is prepared to pay for them. The prices of these services can consist of a standard flat fee and a service charge. Nonfinancial factors such as loss of privacy or, possibly, intrusive marketing promotions also need to be balanced in this pricing process. There is an ongoing need to balance flat-fee tiered pricing, in which a fixed charge is applied for a given quota of airtime, with pricing based on the quantity of data transferred. This is so because customer billing is based on only one aspect, say, the data quantity, and an unaware customer may end up with unexpected bills. On the other hand, subscription-based pricing can be easy to understand, but such pricing may have limitations on the value the network carriers can generate, particularly if the customer is a heavy user of the service.

Availability of a large number of services is usually not perceived as valuable by customers. Further, as correctly stated by Williams (2003), a common standard approach to pricing for different types of customers without segmenting the market and differentiating the value of the service based on location, as perceived by the customer, may not lead to improved financial performance. For example, a roadside emergency service that can guide a driver in distress may be very important for frequent travelers and soccer moms but perhaps not for college-going students who may construe such facilities as limiting their independence. Alternatively, applications developed for niche segments such as outdoor enthusiasts (e.g., campers, hunters, fishers) may hold considerable potential (Rao and Minakakis 2003) in providing services and facilities that are considered valuable by users.

Service providers have greater flexibility in setting their prices when consumers have independent and unrestricted access to services without additional charges from network operators. The effects of advertisement costs, which are packaged together by service providers with network operators, also need to be considered because they have an impact on the overall pricing of services. The pricing issue is particularly relevant as marketers want to use location-based advertising and promotion to drive traffic to a storefront. Marketers and promoters want to encourage location-specific mobile-shopping behavior that can be dynamically customized to the needs of the location and time. MET needs to provide formal strategies to attract customers to stores by providing personalized promotional offers together with services that are available at reasonable prices. Consider, for example, half-priced umbrellas being offered in a shopping mall when it has just started raining outside. The situation is likely to more than double the sale of umbrellas. However, the revenue generated from sales need to be shared between the provider of the umbrellas and the wireless network operator who transmitted the messages on the mobile phones of potential customers in the mall at the time it started raining. The involvement of multiple parties in conducting successful mobile transactions requires creativity and innovation in pricing strategies; however, currently, there appears to be a dearth of alternative pricing strategies. As alluded to earlier, perhaps there is an opportunity to consider separate pricing for mobile voice services versus mobile data services, and a need to consider the impact of high-speed networks (such as 3G and 4G) in pricing them. Prem (2002) has discussed some of these alternative payment options such as pay-per-use, prepaid usage, service-specific subscription fees, rates depending on the time of day or volume of usage, and so on. These payment options need to be further investigated and modeled on the high-speed networks to come up with a good collaborative business model for the success of mobility in business. There is an argument here to create price differentiation based on location, time, and context, wherein a customer at a specific location is keen to get that service at that particular time and location and is less concerned about the price. Finally, even comparative information on pricing can be made available to customers if the business is confident of the value of its offering. Overall, however, it is better for service providers to align themselves with network operators and bundle their services together with those of the operator. This is so because network operators have a much wider and readily available audience, with a higher penetration rate and better chance of promoting the services over their networks than service providers trying to go it alone through local or proprietary networks.

Balancing Personal Services with Privacy

There is evidence from the earlier E-commerce experience that users are willing to provide personal information in exchange for personalized services (Beinat 2001). Another study reveals that mobile customers are more concerned about usefulness and degree of personalization of service than privacy threats (Ho and Kwok 2003). However, the potential for misuse of personal information is real and raises several questions such as these: Who would have access to the location information? Can the user not have his location tracked? How secure is the information (Fink 2002)? The mobile business has to be proactive in creating and following good practices regarding management and use of location data. This practice not only builds trust with consumers but also serves to avoid a more restrictive regulatory climate that may eventually come about if self-regulation does not work.

MET Methodological Framework

There are risks in adopting the new technology as soon as it is available in the market. This risk is because the technology is unknown and untried, and there could be numerous unresolved issues. This is particularly true of mobility, as there is a need to consider the unique challenges of mobility in terms of devices, networks, security, and presentation. There are also significant issues in embarking on mobility, related to the high cost involved in all introductory levels of any new technology.

The immediate question in setting up a MET framework is whether it should be an evolutionary, gradual process or an immediate and radical transformation. The experience of numerous professionals, especially those involved in change management, is that the practical transition is always a combination of revolution and evolution—revolution so that the organization should not fall behind by not remaining competitive in the market, and evolution to reduce the risk of not having a successful E-transformation. According to Murugesan et al. (2001), the development and transformation of an organization could be classified as follows:

> The choice of a suitable development model, according to practitioners and researchers, should be based on its site (and applications), its document orientation, content and graphics design, budget and time constraints and the changing technology.

The risk in adapting the new technology as soon as it is available in the market is that the technology is unknown, with numerous unresolved issues. Another factor in the early-stage entry of business is the high cost involved in all introductory levels of any new technologies.

However, if a business is late in adopting mobility during a specific period of time and its competitors do so, then there is a great chance that the business is left behind in terms of technology adoption, and it may not be able to catch up with its competitors. These are some issues that management is facing today.

Organizations must let internal and external parties involved know that some changes are going to take place. In view of people's general resistance to change, this will give the parties some time to prepare for and adjust to change. The core training is meant for internal parties in the organization; however, it is very important to provide sufficient information to external parties and advise them about change. Organizations must plan and manage change (cultural, technological, internal, and external) and understand the key areas associated with dangers related to their working environment that others have discovered and faced. Implementation of mobile business applications must be rapid, and each project should ideally be phased to be delivered in a maximum of three months. Build quickly and move to the learning stage; then build the next stage and fix the previous ones based on what you have learned.

The transition must remain persistent alongside the development of individual clusters and with detailed communication between them. According to Brans (2003), mobile transition generally takes place by distinguishing what kind of portable devices, networks, application gateways, and enterprise applications are required.

The earlier discussions provide the backdrop for understanding and creating the MET methodological framework. Thus far, various strategic factors influencing mobile transitions have been discussed. There is now a need to outline the overall framework that will enable a strategic transformation of the enterprise to a mobile enterprise. When an organization decides to incorporate mobility into its business, it is a strategic decision that is based on the primary question of *why* "mobilize." This strategic decision is followed by the instantiation of a MET process framework, which is discussed here. The process framework is made up of four major dimensions of a process (Devereans and Johansen 1994). They are the economic, technical, process, and social dimensions, which deal, respectively, with the why, what, how, and who of any transition framework. MET facilitates the incorporation of mobile technologies in business processes, which results in pervasive business activities independent of location and time. Practical experience in dealing with MET issues as discussed by Unhelkar (2003b), Ginige et al. (2001), Subramanium et al. (2004), as well as earlier research conducted by Arunatileka and Unhelkar (2003), suggests that MET encompasses, in addition to mobile processes, technical issues as well as the sociological impact of mobile transformations. Furthermore, as mentioned in the goals of MET and also based on practical experience in dealing with it, a business hardly ever embarks on this transition unless there are sufficiently justified business reasons to do so.

Thus, conceptually, the MET framework can be said to consist of four major aspects—economic, technical, process, and social dimensions. The process of designing a research instrument for setting up a MET (discussed later in this chapter) also reveals the need to understand the demographics of the organizations undergoing MET. These demographics in terms of location, size, and related factors provide a significant insight into the goals and drivers of MET.

Economic Dimension (Why)

The business drivers for incorporation of mobility in business are strategic decisions based on the primary question of "why" to "mobilize." These strategic decisions lead to instantiation of a MET process framework that can take the business to a global mobile playing field. This decision to adopt mobility by the organization is a part of the business dimension of MET. The business/economic dimension of the MET framework is primarily concerned with the costs, competition, customers, employees, convenience, and usage of mobility. These business aspects form part of the survey and are further listed in Table 2.3.

Technical Dimension (What)

The technical dimension focuses on "what" technologies form the creative cause of MET and "what" deliverables are produced at the end of the process. Issues discussed in this dimension include devices/gadgets, programming, databases, networking, security, and architecture of mobile technologies participating in MET. Thus, the process technical dimension includes the understanding and application of various mobile hardware devices and gadgets, issues of GPS-enabled gadgets (3G), and wireless networking and security, as related to MET. There is also an underlying need to prioritize these technical drivers in terms of their relative importance for the organization as it undertakes mobile transition. These technical drivers are summarized in Table 2.3.

Table 2.3   Mobility considerations in mobile Internet usage by business

	M-informative	M-transactive	M-operative	M-collaborative
Economic (why)	Costs Nuisance	Profit sharing Alliance formation	Costs Inventory	Trust Legal mandates
Technology (what)	Device availability and access	Networking—Internet connectivity Reliability Security	Intranet Extranet Groupware Reliability	Portals Groupware Standards and interoperability
Methodology (how)	Personal process	Business process reengineering (BPR)	Organizational policies, BPR	Industrial process reengineering Business collaboration
Sociology (who)	Privacy, access	Security Confidence Convenience	Security Trust Workplace regulations Ethics	Security Trust, sociocultural issues

Process Dimension (How)

The process dimension of the MET methodological framework deals primarily with the question of "how" to model and conduct business transactions, how to ensure quality, and how to manage the changing relationship of the business with its customers and employees. It is concerned with business processes, their modeling and "engineering," and how adoption of mobility by business affects the customer. The process drivers are summarized in the third row of Table 2.3.

Social Dimension (Who)

The social dimension of the transformation process focuses on "who" the players in MET are and how they influence and are influenced by the MET process. Typically, these are clients, employees, and other "users" of the business. The issues that face the users when they interface with a mobile business include usability and privacy, and the way their relationships change with the organization. The changes to work formats, including telecommuting and changing organizational and social structures, are all part of this social dimension of MET. Furthermore, this social dimension also considers the nature of wireless connectivity, as discussed next, which indicates the highly "individual" nature of mobile gadgets and their ability to be location aware (see Adam and Katos [2005], and Elliott and Phillips [2004], for the individual nature of a mobile gadget). These social factors are summarized in Table 2.3 in the last row.

Figure 2.5 shows the four mobile dimensions. Figure 2.6 also shows the four evolutionary and revolutionary tiers of mobile business transitions—m-informative, m-transactive, m-operative, and m-collaborative. As the organization evolves from one usage to another, it also maps with the four dimensions of MET. Table 2.3 maps the four transition dimensions with the evolving mobile usage by business and provides some thoughts on that mapping (which is shown in Figure 2.6).

The Unique Nature of Mobility

The personalized nature of mobility implies that it needs to be separately considered at various levels; first, at the individual level, where it affects the way in which an individual user uses the device; second, at the organizational level, where the issues related to the organization and the relationship of an individual user (such as an employee) with the organization comes into play; and finally at the collaborative level, where the relationships between various organizations as well as individuals need to be considered simultaneously.

Electronic business transitions have been studied, among others, by Ginige et al. (2001) and Lan and Unhelkar (2005). However, the uniqueness of mobile technologies and transitions and how they extend and apply electronic transitions in terms of their impact on business have been discussed by Marmaridis and Unhelkar (2005), Unhelkar (2003b), Godbole and Unhelkar (2003), and Elliott and Phillips (2004). These authors have focused on the specific nature of mobility, which can be extended as shown in Figure 2.7 and is discussed here. The inner square in this figure indicates land-based connectivity between enterprises, functional units, and other fixed devices. This connectivity evolved from the initial centralized connectivity of the mainframe, followed by client/server connectivity and finally resulting in Internet connectivity (business-to-business—B2B, and business-to-customer—B2C). Internet-based connectivity is further augmented by eXtensible Markup Language (XML) to facilitate the Internet as a medium of computing, rather than merely a means of communication. However, as depicted by the outer square in Figure 2.7, external wireless connectivity, by its very nature, is between

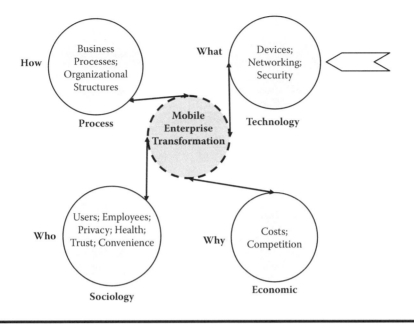

Figure 2.5   The four dimensions of a MET framework.

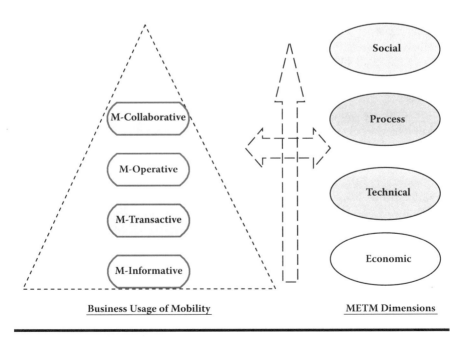

Figure 2.6   Mapping business usage of mobility with MET dimensions.

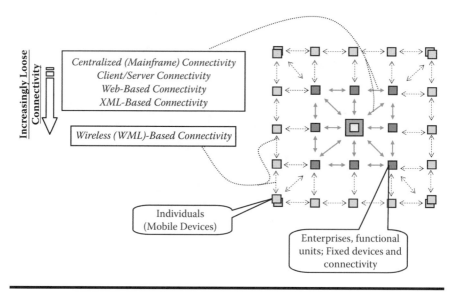

Figure 2.7   Considerations of the nature of mobile "wireless connectivity" and mobile devices.

an individual and the business or between two individuals. As correctly stressed by Elliott and Phillips (2004), a mobile phone is a far more personal device (than, say, a desktop personal computer) as it can be carried by an individual.

This nature of wireless connectivity needs to be understood and incorporated in the dimensions of MET mentioned earlier. For example, technically, it is essential to consider the "individuality" of the mobile gadgets and their ability to be location-aware (see Adam and Katos [2005] for the resultant challenges of security and privacy of individuals, which is different from the challenges in corresponding land-based connections). The economic dimension needs to consider the cost of individual mobile devices and the network's operational costs. The activities and tasks of the process dimension should be created in a way that properly exploits handheld gadgets; socially, mobile transitions need to consider the impact of mobility on the sociocultural fabric of society and the corresponding changing value systems such as work ethics and social protocols. Thus, when businesses transition from the land-based connectivity paradigm and incorporate wireless connectivity in their business practices, they have to ensure that the individual is considered in all their process dimensions.

A customer looks at a mobile business as more than a business that is merely converting its existing services to mobile services. He or she wants the business to provide new and unique services that will make formal use of the location and time independence provided by mobility.

A customer is keen to have highly personalized services provided to him or her when services are delivered on a mobile gadget, especially when they have the potential to target a specific individual. Personalization is one of the unique advantages

Table 2.4 Mobility considerations at individual, organizational, and collaborative levels

Mobile	Individual (customer, employee)	Organization (small, large, global)	Collaboration (vertical, horizontal, dynamic)
Economic (why)	Unit cost—devices and transaction	Infrastructures Operations	Alliance, legal
Technology (what)	Gadgets Usability	Networking Intranet	Web services
Process (how)	Personal process	Business processes	Industrial processes
Sociology (who)	Privacy Telecommuting	Access Usability	Dynamic social cluster/groups

of mobile technologies for customers. The personalized nature of mobility means that it needs to be separately considered at the individual level, then at the organizational level, and finally at the collaborative level. These levels of consideration are shown in Table 2.4, together with the four MET dimensions.

MET Project Management Considerations

MET is a project and should be considered as such. Its project management aspect during enactment is discussed in detail in Chapter 7. Here, its five stages—diagnosis, planning, action, evaluation, and enhancement—are discussed.

Diagnosis

The diagnosis stage of MET involves identifying the business. The interpretation of the current scenario of the business has to be done in a holistic fashion to evaluate the solution. The diagnosis stage is mapped to the mobile transition by trying to identify demographics and mobile maturity. The initial studies, interviews, and meetings with the organizational representative provide information during this diagnostic stage on the state of the organization.

Planning

Accurate diagnosis leads to accurate planning. Therefore, in MET, the project plan is drafted on the basis of the diagnosis. The planning stage specifies how the diagnosed problems can be solved. The planned actions are guided by a framework that indicates a desired future state to be achieved by the organization under consideration. The plan also establishes the target for change and the approach to bring about that change in the organization.

Action

The action stage implements the planned actions. This stage in MET is the specific acting out of the plans. The organization has to work in synergy to implement the planned changes. During this action stage, many existing processes are modeled and refined, the organizational structures change, and hands-on project management comes into play.

Review and Feedback

At the completion of the action stage, the organization evaluates the outcome of the MET transition. The implemented software and system solution is evaluated, and the effectiveness of the transition is measured. This measure is reported as review and feedback to those responsible for the transition and also to business stakeholders.

Enhancement

Enhancing the MET process is an important last action of the business after the transition has taken place. The experience gained from and the issues discovered during the transition need to be incorporated in the MET framework. The resulting enhancements are of immense value to the MET framework.

MET Research: Questions, Results, and Discussions

The MET framework outlined thus far is based on investigative research to create a systematic process for transition. The approach to creating the framework for MET and its corroboration is based on a research survey as well as action research. The theoretical foundation of the MET framework is based on a literature review and practical experiences of the author. This framework, the relative importance of the factors, and their sequencing is carried out by a quantitative research survey carried out across multiple geographical regions.

The MET Research Instrument

The quantitative aspect of this research is made up of a comprehensive research questionnaire that has been formulated and distributed to voluntary participants globally. They were chosen from a wide range of geographical regions—Australia, Europe (including the United Kingdom), North America (including Canada), India and Sri Lanka, Japan, Singapore, and China, and others.

The study is carried out in two parts, with an initial analysis based on responses, most of which are from Australia and some from India. The survey participants included senior management, project management, sales and support, consultants, technical personnel, and others. They belong to small, medium, or large organizations. Participants are also quizzed on the type of business (products versus services) and the industry category they belonged to (education, construction, professional services, manufacturing, banking and finance, information technology, health, government, and others).

The survey is divided into four major parts corresponding to the four aforementioned MET dimensions. Furthermore, the demographics of the participants were also elicited to understand the underlying reasons for their choices in terms of the four MET dimensions. Each of these four MET dimensions is discussed here based on specific questions that deal with MET. Initial results provide invaluable insight into the reasons for MET and the subsequent real and perceived needs as well as risks associated with such transitions. These MET-specific questions are as follows:

a. What are the core drivers for businesses to transition to mobile business? What is their importance in terms of their sequence as core drivers?
b. What are the major technological influences that force businesses to consider adopting mobility? What is the sequence of importance of these technological influences or drivers on the transitioning mobile business?
c. What are the major effects of mobility on the business processes of the enterprise? What is the sequence of importance of this process aspect of mobility to the business?
d. What are the influences of mobility on social aspects of a business? What is the sequence of importance of the social aspects to a mobile business?
e. How do the aforementioned four major areas of influence of mobility on business change with the demographics (as perceived by different roles, for different company sizes, etc.)?

These questions translate into the research survey shown in Appendix A. There are some additional bits of information that emerged from the participants of the survey through subjective responses provided by them. For example, the effect of mobile maturity of an organization on MET was brought home by subjective discussions by the participants. Similarly, the ever-growing importance of the environment and environmental issues are incorporated in MET as a result of additional discussions with the participants.

Initial Research Results on MET

MET derives its basis from earlier electronic business transitions that have been studied, among others, by Ginige et al. (2001) and Lan and Unhelkar (2005).

Although global enterprise transitions provide the basis for the depth of the current process, there is still some uniqueness of mobile technologies that enable businesses to not merely globalize but do so independent of location as a result of mobility. Thus, the impact of mobility on globalization is unique in terms of its location independence, which has been discussed by Marmaridis and Unhelkar (2005), Ginige et al. (2001), and Elliott and Phillips (2004). In this chapter we are outlining the approach to the in-depth survey that extends the concepts of globalization to mobile globalization of enterprises.

A sample of 70 respondents was initially listed, primarily derived from Australia and India. The demographics of the respondents, in terms of their professional roles, are evenly distributed, and currently kept outside the scope of this analysis. These initial results from a sample of the participants are also being discussed here with the aim of laying the foundation for immediate ensuing work in the collection and analysis of the remaining data that is derived from other geographic regions, and which provides a wider cross section of demographics. The current 70 respondents, however, provide an indication of what is considered important in terms of the four dimensions of MET discussed.

Economic Drivers

From among the business drivers, 58 percent of the respondents considered the gadgets as more important (35 percent) or most important (23 percent) business drivers for MET, whereas 68 percent considered costs as more or most important. The trend of this response appeared to be in line with an earlier study presented by Deshpande et al. (2004) in the Device Independent Web Engineering workshop, wherein they described how the dramatic reduction in costs of mobile devices is becoming a crucial factor in the adoption of mobility in business. In regard to competition, 46 percent considered it to be the more or most important factor in driving business toward MET.

Technical Drivers

In regard to technical drivers for MET, 79 percent of the respondents considered mobile gadgets (phones, etc.) as more or most important, and 71 percent considered networks as the technical driving force behind MET. Also, 79 percent considered standards as vital to MET, and 70 percent considered infrastructure as crucial to the success of MET. The phenomenal importance of networks and infrastructure seemed justified because these significant issues formed the basis of all track, conference, and journal themes related to wireless networks and grids (McKnight et al. 2004; Unhelkar 2004a). Mobile agents and mobile Web services also play a crucial part in MET, based on discussions by Subramanium et al. (2004) and Godbole (2003).

Process Drivers

The dynamic business processes that change depending on the adoption of mobility are considered important in MET—with 83 percent of respondents considering business processes as crucial to successful MET. For 77 percent, reengineering of business processes to adopt global mobility was crucial, and 64 percent considered security more or most important. Thus, when it comes to engineering of business processes with mobility, as discussed by S'duk and Unhelkar (2005), an entire business sector made up of a group or collaboration of businesses starts interacting with each other through wireless applications and networks, resulting in a need to reengineer processes that crisscross an industrial sector. This results in what can be called industrial process reengineering (IPR; also process aspect discussed earlier by Unhelkar 2003a), which leads to mobile collaborative businesses (also Unhelkar 2004b). Finally, 64 percent gave importance to costs of application development as an important methodological characteristic of MET.

Social Drivers

Finally, analysis of social factors indicates that 69 percent of respondents give importance to attitude (see Kanter's [2003] arguments on context), whereas a large 87 percent give importance to usability. The importance of usability even in normal (i.e., nonmobile) software applications was identified by Constantine and Lockwood (1999), as far back as a decade ago. Now, it appears that users consider usability as crucial to the success of MET. Privacy was a concern for 57 percent, leading to the conclusion that the functionalities available through mobility are more important than privacy concerns, although privacy does remain important to respondents. Finally, only 39 percent gave importance to changes in the organizational structure, indicating that from a MET viewpoint, perhaps changes to internal organizational structure are not as important as some of the other factors discussed in this survey.

Discussion on MET Initial Results

These initial results have indeed undergone some changes during analysis of the full results, as has been carried out for each of the aforementioned four dimensions in Chapters 3 through 6, respectively. Although most of this initial data seems to suggest that more than 50 percent of the participants are in agreement about the importance of the factors listed in the survey, in choosing the more and most important factors, there was still an opportunity to investigate further in terms of the responses and map them, perhaps to the demographics of the participants. Such further investigations have since been carried out and are reported in subsequent chapters. The initial results also indicate that the four process dimensions of MET are not exclusive to each other. When applied in practice, they are likely to overlap each other, resulting in a cohesive transition process. The cohesive transition process and its enactment are discussed in Chapter 7. However, separate understanding of each of these dimensions is helpful in creating the MET framework in the first place. The in-depth analysis first validates the MET framework and then provides a sound basis for the strategic adoption of mobility in global organizations.

Detailed Survey: Organizational Demographics

As mentioned earlier, the initial survey, discussed in the previous subsections, was followed by a detailed survey, which is analyzed in Chapters 3 to 7. The discussion is spread across all the aforementioned chapters because the demographic data on the survey participants applies to all dimensions. Hence, these demographics factors are shown in Figure 2.8.

Figure 2.9 shows the overall spread of participants and their demographics in the survey. Figure 2.9A shows the spread of roles with senior management accounting for 22 percent, project management 26 percent, sales and support 6 percent, consultant 26 percent, and technical 20 percent. Figure 2.9B shows company size; large companies that have more than 200 workers constitute 36 percent, and small companies that have less than 20 employees 13 percent. Those in between (20–200 employees) belong to the medium category, accounting for 51 percent. Figure 2.9C shows the business type of the company; 73 percent of them are selling services, 15 percent, products, and 12 percent, both services and products. Figure 2.9D displays the industry category; IT participants at 21 percent constitute the largest group in this survey, followed by those from professional services at 20 percent. There are participants from other domains, too: education and training (16 percent), banking and finance (14 percent), manufacturing (7 percent), health and community (7 percent), government (6 percent), building and construction (2 percent), others (6 percent). Figure 2.9E displays the spread across regions with Australia and New Zealand accounting for 39 percent, Europe, including the United Kingdom 2 percent, the United States and Canada 18 percent, the Subcontinent (India and Sri Lanka) 38 percent, Japan, Singapore, and China 1 percent, and others 2 percent. This spread of data can be important in analyzing and interpreting the results in

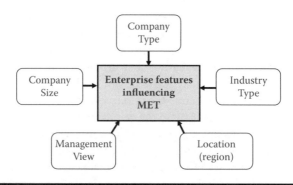

Figure 2.8   The organizational demographic factors in MET.

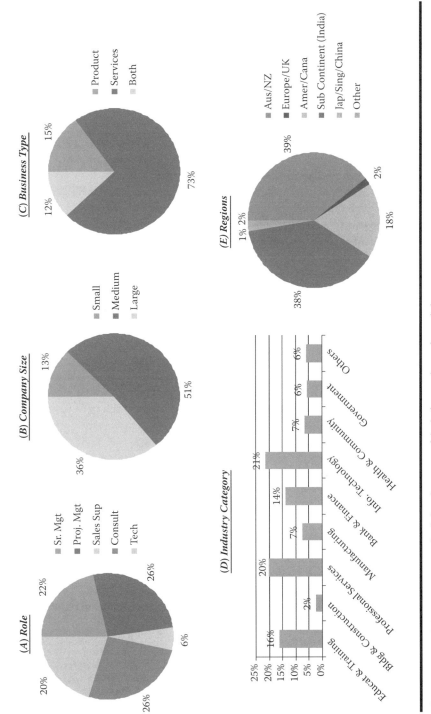

Figure 2.9 MET survey spread of the demographic information of participants.

terms of MET. However, the analysis in the subsequent chapters is a basic analysis carried out to understand the relative importance of the MET drivers. Further studies and analyses that correlates the drivers with some of the specific demographics described here is out of the scope of this book.

Discussion Points

1. Discuss the internal and external factors that force a business to adopt mobility. Also discuss the difference between what would be considered as a mobile-equipped business, as against a fully mobile enterprise.
2. What is the role of business process reengineering (BPR) in METs?
3. Why is the mobile business so heavily dependent on its clients and suppliers? Also, what is the challenge faced by a mobile business in pricing its services when it comes to its dealings with the mobile network operators? Discuss in the context of the layers and players of mobile service delivery.
4. Discuss the four core dimensions of METs with examples of the driver factors that make up each of these dimensions.
5. How do the four dimensions of MET map to the mobile business usage (see Figure 2.6 on mobile usage triangle by business)?
6. What is the fundamental nature of mobility that is different from all previous communications technologies such as the Internet?
7. What are the likely effects of the changing demographics of the users—in terms of their company size, their role in the company and the geographical region from where they come—in terms of their perception of MET drivers?

References

Adam, C. and Katos, V. 2005. The ubiquitous mobile and location-awareness time bomb, *Cutter IT Journal* 18(6): 20–26.

Akcayli, E., Brooks, D., Laszlo, J., and McAteer, S. 2001. Location-Aware Applications—Improving End-User Value Despite Carrier Hesitation, *Jupiter Research* 3 (November 20).

Arunatileka, D. and Unhelkar, B. 2003. Mobile Technologies, providing new possibilities in Customer Relationship Management, *Proceedings of 5th International Information Technology Conference*, Colombo, Sri Lanka, December 2003.

Beinat, E. 2001. Privacy and Location-Based Service, *Geo Informatics,* September.

Brans, P. 2003. *Mobilize Your Enterprise: Achieving Competitive Advantage through Wireless Technology.* Upper Saddle River, NJ: Prentice Hall PTR.

Constantine, L. and Lockwood, L. 1999. *Software for Use: A Practical Guide to Models and Methods of Usage-Centered Design.* Boston: Addison-Wesley. Also see www.foruse.com.

Deshpande, Y., Murugesan, S., Unhelkar, B., and Arunatileka, D. 2004. Workshop on device independent Web engineering: Methodological considerations and challenges in moving Web applications from desk-top to diverse mobile devices, *Proceedings of the Device Independent Web Engineering Workshop,* Munich.

Devereaus, M. and Johansen, R. 1994.*Global Work: Bridging Distance, Culture and Time*. San Francisco: Jossey-Bass, 38–39.

Elliott, G. and Phillips, N. 2004. *Mobile Commerce and Wireless Computing Systems*. Harlow, England: Addison-Wesley.

Fink, S., 2002, The Fine Line Between Location-Based Services and Privacy, Public Safety Report, *Radio Resource Magazine* (August) 17(7).

Ginige, A., Murugesan, S., and Kazanis, P. 2001. A road map for successfully transforming SMEs into E-businesses, *Cutter IT Journal* 14(5), 43.

Godbole, N. 2003. Mobile Computing: Security Issues in Hand-Held Devices, Paper presented at NASONES 2003—National Seminar on Networking and E-Security by Computer Society of India.

Godbole, N. and Unhelkar, B. December 2003. Enhancing Quality of Mobile Applications through Modeling, *Proceedings of Computer Society of India's 35th Convention,* Indian Institute of Technology, New Delhi, India.

Harmon, R. R. and Laird, G. 1997. Linking Marketing Strategy to Customer Value: Implications for Technology Marketers, in *Innovation in Technology Management: The Key to Global Leadership,* PICMET Proceedings, ed. Kocaoglu et al., 896–900.

Hazra, T. K. December 2006. Smart sourcing: Myths, truths, and realities. In *Cutter IT Journal*, issue "Sourcing: out or in?," 19(12).

Ho, S. Y. and Kwok, S. H. 2003. The attraction of personalized service for users in mobile commerce: An empirical study, *ACMSIGecom Exchanges*. 3(4): 10–18.

Hsu, H. Y. S., Burner, G. C., and Kulviwat, S. 2005. Personalization in mobile commerce, *Proceedings of the IRMA Conference 2005*, San Diego, CA.

Kanter, T. 2003. Going wireless, enabling an adaptive and extensible environment, *Mobile Networks and Applications,* 8(1): 37–50.

Lan, Y. and Unhelkar, B. 2005.*Global Enterprise Transitions*. Hershey, PA: IGI Press.

Marmaridis, I. M. and Unhelkar, B. 2005. Challenges in mobile transformations: A requirements modeling perspective for small and medium enterprises, *Proceedings of the International Conference on Mobile Business,* ICMB, Sydney, 2005.

McKnight, L. and Howison, J. 2004. Wireless Grids: Distributed Resource Sharing by Mobile, Nomadic, and Fixed Devices, *IEEE Internet Computing,* July/August 2004 issue, http://dsonline.computer.org/0407/f/w4gei.htm (last accessed July 19, 2004).

Murugesan, S., Deshpande, Y., Hansen, S., and Ginige, A. 2001. Web engineering: A new discipline for development of Web-based systems, in *Web Engineering: Managing Diversity and Complexity of Web Application Development*, eds. S. Murugesan and Y. Deshpande. Berlin: Springer-Verlag.

Prem, E. 2002. Innovative Mobile Services and Revenue Models, *EUTEMA Report*, February.

Ranjbar, M. and Unhelkar, B. 2003. Globalisation and Its Impact on Telecommuting: An Australian Perspective, presented at IBIM03—International Business Information Management Conference (www.ibima.org), Cairo, Egypt.

Rao, B. and Minakakis, L. 2003. Evolution of mobile location-based services, *Communications of the ACM* 46(12): 61–65.

S'duk, R. and Unhelkar, B. 2005. Web Services Extending BPR to Industrial Process Reengineering, *Proceedings of International Resource Management Association (IRMA) Conference*; http://www.irma-international.org, San Diego, California. May 15–18.

Subramanium, C., Kuppuswami, A., and Unhelkar, B. 2004. Relevance of State, Nature, Scale and Location of Business E-Transformation in Web Services, *Proceedings of the 2004 International Symposium on Web Services and Applications* (ISWS'04: June 21–24, 2004, Las Vegas, Nevada; http://www.world-academy-of-science.org).

Unhelkar, B. 2003a. *Process Quality Assurance for UML-based Projects.* Boston: Addison-Wesley.

Unhelkar, B. 2003b. Understanding Collaborations and Clusters in the e-Business World, We-B Conference (www.we-bcentre.com; with Edith Cowan University), Perth, Australia, November 23–24.

Unhelkar, B. 2004a. Paradigm shift in the process of electronic globalisation of businesses resulting from the impact of Web services based technologies, paper presented at the IRMA 2004, USA.

Unhelkar, B. 2004b. Globalization with Mobility, presented at ADCOM 2004, 12th International Conference on Advanced Computing and Communications, Ahmedabad, India.

Unhelkar, B. 2005. Transitioning to a mobile enterprise: A three-dimensional framework, *Cutter IT Journal* 18(8): 5–11.

Unhelkar, B. and Dickens, A. 2008. Lessons in implementing "Green" business strategies with ICT, *Cutter IT Journal,* February 2008.

Unni and Harmon, 2005. Location-based services—opportunities and challenges, in *Handbook of Research in Mobile Business: Technical, Methodological and Social Perspectives,* ed. B., Hershey, PA: IGI Global.

Williams, D. H. 2003. It's the (LBS) applications, stupid! *White Paper* (www.e911-lbs.com).

Younessi, H. 2008. Strategic view on creating business value through mobile technologies, chapter 1 in *Handbook of Research in Mobile Business: Technical, Methodological and Social perspectives,* 2nd ed., ed. B. Unhelkar. Hershey, PA: IGI Global.

Chapter 3

Mobile Enterprise Transitions: Economic Dimension

Method goes far to prevent trouble in business.

William Penn

Chapter Key Points

- Presents the economic dimension of Mobile Enterprise Transition (MET)
- Stresses the strategic importance and use of mobility in business (as against tactical or routine use)
- Discusses and analyzes the importance of the cost factor in MET, including costs of mobile gadgets, mobile transactions, infrastructure, and operations
- Discusses and analyzes the importance of the competition factor in MET, including sophistication in services, excellence in content, and marketing by the competitor
- Discusses and analyzes the importance of the customer factor in MET, including the demand for mobile services by customers
- Discusses and analyzes the employee's ability to provide enhanced, improved service to customers and manage employee processes better than before

- Discusses and analyzes the importance of the convenience factor in MET, including local and global connectivity
- Analyzes survey data in terms of understanding the relative importance of economic factors and their position in creating a MET project plan
- Analyzes survey data to understand the best sequence of economic factors and place them in an economic sequence
- Discusses the informative, transactive, operative, and collaborative use of mobility by business in the context of the economic dimension
- Highlights the strategic advantage of mobility as compared to normal advantage resulting from the use of a disruptive business technology

Introduction

This chapter discusses a systematic approach to understanding the economic dimension of MET and the application of the economic factors within that dimension to MET. These include costs and competition,* which are usually the two primary drivers that compel a business to undertake MET. For example, a stockbroker using mobile technologies is likely to be more competitive compared with those relying only on electronic transactions; competitiveness is enhanced and costs are reduced with the use of mobility through timeliness of transactions. Along with other strategically important economic reasons, these drivers are significant in the decision-making process of the senior management of an organization as it contemplates MET. This is so because the decision of the senior management with regard to MET is based on the overall value of MET to business and customers, and not necessarily on how radical or impressive the features of mobile technologies themselves might be. In fact, without a proper understanding of the return on investment (ROI) on MET and the business opportunities it entails, formal mobile transition may hardly ever happen in the industry. Alternatively, without the benefit of analysis in this economic dimension, the senior management of an organization may even inadvertently assume that the organization is indeed mobile. A compelling need for MET is felt when the cost–benefit analysis of mobility and the strategic benefits likely to accrue from MET are brought to bear in the early decision-making process of the business. This chapter argues for a formal consideration of these economic drivers, and studying, incorporating, and using them in the MET framework. These formal economic drivers include, apart from cost and competition mentioned earlier, the financial opportunities that the mobile business can create and exploit because of the nature of mobility and an understanding of the effect of possible lost business opportunities for not considering mobility

---

* Although profit is also an important economic driver, in this discussion profit is spread between costs and competition. MET can reduce costs and thereby increase profit margins. MET, by enabling the business to be competitive, is certainly aiming to increase profit.

in a formal and strategic manner. This chapter starts with a discussion of the importance of these cost factors from both the business's and the customer's viewpoint. It is followed by a discussion on the effect of competition on the economic performance of the organization. The highly significant discussion on the needs, demands, and capabilities of the customer as well as the corresponding advantages of mobility to employees in a mobile business ensues. Next, the ease of use or convenience accorded by global and local mobile connectivity is discussed from an economic perspective. The usefulness of mobility, especially its perception by the various users, is discussed to enable the transitioning organization to tap into the business opportunities that can result from such perception. The discussions on the various important economic factors are then followed by an analysis of these factors from the point of view of their priorities and relative importance in the transition. This analysis is based on the survey data collected during the research phase of the writing of this book, and it results in the formation of a project plan within the economic dimension of the MET framework. These economic factors of MET are then placed within the context of the discussion on "business usage of mobility" (as discussed in Chapter 1, Figure 1.3). Finally, a suggested approach to calculating and understanding the strategic benefits resulting from MET is discussed, particularly to understand this strategic advantage as different from the normal or nonstrategic advantage of mobile technologies.

Economic Dimension (Why)

The economic drivers of MET are aimed at understanding the primary business question of "*why* mobilize the business?" From an economic viewpoint, these drivers include the costs incurred in the transition and the corresponding benefits to the business that is undertaking MET. However, as a strategic business activity, there are many tangible and intangible aspects of such transition that add "value" to the business. The intangible value addition to the business due to mobility is mostly indiscernible. Therefore, it is important that the transitioning business consider such intangible benefits in its calculations of mobile benefits, ensuring that it does not view the cost–benefit calculations as a short-term benefit to the business. The more strategic an approach in adopting mobility by business, the more long term is the ensuing advantage to it. A detailed understanding of "value" creation by the mobile business is provided in the discussions in Chapter 8. Although the strategic adoption of mobility enables the business to sustain itself profitably over a long period of time, this long-term sustainability of the transitioning mobile business needs to keep the overall business "ecosystem" in mind. Chapter 9 in this book has a detailed discussion on the sustainability of business. The three other drivers of MET that are also related to this economic driver (namely, the technical, process, and social drivers), are discussed in detail in Chapters 4, 5, and 6, respectively. Although this chapter focuses on the economic drivers, in practice, they do not

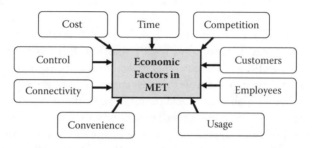

Figure 3.1 Economic factors driving MET.

operate in isolation from the other three. Therefore, once these four MET drivers are understood, then their combined dynamic influence during the enactment of MET is studied and applied in Chapter 7. Figure 3.1 summarizes these economic factors that drive MET. These economic factors that influence MET and that need to be considered during MET are cost, time, competition, control, connectivity, convenience, customers, employees, and usage.

> Costs and competition are compelling drivers for mobile enterprise transitions. Costs and competition are compelling drivers for mobile enterprise transitions. However, mobility provides advantages to customers and employees in terms of personalization and location independence, providing users with value in leisure and work. The strategic advantages of mobility far outweigh the "normal" advantages derived from the technology as mobility is a "disruptive" technology. The economic drivers continue to force the business to think "why" it should undertake MET.

Why should a business embark on MET? Figure 3.1 depicts the various economic reasons for undertaking the MET project. The primary and obvious reasoning from an economic viewpoint starts with costs. Will the cost of conducting the business be cheaper if mobility is adopted in a strategic manner? What are the various types of costs involved in becoming a mobile business? What is the relative importance of these costs with respect to MET? The answer to these questions deal with the costs associated with the mobile devices and the operational costs associated with their use. Competition is another significant economic factor to be considered in MET. Businesses that do not "mobilize" themselves ahead of their competition are left behind by their competitors and are likely to lose their turnover and profit margins. Competition in mobile business can originate from various directions such as the type of service, the type of content, and the manner in which that content is offered, especially by the competition. The business undergoing MET needs to consider the costs of creating as well as offering such mobile content and the opportunity costs of not offering them. Customers are increasingly becoming sophisticated in their demand for mobile services from businesses. Employees also see opportunities for providing better service to customers through mobility, as well as for improving their own internal business processes that enhance the quality of their working lives. Furthermore, with the advent of mobile Web services (discussed in Chapter 4), there is an urgent need for the business to understand the importance of strategically collaborating with other businesses, rather than merely competing with them, to satisfy their customers' demands. These customer demands as well as demands for mobility by business partners form part of the economic decision-making process by the business undertaking MET, as depicted in Figure 3.1.

Mobile connectivity, another important MET factor, can be understood from an economic viewpoint as either local or global. There are numerous business opportunities that are associated with local and global connectivity, because these connectivities provide varied degree of convenience and ease of use to customers. For example, with such mobile connectivity, the business gets the opportunity to tap into the user's leisure and work spaces. Local connectivity provides immediate short-term sales, and global connectivity provides roaming business advantages. However, there are also costs associated with setting up the facilities to provide varying levels of connectivity services to the users. The arrangements and contracts that are inevitably required when participating in a global mobile playing field also need to be considered carefully in this economic dimension of MET. Finally, the usage of mobility in emergency services needs to be considered from the economic as well as social aspects. These services reflect not only legal requirements but also that of the businesses as good corporate citizens. Table 3.1 summarizes the economic drivers that form part of this economic dimension of MET and some of the key transition issues within each of these drivers.

The transition issues listed in Table 3.1 that correspond to the economic factors in MET are examples of some transition issues in the economic dimension. Many more issues are discovered during the practical enactment of MET, as discussed in Chapter 7. These aforementioned economic factors listed in Table 3.1 that influence MET are now discussed in greater detail in this chapter. The following section starts with a discussion on the costs viewpoint within MET. Other economic factors are discussed, followed by a detailed analysis of the research survey data on the priorities of these cost factors. Following this is a discussion on how these factors can be gradually applied to a transitioning organization, ranging from m-informative, m-transactive, and m-operative to using mobility in an m-collaborative organization.

Cost

Costs associated with MET range from the costs of the mobile device, transactions, and infrastructure, to the operational costs that are incurred in deploying these devices. The costs associated with the actual mobile devices are rapidly falling and are now a fraction of the operational costs of the device over a year. Thus, costs play an important part in the decision-making process for MET as they lead to many interesting permutations and combinations in terms of both costing and pricing mobile products.

The costs of running a business are traditionally well known, relatively easily measurable, and understandable by the various stakeholders in the business. There are various types of cost calculations involved in MET, including the costs associated with the physical mobile gadgets, the costs of using and operating those gadgets (e.g., making calls and sending or receiving messages [SMS]), costs associated with setting up the mobile infrastructure, and ongoing costs of running mobile business operations. The regular costs of running a business and the impact of mobility on these costs are highly significant economic initiators for undertaking MET.

The senior management and shareholders of the business usually demand cost reductions associated with the introduction of a new technology. Management, in fact, is continuously looking for ways to optimize business processes and business organization that will enable them to cut down the operating costs of the business. Therefore, cost reduction becomes a major justification for formal adoption of mobile technologies in business. Mobile technologies also provide a wide range of opportunities to achieve cost reduction. Such opportunities to achieve cost benefits include, for example, an improved customer relationship management system, a tightened supply-chain management system, and better control of business by management due to enhanced timeliness of these processes. There are also the costs associated with the actual enactment of MET and the costs of ongoing operations of the mobile business that need to be considered in analyzing the costs versus benefits scenario for undertaking MET.

Mobile Gadgets

Mobile devices are available in abundance in today's mobile markets. They play a crucial role in influencing METs. Figure 3.2 shows the range of mobile devices available in the market and highlight the smallness of their size, the increasing level of convergence of multimedia features on them, the wirelessly connected

Table 3.1 Economic drivers of MET

Economic drivers of mobile enterprise transitions (Why?)		*Transition issues*
Costs	Mobile gadgets (phones/PDA/BlackBerry, etc.)	Business costs, cost–benefit
	Costs per transaction (calls, SMS)	
	Upfront setup costs (networks, infrastructures)	
	Operational costs (regular, ongoing)	
Competition	Sophisticated mobile services offered by competitor	SWOT, balanced scorecard
	Excellence in mobile content offered by competitor	
	Advertisement/marketing of mobility by competitor	
Customers and employees	Customers' demands for mobile services	Quality of working life
	Business partners' demands for mobile processes	
	Employees' ability to provide better services to customers	
Convenience	Local connectivity (location independence)	Quality and value of service
	Global connectivity (roaming)	
Mobile usage	Leisure (e.g., sports, entertainment)	Managing changes based on status, need, and legal compliance (in emergency services)
	Work (e.g., keeping contact with employees)	
	Emergency services (e.g., fire, police, ambulance)	

non-handheld devices such as laptops, and the wallet-sized smart cards—all available to MET. There is a need to handle a number of cost- and functionality-related issues to make the use of these devices successful in MET. First of all, businesses are keen to find the costs associated with procuring mobile gadgets and providing them to employees for use. Businesses may also have to consider specific, custom-made, handheld devices that are used for emerging functions using dedicated network channels. The MET questions on mobile device usage are: What are the costs of procuring mobile devices? What are the advantages in doing so? How is the cost of these gadgets likely to influence the success of a business? Who bears the costs of

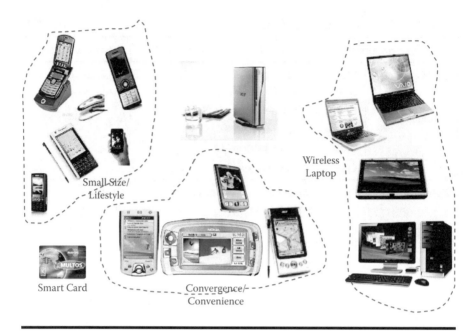

Figure 3.2   Range of mobile devices influencing MET.

procuring and operating these gadgets? What are the costs in swapping or upgrading these mobile devices? These questions are asked by a business upfront when it undertakes MET. More often than not, employees and customers of the business already have mobile gadgets available at their disposal. Therefore, depending on their ownership, the transitioning business may not be required to procure these devices, and may not have to worry about device cost. However, if customers and employees do not own these handheld devices, then they are likely to be "owned" by organizational entities (such as corporates and businesses). The transitioning business has to understand the cost of the mobile gadgets with respect to their ownership and upgrade possibilities during MET. For example, a service business or a network operator may find it worthwhile not charging at all for the device, considering the returns generated by the usage of their service.

The costs of mobile devices are also related to their features and need to be understood by the transitioning organization. For example, the voice-call facility is only one important yet small part of the overall features of a mobile "phone" today. Modern mobile gadgets are laden with incredible additional features that provide value to their users, which go far beyond the use of the gadget in making a voice call. For example, most of them have, in addition to the voice-call facility, short messaging service (SMS); personal calendar–clock–alarm; GPRS and navigation services; radio, photo, and video; and electronic calculator features to name but a few. Most personal digital assistants (PDAs) have, in addition to the mentioned features, integrated wireless modems with excellent Internet-browsing capabilities and ability to execute software applications, securely conduct authenticated transactions, and provide sophisticated entertainment to the user (e.g., through games). A smart card, also shown in Figure 3.2, on the other hand, can employ infrared technologies to enable micropayments that can be used in varieties of ways such as seamlessly operating transit cards, purchase of small goods such as newspapers and soda, and exchanging small-value amounts with fellow users of smart cards. Note that all these mobile devices remain predominantly personalized and can be identified with a specific user.

A key driver for the growth of the mobile business is the high level of penetration of these personalized devices in the markets and, in fact, even in general society. Therefore, mobile enterprises have the potential for realizing the benefits that can be achieved with personalized mobile solutions for users. The dramatic reduction in the costs of such mobile devices, their availability in abundance, and the immense potential for personalization lead to a combination of significant economic drivers for MET. The growth in the availability and usage of mobile devices, particularly of the smart and feature-rich handheld ones, enable businesses to offer services on a chargeable basis. The growth numbers in mobility, also discussed in Chapter 1, are regularly being reported as growing by many market research companies. For example, earlier, in 2006, Gartner had estimated a massive sale of over 84 million mobile units, including PDAs and smart phones sales worldwide (Gartner, Inc. 2006). The markets came very close to these sales figures. Subsequent financial years are reporting growth in large number of gadgets that also cover corresponding individual users through personalized mobile services. IDC (2007) market research predicts the total sales of smart mobile devices to reach 1 billion units by the first quarter of 2011. These figures, if they turn out to be true, will have covered a large cross section of people over wide demographics. The needs of these users of mobility globally are providing rich opportunities for transitioning businesses.

Phenomenal growth in mobile devices is occurring in the so-called BRICs (Brazil, Russia, India, China). Low costs, economic reforms, and vast market base mean these countries' markets are already exploding from a mobile business viewpoint. The needs of a large number of personalized mobile users are a major source of opportunities for transitioning mobile businesses in these markets.

Furthermore, it is worth paying attention to the regions where this growth in mobile devices is occurring—predominantly in the so-called BRICs (Brazil, Russia, India, China). These regions are of particular interests to MET because they not only use mobile devices for conducting businesses but are also regions where the mobile "gaming market" is set to explode (Kamdar 2007). A report by Global Insight says that China and India will continue to lead phenomenal growth in the mobile phone sector; in the case of the latter, the total number of mobile phones already has outstripped the number of land-based connections. This growth has repercussions in a global roaming market where travel and tourism, for example, have a complete new look and feel that is also seamless to geography. There are a number of political and economic factors that are being attributed to this growth in mobile markets in BRIC regions. Some of these factors include (http://www.unpan1.un.org) the opening up of these markets, resulting from rapid economic reforms, reengineering of the telecommunication sector leading to fierce competition, and the massive inherent momentum of these markets due to their large consumer base compared to the rest of the world. The transitioning business needs to "plug in" to this growth of mobile devices—especially as their costs are plunging—to carry out MET successfully.

Another major impact on the sophistication of services in the mobile industry is created by Apple's iPhone, launched in mid-2007. The iPhone has Wi-Fi access that enables loading of external content, such as from iTunes. Interestingly, this facilitates the bypassing of network operators. As a result of this feature, mobile business is now able to conjure additional and location-specific services that do not depend on network operators. Furthermore, Apple also provides a software developer's kit along with its iPhone, which opens it up to third-party software developers for mobile applications development (Kharif 2007).

Costs per Mobile Transaction

The cost of mobile devices as discussed earlier form one significant part of mobile business calculations. Another significant cost associated with mobility, which a mobile business needs to consider, is the "unit cost" of mobile transactions. The costs associated with offered facilities and services on mobile devices are different from the cost of the devices themselves. The charging of mobile facilities and services based on a unit of time, data, or other such feature requires a very creative approach on the part of the transitioning mobile business. Availability of packet-switched networks, as compared with the earlier circuit-switched ones, opens up greater opportunities for network operators to be creative in terms of their charging methods. However, they also need to have a good understanding with service providers in arriving at charging methods. Increasingly, mobile businesses are moving away from charging their customers based on time usage, and instead, they are moving toward charging based on data or "quantity" usage. For example, the charge for SMS depends on the amount of data being sent in a message and not on how long it takes to transmit it. The nature of mobility also mandates that the mobile devices participating in the transition are continuously moving. Therefore, mobile business service providers and operators also need to factor in the location of the mobile gadget in terms of both transmission and reception in calculating the costs per mobile transaction. Local versus roaming features that result from global mobility incur different charges. These costs per transaction unit, depending on device location, accrue on an ongoing basis; they have a significant influence on the mobile business and need to be considered carefully in MET.

Upfront Setup Costs

The cost of mobile devices and the unit cost of mobile usage are both dependent on the individual mobile user. However, the upfront infrastructure setup costs are borne by the transitioning business itself, which MET needs to consider in transitioning to the mobile business. These costs, at various levels of infrastructure, range from setting up short-range mobile transmitters to the organizational and industry-level costs associated with setting up networks and servers, as well as the costs of national and international mobile communications infrastructures that facilitate transmissions across vast geographical regions. Occasionally, the miniscule cost to individuals of having a battery recharger has also been considered an infrastructure or background cost in mobile usage. The levels of infrastructure costs to be considered depend on the type of mobile business and its mobile maturity. Repeaters, speed of transmission, and level of security required on the networks are all part of this cost. However, the most important upfront costs at the business level are that of setting up servers (such as content and application servers), hiring the publicly available network infrastructure, and providing a support structure (such as a call center). MET requires that these costs in setting up the mobile business infrastructure be listed to justify the transition from an economic viewpoint. Partnering with infrastructure providers, sharing infrastructure with other businesses, and setting up joint ventures in the area of mobile content and services can potentially reduce the upfront setup costs in a significant way.

Operational Costs

A mobile business that is operational has to transcend the calculations associated with setup, such as the costs of individual mobile gadgets and hiring of mobile networks and carriers, and start considering the ongoing cost of operation—maintaining the infrastructure and usage of wireless networks, corresponding computing servers' operational costs, etc. MET suggests the factoring in of operational costs at the start of the transition process as an important economic factor for the transition.

Analysis of the Importance of the Cost Factor

The various cost factors in MET have been described thus far in this chapter. This section considers their relative importance with respect to MET as investigated by means of the research survey (see Chapter 2 for the outline and demographics of this survey).

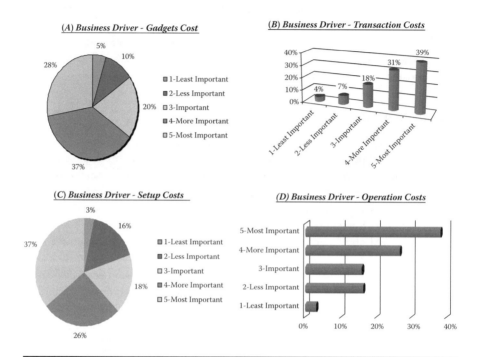

Figure 3.3   Analysis of the importance of the cost factor in the economic dimension of MET.

Figure 3.3 shows the relative importance of the various cost factors in the economic dimension of MET. Figure 3.3A shows the importance of the costs of gadgets within the overall cost factors. The result of the survey, as appearing in this figure, indicates that 37 percent of the participants think that gadget costs are most important, and 28 percent think they are more important. A total of 65 percent think that gadget cost factors are more to most important. Only 5 percent think of them as least important cost factor in the economic dimension of MET. Although this result itself is not surprising, it does underscore the importance of considering the costs of mobile gadgets by transitioning organizations.

Figure 3.3B shows the importance of the transaction costs in MET. The result of the survey in this figure indicates that 39 percent of the participants think that the transaction costs are most important, and 31 percent think they are more important. A total of 70 percent think the transaction cost factors are more to most important. Only 4 percent think they are the least important cost factor in the economic dimension of MET. These numbers indicate that transaction costs are considered by the participants to be even more important in a MET than device costs. This is understandable because transaction costs drive the use of mobility more than device costs, which are rapidly falling anyway.

Figure 3.3C shows the importance of setup costs in MET. The result of the survey, in this figure, indicates that 37 percent of the participants think that setup costs are most important, and 26 percent think they are more important. A total of 63 percent think that the setup cost factors are more to most important. Only 3 percent think of them as the least important cost factor in the economic dimension of MET. These numbers indicate that setup costs are comparable in importance with the two previously discussed costs, although only slightly less in percentage importance.

Figure 3.3D shows the importance of operations costs in MET. The result of the survey in this figure indicates that 38 percent of the participants think that operations costs are most important, and 27 percent think they are more important. A total of 65 percent think that the operations cost factors are more to most important. Only 3 percent think of them as the least important cost factor in the economic dimension of MET. Operations costs are specifically incurred by the business and not usually by the clients and other business partners.

Competition and Mobile Advantage

As mentioned at the beginning of this chapter, competition, similar to costs, is a major driver for MET. When a competitor starts applying the principles of MET in a strategic manner, there is pressure on every other associated business to follow suit. A vital ingredient of this competitive approach to the mobile business is a strategic plan. It helps align the goals of the business with the goals of MET (as discussed in Chapter 2). The more strategic an approach is adopted by the business toward MET, the more value it is likely to derive from mobile usage. The strategic plan for MET includes, apart from the goals, the demographics of the business, its technology approach, and its maturity in terms of both quality and mobile usage. Such strategic planning becomes an important upfront activity for MET. The principles and models of strategic planning, such as those discussed by Porter (2001; e.g., the Five Forces model and the Value Chain models) are applied by mobile businesses in identifying and dealing with competition (Atkins and Ali 2009).

A typical strategic planning approach starts with a strength–weakness–opportunity–threat (SWOT) analysis of the business. Alternatively, a political–economic–sociocultural–technical (PEST) analysis may also be undertaken by the business in the context of MET. A third alternative is to use a balanced scorecard, although such a management technique is slightly further down the track in the economic dimension. These strategic analyses can lead to an understanding of the level of the business in the "mobile business usage" triangle (Figure 1.3) and its mobile maturity, which also indicates its ability to capitalize on mobility. A SWOT analysis, such as the one shown in Figure 3.4, reveals the strengths and weaknesses of the business as well as the opportunities and threats posed to it as it contemplates the use of mobility. For example, the business in Figure 3.4 has strengths in terms of its technical capability in high-speed networks, but it is weak in terms of its current

Strengths	Weaknesses

• Technical sophistication
• Customer acceptance
• Global presence
• Business alliance
  (with operators)
• Funds
	• Inaccurate contents
	• Informal/casual process
	• Hierarchical
	  organizational structure
	• Rigid infrastructure

Opportunities	**Threats**
• Create new contents • Reduce cost of service • From global alliances • Re-engineer processes	• Competition • Open global market • Virtual (email) business • Lack of security of contents

Figure 3.4   A typical SWOT for mobile business.

mobile content. The opportunity available for the business to grow may come about by merging with other businesses. Such strategic mergers between multiple businesses may help them to cut their infrastructure and operational costs as they transition to the mobile business. Competitors proceeding with the mobile business, opening up of the global market, virtual business facilities, and lack of security of content are typical emerging threats to a transitioning business. The focus of the strategic analysis, therefore, is also on players that help it to ameliorate its risks such as its business partners, suppliers, and even government agencies. Therefore, strategic analysis of the business for mobile transition should be undertaken by keeping the business and social environment of the business in mind, and provision should be made for rapid changes in these business and social environments.

The concept of the balanced scorecard mentioned earlier is used by business decision makers to ensure that the implementation of strategies and their policies are in balance with each other. The concept of the balanced scorecard, as shown in Figure 3.5, is built on four perspectives: financial, internal business processes, customer, and learning and growth. These surround the vision and strategy of the organization, which remains at the center of the balanced scorecard. Thus it is also an appropriate management tool for MET.

Figure 3.5 shows this balanced scorecard for MET, as well as the interplay of influences of the four aforementioned perspectives. These are as follows:

The financial perspective is used to assess the business activities and financial standing of the organization, which assist in identifying its strengths and weaknesses. Therefore, in a way, this perspective is similar to a cost–benefit analysis (as also discussed by Atkins and Ali 2009). It also investigates the financial performance record of the organization. The investigation includes a measure of the transitioning organization's business activities, its objectives, and the method of measuring those objectives. Senior management

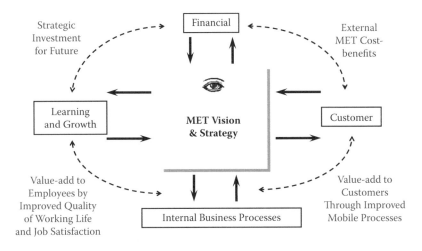

Figure 3.5 Applying the balanced scorecard to MET (part of economic dimension).

can undertake this activity at the start of the MET project, and discuss and comment on the overall mobile initiative of the organization. Later, the feedback on the transition provides information to the business, which enables it to ascertain whether it has achieved its intended MET objectives or not. Comments on the need for any additional mobile business processes are also noted. An understanding of the financial perspective helps a business measure its performance in the economic dimension of MET.

The financial perspective of the balanced scorecard is followed by the profiling and understanding of the demographics of the customer. It is primarily an understanding of the objectives of the customer in dealing with the mobile business. The manner and extent to which the customer uses the business indicates the influence of the customer on the business. The customer's details and influence are recorded in this part of the analysis.

The internal business processes that comprise the operative aspect of the transitioning business are then recorded in the balanced scorecard. These internal business processes include, for example, the inventory, time sheet, and payroll functions. They also include the internal aspects of the "external" customer functions. For example, one internal business process of the organization may use the mobile RFID to enhance its inventories and stock- location processes. This improved internal process due to mobility may result in improved order fulfillment for the customer.

Finally, the balanced scorecard procedure investigates and records the learning and growth of the organization resulting from MET. This learning and employee experience from being mobile is of immense intangible benefit to the organization as it improves the quality of its employees' working life. Thus, the management technique of a balanced scorecard comes in handy in dealing with MET. Further discussion on the calculation of strategic benefits appears later in this chapter.

As the cycle of the balanced scorecard is repeated, the MET vision and strategy are assessed and recorded to monitor the effects of implementing mobile technology in the business.

Sophistication in Mobile Services

Competition among businesses is concentrated on content and promotion that are presented to users in a sophisticated way. The sophistication with which such services are provided to mobile users forms a significant driver for the mobile business. Three significant mobile companies are vying in the mobile market through a combination of devices and service. They are dealing with wireless network operators, creating innovative service applications, and merging the devices. These companies (also discussed by Harmon and Diam 2009) are Apple, Nokia, and Google. The business models followed by these organizations are worth discussing here from the mobile perspective, as they also provide hints to the transitioning mobile businesses in terms of how to structure their business partnerships. The Internet-driven computer industry, for example, provides the starting point for these mobile models. Nokia finds that merely becoming a device manufacturer is not the way to grow its market share in the mobile domain. Therefore, Nokia as well as Apple and Google are attempting to provide services, generate their own content, and also become an integrator of these services and content. However, such attempts to integrate services and content are not favored by mobile network operators (this scenario was earlier discussed in detail in Chapter 2) such as AT&T, Telstra, and Optus because they are keen to keep a major share of the service proceedings for themselves.

Thus, there is an interesting and growing challenge and complexity in the sophistication of services, and packaging of the content together with the services that then ride on the corresponding network operators. For example, Google wants to combine its phenomenal search engine capacity, which is part of its service sophistication, with its content revenue, and that in turn requires use of the mobile network. The mobile Internet, not "open" and free yet, has costs associated with it. An open mobile Internet superhighway or "freeway" can change the entire complexion of the "mobile service" game and be of immense benefit to customers and application providers. Google, in fact, aims to synergize its software and services on mobile networks together with its gPhone, its GPS, Google Maps, contact lists, and Web browsing. Thus, Google's entry into the mobile service market is having a profound impact on the shape of the current and future mobile industry.

Nokia, which has close to 40 percent of the device market with its handsets, is also embracing a service-oriented strategy that provides a convergence of devices, services, and applications to users. For example, it is looking to combine a music store, games, Web communities, maps, and location services and provide them on its Internet-enabled devices to consumers. Nokia has the advantage of over 200 million music-capable handsets that are already in the market. Its navigator phone comes with GPS capability. Users can download navigation software and maps; view their current location on a map; search for destinations; plot specific routes; and locate services such shops, hotels, gas stations, and restaurants (Reardon 2007). Services such as voice directions and live traffic updates are now being made available by Nokia for a fee. Furthermore, similar to Apple, Nokia has also opened its services platform to third-party developers, resulting in thousands of registered developers (Kharif 2007). Thus, the transitioning mobile businesses need to adopt a service strategy initiative to develop closer relationships with end users and capture a higher share of the mobile services market (Schenker 2007).

Excellence in Mobile Content

Mobile content provides yet another important economic factor that needs to be considered seriously in light of competition. The initial focus of a mobile business is on creating and delivering relevant content to its users. However, sourcing of content from various content providers in both vertical and horizontal markets is vital for them to be of value to users. Excellence in the providing of content by mobile businesses is based on how current and relevant they are to the user. Relevance changes rapidly in the mobile business with the change in the location of the user. Therefore, both sourcing and usage of mobile content are dynamic, as compared with nonmobile content. Mobile Web services also open up opportunities for real-time updates of external content. Finally, there is also a need to balance the cost of the content with its quality, accuracy, and currency.

Advertising and Marketing

Advertising and marketing by mobile businesses is primarily done by pushing information onto the mobile devices of its customers. Mobile devices have changed the nature of mass media communications and advertising due to their personalized nature and dynamic composition. As such, mobile marketing is a vital ingredient of MET. Promoting and marketing the content and services of the transitioning mobile business through other nonmobile channels such as the Internet or even physical paper-based channels are important and need to be considered in combination with mobile advertisements. Nonetheless, immense care needs to be taken in using the mobile channels themselves for advertising and marketing the products and services of the business. This is so mainly because of the personalized nature of the devices. Advertisements on the mobile devices of customers need to be carefully scrutinized by providers for their *added value*. Increasingly, it is being discovered that customers are not keen to receive unsolicited advertisements and promotional materials on their mobile devices. This dislike of unsolicited material—even more than unsolicited e-mails or spam on the Internet—is based on the "personalized" nature of mobile devices. Promotions on mobile devices can be particularly counterproductive when the customer is utilizing the roaming facility. It requires the user to pay for the promotional messages on phone calls, especially when he or she is away internationally. At the same time, material that is of value to the customer, such as sports information and weather details, can be combined with subtle promotions, and that combination is more acceptable to the customer than direct advertisements.

Google is significant even in this mobile advertising and marketing space. The number of mobile phones in use exceeds the number of personal computers, laptops, and televisions combined, providing huge potential for location-based advertising and marketing. Google would prefer "net neutrality" and "open access" where any handset could be used on any mobile network with any application (Jenkins 2007) that would enable not only advertisements and services but, as per Babcock (2007), also enable software developers to create reusable components and applications that can be used across devices and networks. Google has recently announced the formation of its "Open Handset Alliance," that includes mobile operators, handset makers, service providers, software firms, and semiconductor firms (Delaney and Sharma 2007).

Analysis of the Importance of the Competition Factor

Figure 3.6 shows the analysis of the importance of the competition factor in the economic dimension of MET. The data have been collected and analyzed from the survey described in the research section of Chapter 2.

Figure 3.6A shows the importance of the mobile service offered by the competitor within the overall competition factors in MET. The result of the survey, as appearing in this figure, indicates that 37 percent of the respondents think that service competition factors are less important. Ten percent think that these factors are most important, whereas 21 percent think they are more important. Thus, a total of 31 percent think the service competition factors are more to most important. Only 8 percent think of competition as the least important factor in the economic dimension of MET. These results indicate that the services offered by the competition, although reasonably important, are not a compelling driver for a business to undertake MET.

Figure 3.6B shows the importance of the mobile content offered by the competitor within the overall competition factors in MET. The result of the survey, in this figure, indicates that 13 percent think of content competition as the most important competition factor in the economic dimension of MET, and 22 percent think it is more important. A total of 35 percent think it is more to most important,

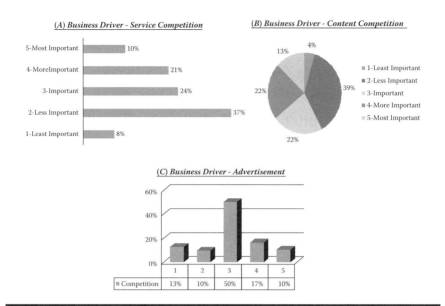

Figure 3.6   Analysis of the importance of the competition factor in the economic dimension of MET.

and 38 percent of the participants, which is the highest percentage in the survey, think that content competition is less important. Only 4 percent think of it as least important. Thus, this factor, similar to the previous factor, indicates that mobile content is reasonably important in order for a business to be competitive, but it is not an entirely compelling factor on its own for MET.

Figure 3.6C shows the importance of advertising/marketing of mobility by the competitor within the overall competition factors in MET. The result of the survey, in this figure, indicates that 50 percent of the participants think that competition is important, 10 percent think it is most important, and 17 percent think it is more important. A total of 27 percent think it is most to more important. Only 10 percent think it is less important, and 13 percent think it is least important. A total of 23 percent think that the advertisement competition is the less to least important factor in the economic dimension of MET. A comparison of the competition factor with others indicates a bell curve for all three factors considered here in MET. The majority of participants in the survey indicate that competition is an important transition factor, but perhaps not as high as costs.

Customer and Employee Management

Customers, employees, and business partners need to be managed properly in MET. Each of these three players influences the transitioning mobile business differently. This section discusses their importance individually, and follows that up with the analysis of the data from the survey on the relative importance of these factors. The earlier discussion of SWOT analysis of the business as well as the use of a balanced scorecard for internal business processes can be used to analyze these various players in MET.

Customers' Demands for Mobile Services

There is interplay between the demands of the customer and the vision and strategy of the transitioning business. Demographics of the customer are as important as that of the business in analyzing customer demands, such as provision of specific location-based services by the mobile business. The challenge to providing these demands comes from the dynamics of change with time and place. Customers are also increasingly asking for the combination of content and services at informative, transactive, and collaborative levels of the mobile business. There is also need on the part of customers for facilities and opportunities to develop applications on their mobile gadgets by combining various software and service components and mobile agents made available by the business.

Business Partners' Demands for Mobile Processes

Business partners of transitioning businesses are likely to demand business-to-business (B2B) mobile processes that are configurable. These business partners demand configurable services and service components from each other that can be put together to provide new and dynamic services to customers. The configurability of processes enables the businesses to collaborate with each other rather than provide complete solutions on their own. The collaborative mobile business usage requires businesses to support each other in enabling and providing mobile Web services.

Employees' Ability to Better Manage Themselves

Customers and employees of a business were never before so well connected with each other than in today's mobile era. Mobility provides employees with immense opportunities to manage themselves better and improve their quality of life or work. Mobility also helps employees to enhance customer service.

Mobility enables employees to manage themselves better and also provides them with the opportunity to improve services to their customers. The personalized nature of mobile devices also means that there is considerable ease with which human resources (HR) functions can be handled on them. For example, mobile devices can be used in the payroll function to provide timely update to the employees on their payment slip data in a secure manner.

Businesses have an ongoing need to optimize labor costs by enhancing their workforce management solutions. These enhancements can be achieved by applying mobility to create flexible scheduling capability that can accommodate rapidly changing demands. Mobility can also be used to schedule task lists and update the rest of the team with it. Visibility of time and attendance data to help management decision making, optimize resource utilization, and improve the quality of work play a significant role in managing employees and enabling them to manage themselves.

Mobile time management is another significant HR function that is extremely helpful to organizations as they adapt mobility. Coupled with task management it helps in optimizing labor costs because the business has an opportunity to match these costs with market demands in real-time. These time and attendance systems help in employee scheduling, shift tracking, and controlling overtime costs, and result in better management of time calculations in mobile solutions.

Employees' Ability to Provide Better Services to Customers

Mobility enables employees to be in direct and personal contact with customers. Notwithstanding the challenges of privacy and security, this enhanced access, which allows employees to respond to the changing demands of customers based on their location, is a special value of mobility. For example, a road runner providing help in a car breakdown service is now directly able to take a "rerouted" call from a stranded driver and provide timely help. This rerouting is based on the dynamic location of the employee as well. A courier with the responsibility of delivering a package is able to contact the addressee and drop the package even in a location different from the one on the address due to mobile connectivity. These services are required to be supported by excellence in timeliness and value of the content, mobile CRM, and reliable connectivity.

Analysis of the Importance of Customers and Employees Factors

Figure 3.7 shows the importance of customers and employees as factors in the economic dimension of MET. There are three factors analyzed in this section: customers, business partners, and employees. The relative importance of these factors in this economic dimension of MET are studied here.

The left column in Figure 3.7 displays the result of the survey in the area of customers' demands in MET. There, 19 percent of the participants think that demands of customers are most important, and 26 percent think they are more important.

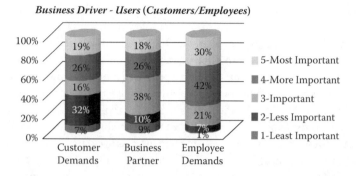

Business Driver - Users (Customers/Employees)

Figure 3.7 Analysis of the importance of customers and employees factors in the economic dimension of MET.

A total of 45 percent think that customers' demands are most to more important. Most people (32 percent) think this factor is less important, and only 7 percent think it is least important. Thus, there is a relative spread of importance in terms of customer demand for MET.

The middle column in Figure 3.7 displays the result of the survey in the area of the business partners' demands in MET. There, 18 percent of the participants think they are most important, and 26 percent think they are more important. A total of 44 percent think they are most to more important. Most people (38 percent) think these are important, and only 9 percent think they are least important.

The right column in Figure 3.7 displays the result of survey in the area of the employees' ability to provide better services to customers. There, 30 percent participants think it is most important, and 42 percent think it is more important. A total of 72 percent think it is more to most important. Only 1 percent thinks it is the least important factor in the economic dimension of MET. Based on these responses, it is amply clear that employees are keen to exploit the potential offered by mobility to improve their overall quality of work—both internally in relations to themselves and externally with the organization's customers.

Mobile Connectivity and Convenience

Mobile connectivity offered through wireless networks and infrastructure can be categorized in two major ways. These are long-distance satellite-based cellular networks and short-range Wi-Fi ones that also combine with cellular networks. A detailed discussion of the technical aspects of these wireless networks follows in the next chapter. From an economic viewpoint, though, this connectivity can be understood as local and global. Local connectivity provides location independence within a localized region, whereas global connectivity enables communication over different and dispersed geographical regions.

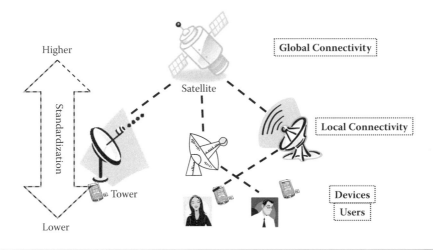

Figure 3.8 **Local and global connectivity offering different types of convenience to users.**

Local Connectivity (Location Independence)

Figure 3.8 provides an understanding of wireless local connectivity versus global connectivity. This discussion focuses on the business aspect of local connectivity. It provides the business use of the short-range wireless connectivity in and around offices and households, and combines it with cellular connectivity offered by cellular network operators within a slightly wider geographical region. As can be noticed here, local connectivity can be in two tiers. Local, short-range mobile connectivity can be configured by the users themselves.

Global Connectivity (Roaming)

Global satellite-based connectivity is the long-range connectivity that offers seamless roaming features to the user. Global connectivity offered directly through satellites has wide-ranging application in defense, shipping, weather forecasting, etc. Seamlessness security and quality of service (QoS) are its vital ingredients. Ruhi and Turel (2005) have studied connectivity and its effect on mobile technology applications. Mobile connectivity is able to provide an opportunity to fulfill context-sensitive voice and data transmission needs. The connectivity requirements differ from city locations to remote locations, where fixed landlines and other forms of communication are not available. There is a need to provide a seamless wireless infrastructure that enables transmission of wireless voice and data across a combination of wired and wireless networks.

Global wireless connectivity bridges the gap between developed and underdeveloped countries as it facilitates and promotes business interchanges across geographical borders. For example, the wireless infrastructure in China, which has already surpassed the fixed-line infrastructure in terms of penetration and coverage (GSM Association 2004), implies that businesses and people from other countries are more likely to engage in commercial transactions with firms located in China through mobile communication networks. Similar wide land areas are connecting India and Sri Lanka through mobile connectivity in Sri Lanka. The ascent in mobile penetration in developing countries obviates the need to set up large land-based infrastructures such as copper wires and supporting physical power. This is because once a mobile infrastructure (such as a mobile transmission tower) is set up, it does not require any additional work such as installation and maintenance of landlines for communication.

Furthermore, mobility started off as a predominant characteristic of knowledge workers, and its widespread availability and standardization of roaming capabilities result in these knowledge workers being able to collaborate with other knowledge workers and their businesses. The seamlessness in wireless connectivity that results from local and global networks provides uninterrupted wireless connectivity to the roaming user to enable him or her to execute mobile applications and source-dispersed contents. Finally, global connectivity also provides impetus to outsourcing.

Analysis of the Importance of Connectivity Factors

Figure 3.9 shows the importance of connectivity factors discussed thus far as a driver in the economic dimension of MET. Figure 3.9A shows the importance of local connectivity (location independence) within MET. The result of the survey in this figure indicates that 31 percent of the participants in the survey think that local convenience is most important, and 52 percent think it is more important. A total of 83 percent think that the local convenience factors is most to more important. Only 2 percent think it is least important. Thus, the importance of local connectivity needs to be considered with great care and attention by the transitioning organization.

Figure 3.9B shows the importance of global connectivity (roaming) within the overall convenience factors in MET. The result of the survey in this figure indicates

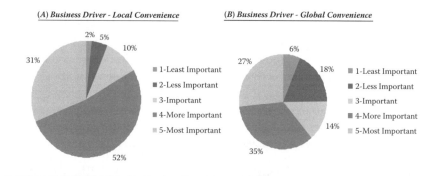

Figure 3.9 Analysis of the importance of connectivity factors in the economic dimension of MET.

that 27 percent of the participants think that global convenience is most important, and 35 percent think it is more important. A total of 62 percent think the
global convenience factor is most to more important. Only 6 percent think it is
least important in the economic dimension of MET. The relative importance of
local connectivity as compared to global connectivity is considered much higher by
the survey participants. This is perhaps because of the ease of network availability,
device availability, and availability of applications on local networks. The ability of
users to configure short-range wireless networks together with the wired Internet
should be of particular importance here.

Mobile Usage as Lifestyle

The way in which mobility is used by individuals has a great bearing on mobile
services that can be offered by the transitioning business. Three types of usage are
studied here from a MET viewpoint: leisure, work, and emergency.

Leisure (e.g., Sports, Entertainment)

The use of mobility for leisure is very common for certain demographics of users
such as adolescents (Gala 2009). Leisure use provides opportunities for transitioning
business to combine it with subtle promotions of its products and services. Examples
include downloading and streaming of movies, sports scores, sports updates, music,
videos, and photos. The leisure use of mobility in MET is ideally started by the
informative use of mobility, wherein leisure contents are primarily "pushed" by the
business to users. The need for two-way or multiway transactions is minimal in the
initial phase of mobile transition when leisure usage is being considered.

Work (e.g., Keeping Contact with Employees)

Mobile usage also influences the working lifestyle of the user by dealing with
work practices with improved means of communication between employees of
the business and customers. Examples include time sheets, inventory, and payroll.
Personalized mobile devices enable workers to upload their time sheets, have the
latest information on their stocks, and have their payroll figures delivered to them.
It also creates social opportunities for workers, which depends on their interest
groups, abilities (such as problem solving), and needs (such as peer support).

Emergency Services (e.g., Fire, Police, and Ambulance)

Mobile usage for emergency services has changed the fabric of society. Equally
importantly, emergency support features have changed the lifestyles of users and
their supporters. Mobility, as an emergency usage, is considered in this economic
dimension from the point of view of costs to service providers. Common examples
are that of fire, police, and ambulance services. Each of these services is governed by
its standards and available in various geographic regions at the press of a three-digit

emergency code (e.g., 000 in Australia; 911 in the United States). The U.S. government mandates EC911 standards for cellular networks, which requires that network operators provide location-specific services within a certain range (technical details are discussed in Chapter 4).

Analysis of the Importance of the Mobile Usage Factor

A transitioning business must consider all three usage types of leisure, work, and emergency services in its strategic MET plans. As leisure usage of mobility changes the way in which mobile businesses can offer services, work usage changes the internal social networking of workers. The emergency services provision is regulated by the government, and the network operators need to comply with those requirements, together with service providers.

Figure 3.10 shows the importance of mobile usage in the economic dimension of MET. The nearest bar displays the importance of leisure (e.g., sports, entertainment, etc.) usage. The highest percentage response in this category is 36 percent, and these respondents think that the leisure factor is less important for transitioning. This data indicates that the leisure usage of mobility is not considered very important in MET. The middle row of bars shows the importance of work (e.g., keeping contact with employees). The highest percentage, 49 percent, think it is more important, indicating that work usage is considered significant by almost half the respondents when it comes to MET. The farthest bar displays the importance of emergency services (e.g., fire, police, and ambulance) usage in the economic dimension of MET. The highest percentage, 45 percent, think it is most important.

Mobile Transition Framework (Economic Dimension)

Costs are the primary economic driver for MET, as they are in most other business activities. There is a need for the business to consider the costs of undertaking the formal transition to a mobile business to receive the corresponding benefits accruing from it. Costs in MET include those of the MET project, devices, networks, creation of content, security, safety of individuals, and setting up alliances with other service providers and network operators.

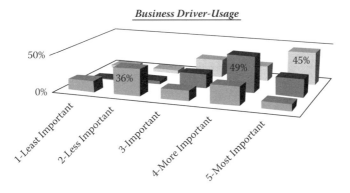

Figure 3.10   Analysis of the importance of the mobile usage factor in the economic dimension of MET.

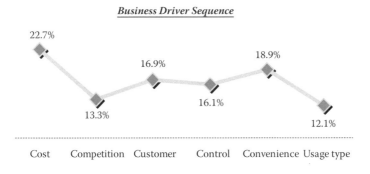

Figure 3.11   Analysis of sequencing of economic drivers in the economic dimension of the MET framework.

Figure 3.11 shows the relative importance of all the economic drivers in the MET framework. It provides information in terms of their priority and how they can be sequenced in the framework. A total of 22.7 percent of the respondents indicated that costs should be the primary driver, whereas 18.9 percent said that convenience needs to be considered first. These then are the first and second important factors in the economic dimension of MET based on the result of the survey. The importance of the customer is next, with 16.9 percent, and improved business control is 16.1 percent, whereas the influence of competition is 13.3 percent. However, only 12.1 percent of the participants think of mobile-usage type as the most important factor driving mobile business. These priorities are also summarized in Table 3.2.

Table 3.2 is based on the sequences of economic factors as indicated by the survey listed in Appendix A, wherein participants provide numbers from 1 to 6 in terms of their view on the relative importance of these factors in MET. The number 1 indicates

Table 3.2 Summary and analysis of the economic dimension survey

	Cost (%)	Competition (%)	Customer (%)	Control (%)	Convenience (%)	Usage type (%)
1	38	9	24	8	18	2
2	26	15	12	18	17	12
3	23	7	8	9	29	23
4	5	15	14	40	21	5
5	2	21	34	17	12	13
6	5	33	7	7	3	44
Total value (after weighting)	22.7	13.3	16.9	16.1	18.9	12.1
Result	1	5	3	4	2	6

Note: 1 should be considered first; 6 should be considered last.

the highest importance and the most urgent of the six factors, and the number 6 the least important of the six factors. Weighting factors are then applied to the data listed in the first six rows in Table 3.2 to arrive at the "total value" to indicate the importance of these factors. This table and the subsequent interpretation of the data therein lead to the creation of a MET framework in the economic dimension.

Figure 3.12 shows the various drivers in the economic dimension of the MET framework. This framework is arrived at based on the analysis of the prioritized economic drivers discussed and presented in Table 3.2. The research survey and the analysis of their priority sequence indicate that costs need to be considered right at the very beginning in MET. In this economic component, typical roles are played by the senior business manager, customers and employees, and business partners, as shown in three separate rows in Figure 3.12. It further shows the sequence of the activities in MET, based on these economic devices, corresponding to the roles mentioned. The sequence of activities in the economic dimension of MET are read from left to right in Figure 3.12 as follows:

1. Cost and time are the very first activities undertaken by the senior business manager together with the accounting department. The issues discussed earlier in this chapter on cost of transition, devices, operational cost, etc., and corresponding benefits from the transition, are considered in this activity.
2. Convenience and connectivity appear as the next important part of the MET framework from the economic dimension. Therefore, the transitioning business needs to consider these next, after the cost and time factors.

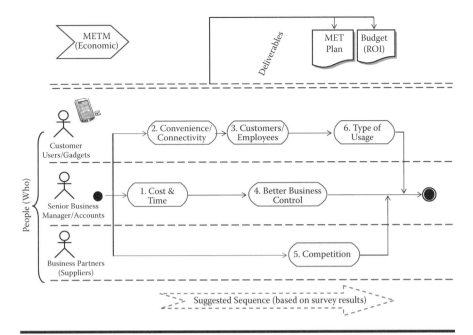

Figure 3.12 Mobile transition framework (economic dimension) based on the study of sequence.

3. Customers and employees are considered next in the MET project, with the advantages and challenges derived by them providing valuable input to the transitioning business.
4. Better business control can result from prudent use of mobility, as it allows real-time input of data on inventories, time, etc. The timely value of business control, therefore, needs to be considered at this stage of the MET project.
5. Competition is considered next, based on the results from the survey. Although, throughout the literature study carried out for this book, competition was considered one of the significant factors in driving MET (and still is), when it comes to sequencing this competition factor, it comes in at fifth place, based on the survey.
6. Usage type is the last in the sequence but an equally important factor that drives MET from an economic viewpoint.

These activities then produce the deliverables of the MET plan together with their budgets. These deliverables, shown in Figure 3.12, incorporate the ROI. The MET transition framework in Figure 3.12 is only depicting the economic dimension. Similar framework components are created for the technical, process, and social dimensions in the next three chapters of this book. Eventually, all four component frameworks are put together in an enactable project plan in Chapter 7 that is then enacted in practice.

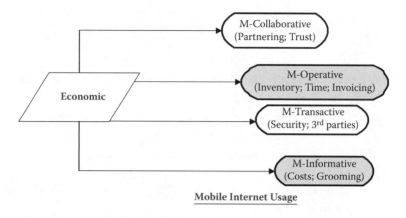

Figure 3.13   Mapping the economic dimension of MET to mobile Internet usage.

Economic Factors in Mobile Business Usage

The discussion thus far in this chapter has been on the various economic factors, their perceived importance, and their sequence in arriving at the economic component of the MET framework. Now we discuss how they come into play with respect to the informative, transactive, operative, and collaborative use of mobility as an organization undertakes MET. These four levels or tiers of mobile business usage, as discussed in Chapter 1, are mapped to the economic dimension of MET as shown here in Figure 3.13.

> The economic factors in MET should be considered in light of the gradually increasing complexities of informative, transactive, operative, and collaborative usage of mobility by business. This stepwise approach to adoption of mobility reduces the risks in MET as it enables the business to "adjust" to the changes resulting from mobility at each step.

Economic–Informative

The economic considerations in the informative aspects of mobile business are primarily the costs of, and competition in, providing information on mobile gadgets. This provision is the easiest of the four usages of mobility because it mostly involves the "push" technology requiring a one-way access to the mobile device. Therefore, in considering the economic aspect of the informative usage of mobility, the business is interested in the cost of "pushing" this one-way information into the mobile devices of users. Examples are an airline that provides flight schedules to passengers, or a hospital providing service information to patients or doctors. The business is interested in finding out the cheapest way to provide this information. The economic factor that comes into play in this informative usage, other than cost and competition, is that of lifestyle. There are lesser issues of security in this one-way usage of mobility by business as compared with the subsequent two-way usage. However, at the same time, there are privacy issues to be considered.

Economic–Transactive

The economic dimension of MET, when dealing with the transactive aspect of business usage of mobility, is in effect mobile commerce. It is the conducting of two-way or multiway transactions on mobile devices using mobile networks between various parties involved. These commercial transactions are external ones conducted outside the boundary of the organization. Therefore, there is a need to set up business alliances to enable these two-way transactive capabilities of mobile business to be effected in practice. Although the cost comes into play here as well, even more important are the additional costs involved in ensuring the security of these transactions. It should be noted that the infrastructure costs of mobile networks remain the same for transactive usage as with informative usage. The economic issues in a two-way transaction include formal identification of both parties, creating a formal deal between them, and ensuring that the deal is legally binding on the parties (Neely and Unhelkar 2005). This elaborate approach to two-way transactions ensures that customers have confidence in using those services.

Economic–Operative

The economic–operative use of mobility by business focuses on providing quality of working life to employees and reducing the cost of operations of the business. In this operative usage, the business transforms its internal business processes and makes them mobile enabled. For example, time management and invoicing are made "mobile," which also enhances the quality of employees' working life. It also leads to better control of the business by management as the data is available in real-time through mobility.

Economic–Collaborative

Strategic planners of the organization need to balance between competition and collaboration. However, the mobile business almost mandates collaboration among businesses or competition of a unique kind. This is so because the mobile customer is only interested in the visible aspect of the final content and services being delivered to him or her, whereas the business needs much more, such as associated businesses to collaborate with in the background to provide the content and services desired by the customer. For example, a customer looking for a hotel for night accommodation goes to his "network operator" to provide him with the nearest convenient hotel. The network operator has no idea where to find the relevant information, so he or she, in turn, collaborates with one or more service providers in the hotel business to provide that information. The driving direction to the selected hotel would come from the map services using General Packet Radio Service (GPRS) navigation systems. The need for mobile businesses is thus increasing more than land-based operations, leading to greater mobile collaborations and clusters (m-alliances). There are a large number of deals that are continuously happening in both vertical and horizontal markets, resulting in dynamic collaborations to provide unique combinations of content and services. These are also needed for the provision of emergency services that may be mandatory, especially for network operators.

Measuring the Strategic Benefits of MET

The economic dimension of MET is concerned with the strategic benefits resulting from the transition. These accrue over a long time and are benefits over and above the normal ones. A simple metric can be used to make these strategic benefits more convincing to the senior management of an organization. This is a discussion on what can be considered strategic benefits that can then be applied in ascertaining mobile transition benefits. The time factor is an important element in understanding mobile strategic benefits, and is also further discussed in Chapters 8 and 9.

An initial measure of MET's benefit to the business can be called the *advantage factor*. It is based on the current operations of business that may be carried out without any particular use of mobile technologies. The MET exercise has certain costs associated with it. However, at the same time, MET can provide greater satisfaction and value to the current clients. Therefore, the immediate advantage of MET can be expressed as follows:

$$\text{Advantage factor} = \text{Cost of lost business/Cost of MET} \qquad (3.1)$$

For example, if the opportunity costs to the organization due to lack of MET (which is the cost of lost business by not incorporating mobility strategically in business) is $2 million, and if the cost of the MET project is $250,000, then the advantage factor based on Equation 3.1 is as follows:

$$\text{Advantage factor} = \$2M/\$250,000 = 8 \qquad (3.2)$$

The number in Equation 3.2, however, simply highlights the advantage of not losing out to competitors. Strategic advantage further implies advantages that are derived *over and above* the normal advantage of using mobility. The calculations of strategic advantage need to consider the benefit that is derived over a sufficiently long period of time. Thus, to arrive at the strategic advantage factor, it is essential for us to look at the advantages of MET that provide value to the transitioning business, which is beyond simply loss prevention. These *additional* advantages of MET can be summarized as the "revenue" accruing from the use of mobility in business. Such new revenue streams generated from MET can come from new mobile business processes, additional business generated from existing customers and, of course, reduction in the cost of internal business operations due to use of mobility. All these advantages are in addition to the routine advantages of not losing business. Thus, again in an informal way, the formula shown in Equation 3.1 can now be rewritten as

$$\text{Strategic advantage factor} = (\text{Cost of lost business}$$
$$+ \text{Revenue by new mobile business}$$
$$+ \text{Operational cost reduction})/(\text{Cost of MET}$$
$$+ \text{Cost of creating extra new business}) \qquad (3.3)$$

For example, if the cost of lost business due to loss of opportunities is $2M, the revenue from new mobile business processes, including content and services, is $3M, and the operational cost reduction due to use of mobility is $1M; and the cost of MET ($250,000) is added to the cost of promoting and operating the new part of the business, which is $750,000. Then, placing these figures in formula 3.3 (along with the figures from formula 3.2) gives

$$\text{Strategic advantage factor} = (\$2M + \$3M + \$1M)/(\$250K + \$750K) \quad (3.4)$$

This gives a strategic advantage factor of 6.0, which may or may not be an improvement over the advantage factor of 2.5 initially, especially in a short period of time. However, there is a need to bring in the time factor to understand the strategic advantage correctly. This time factor implies the length, in terms of number of years, that the business can sustain itself with strategic advantage as against normal advantage or no advantage at all. Sustainability is specifically discussed later in this book, in Chapter 9. Thus, although an ad hoc use of mobility can provide some value to the business, MET works toward a sustainable and managed use of mobility for long-term advantages.

MET Strategic Benefits Accrue in Time

The strategic benefits of mobility are over and above the normal advantages of using new technologies. However, these strategic benefits always accrue in time and are not instantaneous. There is a need to consider the value of mobility from a strategic viewpoint to derive full benefit from this technology.

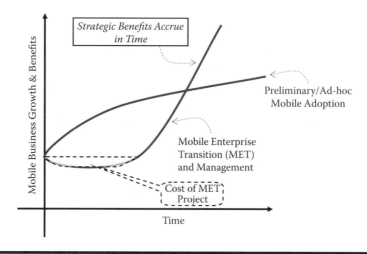

Figure 3.14   MET strategic benefits accrue in time.

Calculation of the strategic benefits of MET can be made into a formal process for evaluating the alternatives. However, it can also require effort in terms of measuring the advantages. An organization may not be in a position to ascertain the advantages of MET before it has embarked on it. Therefore, a certain amount of educated guesswork is required in calculating the strategic advantage factor. However, if data can be collected across the industry and for similar types of organizations, then some valuable indicators can be obtained for an organization before it launches MET. The advantages of MET are both direct as well as spin-offs, and the benefits are tangible as well as intangible.

However, these advantages take some time to accrue. As shown in Figure 3.14, when an organization undertakes MET, the cost of that exercise needs to be factored in the calculations. This is not much different from what happens when an organization decides to reengineer itself. During a reengineering exercise, old processes are given up and new ones are introduced. The result is an initial drop in productivity until the new processes "mature" as people get trained in them and start serving the customers of the company.

Formal MET encourages the organization to reinvent itself in myriad ways by examining its processes, people, and technologies. Thus, as new mobile business processes are created, the old and possibly redundant processes are eliminated. The benefits of these reengineering of processes eventually provides greater "value for money" from undertaking MET than the ad hoc use of mobile phones.

The arguments for strategic advantage discussed here are based on the understanding that whenever we take a strategic view, it implies major upfront expenses (or even possible losses in the present) for the sake of potential profits in the future. Strategic decisions usually imply a nonlinear relationship between inputs and the returns, and there is a long-time factor involved before returns climb above input. That is the reason why strategic decisions are difficult to make, as compared with short-term tactical decisions.

Discussion Points

1. Compare the cost factors with the competition factors in driving MET.
2. You are asked to modify the MET framework's economic dimension (Figure 3.13) because you are dealing with a small business (e.g., furniture manufacturer). Discuss how the framework can be tweaked without losing the value of its sequence when applying it to a small-time furniture manufacturer.
3. SWOT and balanced scorecards are suggested in this chapter as two ways of ascertaining competition. What are the other management techniques you have used for analyzing competition in business that you can apply to MET?
4. Why, according to you, is the convenience factor in Figure 3.12 much higher than the competition factor in driving the sequence?
5. What are the various important issues highlighted from a customer's angle in terms of driving MET? Which of these issues are strategic as compared with routine and known issues related to the customers?
6. How does mobility add value to an employee's working life? Discuss both from the personal and business viewpoint.
7. The business usage of mobility is increasingly involved and complex as the business transitions through the informative, transactive, operative, and collaborative use of mobility. Consider some examples of this increasingly involved usage from an economic viewpoint.

References

Atkins, T. and Ali, H. J. 2009. Mobile strategy of strategic E-business solution by Dr Tony Atkins and Hairul, A. K., Nizam, P. G., Ali, H. J., chapter in *Handbook of Research in Mobile Business: Technical, Methodological and Social Perspectives,* 2nd ed., ed. B. Unhelkar. Hershey, PA: IGI Global.

Babcock, C. 2007. Software Ecosystems: Can Salesforce, Google, and Facebook Be Fertile Grounds for Third-Party Development? We Are About to Find Out, *Information Week* (May 2007) 31–33.

Delaney, K. J. and Sharma, A. 2007. Google, Bidding for Phone Ads, Lures Partners, *The Wall Street Journal,* November 2007.

Gala, J. and Unhelkar, B. 2009. Impact of mobile technologies and gadgets on adolescent's interpersonal relationships, chapter in *Handbook of Research in Mobile Business: Technical, Methodological and Social Perspectives,* 2nd ed. Hershey, PA: IGI Global.

Gartner, 2006. Worldwide Combined PDA and Smartphone Shipments Market Grew 57 Percent in the First Half of 2006. http://www.gartner.com/it/page.jsp

GSM Association, 2004. GSMA Statistics Q1 04. Dublin, Ireland: GSM Association, http://www.gsmworld.com/technology/

Harmon, R. and Diam, T. 2009, Assessing the future of location-based services: Technologies, applications, and strategies, chapter in *Handbook of Research in Mobile Business: Technical, Methodological and Social Perspectives,* 2nd ed., ed. B. Unhelkar, Hershey, PA: IGI Global.

IDC, 2007, http://www.idc.com/.

Jenkins, H. W. 2007. Sort of Evil, *The Wall Street Journal,* A14, July 18.

Kamdar, M. 2007. *Planet India: How the Fastest Growing Democracy is Transforming the World.* New York: Scribner.

Kharif, O. 2007. Apple, Google vs. big wireless, *Businessweek.com,* from http://www.businessweek.com/technology/ content/oct2007/.

Neely, M. and Unhelkar, B. November 2005. The role of a collaborative commerce legal framework in IT-related litigation, ed. by E. Yourdon. *Cutter IT Journal* 18(11): 11–17.

Porter, M. E. 1985. *Competitive Advantage.* London: Collier Macmillan, 33–39, 326–329.

Porter, M. 2001. Strategy and the Internet. *Harvard Business Review,* 63–78.

Reardon, M. 2007. Mobile Phones that Track Your Buddies. *ZDNet News,* 14, http://news.zdnet.com.

Ruhi, U., Turel, O., and Lan, Y. 2005. GISCM, Enabling the glass pipeline: The infusion of mobile technology applications in supply chain management, *Global Integrated Supply Chain Systems*, eds. Lan and B. Unhelkar. Hershey, PA: IGI Global.

Schenker, J. L. 2007. Nokia Aims Way beyond Handsets, *Business Week* 38, www.balancedscorecard.com.

Chapter 4

Mobile Enterprise Transitions: Technical Dimension

> Progress lies not in enhancing what is, but in advancing toward what will be.
>
> **Khalil Gibran**

Chapter Key Points

- Introduces mobile technology enabling modern mobile businesses globalization and collaboration
- Presents and discusses the technical aspect of Mobile Enterprise Transition (MET) especially in relation to mobile gadgets, networking, contents, and security
- Discusses mobile Internet and its accessibility and relevance in a collaborative mobile business
- Discusses mobile Web service (MWS) together with the components that comprise eXtensible Markup Language (XML), Simple Object Access Protocol (SOAP), Web Service Description Language (WSDL), and Universal Description, Discovery, and Integration (UDDI)
- Outlines mobile system architecture and mobile middleware in the context of MET

■ Analyzes the surveyed data to ascertain the priority and sequencing of technical drivers of MET
■ Presents the increasingly involved informative, transactive, operative, and collaborative use of mobility by mapping it to the technical dimension of MET

Introduction

This chapter discusses in detail the technical dimension of Mobile Enterprise Transition (MET), comprising among other things, mobile devices, networks, services, contents, etc. The resultant technical challenges include limitations of mobile gadgets, the need to provide reliability of connections, the importance of security of transactions, and the ability to develop suitable mobile services and applications. Mobile technology is a creative and disruptive emerging technology that makes change imperative for a business; it forces the business to adopt location independence at all levels of operation both internally and externally. Therefore, the economic reasons for MET discussed in Chapter 3 become all the more compelling when combined with the technical factors of mobility discussed in this chapter. Mobility is also fraught with numerous technical challenges. This chapter discusses such challenges and also presents the sequence of activities involved in this dimension. Such sequences are based on statistics gleaned from the research survey mentioned in Chapter 2 (and listed in Appendix A). This survey was conducted globally as a part of the study discussed in this book. Data from the survey is presented and analyzed to validate the sequencing of activities in the technical dimension of MET. Finally, this dimension is mapped for the informative, transactive, operative, and collaborative use of mobility by business.

Technical Dimension (What)

The discussion on the technical dimension of MET focuses on "what" emerging technologies form the creative cause for enabling MET (see Figure 4.1). It starts with an understanding of the disruptive and enabling technologies of communication (i.e., mobile technologies in this case) that influence the business world. This impact of technologies on business provides the impetus for business collaboration and globalization in the context of mobility. The technical dimension of MET further delves into discussions on mobile devices (gadgets), programming, databases, networking, security, and architecture of mobile technologies. Further, the role and significance of various mobile hardware devices, wireless networking, security, and contents (databases) to business are discussed. Participants in the research survey mentioned earlier were asked their opinions on the relative importance of these technical issues with respect to MET. Table 4.1 summarizes these technical issues together with the transition focus.

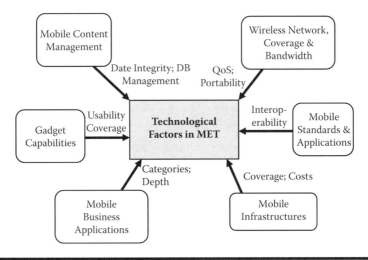

Figure 4.1 Technical dimension of MET.

Enabling Mobile Technologies Landscape

The emerging mobile technologies play a significant role in enabling global business communications and globalization. They not only influence the organizational structure of a business but also play a role in facilitating the application of principles and practices of management. For example, management control, distribution of authority, management of deliverables across geopolitical boundaries, and application of legal and tax principles all undergo change in a global environment resulting from these enabling technologies. Therefore, such technologies need to be studied within the technical dimension of MET. The emerging mobile technologies, as shown in Figure 4.2, are

- Mobile devices and gadgets that present contents and services to users.
- Mobile networks, including mobile Internet, and corresponding transmission infrastructures such as mobile towers, repeaters, etc.
- Mobile applications that analyze and present useful information and knowledge to users.
- Mobile middleware that builds upon existing ones and facilitates communication across varied application platforms.
- Mobile Web services that facilitate interoperability and opportunities for collaboration among business applications and different business departments; for example, billing systems will need to communicate to customer addresses.
- Mobile groupware applications that facilitate creation and operation of virtual teams.
- Mobile system architecture that incorporates technical aspects of mobility in a development platform to facilitate rapid and robust mobile system development.
- Mobile contents and content management systems (CMSs) that enable secure storage and retrieval of mobile contents including data, voice, and video.

Table 4.1 Technical drivers of MET and the transition focus

Technical drivers for mobile enterprise transitions (What?)		
Drivers	*Comprising aspects*	*Transition focus*
Mobile devices (gadgets)	Mobile phones PDA (wireless enabled, BlackBerry) Wireless laptop/tablet PC Wi-Fi devices (printers, speakers, phones) Look and feel (e.g., color, shape)	Convergence Usability Reliability
Mobile networking and security	Wireless broadband network (3G) Wireless local area network (IEEE) Infrared Bluetooth WiMax Radio frequency identification (RFID)/e-Tag Mobile satellite networks	Quality of network Security Reliability
Mobile standards and applications	Mobile network standards (IEEE) Vendor's desire to comply with standards Customer's desire to use applications Availability and development of mobile applications	Interoperability Development
Mobile infrastructures	Transmission towers Satellites Power lines	Architecture Use of infrastructure Coverage
Mobile content management	Uploading vendor contents Pushing contents to customers Enabling customers to pull contents Multimedia aspect of contents	Database management Integrity Conversion

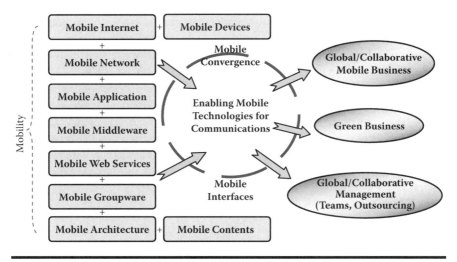

Figure 4.2 Enabling mobile technologies for global business communication (leading to globalization and collaboration between businesses and enhanced global management).

Mobile technologies have far-reaching implications for businesses in terms of their globalization, collaboration, and even environmental responsibilities. The technical drivers of MET mandate these changes in both the structure and dynamics of organizations.

The aforementioned technologies form the backbone of business communications. Lan and Unhelkar (2005) discuss how Internet and related communication technologies influence globalization. That discussion is extended and applied here to mobile communication technologies and their effects on global and collaborative mobile businesses. The communication technologies depicted in Figure 4.2 are the technical drivers and enablers for transitioning a business to a mobile one. This transition can also lead to and enhance the collaboration and globalization of enterprises. Figure 4.2 also shows pictorially the resultant influences of such technologies on business:

- They result in global and collaborative businesses that also expand rapidly.
- They create collaborative management strategies that influence the creation of virtual teams and management of outsourced/smart-sourced projects.
- They have a positive impact on environmentally responsible "green" business strategies that handle the growing significance of "green" business.

Mobile technologies, however, do not exist or operate in isolation. They form a suite of interrelated components that depend on each other to collect, store, retrieve, analyze, and disseminate information and knowledge. Interrelated mobile components enable information and knowledge dissemination. As a result, businesses can plan, control, coordinate, expand, and improve the services offered to their customers. They also reap the advantages of mobility internally in their operations, decision-making processes, and people or human resources (HR) management. Decision support systems (DSSs) are enhanced by advances in mobile communications, their location and time independence, and their ability to correlate otherwise unrelated silos of information. These technologies are discussed in greater detail in the following sections to understand how they help in METs.

Mobile Internet

Mobile Internet extends the Internet by making it available on mobile devices using wireless connectivity. The Internet has been understood as a network of computers without any central control or organization. Occasionally it has also been referred to as a "mind map," providing ideal conduit for communications between individuals, organizations, and governments. Mobile Internet, which forms the underlying basis for many of the technologies depicted in Figure 4.2, provides further unique opportunities as well as challenges in terms of information processing and communication capabilities for business. This is because mobile Internet capitalizes on the existing Internet communication protocols, applications, and contents by rapidly evolving and adopting features to suit the modern mobile business requirements. Internet Protocol (IP) provides the basic network and routing services for Transmission Control Protocol (TCP). TCP enables reliable data transportation between two parties at the ends of a network connection. This delivery service is crucial for mobile transactions. IP and TCP require significant modifications for adapting to the mobile Internet communication. The advantages of using TCP/IP are that they can carry voice and data traffic, and they can be used for voice over broadband or for just mobile broadband.

Mobile Internet needs to be considered in MET because it influences the system architecture, software and applications, database and connectivity, hardware, security, as well as telecommunications. Together, they can be referred to as a "mobile development platform" on which mobile business applications can be developed and deployed on a real-time basis.

The Internet also needs to be understood in the context of two of its variants—the extranet and the intranet. The intranet defines the boundary of the organization for Internet communication purposes and limits communications within that boundary. Therefore, to make use of the Intranet for mobile communications, there is a need to define the boundary and scope of its use. Mobile Internet and intranet communication mechanisms need to be defined in the early stages of development of mobile applications to ensure flexibility and security. Extranet extends the scope of the intranet to provide a controlled access of the organization's data to the applications belonging to authorized external organizations. The access authorization for this extranet is created and maintained dynamically in the mobile communication platform.

Mobile Devices

Mobile devices play a far more crucial role in mobile enterprise transitions than desk-bound machines in corresponding electronic transitions. The ever-increasing capability of mobile gadgets having small and compact sizes is a revolution in itself that influences all the dimensions of MET. Capabilities of mobile devices need to be correlated to the mobile Internet, mobile contents, and wireless network infrastructures so that they are of maximum value to the business. Over the past few years, availability of the easier and cheaper electronic (notably, the chip) technology has led to a plethora of developments in the area of mobile communication equipments and handheld gadgets. These ubiquitous and pervasive equipments and gadgets are now being complemented by an equally supportive network communication infrastructure. Therefore, when developing these gadgets, the wireless network infrastructure, the operating system that will operate the device, and the specific mobile applications should be considered.

Mobile devices are influenced by both hardware and software factors. Mobile system architecture also influences devices; a thick client model will require the devices to run sophisticated operating systems and applications.

While discussing the hardware aspect of mobile devices, it is necessary to consider their physical characteristics such as size, weight, ruggedness, and battery life, for example. The software aspect includes applications, usability, and operating systems. For example, the sophisticated BlackBerry devices are built on a Java-based operating environment, executing Java applications. Mobile devices also include Web browsing features, which use Hypertext Markup Language (HTML) and Wireless Markup Language (WML) Web pages, and use languages such as .NET, Java, Web Services, C#, and ASP/JSP. Mobile devices also need support from server-side applications, and are influenced by system architectures such as thin client or thick client. These two hardware and software aspects of mobile devices and applications are also interrelated. Most new mobile applications consume a significant amount of battery power, almost to an extent that users end up charging their devices on a daily basis. These devices (or gadgets) are discussed in greater detail later in this chapter.

Mobile Networks

The range, strength, security, and types of mobile networks need to be considered when an enterprise transitions to a comprehensive mobile one. The mobile networks can range from the wireless local area networks (WLANs) to the cellular and satellite communication networks. Therefore, mobile networks in a way complement the mobile Internet discussed earlier. Increasingly, wireless networks are becoming as fast and reliable as land-based connections. Therefore, wireless connectivity is enabling mobile business activities inside and outside organizations.

Mobile networks include cellular and Wi-Fi networks, which cover long- and short-range communications. Cellular networks are made up of a combination of fixed and dynamic transmitters and receivers for sending and receiving messages to a base station. Repeaters can be used to cover a wider area of transmission than is possible with a single transmitter; they are used for mobile phone and data communications over long distances. Wi-Fi is a short-range mobile network made up of communication mechanisms such as infrared, radio frequency, and Bluetooth. These networks use communication technology standards of IEEE 802.11 and its variations to provide wireless connectivity over relatively short distances. Wi-Fi connectivity provides a reliable and secure mechanism for transmitting and receiving data and information. The Wi-Fi network has a base antenna to transmit signals in a relatively small physical area; this antenna is also linked to a broadband Internet connection. The receiving device, which can be a mobile personal digital assistant (PDA) or a tablet PC, is able to receive the signal transmitted by the antenna within a local area such as home or office. Thus, usually, there is a two-tiered connectivity between the Wi-Fi device and the transmitting/receiving device, which in turn is connected to the land-based or wireless broadband Internet. This arrangement of networks can be used to connect a set of machines, which may include laptops, PDAs, and other mobile gadgets, initially to a Wi-Fi network and then into the Internet. Such networks have a limited range of about a hundred meters. The strength and quality of a signal can rapidly deteriorate with increasing distance from the base antenna. The latest Wi-Fi signals, however, have a much bigger coverage, with the signal strengths lasting well up to a few hundred meters. Such a network functions similar to a Wi-Fi Internet within a stipulated range, opening up enormous business opportunity. An example of such a combined implementation of Wi-Fi and cellular networks is T-Mobile. Wi-Fi networks are usually used by laptops and PDAs, whereas cellular networks are typically used by mobile phones. However, devices that provide a combination of network functionalities and can work equally well on cellular as well as Wi-Fi networks are also becoming available. Telecommunication providers such as Hutchison have opened up Voice-over-IP (VoIP) calls over cellular networks. This has bridged the gap between PC-based applications and mobile applications. Mobile devices and VoIP applications, such as Skype (source: http://www.three.com.au), can now be converged in a network that uses both mobile and land-based communication networks.

Mobile Applications

Mobile applications range from back-end server-side business applications that store and process large amounts of data and information, to numerous applications that offer ever-increasing functionality on tiny handheld devices. Such mobile application functionalities require the processing and presentation of data, the ability to customize language features, and the ability to connect to back-end applications. Categories of mobile applications include business, entertainment and informative, emergency help and support, and so on. Sophisticated user groups are also demanding flexibility and functionalities from service providers that will enable them to create their own applications. These applications and categories are discussed in detail from a process viewpoint in Chapter 5.

Mobile Middleware

Mobile middleware technologies bring together or "gel" the various parts of a mobile software application. The need for mobile middleware is felt due to the evolving, dispersed, global system environment. These dispersed business computer systems are made up of multiple computers, systems, applications, and services interconnected with one another so as to provide value to a business (see Figure 4.3). Middleware technologies enable interactions among these systems by creating and using common interfaces. Wireless Application Protocol (WAP) and i-Mode are the two well-known mobile middleware protocols used in mobile application development. WAP and i-Mode middleware platforms are built on top of the

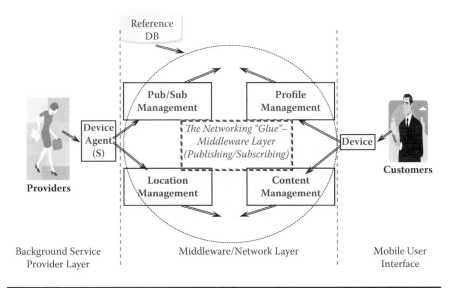

Figure 4.3   Positioning mobile middleware in a mobile architecture.

Table 4.2 Mobile middleware in mobile system development

Technical viewpoint	WAP	i-Mode
Developer	WAP Forum/alliance	NTT DoCoMo
Implementation	A (standard) protocol	A complete mobile Internet service
Programming language	WML (Wireless Markup Language)	CHTML (Compact HTML)
Technology platform	WAP gateway	TCP/IP platform
Features	Widely adopted and flexible	Highest number of users and easy to use

existing network protocols of Transmission Control Protocol (TCP) and Internet Protocol (IP) suites.

WAP is an open, global, and flexible standard that allows users to access and interact with service providers using most operating systems (such as PalmOS, Windows CE, and JavaOS), and uses wireless networks such as code division multiple access (CDMA) and Global System for Mobile (GSM). The WAP gateway, which forms the technology platform, translates requests from WAP and submits them to Web servers. Responses are translated back to enable the initiating devices to understand and use them.

I-Mode (2003) is a packet-switched middleware Internet service for cellular devices, which is highly popular in Japan. This service, offered by NTT DoCoMo, enables cellular phone users to access the Internet: e-mails, mobile shopping and banking, ticketing, and personalized ring tones. Users are charged on the basis of the volume of data transmitted rather than the amount of time spent connected. Wideband CDMA (W-CDMA) services that support higher speeds also enable users to download videos and other intense content. Table 4.2 summarizes the various WAP and i-Mode features from a technical viewpoint.

Mobile Web Services

Mobile Web services enable publishing and consumption of service offerings over mobile networks irrespective of the underlying platforms. They herald a new paradigm in businesses that is based on collaboration rather than competition. They also provide a unified view of myriad services to a user, thereby hiding the underlying complexities.

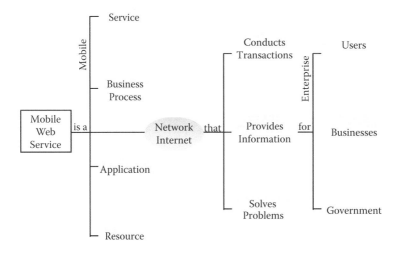

Figure 4.4   A mobile Web service.

Web services (WSs) provide a standardized mechanism for communication between various software applications operating on different computing platforms across various wired and wireless networks. They open up genuine independence for businesses by enabling easy interaction and collaboration among them. Mobility using WSs results in mobile Web services (MWSs), which create opportunities for multiple organizations to interact with each other under the umbrella of a unified application. The WSs initiative effectively creates computational objects that offer service capability over a network (Davies et al. 2004). MWSs extend the WSs on wireless networks, heralding a new paradigm in the way mobile applications are used to add value to business. Figure 4.4 shows what comprises an MWS. An MWS is a service, process, application, or resource that uses the Internet to conduct transactions, provide information, and solve business problems that are of value to businesses, users, and governments. It facilitates direct interface and interactions between multiple mobile applications, obviating the need to interact and conduct individual business transactions. Thus, in a way, MWS is an advancement on the previously discussed mobile middleware, as it goes beyond simple interactions between two applications and moves to the collaborative use of mobility by businesses (discussed later in this chapter on collaboration).

According to the Australian Computer Society's (ACS 2005) report on MWS, with WSs, mobile phones now have the potential to actually consume useful services. This consumption of services through Simple Object Access Protocol/Hypertext Transfer Protocol (SOAP/HTTP) requires the SOAP client on the mobile device to process both HTTP and XML commands. This can result in reduced data speeds and potential performance issues. Mobile devices aiming to use WSs can hide their complexity by providing a unified front-end interface to all their underlying services.

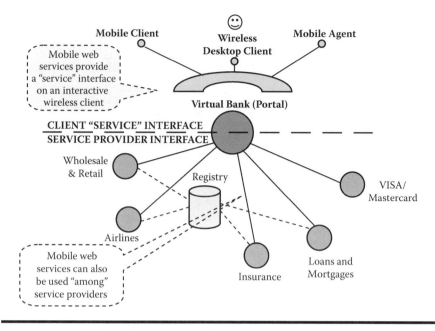

Figure 4.5   Mobile Web services in collaboration.

The layered approach to WSs enables mobile users to leverage these underlying services and complex technologies relatively easily. An example of hiding complexity using MWS and presenting a unified view is shown in Figure 4.5. In the figure, the client (either wireless or desktop) has a range of services available to him or her from the service providers. Service providers include retailers, airlines, insurance, loans, and visa cards. WSs enable each of these services to collaborate with one another, and together they provide a unified interface to the user. The user approaches these services through a single virtual bank (portal). Architecturally, utilization of WSs requires a gateway between the phone and the portal's (WS-enabled) servers to handle transmission and conversion of messages (http://www.acs.openlab.net.au/).

Mobile Groupware

Groupware can be understood as a combination of technology and applications that facilitate communication among a number of individuals who need to work in a group. Mobile groupware applications bring together e-mails, task lists, calendars, newsgroups, and conference calls (audio and video) for multiple and dispersed users. Further, because of its location independence, mobile groupware technologies can create dynamic groups, such as a group of people traveling in a bus together or strolling in a mall. The creation of dynamic user groups is discussed in detail in Chapter 5. However, in most cases, groupware technologies are put to good use by creating virtual working groups that are effectively managed remotely. This remote management of groups enables even small organizations to increase their global reach and operate effectively from a distance. Groupware technology solutions, which combine mobility with the Web, facilitate video-/teleconferencing, instant messaging, and collaborative decision making. They minimize the need for face-to-face interactions, thereby reducing the travel needs of employees within such companies. Mobile groupware technologies can create virtual groups within or outside organizations that can cooperate with each other, communicate easily, compete, entertain (i.e., play games), coordinate (such as in event management), and negotiate. These, however, need to be used with caution as they do not always provide the same value as a face-to-face conversational experience. Nonetheless, mobile groupware does enhance collaboration and communications, enriching the professional and social working environment.

Mobile Enterprise Architecture

A mobile system architecture extends and expands the known concepts of standardized information technology (IT) system architecture, with specific focus on mobile technologies. Mobile system architecture is thus an IT architecture that incorporates location and time independence, nuances of content management, and issues of reliability and security of wireless transmissions, as well as provides the flexibility required by developers of end-user mobile applications (Unhelkar 2008a). It also encompasses issues and constraints related to the functionality of an application, the availability and speed of the mobile network process related to software development, and the incorporation of mobile security. Mobile functional architecture deals with business processes and organizations. The network architecture provides for network technology constraints imposed by the organization (such as availability of bandwidth); the mobile software development strategies within the architecture using those constraints; and the mobile security architecture that applies to all aspects of the system architecture: functional, network, and software. Thus, a good mobile system architecture is based on patterns of business processes, network configurations, and software development.

Figure 4.6 shows an example of a Mobile Service-Oriented Architecture (MSOA). It shows a specific instantiation of a reference architecture in practice, which is divided into four major parts: the mobile device and user, the network, the servers and applications, and the contents. The purpose of such an architecture is to enable the applications to offer services through network connections using, for example, Active Server Pages (ASP) or Common Gateway Interface (CGI) scripts. The user, through a mobile browser, accesses the server using the scripts. The server hosts the application programs. The database server goes further to the content management system (CMS) to access data or information. This data or information is processed by applications on the application server and sent to the end user. Such mobile enterprise architectures provide support for managing message queues, message distribution, and also helps location management. For

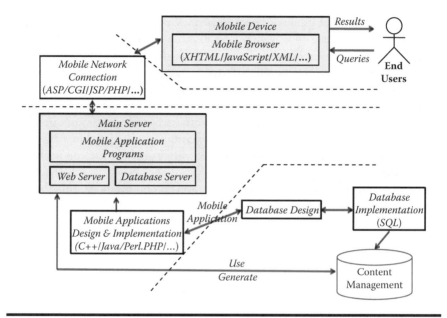

Figure 4.6 **Mobile service-oriented architecture.**

example, the Publish/Subscribe middleware systems in this architecture address the challenge of queuing messages by analyzing the adaptation of a centralized and distributed Publish/Subscribe architecture using mobility (for further discussions, see Vyas and Yoon 2005).

Figure 4.7 describes another important transition aspect of mobile architecture. The mobile architecture evolved from system architecture, which, itself had evolved through the various tiered architectural approaches shown in Figure 4.7. For example, the initial system architecture had no tiers at all, and both the data and application were put together on one machine in a single technical space. Later, the application and data were split—resulting in a two-tiered client/server architecture. A three-tiered architecture aimed to further separate the rules from the presentation of an application. In the case of mobile system architecture, the client, application server, and content management reflects the three tiers of the earlier system architecture, middleware and security playing an important role in their connectivity (as shown in Figure 4.7).

Mobile Contents

Mobile contents deal with the provision and use of data and information through one or more databases in a mobile business. "Contents" is a generic term that refers to data and information in various forms, including standard text, audio, video, charts, and other multimedia formats. Although there are a number of commercial CMSs that are based on available database technologies, using these systems in

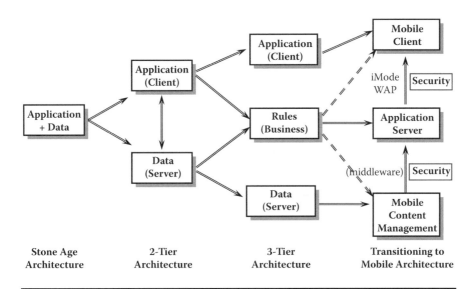

Figure 4.7 Transitions to mobile enterprise architecture.

mobile business applications requires specific analysis and design of the databases. This specific analysis needs to consider the sourcing, storage, provision, and security of contents. For example, the content to be delivered on a mobile gadget needs to be filtered for features that are irrelevant or not easy to transmit to a small-screen handheld gadget. CMSs need the ability to create layers for storing and retrieving data depending on factors such as the type of gadget being used and the urgency and accuracy of data or information required. Provision and loading of contents from various sources, such as customers, employees, third-party content providers, government agencies, and so on needs to be factored in during the design of a CMS. But there are telecommunication providers who may leave the choice of content management entirely to the users. Users may either choose to browse the Internet and download or use applications through their mobile devices that may not be fully supported, or in other cases use applications solely provided by the telecom operator who guarantees support for the device. In the former case, the user will not be eligible to lodge a support call to the telecom provider in case the application does not work on his or her device, as opposed to applications and services provided by the telecom operators themselves.

Mobile Convergence

Mobile convergence deals with the convergence of devices, telephony, applications, and networks. It is an ongoing process that brings together the aforementioned technologies (shown in Figure 4.2) to deliver contents and services on a single handheld device. For example, converged handheld global positioning system (GPS) mobile devices make use of travel planning applications, maps of interesting places, driving directions, and weather information combined in real-time and delivered on an integrated GPS to guide tourists. Vanjara (2005) describes *Streets and Trips 2005*, a converged Microsoft product that, together with the handheld GPS locator and plug-n-play receiver hardware component, makes it easy to create travel and tourism events and packages. The potential advent of handheld nanodevices, with their greater processing power, superior features, larger storage, and longer battery life, is likely to provide immense opportunity for converged services that are made available to the user on a single device with a unified interface. Convergence of mobile technologies empowers and enables users to bring together work and pleasure-related activities efficiently and effectively.

Mobile Interfaces

Mobile interfaces, as illustrated in Figure 4.2, include network interfaces and their standardized protocols, interfaces to content management systems and, most importantly, the interface between the user and the mobile device. Device-to-user interfaces have gained maximum attention mainly because of the challenges associated with the smallness of their (physical and screen) size. A mobile device does not have the privilege of using an elaborate keyboard or a mouse; therefore, voice, visual, and handwriting recognition interfaces play an important role in communicating with the user. The small keypads of handheld devices make it difficult to input large content; voice and handwriting recognition, however, create opportunities to address this issue by providing voice commands, visual clues (outputs) instead of text, and by reading hard scans. Ease of entering large SMS text messages is a subjective issue; most teenage and younger users are able to do it easily (see http://www.naturalinteraction.org).

The discussion thus far has been on mobile technologies and their influence on business. The next section organizes these technologies into understandable and manageable layers from a business viewpoint. These layers influence the various *types* of mobilities; therefore, an understanding of the layers is important for successful METM.

Mobile Technology Layers for Business

Mobile technology layers provide the basis for mobile architecture. The mobile networks, databases, middleware, business applications, and devices need to be considered individually and then together to provide a sound basis for a mobile business. Each layer has its own mobility issues as well as issues influencing all other layers.

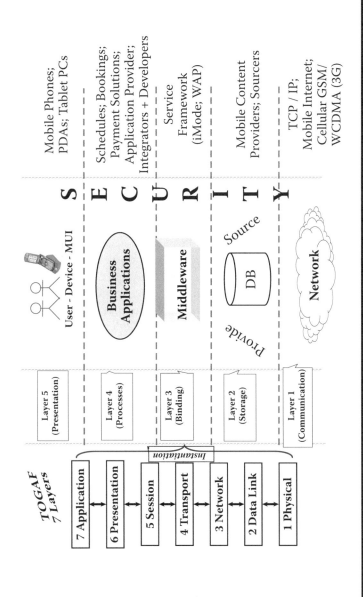

Figure 4.8   Mobile enterprise technology layers (based on www.methodscience.com).

Mobile technologies can be best understood from a business point of view as being made up of layers with each layer having a corresponding impact on the business. Figure 4.8 shows these layers from a business viewpoint. They are expansions of the basic mobile technology layers shown in Figure 2.3 (see Chapter 2). These layers can also be mapped with the well-known architecture reference frameworks such as The Open Group Architecture Framework (TOGAF), as shown roughly in Figure 4.8 (for details, read the *Cutter Executive* report, Unhelkar 2008). METs can consider these technical layers as contributors to the successful transition of devices, users, and sessions.

Layer 1: Transport/Network Layer

The first layer of the aforementioned mobile architecture is the network and communications layer. This layer provides the fundamentals of telecommunications on which cellular GSM networks operate. This layer can also be called the data-link layer. It enables the Mobile Internet Protocol version 4 (MIPv4) (Pedrasa et al., 2009; Perkins et al. 2002) and rides on top of the standard communications protocols of TCP/IP. However, in case of mobile networks, this layer also uses the MIPv4 and related mobile protocols. Mobility of a session at this layer is retained by maintaining the home address of the device within the network while the mobile device roams on the host and foreign networks. Johnson et al. (2004) discuss the MIPv6 host, which continues to use a single permanent home address while it moves around the Internet. Integration of mobile support in MIPv6 makes it a more efficient network protocol than MIPv4. The MIPv6 network protocol is also able to support a moving network, which is a group of nodes moving as a unit, by using a mobile router.

Layer 2: Content Layer

The content or database layer controls and manipulates contents presented to mobile users. This management of data includes sourcing of news materials, and audio and video streams (in the case of 3G), and providing handset self-service, to name but a few. The database has two major parts to its functioning: (1) sourcing of contents from a variety of sources including mobile users and (2) providing contents to users. Modeling of data, the storage and retrieval of contents, and their security are all part of this layer of technology.

Layer 3: Middleware Layer

The middleware layer provides the "glue" between the transport layer, content layer, and one or more applications. Two such technologies discussed earlier were WAP and i-Mode. These middleware technologies handle mobile user requests that are sent as universal resource locators (URL) through the network to the server via the

WAP gateway. This Web server then sends back responses to the WAP gateway. These responses, in HTML, are translated to Wireless Markup Language (WML) before being forwarded to the mobile devices. WML is a markup language based on XML that specifies the content and user interfaces for mobile devices with minimum demands on the memory and processing power of devices, as it strips the contents of unnecessary features.

I-Mode provides users with access to services that are integrated on an i-Mode gateway that is similar to the WAP gateway. However, it differs from WAP in that it uses compact HTML (c-HTML) as the markup language to deliver contents. c-HTML is a subset of HTML that filters images, tables, maps, multiple-character fonts and styles, background colors or images, frames, and cascading style sheets before delivering them onto devices. Japan, particularly, had phenomenal success with i-Mode that has led to collaborations between content providers, gadget manufacturers, back-end supporters, and global network operators. The i-Mode service platform enables content providers and sophisticated users to develop applications easily. Thus, it provides a middleware service on the mobile Internet.

Layer 4: Application Layer

The application layer provides software application support for a user/ device. Its management is based on Session Initiation Protocol (SIP; Rosenburg et al. 2002), which makes use of a registrar server and a location services server to keep track of the various connections and devices associated with a given user. The application layer provides support to the mapping of connections and routing of services. Thus, mobility in this layer is supported by e-mail-style identification of users and their connections.

Increasingly, the application layer has to provide for interoperability of applications between networks. For example, applications such as Skype provide Voice-over-IP (VoIP) calls to other online Skype users. As mentioned earlier, in such applications, the use of cellular networks for mobile connections is judiciously combined with features of the broadband Internet.

Layer 5: User and Device Layer

Some service providers use hardware codes or locks on the mobile devices provided by them to users. These codes prevent the device from being used on "other" networks and thereby hamper device mobility. Usually, the use of WAP handsets is limited to senior managers; but relatively new companies are equipped with WAP for use in their data applications. Further, there is a dearth of customer relationship management (CRM), enterprise resource planning (ERP), supply-chain management (SCM), etc., in WAP space. The main reason for deploying mobile Internet solutions is to implement applications using SMS solutions. Mobile Internet is also used by some companies in CRM, ERP, SCM, and E-procurement.

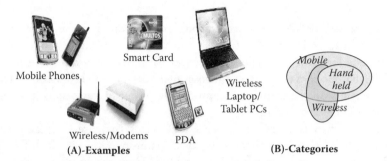

Mobile Phones

Smart Card

Wireless Laptop/ Tablet PCs

Wireless/Modems   PDA

(A)-Examples

Mobile

Hand held

Wireless

(B)-Categories

Stage 1: Routine use of mobile devices to activate and text
Stage 2: Incorporating mobile devices in existing processes
Stage 3: Innovative and storage use of mobile
Stage 4: Environmentally responsible use of mobile devices

Figure 4.9   Mobile devices in MET.

The discussion thus far lays the foundation for emerging mobile technologies in the context of mobile business. Now we discuss each specific factor listed earlier in Table 4.1. Each discussion is followed by presentation of results from the survey conducted for MET and a corresponding practical insight into the results.

Mobile Devices

Device Range and Categories

A range of mobile devices are shown in Figure 4.9A. These devices include ubiquitous mobile phones, PDAs, wireless laptops, tablet PCs, smart cards, and wireless modems. These modern mobile devices have excellent portability, data security, battery life, and operating time compared to earlier ones. Further, these devices are also equipped with high-performance processors, high-resolution colored displays, photo and video cards, nonvolatile flash, backup storage, and increasingly reliable transmission capabilities. Transcending the wireless phone and the simple PDA, now there is a plethora of devices ranging from high-end PDAs with integrated wireless modems down to small phones with wireless Web-browsing capabilities. Even the simplest of handheld devices provide enough computing power to run small applications, play games, and, of course, make voice calls. This combination of size, power, and flexibility, which is available in today's mobile devices, is a key enabler for MET. Furthermore, as more personal devices find their way into the enterprise, corporations are realizing the benefits that can be achieved with mobile solutions. Thus, proliferation of devices is a key factor in the growth of mobile solutions in the enterprise.

Mobile devices may be categorized in different ways. Figure 4.9B gives this categorization as mobile, wireless, and handheld devices. Each of these terms differ slightly in meaning. For example, a wireless device need not be mobile and vice versa; handheld devices are usually mobile, but need not be used as such, for example, a handheld scanner or bar-code reader connected to a desktop machine.

Mobile devices are the most crucial aspect of a mobile business. Their processing capabilities influence the architecture (thin versus rich client), usability, and security requirements. This mobile device usage is given due importance in MET, starting with phone and text usage, through to the incorporation of devices in business processes. Eventually, mobile devices also become part of the "green mobile" aspects of a business.

Nanodevices

A significant advancement in mobile devices is their dramatic reduction in size. Mobile devices are moving from micro to nano as the emerging nanotechnology influences their manufacture and use (Vanjara 2005). Nanotechnology (Wilson et al. 2002) is considered as the foundation of future mobile hardware as it opens up opportunities for storage and retrieval of several gigabytes of data on a millipede nanodrive the size of a postage stamp (Future Technology 2005). This reduction in size provides the opportunity to incorporate these devices in processes requiring less space such as in pharmaceutical drug laboratories, minute automobile dashboard controls, and delicate medical equipment.

Projection Technologies

Presentation technology currently uses liquid crystal displays (LCDs) that are coupled with touch-screen technologies in smart-phone displays. However, LCDs are increasingly being superseded by organic light emitting diodes (OLEDs), which are lighter and thinner and provide wider viewing angles as compared with LCDs (Harmon and Diam 2009). OLED displays are used in mobile music players, cell phones, and laptops. Currently, OLEDs suffer from a relatively short display time, but this is expected to improve as the technology matures. The presentation mechanism on mobile devices is undergoing another revolution in terms of holographic projection of images. Holographs, coupled with nanotechnologies, pave the way for dramatic changes in the mobile device domain. Thus, the current restricted displays due to smaller sizes of mobile devices such as PDAs and phones will be overcome by these kind of display technologies. This will eventually give way to new types of mobile devices such as buttons, rings, and threads that will not be hampered by the display limitations. Smart diagnostic devices in the medical field, such as "smart pill," wirelessly provide information on the state of the insides of a patient to an outside tracking device. Unhindered by the limitation of size of the actual mobile device, holographic projections create interfaces that are comfortable from a user's viewpoint.

Device Convergence

Device convergence implies convergence of multiple functionalities, services, and related offerings on a single device. It also implies the convergence of mobile devices with supporting wireless network infrastructures, which enables seamless transitions and portability of devices. Device manufacturers need to map the various network protocols to the operator's network infrastructure so as to ensure interoperability of devices and applications. Device vendors (such as Nokia, Motorola, and LG) are continuously undertaking research and development in the area of mobile handsets, which would enable them to enhance the area of convergence by the devices. A converged mobile device can enable digital creations and, thereby, enhance the educational and entertainment experience of users leading to what Bolter and MacIntyre (2007) call augmented reality (AR) applications. For example, Nokia's mobile AR application integrates a phone, camera, GPS, accelerometer, and compass on a single converged device that can then provide guidance to a traveler including images of sightseeing locations and tourist attractions.

Device convergence also results in network convergence: when a device is capable of handling multiple networks, network types such as GPS, Wi-Fi, VoIP, and WiMax lose their boundaries. Smart phones enable users to bypass network layers such as cellular networks and use either local networks or the broad WiMax seamlessly. Companies such as Google, with a regulatory boost from the Federal Communications Commission, are pushing to disrupt the market with a "network-neutral" open cellular system in the 700-MHz band (Gapper 2007; Harmon and Diam 2009).

Mobile phones already have enough memory to allow users to simply download an entire audio or video entertainment catalog from the mobile Internet, store it, and replay it as many times as desired. Similarly, preloaded maps provide location features with ease.

Convergence of features on mobile devices results in the devices having both fixed and mobile functionalities. 4G networks, discussed later, eliminate distance- and voice-based pricing, with users paying the same price for unlimited phone calls and data services. Smart phones have features for remote car keys, monitoring of medical conditions, and so on.

Device Independence

The device independent working group (DIWG) of the World Wide Web Consortium (W3C) started its work with a vision "to allow the Web to be accessible by anyone, anywhere, anytime, anyhow." With continuing advances in mobile communication capabilities and dramatic reductions in costs of mobile devices, the demand for Web access from many different types of mobile devices has gone up substantially. The range of markup languages that enable delivery of Web content on vastly different devices also continues to grow. Consequently, making Web sites and applications available to users on different and multiple mobile devices poses both new opportunities and challenges to mobile application developers and enterprises (Deshpande et al. 2004).

Stages in Mobile Device Usage

MET incorporates increasingly sophisticated uses of mobile devices. Figure 4.9 lists these usages in four stages:

Stage 1: Mobile devices are used in a routine manner in this stage, that is, for voice calls (which is now accompanied with text facilities).

Stage 2: In this stage, mobility can be incorporated formally in an existing business process to generate an entirely new engineered process for the business. This usage of mobile devices is more involved, and it may require some training and help.

Stage 3: This stage involves the innovative use of mobility that allows a business to make strategic use of mobile devices. Such usage requires strategic planning, prototyping, and, for large businesses, working in collaboration with the device manufacturers and network service providers.

Stage 4: In this stage, a business breaks out of the "profit-making" mode and moves toward other dimensions such as environmental intelligence and sustainability.

Analysis of the Importance of Mobile Devices in MET

Figure 4.10 shows the importance of devices in the technical dimension of MET. Figure 4.10A shows the importance of different mobile gadgets, including mobile phones, PDAs (wireless-enabled and BlackBerry), wireless laptop or tablet PC, and Wi-Fi devices (printers, speakers, phones, etc.), which were discussed earlier in Figure 4.9 within the overall technical dimension of MET.

The result of the survey in terms of the importance of mobile phones in the technical aspect of MET, shown in the lowermost icons in Figure 4.10A, indicates that 43 percent of the participants think mobile phones are most important and 31 percent think they are more important. Thus, a total of 74 percent participants think that mobile phones are more or most important. Only 2 percent think of mobile phones as the least important devices in the technical dimension of MET. These results underscore the accepted importance of mobile phones in MET.

The result of the survey in terms of the importance of PDA in the technical dimension of MET, shown in the second last row of Figure 4.10A, indicates that 16 percent of the participants think that PDA is the most important factor and

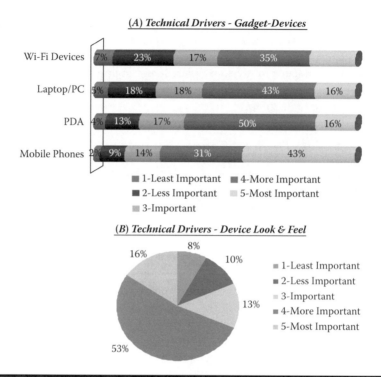

Figure 4.10 Analysis of the importance of mobile device factor in technical dimension of MET.

50 percent think it is more important. Therefore, a total of 66 percent think the PDA device is more or most important. Only 4 percent think of it as a least important device in the technical dimension of MET. These figures establish that the importance of PDAs is similar to that of mobile phones discussed earlier; however, because of the analog history of mobile phones, other devices are understandably slightly less important than the ubiquitous phone.

The result of the survey relating to the significance of laptop/PC in MET, shown in the third bar from the bottom of Figure 4.10A, indicates that 16 percent of the participants think that laptops/PCs are most important, and 43 percent think that they are more important devices. Thus, a total of 59 percent think the laptops/PCs are more or most important. Only 5 percent think of them as least important devices in the technical dimension of MET.

The result of the survey relating to of Wi-Fi devices such as printers, speakers, and Wi-Fi-enabled processes, shown at the top of Figure 4.10A, indicates that 18 percent of the participants think that such devices are most important and 35 percent think that they are more important. Thus, a total of 53 percent think the Wi-Fi devices factor is more or most important. Only 7 percent rate them as a least important device factor in the technical dimension of MET.

Finally, Figure 4.10B shows the importance of the look and feel of devices, particularly their colors and shapes, from the technical aspect of MET. The result of the survey, as shown in the figure, indicates that 16 percent of the participants think that the look and feel of devices are most important and 53 percent think they are more important. Thus, a total of 69 percent think the look and feel factors are more or most important. Only 8 percent think that they are least important in the technical dimension of MET. The significance of the look and feel factor will change depending on the age of the users. Although that particular analysis is out of the scope of this research, it is most likely that this factor will be rated highly by adolescents.

The overall survey indicates that devices are considered more to most important on all counts. Therefore, mobile devices must be taken into account early on in the MET framework. The relative importance of the device factor is further highlighted by the analysis of the sequence of their relative importance later in this chapter.

Mobile Networking and Telecommunication

METs need to consider the effects of mobile networks and telecommunication on the transitioning business. Mobile networks, together with mobile middleware and devices, provide support for a mobile platform that comprises the wireless Internet, smart clients, and mobile messaging architectures. Software vendors have made significant advances in providing reusable components and frameworks that sit on top of the mobile platform and facilitate rapid mobile application development. These applications make use of wireless networks, the mobile Internet, wireless application server frameworks, device emulators, WAP, and the corresponding development tools for mobile business solutions.

Wireless Networks and Conversions

Wireless networks are broadly grouped into short- and long-range networks. LAN, MAN, and WAN stand for local area network, metropolitan area network, and wide area network, respectively. The Wi-Fi network standard is for WLAN. The IEEE 802.11b (Wi-Fi) system is also a popular wireless network, widely used in offices, homes, and public spaces such as airports, shopping malls, and restaurants. IEEE 802.11a and 802.11g are standards with much higher speeds, and they may replace Wi-Fi in the near future. Bluetooth technology, having limited coverage and throughput, is suitable for applications in personal area networks (PANs). Cellular networks provide longer transmission distances and greater coverage, but they have a much lower bandwidth (less than 1 Mbps) compared with Wi-Fi standards. A recent trend in cellular systems is for "third generation" (3G) standards to support wireless multimedia and high-bandwidth services.

Cellular systems are evolving from analog to digital and from circuit-switched to packet-switched networks. However, 3G systems need to enhance their quality of service (QoS) to provide meaningful content and user satisfaction. The two main standards for 3G are wideband CDMA (WCDMA) and CDMA2000. Both standards use direct sequence spread spectrum (DSSS) in a 5-MHz bandwidth. The technical differences between these two standards include their different chip rate, frame time, spectrum used, and time synchronization mechanism. The WCDMA system can internetwork with GSM networks and is strongly supported by the European Union, which calls it the Universal Mobile Telecommunications System (UMTS). CDMA2000 is backward compatible with IS-95, which is widely deployed in the United States.

When converting a GSM to a UMTS, the technology to consider is the General Packet Radio Service (GPRS), which provides a starting point for 3G services. Through GPRS, the device is connected to the network all the time. This connectivity provides opportunities for new businesses and services that depend on the subscriber being online all the time. The GPRS experience and investments have to be used in transitioning to UMTS. Transitioning from second generation (2G) to 3G can follow different paths. For example, in Europe, the transition from GSM to UMTS occurs when GPRS is introduced in GSM. However, in North America, the evolution starts with Time Division Multiple Access (TDMA), then transitions to Enhanced Data rates for GSM Evolution (EDGE), and then eventually to UMTS. Transitioning using EDGE is relatively easier, as the existing frequencies and infrastructure of GSM networks can be reused.

The Long Term Evolution (LTE) as a fourth-generation (4G) technology is being promoted by Ericsson and Nokia as an advancement over the popular GSM cellular networks. Qualcomm, however, is promoting Ultra Mobile Broadband (UMB) as a transition path in the 4G space for CDMA networks. Companies such as Intel, Cisco, Sprint, and Samsung are bypassing the cellular space and, instead, supporting the mobile WiMax (Allison 2007). Similarly, Verison Wireless is thought to be testing UMB and WiMax and, at the same time, it is also considering LTE. Verizon, Qualcomm, Alcatel-Lucent, Nortel, LG, and Samsung together seem to be creating the CDMA ecosystem (Schenker 2007). AT&T is committed to LTE, and T-Mobile is likely to do so as well.

Wireless networks are short range and long range. However, their integration with devices and applications is the key mobile business driver. Companies such as Verizon, Qualcomm, Alcatel-Lucent, Nortel, LG, Samsung, AT&T, and T-Mobile form the wireless network ecosystem. Wireless networks are expressed as generations: 2G, 2.5G, and the recent 3G are well known. MET has to consider the transition from the current generation used by an enterprise to a new generation of networks. This transition includes not only switching to a new type of network but also the smooth transition of devices, applications, contents, and the use of middleware to achieve it.

Transition from 2.5G and 3G networks to the 4G technology is likely to pick up momentum around 2010. This is because the International Telecommunications Union (ITU) is likely to release a standard definition for 4G by 2009 (Harmon and Diam 2009). The primary 4G technologies are expected to be LTE, UMB, and IEEE 802.16m-WiMax (Mohney 2007).

Characteristics of 4G

Fourth-generation, 4G, wireless networks provide for convergence of voice, data, and streamed multimedia, which enable "anytime, anywhere" services to users with higher data rates than previous generations. Applications in 4G include wireless broadband access, multimedia messaging services, video chats, mobile TV, high-definition TV content, and digital video broadcasting (DVB). (See Unhelkar [2008a] for discussions, in particular on IP Multimedia Subsystem (IMS) applications.) Thus, 4G can be characterized as a fully IP-based integrated system that also converges wired and wireless technologies. It should be able to offer all types of services at an affordable cost with premium quality and high security. According to the 4G working groups, infrastructure and terminals of 4G will encompass all standards from 2G to 4G, interfaces with legacy systems, and an open platform for extensions. Transitioning to 4G will require allocation, availability, standardization, and innovation decisions related to the network. Further, there is also a need to provide for switching enhancements and collaborations (intervendor cooperation) before the vision of 4G materializes (http://www.mobileinfo.com).

Long-Range Mobile/Wireless Networks

Long-range mobile networks are the well-known cellular networks. Mobile devices connect to these mobile networks over much greater distances than the local in-house or office networks. Further, these networks operate in conjunction with satellites that are used in global positioning systems (GPSs), thereby determining the precise location of the mobile handsets. The GPS-based locating system is able to make use of satellites (currently three) to ascertain the location of mobile gadgets to an accuracy of 10 to 15 m. The satellite infrastructure and GPS networks combine to provide long-range communication services to users. Transitions to, and within, the network technologies typically require considerable expenditure as these transitions tend to be infrastructure projects; however, with the sophistication and hybrid network-handling capabilities of mobile devices, the enterprises themselves that are undergoing transitions may not incur infrastructure expenses but will have to deal with expenses related to modifications on mobile devices and installation of new applications on them.

Short-Range Wireless Networks

Short-range wireless networks include Ethernet-based wireless WLAN, Wi-Fi, Bluetooth, infrared, and radio frequency identification (RFID). Networks typically based on standards such as the IEEE 802.11 provide opportunities for the creation of short-range services within offices or households; they need to be formally considered by the transitioning business. However, their limited coverage implies that they are in a different category as compared with GPS networks. The key to the commercial use of both short- and long-range networks is their convergence. Seamless connectivity among various types of networks is required for their commercial use, and transitioning organizations need to incorporate these issues in their technical transition plans. Mobile devices that are not sophisticated enough would require further modifications and extensions to both their hardware and software to enable the use of seamless transition capabilities of the networks.

Bluetooth technology uses a 2.4 GHz transmission band and is able to operate within a radius of approximately 10 m for data and voice transfer, irrespective of the line of sight. Thus, Bluetooth can be used to identify and communicate with a customer in a business establishment (such as a coffee shop). However, an infrared transmission requires a corresponding line of sight. The FCC standards for location specification are not mandatory for these short-range technologies.

Bluetooth-enabled electronic devices connect and communicate wirelessly through short-range ad hoc networks, known as piconets. Each device can simultaneously communicate with up to seven other devices within a single piconet; it can also belong to several piconets simultaneously. Piconets are established dynamically and automatically as Bluetooth-enabled devices enter and leave a radio proximity (Kuppuswami and Unhelkar 2004). The fundamental strength of this technology is its ability to simultaneously handle both data and voice transmissions, thereby enabling the use of hands-free headsets for voice calls, printing out documents, and for sending faxes, and to synchronize PDAs, laptops, and mobile phone applications of users.

Furthermore, these short-range technologies assume special significance when their providers try to use them for long-range communications. For example, the discussion in Chapter 2 on cellular network operators and their tussle with service providers (and vice versa) becomes significant in light of the fact that location-specific service providers (especially when they own the content) try to use short-range transmissions to bypass the so-called walled gardens of cellular or GPS network operators.

IEEE 802.11

This is a short-range standard that uses the wired equivalent privacy (WEP) algorithm for security encryption. WLAN is based on this standard and facilitates communication between the user and the corresponding local server through a wireless network. This obviates the need for laying down unaesthetic or messy network cables through the house or office.

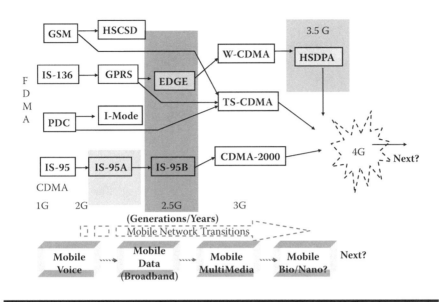

Figure 4.11 Mobile network transition paths (from generation to generation).

IEEE 802.16

This standard (WiMax) facilitates communication over larger distances than the aforementioned standard through networking numerous wireless equipments with proper compatibility and interoperability. Communications between mobile devices using this standard cannot only be accomplished between two devices but also between numerous devices that may be within the range of the transmission, thus, there is an open access similar to the cellular network but with a point-to-point technology. This type of WiMax access has great potential in MET, particularly when the organization has or partners with WiMax users. Small-sized organizations have a need to cater to its patrons in small. localized areas (e.g., restaurant, waiting room in a surgery or hospital, etc.), whereas large, dispersed organizations need to cover wider areas and multiple patrons. Figure 4.11 depicts mobile network transition paths (based on Bhattar et al. 2005).

In the first generation, almost all the networks were analog systems in which voice was considered to be the main traffic. These systems had basic communication facilities and little security. Some of the standards were NMT, AMPS, Hicap, CDPD, Mobitex, and DataTac. During the second generation, the standards for wireless communications moved from analog to digital; examples of some European standards include GSM, iDEN, D-AMPS, IS-95, PDC, CSD, PHS, GPRS, HSCSD, and WiDEN. The third-generation (3G) standards aim to meet the growing demands on network capacity, rates required for high-speed data transfer,

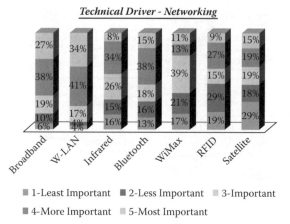

Figure 4.12   Analysis of the importance of the networking factor in the technical dimension of MET.

and multimedia applications. 3G systems enhance previous systems with two supporting infrastructures: one consisting of circuit-switched nodes, and the other, of packet-oriented nodes. The ITU defines a specific set of 3G air interface technologies as part of the IMT-2000 initiative. As the mobile world transitions toward 3G, numerous technologies come into play. These technologies include EDGE and EGPRS (2.5G); CDMA2000, W-CDMA, and UMTS (3GSM); TD-SCDMA (3G); and HSDPA, HSPOA, and LTE (post 3G).

Analysis of the Importance of the Networking Factor

Figure 4.12 shows the importance of networking in the technical dimension of MET. Networking factors in this aspect include wireless broadband network (3G, Next G), WLAN, infrared, Bluetooth, WiMax, radio frequency identification (RFID)/E-Tag, and mobile satellite networks.

The result of the survey regarding the importance of the wireless broadband network in the technical aspect of MET (shown on the left in Figure 4.12) indicates that 27 percent of the participants think that this factor is most important and for 38 percent, it is more important. Thus, a total of 65 percent think the wireless broadband network factor is more or most important. Only 6 percent think of it as a least important networking factor in the technical dimension of MET. These results indicate a strong agreement with the popular belief that wireless broadband is crucial for the growth of mobility in business.

On the importance of WLAN in technical dimension (shown second from left in Figure 4.12), 34 percent of the participants in the survey think it a most important factor, and 41 percent consider it more important. Thus, a total of 75 percent think the WLAN factor is more or most important. Only 4 percent think it least important in the technical dimension of MET. These results indicate that the importance of WLAN is slightly more than that of wireless broadband. It can be attributed to the proximity felt by the respondents to WLAN networks at both home and office. However, the results are not dramatically different enough to cause concern.

On the importance of infrared (shown third from left in Figure 4.12), 8 percent of participants think it is a most important factor, whereas 34 percent consider it as more important. Thus, a total of 42 percent consider infrared as a more or most important networking factor from the technical aspect of MET, whereas 16 percent of the participants think it is least important. These results indicate that although infrared networking capability is important, it is not as important as the previous two factors studied.

The results of the survey regarding the importance of Bluetooth (shown fourth from left in Figure 4.12) indicate that 38 percent of the participants consider it as more important, and 15 percent, as most important. Thus, a total of 53 percent think that Bluetooth is a more or most important networking factor in the technical dimension of MET; 13 percent think it is least important. The responses for Bluetooth and infrared are almost comparable, but their importance is less than that of WLAN and broadband.

The results regarding the importance of WiMax (shown fifth from left in Figure 4.12) indicate that 11 percent of participants consider it most important, whereas 13 percent think it as more important. Thus, a total of 24 percent think it is most or more important. However, 39 percent of the participants think that WiMax is important. Further, 21 percent consider it less important and 17 percent as a least important networking factor. These results imply a bell curve, giving sufficient importance to WiMax, but not as much as that given to all previous factors.

Survey results on the importance of RFID/E-Tag (shown second from right in Figure 4.12) indicate that 9 percent of the participants in the survey consider RFID/E-Tag as most important, and 27 percent think this factor as more important. Thus, a total of 36 percent consider RFID/E-Tag as most or more important in the technical dimension of MET. The factor is considered important by 15 percent and less important by 29 percent. Also, 19 percent consider RFID/E-Tag least important in the technical dimension of MET. These results are similar to the previous results on short-range networks.

The results of the survey on the importance of mobile satellite networks (shown on the right-hand side in Figure 4.12) indicate that 15 percent of the participants consider them as most important, and 19 percent as more important. Thus, a total of 34 percent consider mobile satellite networks as most or more important in the technical dimension of MET. They are considered important, by 19 percent, and 18 percent think they are less important. However, 29 percent consider mobile satellite networks as least important. The overall responses from the survey indicate that the respondents consider the various types and ranges of networks as important to MET and the mobile business. Long-range networks appeared to be of more interest than short-range ones. This may be due to the importance given by respondents to the business use of mobile networks over, perhaps, home use. However, the overall importance of wireless networks has been sufficiently established for transitioning businesses to consider them in the step-by-step transition exercise.

Wireless (Mobile) Standards

Wireless communication networks can be grouped under different standards. These standards form the backbone of mobile communications; but, they change at breathtaking speeds. Variations in standards and the phenomenal rate at which they occur are major impediments to the development of mobile applications and business solutions. This is because as soon as we have applications based on certain standards, the standards themselves change, and the applications become obsolete. Also, knowledgeable mobile users are demanding applications and features that are backward compatible with previous standards. However, as with any new industry, it takes time for standards to develop, and a transitioning enterprise needs to continuously keep in touch with these evolving mobile standards.

In the context of MET, technology generations can be understood as spanning from the very first generation (G or 1G) through to the latest 4G and beyond. Initially, only voice communication was possible with 1G analog technology. With the use of 2G standards, the world turned toward digital technology for wireless communication, and in addition to voice communications, SMS was added. These gave rise to the demand for wireless Internet services, which were provided by the "second and a half generation" (2.5G) technology. Later, 3G evolved to provide fast Internet services, live video and audio streaming, online games, and interactive multimedia. The data rate support of 3G is around 2 Mbps. Therefore, all these services cannot be available at the same time at the desired speed. This limitation is handled by the 4G standards that have ambitious goals, challenging research issues, and above all, never-ending user expectations. Research activities to achieve these goals have already started, and standardization and commercial availability of 4G technology is expected by the year 2010. The following subsections further discuss the generations from the MET viewpoint:

First Generation (1G; 1980s): NMT, AMPS, FDMA

The first generation was based on analog systems, and it was deployed during the 1980s. Nordic Mobile Telephone (NMT) in Sweden and Norway's Advanced Mobile Phone System (AMPS) introduced this generation of mobile devices that supports analog voice. The handsets were bulky, phones had poor voice quality, and there was no data transmission capability. In this generation, voice calls use frequency modulation (FM) and frequency division multiple access (FDMA). Such systems typically use 25 MHz bandwidth for both forward and return links between the base station and handsets. The 1G network standards are gradually phasing out. Issues in transitioning to the next generation appear to be less technical and more business or regulatory in nature. For example, Telstra in Australia was asked by the government to keep its analog networks open.

Second Generation (2G; 1990s): TDMA, CDMA

The 2G networks use higher-order digital modulation techniques that support improved voice quality, network security, and call reliability. For efficient use of the frequency spectrum, 2G standards use multiple access schemes such as TDMA and CDMA. These are two cellular network standards for long-distance communication that are well-known and in use.

GSM is a popular cellular standard for mobile phones developed in the 1980s. It uses the TDMA approach, in which frequencies are divided into time slots with each time slot allotted to phone calls. GSM allows compatibility and interoperability across geographical boundaries operating on the 0.9–1.8 GHz bands (1.9 GHz in the United States). Circuit-switched technology for data transmission enables SMS, which is very popular with GSM.

The second network standard is CDMA, which is based on a spread spectrum method, in which a signal is spread over a broad range of frequencies thereby reducing interference and increasing the number of simultaneous users within a frequency band. With CDMA, each conversation is digitized and then tagged with a code. In contrast to FDMA or TDMA where each user is allotted a particular frequency band or time slot, in CDMA the entire bandwidth is allocated for all users at all times. The use of CDMA technology has several advantages such as improved network capacity, immunity from interference by other signals, reliable connection, improved voice quality, network security, and optimum frequency reuse. For CDMA, a subscriber is attached to two adjacent cells simultaneously, ensuring smooth and seamless transition from one cell to another, which is transparent to the user.

2.5G (Late 1990s): WAP, I-Mode, GPRS

The standards of 2.5G are built on top of 2G standards and have backward compatibility. They support Internet applications with higher data rates, e-mails and Web browsing, and transactions and location-specific services. They have packet-switched as well as circuit-switched implementations.

Although 2.5G standards offer Internet services, their data throughput rates are not sufficient for high-speed broadband Internet and multimedia access. Also, these standards do not offer many services and are not flexible enough.

2.5G standards also support WAP. As discussed earlier on middleware, WAP is a Web-browsing language that supports compressed Web pages on small, portable handheld devices. Before the introduction of WAP, NTT DoCoMo, Japan, deployed the proprietary wireless i-Mode that has the capability to support interactive Internet browsing, color graphics, mobile online games, etc.

High-Speed Circuit-Switched Data (HSCSD) allows individual users to use consecutive time slots. This enables them to obtain high-speed data access on GSM networks as it does not limit each user to a single specific time slot as in the case of 2G GSM standards.

General Packet Radio Services (GPRS) is a packet-based data network on dedicated GSM channels. However, it is not suitable for real-time Internet applications and Web browsing. GPRS networks can be shared by multiple users in contrast to HSCSD, thereby supporting a larger number of users. Transitioning businesses need to consider GPRS carefully, as their QoS might drop down rapidly as more users get connected.

Enhanced Data Rates for GSM Evolution (EDGE) is able to support modulation for higher data rates due to 8-phase shift keying (8-PSK). It facilitates personalized settings for each user that can be dynamically determined. Thus, an acceptable level of quality is quickly attained and maintained using minimum resources with the help of feedback from subscribers.

IS-95B for 2.5G CDMA supports both packet- and circuit-switched data accesses. It is an upgraded version of IS-95 and represents 2.5G technology. IS-95B provides high data rates to individual users by combining multiple orthogonal (coded) user channels on a common CDMA radio channel.

Third Generation (3G; Early 2000s)

The 3G technology standards aim to overcome the limitations of previous ones. They provide capabilities for wide area wireless voice telephony, broadband networks that have high capacities and speeds, and global roaming. 3G applications include VoIP, audio and video streaming, faxing and e-mail, multimedia services on demand, and videoconferencing. These applications, however, when used by global mobile users require global standards to enable mobile interoperability. The ITU attempted to provide such a standard, called International Mobile Telephone 2000 (IMT-2000), which was expected to bring about global interoperability across geographical regions. The standard, however, did not materialize, and the current global standards are the two disparate ones previously mentioned: TDMA, based on GSM, and the competing CDMA. From a transition viewpoint, both these 3G standards maintain backward compatibility with 2G and 2.5G. Technologies that make up the 3G standards are as follows:

UMTS Wideband-CDMA (W-CDMA), also known as Universal Mobile Telephone System (UMTS), provides continuous "always on" accessibility support for 3G networks. The high data rates of 2 Mbps per user enable multimedia applications, live audio and video streaming, and other high-speed Internet services.

CDMA2000 is an evolutionary 3G standard facilitating easier backward compatibility and a smoother transition path for users transitioning from earlier standards. It is being developed by the Telecommunications Industry Association (TIA) based in the United States.

TD-SCDMA stands for Time Division-Synchronous Code Division Multiple Access, and was proposed by the Chinese Academy of Tele-communications Technology (CATT) and the Siemens Corporation. It is adopted by the ITU as a 3G option. It uses the existing GSM infrastructure with several new technologies such as joint detection, dynamic channel allocation, smart antennas, mutual terminal synchronization, as well as additional upgrade tools to obtain higher data rates and support both circuit-switched and packet-switched data.

High-Speed Downlink Packet Access (HSDPA) is an upgraded path to W-CDMA. It provides 8–10 Mbps speed in the 5 MHz bandwidth using adaptive modulation and coding (AMC) techniques, multiple input multiple output (MIMO), hybrid automatic request, and improved cell search and receiver design. It is sometimes referred to as 3.5G technology as HSDPA is an intermediate packet-based data service solution between the 3G and 4G technologies.

Fourth Generation (4G; 2000s)

The 4G standards provide end-to-end IP solutions where voice, data, and multimedia streaming can function at higher data rates with the benefit of anytime–anywhere operations. Further, with high data rate throughputs of about 20 Mbps, which can be maintained for users moving at an average speed of 200 kmph, 4G networks operate in the 2–8 GHz bandwidth. These standards will integrate almost all heterogeneous networks and also make provisions for integrating future networks. Such integration will enable users to communicate and roam freely between networks and stay connected through a single mobile handset. For example, 4G standards will support handovers between CDMA and GSM networks or vice versa with the same handset.

AMC schemes are also considered for 4G technologies in view of the high data rate support required at high vehicle speeds. AMC changes its modulation and coding schemes dynamically according to varying channel conditions and adapt accordingly. A variety of problems will be encountered in high-frequency ranges. For example, in high-frequency bands, the signal becomes distorted or attenuated due to rain and other atmospheric conditions. Therefore, smart antennas will be used to improve the signal strength in the mobile handset.

Multimedia messaging service (MMS) in camera-equipped mobile phones, which are becoming commonplace, demand high bandwidths for transmission and large amounts of memory for storage and display. Further, improved browser technologies are required to effectively handle these MMS content. Issues related to antennas, power control, battery life, VLSI and ASIC technologies, device technologies, etc., are some important considerations in this aspect.

As we can see, 4G has many ambitious goals and exciting promises, even before the 3G technology is fully experienced. The use of GPRS and EDGE of 2.5G for Internet applications has just started, and 3G technologies are yet to be deployed in many parts of the world. So, the full utilization of 4G technologies is still

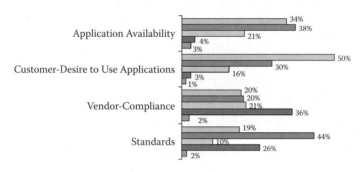

Technical Drivers - Importance of Standards

▨ 1-Least Important ▨ 2-Less Important ▢ 3-Important ▨ 4-More Important ▢ 5-Most Important

Figure 4.13   Analysis of the importance of the standards factor in the technical dimension of MET.

further away. Next Generation Network (NGN) is a sophisticated 3G network evolving from the convergence of the feature-rich Internet and the ubiquitous telephony networks.

Beyond 4G

Advances beyond 4G are too early to contemplate, but transitioning businesses need to keep them in mind from a futuristic viewpoint. Researchers expect fifth generation (5G) wireless systems that converge using a much higher bandwidth, provide global mobility, and incorporate tight security and realize a seamless wireless Internet for commercial use. This generation of mobile communications will deal with issues that are beyond imagination today. However, it is expected that with 5G, it will be possible to download and watch an entire movie while the user is moving. Converged 5G mobile gadgets will have full HDTV features on its screen (or possibly 3-D holographic images). There are immense possibilities in the medical field, with potential applications such as expert surgery support from global experts irrespective of where they may be located. Weather forecasts, sports reports, and entertainment will change with 5G.

Figure 4.13 shows the importance of standards and applications in the technical dimension of MET. Standards and applications factors consider network standards such as 802.11 and 802.22, the vendor's desire to comply with these standards, the customer's desire to use applications, and the availability of mobile applications within the overall technical dimension of MET.

The result of the MET survey on the importance of availability of mobile applications from the technical aspect of MET (appearing at the top in Figure 4.13) indicates that 34 percent of the participants think it most important and 38 percent consider it as more important. Thus, a total of 72 percent think the availability of mobile applications is more or most important; such a high number implies that this factor is likely to play a very important role in MET. Transitioning enterprises need to develop these solutions themselves or partner with developers who do so. Only 3 percent thinks this factor is least important in the technical dimension of MET.

Regarding the customer's desire to use mobile applications (appearing second from the top in Figure 4.13), 50 percent of the participants of the survey think that the customer's desire is most important, and for 30 percent, it is more important. Thus, a total of 80 percent think the factor is more or most important. Thus, enterprises undertaking MET need to focus on identifying and facilitating expectations of customers in terms of using mobile applications. A number of factors from other dimensions of MET (such as usability) also come into play in ensuring that the customer's needs and desires are satisfied. Barely 1 percent of the participants think the customer's desire to use applications is least important from the technical aspect of MET.

With respect to the vendor's desire to comply with standards (appearing second from the bottom in Figure 4.13), 20 percent of the participants of the survey think that such a desire is most important and 20 percent consider it more important. Thus, a total 40 percent of the participants think this factor is most or more important. These results indicate that the customer's desires and needs are considered significantly higher than those of vendors in a MET. In fact, most respondents in this category, around 36 percent, thought that the vendor's desire to comply with standards is a less important factor; as low as 2 percent thought vendor's desire as least important.

On the importance of the use of standards (e.g., 802.11 and 802.22 type standards) in the technical dimension (appearing at the bottom of Figure 4.13), 19 percent of the participants in the survey think that this factor is most important and 44 percent consider it more important. Thus, a total of 63 percent think standards are more or most important. Only 2 percent consider standards as a least important factor in the technical dimension of MET.

Mobile Software Applications

Mobile software applications utilize technical development environments such as C++ and Java, and open source such as PERL. Mobile applications need to consider both the end users including their mobile devices and the corresponding back-end supporting application software that handles the processing and storage of contents. The phenomenal importance given by the survey respondents to mobile software applications indicate that transitioning enterprises should focus on creating value for customers by providing relevant applications on their devices.

Programming languages such as C/C++ and Java that are used for software development are also popular in the development of mobile applications. However, dynamic programming languages such as PERL are also being used, which enable changes in code and logical structures of the software program at runtime. The integration of programming languages, networking, databases, and security needed for mobile applications leads to Integrated Development Environments (IDEs). Examples of such development environments are

- Sun Java Studio IDE: It is a development platform that enables the development and deployment of mobile applications. It features UML modeling as well as instant collaborations among applications and services. The application environment is used to develop, debug, and deploy enterprise applications, Web services, and portal components.
- Microsoft ASP.NET: This is a part of Microsoft's .NET platform that not only allows programmers to create dynamic Web applications but also dynamic mobile applications.
- NetBeans IDE: This is an open source IDE for software developers, which is used to create professional cross-platform desktop, enterprise, Web, and mobile applications.

Mobile ICT Infrastructure for Mobile Business Operations

The mobile infrastructure includes transmission towers, satellite networks, and power lines supporting the transmission. Their existence and availability and the challenges in using or changing them need to be considered by transitioning businesses. The robustness and reliability of the infrastructures and the cost of using them enable mobile businesses to create and offer new and dynamic services to clients. Mobile infrastructures are of tremendous importance in developing nations (such as India and Sri Lanka), where erecting a tower with substantial capacity and range can cover a large geographical area and enable mobile networking and connectivity. Mobile infrastructure is not encumbered with laying copper wires or fiber optics for network connectivity. Participants of the MET research survey responded to the relative importance of different mobile infrastructures as given in the following text.

Figure 4.14 shows the importance of mobile infrastructures in MET. Figure 4.14A shows the importance of transmission towers within the overall infrastructure factors in MET. This figure shows that 23 percent of the participants in the survey think that transmission towers are most important, and 44 percent consider them as more important. Thus, a total of 67 percent think this factor is either more or most important. Only 3 percent consider transmission towers as a least important infrastructure factor in the technical dimension of MET.

Figure 4.14B shows the importance of satellites. Survey results indicate that 16 percent of the participants consider satellites a most important factor, and 39

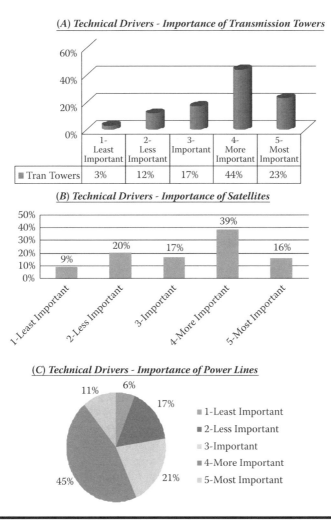

(A) Technical Drivers - Importance of Transmission Towers

	1-Least Important	2-Less Important	3-Important	4-More Important	5-Most Important
■ Tran Towers	3%	12%	17%	44%	23%

(B) Technical Drivers - Importance of Satellites

(C) Technical Drivers - Importance of Power Lines

- ■ 1-Least Important
- ■ 2-Less Important
- ▨ 3-Important
- ■ 4-More Important
- ▨ 5-Most Important

Figure 4.14   Analysis of the importance of the infrastructure factor in the technical dimension of MET.

percent think that they are more important. Thus, a total of 55 percent think the satellites factor is either more or most important. Only 9 percent think it a least important infrastructure factor in the technical dimension of MET.

Figure 4.14C shows the importance of power lines. The result, as appearing in this figure, indicates that 45 percent of the participants think power lines are more important, and 11 percent, that they are most important. Thus, a total of 56 percent think the power lines factor as either more or most important. Only 6 percent think of it as a least important infrastructure factor in the technical dimension of MET.

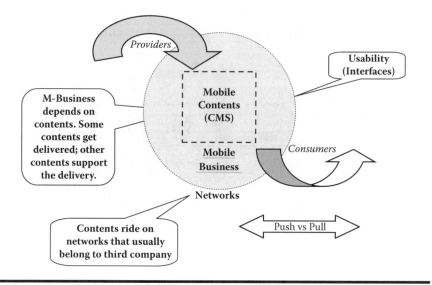

Figure 4.15   Mobile contents: provision and consumption based on networks.

The survey results indicate a reasonable acceptance of the importance of infrastructures in the context of MET. The figures are not exceptionally high or low and, therefore, they do not suggest any unique or specific stress on any part of the infrastructure.

Mobile Content Management

The data related to mobile applications can be voice, video, images, charts, and text. Therefore, it is appropriately referred to as "content" rather than data. According to Goh and Taniar (2006), mobile contents have three separate challenges: sourcing of contents, ensuring their secure storage, and provisioning or "mining" of contents by applications and services. Figure 4.15 shows the provisioning as well as consumption of contents. Content providers comprise not only the organizational providers but also individual users who give information through their mobile devices as well as, many a times unwittingly, their locations. The consumers include users as well as other mobile businesses that rely on the contents sent by the provider. The movement of contents depends on the availability of networks that themselves may belong to an entirely different business with which the transitioning business may have to partner. The foci of mobile contents continue to be location independence and personalization.

Real-time updating and sharing of contents takes place for multiple applications that use a multitude of databases such as a CMS. CMSs, as shown in Figure 4.16, could themselves be residing in a variety of locations, such as internal networks, the Internet, and also specific mobile databases. The many-to-many mapping between applications and databases leads to issues regarding data integrity, as multiple

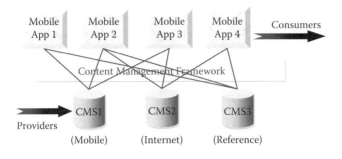

Figure 4.16   Mapping mobile applications to a combination of contents.

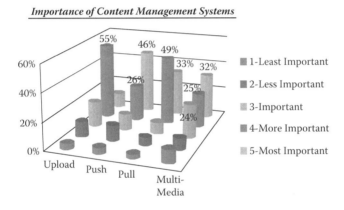

Figure 4.17   Analysis of the importance of the content factor in the technical dimension of MET.

updates can occur simultaneously from mobile users in real-time. For example, the moment the user moves his or her location, the location-specific information (e.g., the location itself) of the source changes. Mobile applications that use location-specific information need to handle not only the conflicts resulting from multiple updates but also identify—in the first place—that there is a conflict even when the sources of data are at two different locations. Mobile database architectures need to reconcile the movement of the client especially when there are multiple entries in a database by one client who is moving. Further challenges of mobile database architectures are that they have to handle the randomness of user connections, ensure the reliability of connections, and maintain the progressive storage and retrieval of data as the applications are executed.

Figure 4.17 shows the importance of CMSs in METs. The CMS factors include the uploading of vendor contents, pushing contents to customers, enabling customers to pull the contents, and the multimedia aspect of contents within the overall technical dimension of MET.

Today, databases have evolved into CMSs that are capable of storing audios, videos, photos, graphs, charts, and many other content formats, which could not be stored in standard relational databases. Therefore, the technical dimension of MET must consider, among other issues, the following:

- The type and nature of content
- The way the location of contents influences the speed and security of downloads
- The duration for which the content is kept before it is replaced or upgraded
- The synchronization of content between mobile devices and back-end servers
- Integration of applications with networks and devices with the mobile contents

The result of the MET survey (shown on the left-hand side in Figure 4.17), indicates that 55 percent of the participants think that uploading vendor contents is a more important CMS factor in the technical dimension of MET, and 11 percent think that it is most important. Thus, a total of 66 percent consider it most or more important factor. Only 4 percent think it is least important.

Survey results shown second from the left-hand side in Figure 4.17 indicate that 46 percent of the participants think that pushing contents to customers is most important, and 26 percent think it a more important factor. Thus, a total of 72 percent think that pushing contents is most or more important in the technical dimension of MET. Only 4 percent think it a least important factor.

Results of the survey, as shown second from the right-hand side in Figure 4.17, indicate that 33 percent of the participants think that enabling customers to pull contents is a most important factor, and 49 percent consider it more important. Thus, a total of 82 percent consider it as a most or more important factor. This figure when compared with the earlier one on enabling vendors to push contents to mobile devices indicates a predominant bent on the part of participants to keep the ability to download contents on the user side. Only 3 percent think it is a least important factor.

As shown at the right-hand side of Figure 4.17, 32 percent of the participants in the survey think that the multimedia aspect of contents is most important, and 25 percent think it more important. Thus, a total of 57 percent consider the multimedia aspect of contents factor most or more important, and 10 percent consider it least important in the technical dimension of MET.

The discussion thus far has been to understand the individual technical factors that contribute to MET. We now consider how these factors are sequenced in terms of their comparative priority and responsibilities.

Mobile Transition Framework (Technical Dimension)

Figure 4.18 shows the relative importance, in terms of sequencing, of technical drivers of the MET framework. Whereas 19.6 percent of the respondents of the MET survey indicated that network coverage and bandwidth should be the primary technical

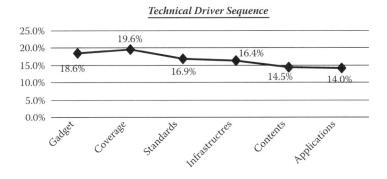

Figure 4.18   Analysis of the sequencing of technical drivers of the MET framework.

driver of MET, 18.6 percent said that mobile gadget capabilities need to be considered first in the transition toward a mobile business. These are the first and second important factors in the process dimension of MET, as shown in the survey. However, only 14 percent of the respondents think that mobile business applications should be the most important driving factor of the mobile business. This is the least percentage of people who think that applications are important in terms of their sequencing.

An analysis of the sequencing factors in terms of their priorities shows how these factors can be configured in a process. The resultant technical process framework is shown in Figure 4.19. As shown in the figure, transition begins with considering mobile network coverage as this is the most important sequencing factor according to the survey participants. This is followed by taking into account the mobile gadgets factor. The mobile network communication standards and their effects are considered next by the architect/designer, and so are infrastructures for transmission and reception of mobile data. Note that not every business needs to set up a mobile transmission infrastructure; however, every transitioning business needs to consider this infrastructure as it comes up with new processes and services for its clients. Mobile content management is taken into account next by the transitioning business, followed by mobile business applications.

Technical Factors in Mobile Business Usage

There are four levels of mobility use by businesses: informative, transactive, operative, and collaborative. They are shown in Figure 4.20, and are discussed in this section from the context of the technical dimension of MET.

Technical–Informative

Technical drivers that influence the mobile business provide the basic impetus for the informative use of mobile technology. The push mechanism, discussed earlier

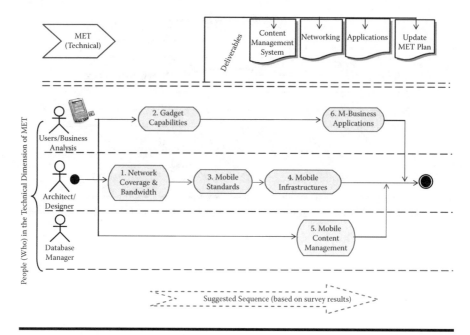

Figure 4.19 Mobile transition framework (technical dimension).

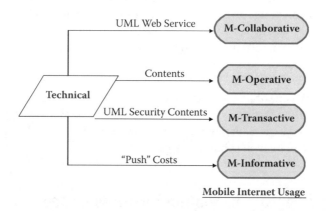

Figure 4.20 Mapping the technical dimension of MET to mobile Internet usage.

in this chapter, is important in this informative use of mobile technology. The informative use can be in two ways: either as a general broadcast, or as an informative service requiring registration. The preregistered informative service would technically require a secure server and will encourage the business to conduct two-way transactions. Note also that for the informative use, technically, the server can register users with the help of even a land-based Internet. Overall, however, this is relatively easy to implement as there are minimum security requirements. Mobile business at this stage will be generating static contents.

Technical–Transactive

Transactive capabilities of businesses come into play when they want two-way transactions with customers. Technically, wireless networks are expected to provide the necessary speed, reliability, and security for such two-way transactions. Further, the mobile applications discussed in Chapter 5 are also required for providing substantial business capabilities for transactions. Mobile agents programs also create opportunities for multiway transactions. Contents at both client and server sides need to be modeled. WML contents can be generated and provided as two-way services.

Technical–Operative

Technically, the operative use of mobility by businesses builds up and expands their transactive capabilities. The operational use requires attention to supply-chain management, inventory management, and all the internal HR functions. Therefore, the operative use of mobile technology calls for attention to content management as it deals with the uploading and dispersal of contents for internal systems. Technically, an enterprise architecture will have to separate the mobile intranet from the Internet, creating multitiered access for employees working within or outside the physical boundaries of the organization. Transitions across various wireless communication standards such as 2G, 2.5G, and 3G need to be considered from the employee's point of view. Network and device transitions in operational use save costs and time, and impact internal technologies.

Technical–Collaborative

Collaborations among businesses and groups of individuals require that their devices and applications be able to communicate with each other seamlessly.

Mobile Web services (MWSs) have collaborative and technical capabilities that are relatively easy to implement compared to the process, economic, and social challenges of collaborative usage. Through mobile Web services (Ghanbary 2006) and Mobile Service-Oriented Architecture (Wu and Unhelkar 2008), software applications are able to communicate with each other across platforms and environments. The XML-based interface of these services enables different mobile devices and applications to communicate with each other, use each other's database/contents, execute remote applications, and facilitate mobile agent execution. This potential offered by technical collaboration needs to be supported by corresponding economic, process, and social capabilities; contents will be dynamically generated, used, or sold by multiple parties.

References

ACS. 2005. www.acs.org.au, the Australian Computer Society's Web site.

Allison, K. 2007. Cisco to purchase WiMAX supplier, *Financial Times*, October 24, 19.

Bhattar, R. K., Ramakrishnan K. R., Dasgupta K. S., and Palsule V. S. 2006. Review of Wireless Technologies and Generations, chapter 11 in *Handbook of Research in Mobile Business: Technical, Methodological and Social Perspectives*, ed. B. Unhelkar, B. Hershey, PA: IGI Global.

Bolter, J. D. and MacIntyre, B. 2007. Is it alive or is it AR? *IEEE Spectrum*, August, 31–35.

Davies, N. J., Fensel, D., and Richardson, M. 2004. The future of Web services. *BT Technology* 22(1), 118–127.

Deshpande, Y., Murugesan, S., Unhelkar, B., and Arunatileka, D. 2004. Device Independent Web Engineering: Methodological Considerations and Challenges—Moving Web Applications from Desk-Top to Diverse Mobile Devices, *Proceedings of ICWE2004,* The 1st International Workshop on Device Independent Web Engineering (the 4th International Conference, ICWE2004) 25 July 2004, Munich, Germany.

Future Technology. 2005. Recent news of a new kind of world, retrieved April 30, 2005, from http://www.globalchange.com/futuretechnology.htm. (article also cited *IEEE Transactions on Nanotechnology*, March 2002; and *Scientific American*, February 2003).

Gapper, J. 2007. Mighty Google rings in the changes, *Financial Times*, November 11.

Ghanbary, A. 2006. Evaluation of mobile technologies in the context of their application, limitation and transformation, chapter in *Handbook of Research in Mobile Business: Technical, Methodological and Social Perspectives,* ed. B. Unhelkar. Hershey, PA: IGI Global.

Goh, J. and Taniar, D. 2006. Mobile user data mining and its applications, in Handbook of Research in Mobile Business: Technical, Methodological and Social Perspectives, ed. B. Unhelkar. Hershey, PA: IGI Global.

Harmon, R. and Diam, T. 2009, Assessing the future of location-based services: Technologies, applications, and strategies, chapter in *Handbook of Research in Mobile Business: Technical, Methodological and Social Perspectives,* 2nd ed., ed. B. Unhelkar. Hershey, PA: IGI Global.

i-Mode. 2003. http://www.nttdocomo.com/services/imode/index.html

Johnson, D., Perkins, C., and Arkko, J. 2004. RFC 3775: Mobility Support in IPv6, retrieved November 4, 2007, from http://www.rfc-editor.org/rfc/rfc3775.txt.

Kuppuswami, A. and Unhelkar, B. 2004. Relevance of State, Nature, Scale and Location of Business E-Transformation in Web Services, *Proceedings of the 2004 International Symposium on Web Services and Applications (*ISWS'04: June 21–24, Las Vegas, Nevada, USA; http://www.world-academy-of-science.org).

Lan, Y. and Unhelkar, B. 2005. Global Enterprise Transitions, IDEAS Group Publishing.

Mohney, D. 2007. October, The Business Case for Enterprise WiMAX, *Von Magazine* 5(3), 26–31.

Pedrasa, J., R., Perera, E., and Seneviratne, A. 2009. Context Aware Mobility Management, chapter in *Handbook of Research in Mobile Business: Technical, Methodological and Social Perspectives,* 2nd ed., ed. B. Unhelkar. Hershey, PA: IGI Global.

Perkins, C. et al., 2002. RFC 3220: IP Mobility support for IPv4, retrieved November 4, 2007 from http://www.rfc-editor.org/rfc/rfc3220.txt.

Rosenburg, J., Schulzrinne, H., Camarillo, G., Johnston, A., Peterson, J., Sparks, R., Handley, M., and Schooler, E. 2002. RFC 3261: Session Initiation Protocol, retrieved November 4, 2007 from http://www.rfc-editor.org/rfc/rfc3261.txt.

Schenker, J. L. 2007. Nokia Aims Way beyond Handsets, *Business Week* 38.

Unhelkar, B. 2008a. Mobile Enterprise Architecture: Model and Application, *Cutter Executive Report*, www.cutter.com, 11(3) April, 2008.

Unhelkar, B. 2008b. Applying Service Oriented Architecture (SOA) in order to create and integrate Application/Services over Internet/IMS, tutorial delivered at *2nd International Conference on Internet Multimedia Services Architecture and Applications (IMSAA-08)* conference, Bangalore, India. http://www.iiitb.ac.in/imsaa2008/tutorial.html#tutorial-1

Vanjara, K. 2005. Application of mobile technologies in healthcare diagnostics and administration, chapter in *Handbook of Research in Mobile Business: Technical, Methodological and Social Perspectives,* ed. B. Unhelkar. Hershey, PA: IGI Global.

Vyas, A. and Yoon, V. 2005. Information management in mobile environments using location-aware intelligent agent system (Lia), chapter in *Handbook of Research in Mobile Business: Technical, Methodological and Social Perspectives,* ed. B. Unhelkar. Hershey, PA: IGI Global.

Wilson, M., Kannangara, K., Smith, G., Simmons, M., and Raguse, B. 2002. *Nanotechnology: Basic Science and Emerging Technologies.* Sydney, Australia: UNSW Press.

Wu, M. and Unhelkar, B. 2008. Extending Enterprise Architecture with Mobility, *Proceedings of IEEE VTC*, Singapore, May 12–15.

Chapter 5

Mobile Enterprise Transitions: Process Dimension

Caution is not an adequate basis for success either ....

John Legge, *Chaos Theory and Business Planning*, 1990, p. 2

Chapter Key Points

- Discusses the process dimension of Mobile Enterprise Transition (MET) wherein the impact of mobility on business processes is understood with the aim of engineering mobile business processes
- Creates an understanding of the "mobile context" of the user in modeling business processes
- Discusses quality-of-service (QoS) issues such as real-time response and coverage from a business viewpoint by balancing it against cost
- Presents the ever-important financial applications with and for mobility, analyzing and creating a sequence of factors that can be put together in a framework for the process dimension of MET

▪ Presents the evolving complexity of the process dimension through informative, transactive, operative, and collaborative use of mobility in this dimension
▪ Presents the relevance of the known process-modeling techniques of UML (activity diagrams and use cases) and BPMN in mobile process modeling
▪ Discusses the mobile business applications, their natures, categories, challenges, and their implementations in mobile CRM and mobile SCM
▪ Outlines the relevance of mobile collaborations to mobile business

Introduction

This chapter discusses the impact of mobility on the business processes of an enterprise and also the positive influence of process modeling on proper utilization of mobility by business. Earlier, in Chapter 3, we discussed the economic dimension, and in Chapter 4 the technical dimension of MET. These earlier discussions focused on "why" to mobilize the enterprise (the compelling economic situation) and "what" causes that mobilization (the technical impact), respectively. This current chapter is focused on "how" the business processes of an organization change and "how" new business processes are introduced as the organization undergoes mobile transition. Modeling of business processes, use of mobile applications and mobile business packages, reengineering of processes, quality of service, and the financial aspects of mobile processes are some of the important parts of the MET process dimension discussed in this chapter. The end result of incorporating mobile technologies in business processes should be of "value" to the customer. These customer "values" accrue when the organization investigates and analyzes the customer in the "context" of the mobile environment in which the customer exists. Therefore, this chapter initially delves deeper into the context of the user. A number of other factors, such as collaborations between employers, and other external systems also come into play in providing value to mobile users. The various aspects of a process, and the way these process aspects are affected by mobility, are shown in Figure 5.1.

Figure 5.1 shows the process of how a user registers in a hospital management system. This figure is based on the use of case diagrams of the unified modeling language (UML; www.omg.org) discussed later in this chapter. The user, equipped with a mobile gadget, transacts with the hospital by crossing the boundary of the hospital management system. Figure 5.1 further shows how the administrator of the hospital can deal with the requests coming from the user with an internal Wi-Fi link to the system. Thus, note how mobility influences the external business process of registration by the user through a mobile device using, possibly, a cellular network, whereas internally the process can be managed using a local Wi-Fi link. There is also the third actor in this process, which is an external system called the "Health Regulatory System," which can be accessed by this process using a WiMax connection as that system may be within the same premises as the hospital

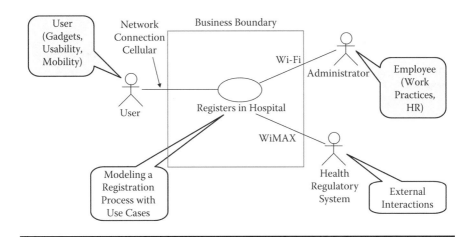

Figure 5.1   Impact of mobility on a business process.

management system. Figure 5.1 depicts only an example scenario for the various ways in which mobility influences business. Each mobile business is made up of numerous business processes, and each of those business processes are affected by mobility in different ways—mostly positive but at times in a challenging manner. These various aspects of mobile business processes are further discussed in the ensuing pages of this chapter.

Modeling of mobile business processes keep the user (customer) firmly in focus, as also shown by the actor notation representing the user in Figure 5.1. This focus on the customer by the mobile business leads to changes in the organizations' applications such as customer relationship management (CRM), human resources (HR), and supply-chain management (SCM). The real-time interaction in these applications comprises mobile initiation and instantaneous response between the business and the customer. This initiation and response between the business and the customer needs to be modeled in the business processes. The main challenges in creating and modeling these mobile business processes are that they are dynamic—changing with the changing location of the customer. Furthermore, there is a need to provide due consideration to personalization of services for mobile users in modeling the processes. Mobile processes open up opportunities for the business to provide one-touch access for users through their handheld devices, equip field workers such as sales representatives and road runners with real-time contents of the business that helps them provide timely service to the customers, and enables dynamic, "on the fly" grouping of users that allows the business to create time- and location-based opportunities to market/sell/serve *changing* groups of customers. These are some of the interesting process-modeling challenges discussed in this chapter. However, we start here by discussing the process drivers for MET.

Table 5.1   Process drivers for mobile enterprise transitions (How?)

Process drivers for mobile enterprise transitions (How?)		Transition issues
Mobile business processes	Mobile business-to-consumer (B2C) context Mobile business-to-business (B2B) Government-to-mobile individual (G2I) Collaborative (M2M)	Relevance to users; context-based modeling
Merging and modeling mobile processes	Creating new mobile processes BPR modeling Reengineering with mobile processes Removing redundant processes Modeling of mobile business processes	Use of modeling standards (UML, BPMN) Quality of process models Collaborative models
QoS: Quality of service	Real-time response when compared with cost balancing Coverage when compared with the cost factors Coverage when compared with security Accuracy when compared with costs	Balancing the various quality factors based on needs (context)
Mobile applications and finances	Applications supporting mobile usage (e.g., bill payments) categories Financial transactions using mobile gadgets modeling Service and support for mobile usage Transparency in mobile charges (call costs) Software Support for lost/stolen mobile gadgets development Costs of developing mobile applications	On-demand services and processes Application development and maintenance Package customizations

Process Dimension (How)

This process dimension of the MET framework deals with the question of "how" to create and conduct business transactions with mobility (Table 5.1). Thus, this process dimension of MET is concerned with the changes to the way in which users (customers, employees, managers) use the content and services of the business, the quality of those services, and the modeling and "engineering" of mobile software applications corresponding to those services, which are listed in Figure 5.2.

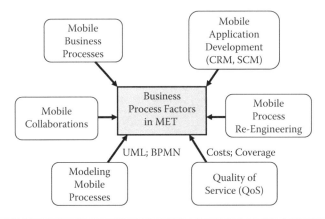

Figure 5.2   Business process factors driving MET.

Table 5.2   Various factors that comprise context in mobile processes

Context factor in mobile applications	Influence on context
User and device position	Distance of device from base station
Activity of the user	Whether the user is static or moving; also the urgency of activity (i.e., leisure or emergency)
Point in time/date	Morning/evening, vacation, past/current/future
Device type/identity	Smart phone, PDA; tablet PC, identifier, and ownership
State of the user	On, off, transmitting, receiving, secured, lost
Environment of operation	Strength of networks, quality and intensity

Table 5.2 lists these important process drivers of MET. The rest of the discussion in this chapter deals with the issues associated with these MET drivers, what influences them, and how to best sequence and apply these process drivers (or factors) for successful mobile transitions.

Mobile Processes Landscape

Context in Mobile Business Processes

A mobile process depends on context, network, and content. Figure 5.3 shows the influence of these factors. However, these influencing factors are intertwined with

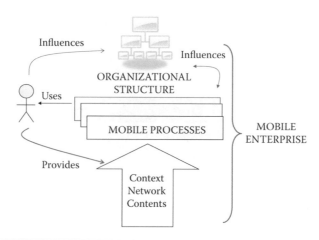

Figure 5.3 A mobile process depends on context, network, and contents.

each other; not independent of each other. Furthermore, the effect of context, network, and content are not limited to mobile processes; there is the further effect of changes to mobile processes on the organization's structure. A number of mobile processes make up a process-based mobile enterprise, and therefore, the organizational structure of the enterprise is also influenced by changes to and reengineering of mobile processes (discussed in greater details in Chapter 6). The starting point for the context, however, is the user, also shown in Figure 5.3.

Therefore, the analysis of the customers in business processes starts with a good understanding of the context of the customers. This is so because the significance of mobile business processes to the user is derived from the "context" in which they are used. The following are examples of context-based mobile processes. A pizza shop beams promotional electronic coupons to potential mobile customers. It can also send information on nearby hotels, motels, and attractions with discounts. Another is a yellow-page service that gives details on nearby services, such as the location of the closest gas stations to where the user is driving, along with gas prices. Additional information such as deals available on rotation of tires, car batteries, etc., at a nearby auto center can be passed to the user while presenting user-required information. The term context refers to a wide range of factors that come into play when the user invokes the business process. These context factors are made up of the location of the user and the device, user's activity, point in time, type and state of device, and the state of the mobile environment in which the device is operating (Vyas and Yoon 2005). These factors and their explanation are summarized in Table 5.2.

The context presented in Table 5.2 comes into play in detail in modeling mobile business processes and applications. Location and time context with respect to mobility implies where a specific service is required and whether the service required is in the present or the future (potential) location of the user. The content and manners in which these services are delivered to the user, also change based on the context. The changing nature of the location of the user plays the most important part in determining the context. However, this changing location of the user and his device are not the only factors that are considered in determining the context of a mobile user. Pedrasa et al. (2009) describe four significant aspects of mobility that help us understand context in a mobile environment.

A mobile user usually moves with the device. However, a user with a unique identity can also move from one device to another. The new device used by a mobile user may have mobile capabilities, but it may not necessarily be moving all the time. The devices can be wirelessly connected but may be stationary. The information on the movement of devices and users is vital, particularly in providing users with relevant information. Such information can include marketing and advertisement; it can also be regarding emergency help such as an ambulance or fire brigade. Furthermore, there are situations wherein the user and the device are maintaining established communication links but the "session" dealing with that communication is moving. This session mobility enables change of location of a session from one device to other in a seamless manner. Thus, the focus of mobile business process modeling is to provide continuity of personalized services irrespective of changes to users' location, device, or session.

Unified Mobile User View

Customer's context and demands need to be incorporated in mobile business processes, and needs to be considered with the basic informative usage of mobility by business and its progress toward transactive and collaborative usage. Informative usage of mobility includes news, entertainment, and driving directions. Transactive usage includes banking, shopping, auctions, advertising, and ticketing. Operative usage is time sheets and inventories. Collaborative usage based on context is the formation and interaction of groups in shopping malls, sports complexes, or even auctions that are part of transactive use. Each of these categories is differently impacted by the context.

Modeling and design of software applications need to consider all of the aforementioned contexts, mobility type, and changes to the customer's location to ascertain the needs of, and the type of product/service offerings that can be made to, the customer. Mobile application, therefore, needs to be designed to incorporate techniques for location detection and direction, continuous connectivity with the location-dependent content residing on the base service server. However, most importantly, these mobile applications have a need to provide a unified view of the business offerings to the customer. Thus, mobile application designs need to bring together the device, network, content, and environment seamlessly through process models to provide value to the user, as shown in Figure 5.4. Mobile applications are challenged continuously by user perceptions about information privacy and security. Therefore, these mobile application designs need to safeguard users'

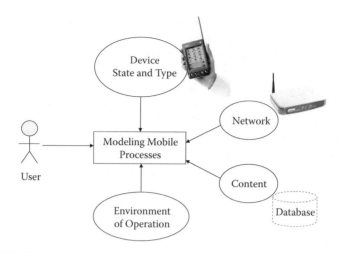

Figure 5.4   Convergence to deliver a unified view of business to the user.

unified privacy and security because, in context-based mobile processes, the location of the user is visible to the system on an ongoing base. The users' personal information is also available to the device, network, and the system. Furthermore, mobile application designs need to enable customization of the mobile content to the specific context or location of the user. Thus, as shown in Figure 5.4, convergence and unification of the context is the "value" that a business can provide to the user, particularly when modeled as mobile processes.

> Mobile application designs need to converge content and location detection to provide "value" to users. Increasingly, one can expect applications that use continuous connectivity with the content residing on the base service server. These mobile application designs need to also cater to user perceptions on information privacy and security.

Location Detection

Detecting the location of the user provides vital input in ascertaining the context of the user, and is thus an important part of mobile applications. It requires a set of supporting network and system infrastructure (Ruhi and Turel 2005). Some of the location detection techniques are Time Difference of Arrival (TDOA), Angle of Arrival (AOA), and Location Pattern Matching (LPM). These technologies compare the times at which a cell signal reaches multiple location measurement units installed at the base stations and thereby determine the location of the devices. The network layout and the density of deployment of base stations determine the accuracy of the locations.

Location detection techniques are combined with various types of wireless networks to ascertain the locations of mobile devices, people, and even inventory items. For example,

- WWAN—Wireless wide area network, for applications in supply chains, shipping, and tracking of courier packages
- Cellular networks—involved in conversations and messaging between people, especially long distance
- P2T—Push to talk, for coordinating deliveries, inventories, and event management within relatively shorter distances of few hundred meters
- RFID—Radio frequency identification, for identifying the location of inventory items based on tags attached to them (the items may be stationary and the reader be mobile)
- WLAN (Wi-Fi)—Wireless local area network that can be used in homes and offices, again within a few hundred meters
- Bluetooth Technology—for short-range communications, barcode scanning, inventory management
- Global positioning system (GPS)—Cost-effective but widely acceptable locating technique, also compatible with most wireless networks as well as information technologies

Wi-Fi and Bluetooth have a limited range, but these networks perform better indoors. These technologies are short-range positioning systems that are highly accurate and provide device-to-device communication in wireless handsets. However, GPS does not function efficiently indoors and in urban areas. An effective location detection strategy combines short- and long-range technologies so that outdoor as well as indoor locations can be effectively detected.

Mobile Application Programs (Software) and Architecture

Mobile applications are software programs that provide system support to the mobile business process and value to users at work or in their day-to-day lives. Additionally, they provide competitive advantage to the mobile business by opening up opportunities to streamline processes, reduce costs, increase customer patronage, and enable timely planning of orders and deliveries. Mobile applications deal with areas including financial, customer, planning, production, customer service administration, and inventory (Lan and Unhelkar 2005). However, value generation is not just dependent on what the mobile business process can offer. As mentioned earlier, the value of mobile applications and services also depend on the perceived value and users' sensitivity. The user sensitivity factors range from usability of mobile applications to confidentiality usage, security of phones, and privacy of individuals. The ease of use of business functionalities associated with primary business processes such as receipt and payment of bills, support of applications, cost of usage, authentication, availability of applications, confidentiality, and traceability (the ability to prove that the transaction has indeed taken place and who conducted it) are some important aspects of value creation in MET. These are some of the external business factors that are considered in mobile application development. The focus of external factors is on value creation and maximization, which is discussed in further detail in Chapter 8.

Mobile business applications also improve the internal availability and reliability of financial information. Internal processes, however, are focused on cost reduction by making use of mobile business applications. Collaborative mobile applications add further dimension to value creation by accessing centralized content management systems that are also linked to other external enterprise systems.

Cost reduction and value creation through mobile business applications is further supported by the generation of a suite of metrics. These metrics allow quality issues to be recorded, tracked, and analyzed. Metrics are helpful in measuring the internal lead times so that ordering can be aligned with available production capacity to maximize utilization. Such metrics enable quicker time-to-market for the firm's products. Mobile system benefits include single point of data entry, simplified order placement with few key touches, order status inquiries, managing delivery, and invoicing and payments.

Table 5.3 summarizes the mobile business applications and highlights the process issues that need to be considered in developing or procuring these applications.

Developing good mobile applications requires due consideration to software architectures, software process models, and quality aspects of development. Therefore, mobile application development can utilize the lessons learned from earlier software development activities. However, it requires excellence in process modeling, which is over and above the due consideration of the mobile gadgets, content, networks, and social context of the user. The modeling of mobile applications has to consider device (client)-side processing besides server-side processes. Thus, the need to model and develop *interconnecting* Web applications that allow internal and external users to communicate seamlessly across existing (potentially legacy) and new mobile networks is increasingly felt by business. Creation of applications based on a mobile enterprise architecture that provides a suite of programs and components that can be configured quickly and effectively to produce mobile applications is a vital step toward MET success. The architecture needs to provide an interconnecting framework of components and applications that interface seamlessly and securely with each other, that are formally modeled and documented, and that can access contents flexibly. A robust architecture for mobile applications enables handling of several XML interchange standards (e.g., RosettaNet, ebXML, LIXI), eliminating the risks in creating collaborative applications and mobile content, and enhancing user experience.

Table 5.3   Major mobile business applications, industries, type of mobile usage, and mobile process issues

Industry	Mobile business applications	Mobile usage type	Mobile process issue (primary)
Advertising	Context-specific informative applications	Messages, video	Informative
Education	Mobile classes and discussion sessions	Voice, chats	Collaborative
Supply chain	Resource management, product tracking and dispatching	Auto/ agents	Operative
Entertainment	Music/video/games, downloads and online gaming applications	Voice, data, browsing	Informative
Hospital management	Patient flow application, doctor management, remote diagnosis	Automated, mobile agents	Operative
Travel and tourism	Schedules, maps, airlines, weather, hotels, car applications	Browsing	Transactive
Insurance	Policies and claims processes	Automated payments	Transactive
Pharmaceutical	Inventory, labs, testing	Short range	Informative
Traffic	Routing, positioning services, toll paying, and traffic advisories	Hybrid, network, direction	Collaborative

Mobile application value is created by modeling the business processes these applications are meant to satisfy. In addition, mobile applications need to consider communication networks, content, and presentation. Mobile applications can be designed to be online and offline, as well as a thin-client or rich-client application. Quality measurements and metrics for mobile applications provide a significant challenge to designers.

A well-constructed architecture for mobile applications development also handles the configuration and implementation of mobile security standards. These enable adherence to corporate policies on security. Devices, networks, and content servers are all subject to these policies at both the manual and systems level. Thus, security on mobile devices can be set from a centralized server rather than by having physical access to the mobile device.

Implementation of mobile systems requires integration and seamless linking with the rest of the enterprise architecture. Mobile software usually requires a significant degree of customization to integrate it to the rest of the organization. Customization of enterprise software is fraught with risk and significant cost for ongoing maintenance. Wu and Unhelkar (2007, 2008, 2009) have demonstrated this challenge by creating a comprehensive Mobile Enabled Architecture (M-EA) model that simplifies the process of incorporation of mobility in security systems.

Mobile Application Categories

Mobile applications belong to different categories such as online and offline applications, type of connecting networks used by the applications, and type of handheld devices required by the applications. In practice, these categories tend to blur and merge with each other; still, an understanding of these "rough" categories of mobile applications influence the way they are developed, tested, and deployed.

Online Applications

The major online mobile applications provide information; check e-mails; enable payments, mobile banking, mobile shopping, mobile education, and general government bulletins; provide messaging; and enable leisure activities. These online applications are executed when the mobile gadgets are connected to the mobile Internet. This connectivity of devices enables an organization to implement applications that make physical movements of people and material easier and smoother than without such mobile application support. Most importantly, though, mobile online applications bring in the *dynamic* aspect of a business process to the forefront, enabling changes to the process as it happens. For example, consider the case of the courier delivering and picking up packages during the day. The route of this courier can be with the help of mobility that results in time and distance benefits to the organization, the courier, and the customer. Mobile online applications that need to ascertain a user's precise location (e.g., emergency services—police, fire, ambulance) make extensive use of telemetric services such as location-based services (LBSs), global positioning services (GPSs), and car navigation systems (CNSs) to create value for their users.

Offline Applications

Offline mobile applications are also an important consideration for business. The major offline services offered by related network providers include personalized diaries, games, ordinary communications, built-in memory, expert systems, remote supervision, and connectivity to local devices through Bluetooth and infrared. These can be extra features on particular mobile devices.

Industry Categories

Mobile applications cover a range of industries such as banking, hospital, gaming, and travel. The type of industry for which a mobile application is developed has a significant bearing on the nature of the application itself. For example, the gaming industry requires mobile applications that are rich in graphics, audio, and video but have relatively less stringent security requirements than, say, an application developed for the banking industry. Applications such as bill payments require the highest standard of security, and applications such as mobile electoral voting and conducting online surveys also require very high privacy. The level of risk within an industry category, influenced by local legislations and business environment factors, plays a role in the categorizing, development, and deployment of mobile applications.

Nature of the Transaction

We have seen earlier, in Chapter 2, the four layers of business usage of mobility. They indicate the nature of the transactions, which depend on whether they are merely informative, or have two-party transaction needs, or involve multiple parties. Another factor to be considered from an architectural viewpoint is whether the transactions are "pushed" to the mobile device, or the device owner is provided the option of "pulling" in the transaction. The nature of the transaction also affects the content of the communication, such as whether it's a two-way banking transaction or an informative weather alert or a personalized digital image for social purposes. Upfront consideration of the nature of transactions helps in designing, testing, and deploying mobile applications.

Nature and Extent of Collaboration

Mobile Web services lead to extraordinary opportunities for businesses to collaborate. Such collaboration is not merely between two people who are interacting through a mobile phone with each other. In fact, increasingly, the human factor in communication between collaborating businesses is becoming less important, and services-oriented software applications are taking up the mandate of collaborating. Thus, apart from people, there are mobile services and components, mobile intelligent agents, and mobile sensors that are initiating and managing communications. The nature of collaborating individuals, services, and sensors needs to be considered in mobile applications development.

Device Types

The range of devices considered in detail in Chapter 4 also plays an important role in categorizing mobile applications. For example, a mobile application designed for common usage by normal cell phones will be different from the one that aims to use smart phones or tablet PCs as the end-user device. The location of the device and the speed with which it is expected to move, the amount of memory it will have, and the expected level of computation at the device end are all important contributing factors in the design of the mobile application.

Challenges of Mobile Business Application

Mobile application development faces some specific challenges in addition to those involving normal software application development. The following factors, elicited mostly from the research questions for this book project, are considered as major challenges in mobile application development.

- Increased complexity due to dynamically changing mobile inputs that affect the way in which mobile applications are used.
- Lack of known and published mobile business process modeling methodologies and techniques.
- Lack of compatibility and integrity between various application development standards.
- Slow speed of mobile applications implementation due to distribution of systems, additional testing, and the extra security required.
- Lack of reliable mobile services and service-oriented issues that prevent collaboration and uniformity of applications.
- Lack of hardware standards that enable different devices to be interchanged; applications need to continuously interpret and understand the type of device they are dealing with.
- Lack of collaboration between competitors (due to understandable "interests") to create a common standard for exchange of contents and services among applications.
- Lack of universal standards for transmission of data and services; therefore, standards should be sufficiently detailed to enable interoperability between applications but flexible enough to allow newer technologies to be adapted.
- Enforcing change in the application development field without access to proper processes aimed at mobile application development.
- Varying speed for transferring data. There is a need to further standardize wireless transmission speeds. However, the nature of mobile transmissions depends on the proximity and movement of users and devices in the context of the base stations, leading to difficulties in standardizing speed.
- Incompatibility of multimedia messaging, including SMS, e-mails, and voice messages; this leads to different weightings or levels of importance being given to varying media.
- Lack of presentation standards; these standards are crucial in enhancing the usability of mobile applications on small handheld devices. Current visual screens need not be the only mechanism to present information.

- Unified Modeling Language (UML) has hardly anything to offer in terms of user interface designs; this UI design takes a bigger challenge in handheld devices, but there are no supporting modeling and process standards that can specifically handle mobile applications development.
- Difficulty in acceptance of applications by users; reaching users and "training" them is currently happening mostly through advertisement and Web site help.
- Lack of user training and the difficulty in imparting such training to mobile users.
- Underdeveloped supporting payment structures for use by mobile Web services that can be plugged into customer-facing applications.
- High costs of applications development and customization; perhaps because of lack of training and experience in the specific mobile techniques for software implementation.
- Testing of application in real-life scenarios provides an interesting challenge for mobile applications. Those that work under simulated "test" conditions are known to have failed in real life because it is very difficult to incorporate all real-life factors in mobile tests.
- Latency in transmission of mobile data. This arises when, after sending a message, the user assumes it has been received.
- Security challenges of devices, networks, and applications when using mobile applications in practice.
- Inconsistencies and competition in the development environment (Microsoft versus Sun/Unix versus Linux) and the ongoing debate as to which application development environment is most suitable for the project.

The Mobile in Customer Relationship Management and Supply-Chain Management

The CRM strategy needs to be aligned with the mobile business strategy of the organization. A good MET approach aims at modeling and developing comprehensive customer-related functions by integrating people, process, and technologies to maximize relationships with all stakeholders. Furthermore, this CRM approach particularly facilitates interaction and relationship among customers that can result in customer groups exchanging thoughts and perceptions of products and services, as well as directing the business with what the customers would really want. Mobility helps in this interaction immensely as it enables it to happen in real-time in an m-CRM.

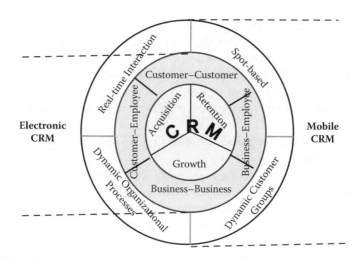

Figure 5.5   Mobile CRM (m-CRM) expands and builds on CRM and e-CRM.

Mobile customer relationship management (m-CRM) is perhaps one of the most significant areas of mobile business applications due to the personalization features of mobility that can be applied to CRM. m-CRM builds on top of e-CRM, which in turn extends and develops the traditional CRM, as shown in Figure 5.5.

Traditional customer relationship management (CRM) is concerned with three main characteristics, namely, acquisition, retention, and growth of customers. The growth of electronic business took CRM to a new dimension. This e-CRM had the main characteristics of various types of relationships: customer-to-customer (C2C), business-to-employee (B2E), business-to-business (B2B), and customer-to-employee (C2E). This concept of e-CRM facilitates the capture, integration, and distribution of data gained at the organization's Web site throughout the enterprise (Pan and Lee 2003). The goal of e-CRM systems is to improve customer service as well as provide analytical capabilities for the decision methods. This capability of e-CRM is further enhanced by making use of the unique mobile characteristics of m-CRM. These, as shown in Figure 5.5, are real-time interaction, spot-based opportunity, dynamic organizational processes, and dynamic customer group. These characteristics are now discussed in detail with the aim of providing the framework for the process dimension of MET.

Real-Time Interaction

Compared with traditional e-CRM, in which the location of the customer is fixed and dependent on a physical connection, in the case of m-CRM the interaction with the customer is dynamic and in real-time. This is so because the customer can be physically moving in real-time and still be connected to the business. Real-time interaction allows customers to interact with the business through a mobile-enabled CRM system. This offers better value than e-CRM for customers because specific problems the customers face can be solved instantaneously. The choice is for the customer to demand the specific actions required or defer such actions. For example, an SMS message is received by a customer from a mobile-enabled parking machine, indicating that the parking meter is about to run out of credit in specific minutes. The customer then has an opportunity to recharge his parking by using the mobile connectivity into the m-CRM system or move the vehicle.

Spot-Based

The customer's physical location or the specific "spot" where the customer is physically present is of relevance to the business. This knowledge of location, as discussed earlier, creates unique opportunities to dynamically combine the physical information on the presence of the customer with the significance of that customer to that location. A common example of this spot-based opportunity is when a customer walking through a shopping arcade with a mobile phone in her or his pocket, which is provided with "spot sales" on hairdressing and nail polishing. Another example is that of mobile phone users within the periphery of a shopping center who can receive an SMS, with the vendor offering 30 percent discount coupons from a burger shop provided the order is placed within the next half hour. m-CRM is geared toward creating these opportunities and then enabling the organization to serve it. These mobile-enabled business opportunities do not exist in a land-based Internet.

Dynamic Organizational Processes

Dynamic organizational processes are the business processes of an organization that change due to mobility, for example, the road service that uses mobile technology to receive information on a customer needing road assistance. The service vehicle out on the road needs to be directed to that customer's particular location. However, depending on the nature of road services required, the location and the time to provide that service is determined. Road-service providers can strategically position their service vehicle in locations where services are most likely to be needed, so that the lead time to such services is minimized. The service process then *dynamically changes,* depending on the context. Thus, for one nonmobile (land-based) process, there are multiple mobile processes that need to be modeled to provide the same service. The dynamic nature of the mobile process requires these various options be available to the business.

Dynamic Customer Group

Mobile-CRM needs to provide opportunities to dynamically create customer groups. Such groups occur in real-time as people get together for various purposes with mobile gadgets in their pockets. They can be served and marketed to at a particular time and location. Such a dynamic customer group further facilitates group marketing. Customer-group-based services provide a selected group of customers with information or transaction capabilities with a specific time window. For instance, the registered members of a frequent-flyer program form such a dynamic group, and they can be notified of a delayed flight—service required within a specific time only. Thus, this dynamic customer group exists only in that point of time before boarding the flight and only for the group of people who are taking that flight. The group and timings will change for the next flight, and so on. Another example is of a group of customers in a shopping center, who can be dynamically created by the mobile CRM as the target group of customers. These groups can be created almost daily, depending on the interests of the customers and, say, the surplus stocks in the shopping center. Prior to the availability of an m-CRM, organizations competed in their geographical areas. By contrast, the mobile business is not only reaching globally but is also dynamically changing. The m-CRM opportunities described in this section extend beyond the known advantages of CRM in the model introduced by Raisinghani and Taylor (2006).

UML and BPMN

UML for the object management group provides a standardized mechanism to model processes in addition to modeling system requirements and design. The last recognized version of UML across both research and industry communities is version 1.4.1, although in practice nowadays, version 2.0 is gaining popularity. This is so because UML 2.0 seems to have been adopted by numerous tool vendors, professionals in the industry, authors, and organizations running various certification courses. The wisdom of using modeling to enhance the quality of processes has been generally accepted in the ICT (information and communication technology) community. The need to communicate using appropriate modeling techniques among the users, business stakeholders, architects and developers, and project managers and testers has never been greater. The UML is such a de facto modeling standard that facilitates such communication in practice. It has resulted from the collaboration of numerous eminent methodologists as well as industry groups, and is supported by many CASE tools. The UML has found acceptance in projects of different types and sizes (Unhelkar 2003), as well as in a wide range of application domains, including insurance, banking, airlines, manufacturing, and telecommunications. Booch et al. (2003) have identified and described four purposes of the UML: (a) visualizing, (b) specifying, (c) constructing, and (d) documenting. These can be applied to visualize business (user) requirements, create system and database design, apply the constraints resulting from system architecture, and even model the testing aspect of a system. The modeling of business processes within mobile business benefits from the use of the UML's use cases and activity diagrams. For details on the techniques of modeling with use cases, use case diagrams, and activity diagrams, see *Practical OO*

Analysis and *Practical OO Design* (Unhelkar 2005a, 2005b). In addition to these, there is also a business process notation of ULM that can be used in modeling mobile business processes. This notation is called the Business Process Modeling Notation (BPMN; www.bpmi.org). It offers a standardized mechanism to create business process diagrams, which represent the activities of the business process and the flow controls exactly the way they are performed. The BPMN diagram is an excellent technique to create the test and validate a mobile business process model.

Mobile Supply-Chain Management (SCM)

Two of the most significant external transactive processes in an enterprise are that of CRM and SCM (supply-chain management). These transactive processes are summarized in Figure 5.6.

CRM can be understood as "an enterprise approach to understanding and influencing customer behavior through meaningful communications to improve customer acquisition, customer retention, customer loyalty, and customer profitability." The fundamentals of the CRM function in an organization are to provide global customer satisfaction. The CRM strategy needs to be aligned with the mobile business strategy of the organization. A good MET approach will aim at modeling and developing comprehensive customer-related functions by integrating people, process, and technology to maximize the relationship with all customers. The basic principles of CRM strategy may involve aligning the organization around customers, sharing information across the entire business, leveraging data from disparate sources to better understand the customers and anticipate their needs, and maximizing customer profitability.

Sales mobile processes include multichannel selling system that might include the direct/automatic delivery of products or services to the customers. The integration

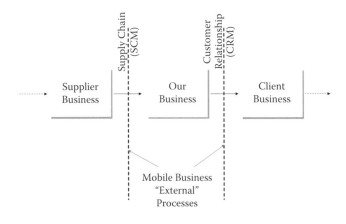

Figure 5.6   CRM, SCM, and their interface with "our" mobile business.

of customer requirements into product channels, and then servicing those requirements, are achieved by collaboration and coordination of mobile networks and applications. Similarly, mobile marketing includes utilizing the mobile technologies for an organization's marketing process, which requires coordination and integration of supporting mobile networks, contents, and marketing applications. Customer mobile processes also integrate customer support centers by converging all customer contact points and necessary services at a single point. Customer support can be a help desk, a call center, or an online support via mobile Internet e-mail or SMS. This support center aims to provide services and support to customers and suppliers who are making use of the SCM system. SCM integrates a number of business processes such as procurement, logistics, production, transportation, warehousing, delivery, and distribution. An effective mobile SCM system not only applies mobility to the aforementioned business processes but also influences, and is influenced by, the use of mobility by their suppliers, retailers, distributors, and consumers to form a supply chain network. Mobility in the supply chain network strategy is an essential factor that reduces costs in material purchases, storage and logistics requirements, and product transportation and distribution processes influencing their business as well as that of their suppliers. Collaboration with suppliers requires sharing of information in a supply chain network, which, in turn, requires the parties to trust each other. Information sharing among all parties in the global supply chain network can be implemented through a mobile Internet that may be managed by either of the involved parties. Based on these various benefits that can be availed through the adoption of mobile SCM technology applications, organizations need a roadmap to implement these technologies in their various business functions and subsequently integrate these into a seamless mobile infrastructure.

Modeling in MET

This section describes what modeling entails, its need in MET, and its advantages and limitations. The aim of MET is to build a mobile enterprise that is flexible and that helps it provide greater value to its customers. This requirement of the mobile enterprise is also that it is able to handle rapidly changing technology that is going to affect it in various ways that cannot be fully comprehended at this stage. Furthermore, because of the significant sociological role that mobility plays in society, it is important to create a process model that also reflects this sociological functioning of the organization.

Modeling serves many purposes in the real world. A model is necessarily incomplete as it cannot incorporate every possible real-life situation. However, modeling is still helpful in understanding reality. Thus, one purpose of modeling a MET is to give us a good idea of what the current real enterprise is. For example, the model of an enterprise relevant to an accountant contains the profit-and-loss accounts and the balance sheets, whereas that of the personnel department is contained in the organizational chart and the hierarchy.

> The purpose of modeling in MET is to provide reengineered and creative solutions by applying mobility even to their routine applications so that they result in a user-focused and unified solution. Models play a tremendously creative role in MET as they help clarify the existing enterprise as well as model the desired mobile enterprise. Process models provide different views on the same reality, enable creation of layers, and eliminate unnecessary details for a specific process.

A good model usually has different views, depending on the need of the user. Thus, a model enables viewing of the same reality from different angles, as also from different levels. When modeling an enterprise, it is particularly important that the models that are created serve the specific purpose of users of that model who are placed at different levels within the organization. There is a need for the model to take the same input and show it in different ways. For example, the accountant's view of accounting information is different from that of the general manager. Therefore, modeling is required to provide a representation of the process *from the viewer's perspective.*

A mobile enterprise depends on its business process. Therefore, to model such an enterprise, it is also essential to model its processes. At the software applications level, modeling also helps in making sense out of the large amount of data and the databases in which the data resides. Modeling further enables analyses of the data and converts it into information. One of the main purposes of modeling is to further take us from an information age to a knowledge age. The tools and techniques of semantic modeling become useful by providing meaning to the data that is stored in the organization's databases. Thus, we see that modeling is a tool that allows us to understand the reality and also view it in many different ways.

The initial attempt at modeling an enterprise is to represent it as it exists now. However, that is not the only purpose of modeling the enterprise and its systems. We also aim to ensure that this meaning or information is a true and creative cause for new and reengineered business processes. Modeling not only provides meaning to the reality that exists but it becomes a *creative cause* for a new and, as yet, nonexistent reality. For example, it is not enough for a model of a branch reconciliation process to show us how that process is carried out now. A model should also help us create a new process that would satisfy the user (in this example the teller and the branch manager) in a way that takes advantage of mobile technology and reduces the hierarchy in performing the job.

The purpose of modeling in the MET exercise is to provide reengineered and creative solutions by applying mobility to even their routine applications such as payroll and accounting so that they result in a user-focused solution. Furthermore, although the prime output of the business systems is their information, modeling helps in many systems that primarily do not deal with data processing. Typical examples are process control systems for power plants or patient monitoring systems in hospitals. The primary purpose of these systems is not the *information* they impart, but the *process* they perform. Modeling can be extremely creative and economical in these systems. The mobile technology used in, say, a process-control system is a means rather than the end in itself. Specific ways, in which modeling serves the purpose of understanding the mobile business and creating new and reengineering mobile business processes, are as follows:

- Process models eliminate all irrelevant matters from consideration. A process model is an abstract representation of the reality. The modeler has a choice of removing things that are not relevant to the purpose for which the model is built. For example, a model of a hospital administration system that provides information to the administrative staff on their mobile gadgets need not present the diagnosis details of a patient on the mobile device.
- Process models enable the modeler to concentrate on the goals by representing the parts of a system or company that are relevant to the purpose for which the model is being created. For example, in discussing payment methods in a mobile application, the modeler can create multiple ways of understanding the same method. The model may not concern itself with other parts of the system that do not deal with payment methods.
- Process models provide a cheap alternative to understanding potential new creations. For example, it is cheaper to build the model of a house and explore its limitations or make changes to it rather than building a new house and then making changes to it. This is equally true of mobile applications and processes, wherein changes at later stages to an implemented process can cost many times that of a change early in the software's life.
- Process models help where we don't have previous experience in handling the situations, as is likely to be the case with mobile processes.
- Process models enhance quality and enable reuse, and provide the end user with a means of giving input before the final mobile process to make sure the product is independent. A model is a means of involving the end user or the sponsor of the product in its creation at an early stage of its life cycle.

Despite its advantages, the use of a process model to model a business process has its own limitations. Awareness of these limitations enables the process models to make best use of the modeling tools, and some of the specific limitations and caveats of modeling in the context of mobile business processes are

- A mobile process model is an abstraction of the reality. Therefore, it does not provide the complete picture of the actual and dynamic situation. A mobile process model is thus subject to the interpretation of the observer, and the process modeler should explicitly state the caveats.

- Unless a model is dynamic, it does not provide the feel for timings. Therefore, process models should provide a feel of the changing reality. A static mobile process model is not able to convey the right meaning to the user.
- The user of the model should be aware of the notations and language used to express the model. Nonstandardized notations and processes can render a model useless.
- A mobile process model may be created for a specific situation. Once the situation has changed, the model may no longer be relevant.

Mobile Business Processes

The discussion thus far provides an understanding of the mobile process landscape. We now consider the specific factors (listed in Table 5.1) that drive this process dimension of MET and analyze them for the MET framework.

Business-to-Consumer (B2C)

Mobile business processes need to be modeled for customers, keeping their context in mind. This context was discussed earlier as a mechanism to understand the relevance of the product or service to the mobile customer. B2C interactions are popular processes even in the electronic era, wherein they represented the interaction between a consumer sitting across an Internet terminal and the business server. B2C business processes deal with information and transaction between the organization and the individual customer. There is greater opportunity for B2C processes to be "mobilized" as the customer remains the personalized owner of the mobile gadget at one end of the process.

Business-to-Business (B2B)

Business-to-business interactions occur between two business entities using a combination of physical, Internet, and wireless connectivity. The land-based Internet connectivity is more prevalent for B2B transactions than wireless connections. This is so because B2B transactions are usually between predefined businesses that have established contacts using either Internet connections or a virtual private network (VPN). When two business applications residing on two separate application servers are communicating with each other, they are not mobile. However, these B2B transactions can benefit by wireless connections such as provided by WiMax. Mobile applications also enable the organization to access external mobile data resources such as the location and status of a shipment or a courier position. Mobile distribution systems especially help in the case of time-sensitive goods and provide many possibilities to improve the efficiency of inventories and supplies.

Government-to-Individual (G2I)

Individuals can easily relate to government through mobility because of the personalized nature of mobile gadgets. This personalized, individualized relationship can open up opportunities for transactions such as mobile voting and referendum, mobile tax enquiries, on-the-spot queries on legality of finance transactions, and so on. Businesses can also relate to government through mobility as it provides avenues to report to government, as well as comply with government rules and regulations using mobility.

Collaborative (Many-to-Many, M2M)

Mobile collaborative processes are between a group of organizations that get together using mobile connectivity tools and mobile Web services to provide service to users. The various tiers or levels of wireless connectivity provide opportunities for collaborations not only among businesses but also between individuals. The promise for collaborations between businesses is the ability of one business to pass on an opportunity that it cannot fulfill (because of, say, lack of access to users) to another business using mobile Web services. Collaborative use of mobility by business requires mobile business applications to interface or even integrate with each other. Complete and seamless integration of mobile business application leads to pervasiveness of mobile business. Gupta and Moitra (2004) characterize pervasive computing as saturating an environment *with computing and communication capability, yet having those devices integrated into the environment such that they "disappear."* Wireless connectivity provides an enormous opportunity for pervasive computing. However, to achieve that pervasiveness, mobile applications need to be driven by their capabilities to enhance internal and external integration. Internal business processes can be integrated through wireless local and personal area networks. External collaboration is achieved by mobile applications using wireless wide area networks (WWAN) to convey relevant information from collaborating parties such as customers, retailers, and distributors. This collaboration between mobile applications results from the use of Web services particularly when a large organization deals with a number of smaller-size businesses. Having thus discussed the various important factors in mobile business processes, we now analyze the importance of those factors, resulting from our research survey.

Figure 5.7 shows the importance of the business processes in the process dimension of driving MET. There are four factors studied for their importance that are included in this section: business-to-consumer (B2C), business-to-business (B2B), government-to-individual (G2I), and collaborative (many-to-many).

The left-hand-side column in Figure 5.7 displays the result of the survey in the area of B2C. There are 46 percent of the respondents who think the B2C factor is most important, and 36 percent think it is more important. A total of 82 percent think the B2C is the more to most important factor in the business process

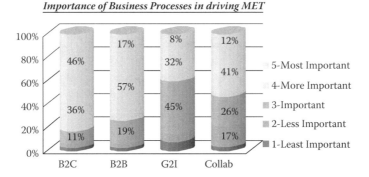

Figure 5.7   Analysis of the importance of the business process factor in process dimension of MET.

dimension of MET. Only 3 percent think this factor should belong to the least important level.

The second left-hand-side column displays the result of the survey in the area of B2B. A total of 17 percent of the respondents think the B2B factor is most important, and 57 percent think it is more important. A total of 74 percent think the B2B is the more to most important factor in the business process dimension of MET. There is only 3 percent who think this factor is least important.

The second right-hand-side column displays the result of survey in the area of G2I. There are 8 percent who think G2I is most important, and 32 percent think it is more important. A total of 40 percent think G2I is the more to most important factor in the process dimension of MET. Most participants (45 percent) believe that this is the important factor, whereas only 8 percent think that it is the least important factor.

The right-hand-side column displays the result of the survey in the area of many-to-many factors. There are 12 percent who think collaborative is the most important factor, and 41 percent think it is more important. A total of 53 percent think it is the more to most important factor in the process dimension of MET. Only 4 percent think it is least important. These figures indicate that the majority of the participants through these process factors are more to most important in MET.

Modeling and Reengineering Mobile Processes

Reasons for Modeling a Mobile Process

Formal modeling of business processes is vital for the success of a mobile enterprise. Business process models provide the "prototype" of the way the business will be used by its customers and partners. There is a need to leverage the opportunity to reengineer the mobile business in a way that will keep it flexible and relevant to mobile technologies.

The process model for the various business processes is relevant to understanding the requirements of the users. Such a model also enables the mobile enterprise to handle the rapid changes in its environment. Modeling of mobile business processes can help a mobile enterprise in the following ways:

■ Enable the mobile enterprise to be as flexible as possible. This would mean that the enterprise is able to handle different types of requirements, which are also changing within its domain, comfortably.
■ Enable the mobile business to move away from a hierarchical organization structure and base itself on a customer-centered model of business.
■ Enable proper understanding of the boundaries between the organization and society by modeling the way the user "uses" the organization. This understanding will enable the organization to influence, and be influenced by, society in a positive way.
■ Enabling the mobile business to absorb rapid changes in the external technical environment. Process modeling enables the organization to preempt and anticipate technological changes.
■ The process model, as against the hierarchical structure model, allows the organization to respond to changes in the external environment in a strategic manner. Instead of large-scale movement of personnel and inventories, and large changes to production schedules, the responses can be in small parts and focused only on the element of the process needing change.
■ Be able to adapt to the technical changes coming from within the organization, such as changes to the method of work.
■ Processes should be fine granular, which also means the supporting systems and modules should be smaller in size. This will enable the organization to manage itself in a much better way as it can change its internal processes quickly if the external processes change, based on its finer granularity.

These characteristics of a process-based enterprise are helpful in understanding the expectations from a mobile enterprise. A process-based enterprise has an internal structure that is not rigid or hierarchical. Instead, mobile enterprises are made up of processes that are flexible enough to absorb large changes from both inside and outside the organization. Furthermore, dynamic and distributed processes also have the characteristics of fuzziness, which render the changes within an organization imperceptible from outside.

Mobile processes provide maximum value when they are not used merely in a supporting or automating role within the existing business processes. Mobile technologies need to be incorporated in new and existing business to ensure that users receive manyfold benefits as against incremental value. These benefits occur with the convergence of processes within these applications. However, MET encourages businesses to rethink radically—not just for a faster or cheaper way of conducting the same business processes using mobile technologies from the point of view of providing "value" to the user. Traditional business applications such as payroll, HR, accounts, general ledger, and inventory need to be reexamined from this mobile process viewpoint.

Internal and external business process integration is an extremely important driver in the transition to mobile business. Internal integration is required particularly of operative mobile business. External integration is helpful with supply chain partners and customers. Availability of mobile Internet and the connectivity accorded by it allow the newer mobile applications to integrate both internal and external processes. Voice communication capabilities of mobile phones on cellular networks as well as the push-to-talk (P2T) features of local wireless devices allow users to effortlessly connect to one another. Convergence of processes that bring together otherwise unrelated parts of information are of particular interest here. Mobile business processes need to be considered from three viewpoints: modeling new business processes with mobility, reengineering existing processes, and removing redundant processes. The known and standard process modeling techniques such as those using UML and BPMN are very valuable here. The importance of modeling techniques in engineering mobile processes requires a separate discussion, as undertaken later in this chapter.

A Mobile Process-Based View

A process-based mobile enterprise is able to cut across its own hierarchy and reach the customer directly on her or his own personalized device. Mobility is a key enabler of processes within an organization as it is a unique way to deliver services to a specific user who is not really interested in the way in which the enterprise is internally structured.

The essential nature of a process model is that it cuts across the hierarchy of a traditional organizational unit and reaches the customer directly on his or her personal device. The process is made up of a collection of activities that take one or more kinds of input and create an output that is of "value" to the customer. Thus, a mobile process model deals with the basic purpose of the organization—to serve the customer. This is achieved by modeling the organization based on the customer's need rather than around the hierarchy of organizational departments and its people.

Thus, in an insurance company, instead of organizing the departments in a hierarchy, they are organized around the basic process of "claims: from application to settlement." The software systems and people within the departments support this basic process. Thus, even if the departments exist, they and all the people

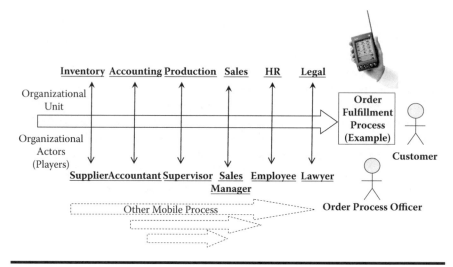

Figure 5.8 A process cuts across hierarchical departments and players in an organization.

within them are organized around the process that supports the business. When a customer makes a claim, he is not concerned with the hierarchies and particular responsibilities of each department. What concerns the customer is the claim and its status. In a process-based organization, when the customer rings to inquire about the claim, it is handled by the process, which may be assigned to a person. Thus, answers to all questions that relate to the claim as well as its status are known through a single process, rather than through four departments.

Figure 5.8 shows another example of a process that cuts across multiple business hierarchical units. The company has a variety of products and services, one of which deals with placement of an order for a product. In a traditional organization, the work is organized in separate departments, each dealing with one aspect of the order. These departments, as shown in Figure 5.8, are the inventory, accounting, production, sales, HR, and legal. Each of these departments is hierarchically organized, together with the organizational actors. Traditionally, these actors have a myopic view of the organization—only their own departments. Therefore, when an order is received from the customer, each department becomes busy with its own responsibilities. Such an order fulfillment process is fraught with limitations. For example, if the customer rings to find out the status of his or her order, the phone call would have to be directed to the departments before the status of the order is ascertained. Each of the departments has a specific job to do, and has its own specific agenda and a budget to support that agenda. Occasionally, the agenda of the separate and hierarchically organized departments can clash, and so would the career aspirations of those who head the departments. The job of the departmental heads is restricted to managing the coordination within the department. This organizational structure is not satisfactory from the customer's viewpoint, as well as from that of the employees of the company. Furthermore, being a coarse granular and centralized organization, it has less opportunity to maneuver in response to external crises. For instance, when the customer is on the move and has a need for rapidly changing order requirements, the rigid hierarchical framework prevents options such as combining orders, changing orders based on locations, and rerouting of orders. Modeling the organization based on mobile processes means cutting across the departmental hierarchies of inventory, accounting, production, sales, HR, and legal to arrive at the common view and provide service to the customer.

Creating New Mobile Processes

Business engineering has been referred to by Jacobson et al. as "burying the old ways of thinking and replacing them with a new approach." New mobile business processes need to be modeled from scratch for the mobile organization. The goals of the process in terms of value to customer or employee are documented at the outset. Mobility is considered across the entire process to see where it adds value. Note that although the processes are new, the people involved in the previous processes, both customers and employees, are still most likely the existing employees. The knowledge and expertise of these users needs to be capitalized in modeling new mobile business processes. This expertise of existing process users is a creative cause for a totally new type of mobile business process that did not exist earlier in the enterprise. This is so because existing users are most likely to be interested in the goals of the process rather than activities within the process. Design of new mobile business processes that emerge because of mobile technologies is considered as forward engineering.

Reengineering Existing Processes

Current Internet-based processes need to be reengineered and merged with the new mobile processes. Some are a combination of "e" and "m," whereas others are purely mobile. Reengineering for mobile business has the challenge of dealing with existing business processes. These are obviously serving some purpose in the business. "Tagging" mobile devices at the end of these processes, as discussed earlier, is an easy but unattractive and mostly unproductive solution for organizations undergoing MET. However, getting rid of the existing processes and replacing them with totally new ones is not easy, especially if the business itself is not new but an existing one. A certain level of formal integration or merger of existing processes are required with the new mobile processes or elements of mobility in existing processes.

Removing Redundant Existing Processes

Formal incorporation of mobility in some business processes will render some other physical and Internet processes redundant. Formal modeling of enterprise-wide processes will highlight these redundant "e" processes. For example, if a bank

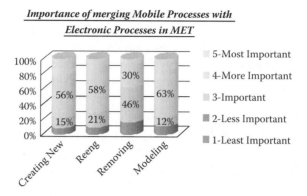

Figure 5.9 shows the importance of merging mobile processes with electronic. The chart shows "Importance of merging Mobile Processes with Electronic Processes in MET" with categories Creating New (56%, 15%), Reeng (58%, 21%), Removing (30%, 46%), Modeling (63%, 12%), and legend 5-Most Important, 4-More Important, 3-Important, 2-Less Important, 1-Least Important.

Figure 5.9 Analysis of modeling and reengineering of mobile processes based on the process drives in MET.

introduces the ability to check account balances through mobile gadgets, then gradually the need to check balances by walking up to a physical bank will not be there. Similarly, once the mobile-based ticketing system for say, a sports event, has matured, the existing paper-based ticketing processes would be redundant.

Figure 5.9 shows the importance of merging mobile processes with electronic ones in the process dimension of MET. There are four factors included in this section: creating new mobile processes, reengineering existing "e" with mobile processes, removing redundant "e" processes, and modeling of mobile business processes.

The left-hand-side column displays the result of the survey in the area of creating new mobile processes. A total of 56 percent of the respondents think that creating new mobile processes is more important, and 21 percent think it is most important. Thus, a total of 77 percent think that creating new mobile processes is the more to most important factor in the process dimension of MET. Only 3 percent think it is least important. This result indicates the phenomenal importance of creating new and relevant mobile business processes for the transitioning enterprise. Modeling, as discussed earlier in this chapter, plays a major role in the creation of relevant mobile processes.

The second left-hand-side column displays the result of the survey in the area of reengineering the existing "e" with mobile processes factors. There are 58 percent of respondents who think reengineering the existing "e" with mobile processes is more important, and 12 percent think it is most important. A total of 70 percent think reengineering the existing "e" with mobile processes is the more to most important factor in the process dimension of MET. Only 3 percent think it is least important. This result, similar to the previous one, again underscores the importance of modeling the existing business process. One can further ascertain that the transitioning business should give importance to the reengineering of existing electronic processes with mobility, and not just focus on new mobile processes.

The second right-hand-side column displays the result of the survey in the area of removing redundant "e" processes factors. There are 7 percent who think removing redundant "e" processes is most important, 30 percent think it belongs to the more important level, and 46 percent (most participants) think it is important. Thus, a total of 76 percent think removing redundant "e" processes is the important to more important factor in the process dimension of MET. There are 8 percent who think it is the least important factor. The survey results here form a standard bell curve, highlighting the importance of formal removal of redundant processes.

The right-hand-side column displays the result of the survey in the area of modeling of mobile business processes factors. There are 14 percent who think modeling of mobile business processes is most important, and 63 percent think it is more important. A total of 77 percent think modeling of mobile business processes is the more to most important factor in the process dimension of MET. There is only 1 percent who think it is the least important factor. Thus, the survey results ratify the significance of modeling of processes as discussed earlier in this chapter.

Quality of Service

Quality of service (QoS) is the expectation of the customer and the fulfillment of service from a mobile business. End-user sensitivity and perception are the most significant factors in QoS. There are a number of factors affecting QoS in mobile applications. Four specific factors discussed here are timing, coverage, security, and accuracy. These QoS factors are, in turn, affected by the rapidity of movements of the users, the urgency, and the load on the network in terms of how busy the wireless is. Congestion in the network clearly depends on the usage, which varies at different times of the day. As expected, during business hours the network load on the Internet service provider is heavy. Thus, each of these QoS factors needs to be balanced by cost when it comes to the perception of QoS by users.

Real-Time Response When Compared with Costs

The QoS of response depends on the time taken by the business system to respond to user requests. The immediacy of responses is based on network capacity and load at that point of time. There is a need to balance the timeliness of response with the costs associated with it. Business, as well as system architecture, needs to carefully distribute the load to achieve higher response times.

Coverage When Compared with Costs

The quality of mobile business applications depends on how well they cover the physical range for users. Coverage can vary from local wireless network coverage for home or office to long-distance cellular coverage. The wider the coverage required, the greater is the challenge to the business in terms of QoS.

Coverage When Compared with Security

Coverage and security requires a balancing act from the service provider. As seen earlier, the wider the coverage, the greater is the perceived QoS by the user. However, the wider the coverage, the greater also is the challenge in providing security. Wider coverage can be mixed in terms of informative service, which requires less security than transactive usage. QoS has a vital role in providing service, especially secure service.

Accuracy When Compared with Costs

More accuracy, including, particularly, more value in terms of video transmission, is an important part of QoS. In ascertaining the accuracy of mobile transmissions, there is a need to consider not only the strengths and bandwidths of the transmission signals but also the need to face the associated challenges of interferences due to weak signals, the speed and mobility of the receiver, and the potential for the user's signals crisscrossing each other due to transmission and reception of multiple mobile signals simultaneously.

Costs, coverage, accuracy, and timeliness of response together form the QoS factor. The specific QoS is determined by a balance of these factors, and its perception can change depending on the location and need of the user.

Figure 5.10 shows the importance of the QoS factor in the process dimension of driving MET. There are four factors included in this section: real-time response when compared with costs, coverage when compared with costs, coverage when compared with security, and accuracy when compared with costs factors.

The result of the survey in the importance of accuracy when compared with costs factors in process dimension, as appearing at the top of this Figure 5.10, indicates that 40 percent of the participants in the survey think that the accuracy when compared with costs factor is most important and 24 percent think they are more important. A total of 64 percent think the accuracy factor is more to most important. Only 7 percent think of the accuracy when compared with costs factors as least important factor in the process dimension of MET.

The importance of coverage, in the result of the survey, when compared with security factors in the process dimension, which appears at the second from the top of Figure 5.10, indicates that 28 percent of the participants think that coverage is the most important, and 38 percent think it is more important. A total of 66 percent think the security factor is more to most important. Only less than 4 percent think that coverage is the least important factor in the process dimension of MET.

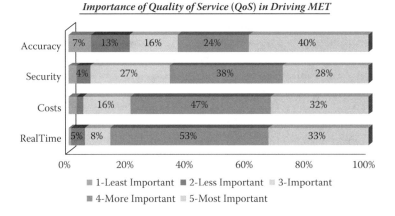

Importance of Quality of Service (QoS) in Driving MET

Figure 5.10 legend:
■ 1-Least Important ■ 2-Less Important ■ 3-Important
■ 4-More Important ■ 5-Most Important

Figure 5.10 Analysis of the quality-of-service (QoS) factors in the process dimension of MET.

The importance of coverage, when compared with costs factors in the process dimension in the result of the survey, which appears second from the bottom of Figure 5.10, indicates that 32 percent of the participants think that it is most important, and 47 percent think it is more important. A total of 79 percent think the costs factor is more to most important. Only less than 4 percent think of coverage as the least important factor in the process dimension of MET.

The importance of real-time response in the result of the survey, when compared with costs factors in the process dimension, which appears at the bottom of Figure 5.10, indicates that 33 percent of the participants in the survey think that the real-time factor is most important, and 53 percent think it is more important. A total of 86 percent think real-time response is more to most important. Only less than 2 percent think it is the least important factor in the process dimension of MET.

Mobile Applications and Financial Aspects

Mobile application categories were discussed earlier in this chapter. One of their important contributions to the mobile business is enhancement of the overall financial transactions and reporting capabilities of the business. Thus, both the customer and the business tend to benefit by the use of mobile applications.

Applications Supporting Mobile Usage

Mobile applications are very handy in helping users manage their own mobile accounts. For example, managing the credit on the account, time-limiting the calls, and payment of the mobile phone bill can all be integrated and presented to the user on the mobile device itself. Further, with the help of service providers—such as an online payment-processing company founded in 1999 (Paypal 1999)—cost-effective payment methods can be implemented by using the mobile Internet. Paypal is used heavily for eBay auction clearance, enabling private sales of goods and services, and facilitation of community payment. Thus, the experience of the customer and the business in dealing with each other is changing rapidly and growing more with mobility. Prepaid, postpaid, timed contracts, limited access, etc., are the various ways in which financial opportunities support the mobile user. For example, payment of prepaid mobile SIM makes it easier for global travelers to buy these cards locally, use them for a short period of time, and then dispose of them. Mobility also enhances new payment methods that are user-friendly, flexible, and secure. For example, using a mobile device as an electronic wireless wallet is an important facilitator of overall growth in the transactive use of the mobile business. Such a mobile device as a means of payment is also likely to have an effect on decision making of the customer and increases the selling opportunities for goods and services.

Financial Transactions Using Mobile Gadgets

Mobile gadgets are now appearing in the market that are capable of performing financial transactions. These financial transactions require not only the capabilities of the device but also the underlying infrastructure, applications, and content to work in synergy to provide users with the capabilities to conduct financial transactions. As this gets written (early 2008), two Australian banks are reported to have enabled financial transaction capabilities using mobile devices (Moses 2008). The National Australia Bank (NAB) and the Australia–NewZealand (ANZ) bank announced that they now have business processes that enable customers to check balances, view mini statements, and transfer funds between their accounts via SMS. The ANZ bank is also enabling users to pay bills and transfer money to third parties using a special mobile phone application. A report released by Juniper Research in February 2008 predicts revolution in the financial services sector with an expectation of 612 million mobile phone users employing these types of financial applications, resulting in $587 billion worth of financial transactions by 2011. Customer privacy and security issues discussed in this book also come into play in these banking services transitions. For example, security in the aforementioned financial applications ensures that none of the customer details are saved on the phone. Instead, the phone number itself is preregistered by the bank and, in case of loss of the phone, the banking service is switched off as soon as the SIM card is deactivated.

Service and Support for Mobile Usage

Mobile users depend on mobile devices to extend where their crucial business transactions or even their life (in case of emergency situation) depends on the device.

Therefore, there is a great need to have the device working all the time and under all conditions. Malfunctioning mobile devices need immediate on-the-spot service and support. It is not an uncommon sight to see public places such as airports and hotels having a suite of "chargers"—made up of free sockets belonging to different mobile device manufacturers such as Nokia and LG—available for users to recharge their devices. Services and support are not merely restricted to fixing devices and recharging batteries. Mobile businesses in the background can provide a range of support services such as language translations, help in "how to use" a certain feature of the device, and so on.

Transparency in Mobile Charges (Call Costs)

Transparency in mobile business means that users are made aware of the costs associated in transacting with the business. Users will be accessing the mobile business through a combination of content providers, service providers, and network providers. These various business collaborations have the potential for creating a maze of charges that may not be clear to the consumer. Further, the variations in contracts and the way in which these contracts between the customer and the business allow the business (particularly the network operator) to charge the customer are the focus of many disputes. Therefore, genuine efforts are also required to ensure that the mobile business adheres to and uses a transparent and proper billing system for its services. Keeping in view that the services are available universally and under heterogeneous systems, proper tracking of mobile usage by the customer can become a real challenge. However, this transparency factor is vital to apportion correct changes across all collaborating businesses and, at the same time, keep the faith of the customer in the mobile business.

Support for Lost/Stolen Mobile Gadgets

The personalized and miniature nature of mobile gadgets places an additional responsibility on the mobile business to ensure support for mobile users. This support includes timely help in handling the common scenario of lost and stolen mobile gadgets. It means locking up of lost phones to prevent their abuse. Occasionally, phones and SIM need to be unlocked to enable their use over other networks.

Developing Mobile Applications

The cost and complexities of developing mobile applications was discussed earlier in this chapter. These costs play an important role in the MET process. The costs associated with the development of mobile applications involves those of analyzing and modeling them, implementing the models, and testing and deploying them. These costs come into play in MET even when the business is implementing an "off-the-shelf" package. The influence of both time and budget factors on mobile application development and customization needs to be factored in the project plan for transition. Mobile technology applications need to be modularized, service-oriented, transportable across platforms, and secured. These requirements may involve the application development team to interact with many other parties, including third-party developers of components, content managers, and network service providers.

Financial Management of Mobile Business Processes

Financial management of an organization and its business processes is enhanced by the use of mobility due to the real-time nature of mobility. As seen earlier, mobility is incorporated in supply chain applications that help the business ascertain its costs, inventories, and current financial information as a part of ongoing business activities, rather than at the end of the day or an accounting period. Technologies such as GPS, telemetry, and RFID can feed real-time data to static tethered information systems. Further, by streamlining the order-to-cash process, mobile technologies can reduce the complexity in the overall supply chain execution (Kalakota et al. 2003). External customer processes also benefit by astute financial management as they help in providing transparency of processes to the management as well as the customer. Mobile businesses are able to use the information obtained by tracking their business customers and their movement, which can provide the management with important financial data that can be used to enhance profits.

> Transitioning businesses need to invest in mobile financial applications that provide users with transparency in terms of their interactions with the business. Furthermore, mobile devices that deal with financial transactions present high risks if they are lost or stolen. Provision for support needs to be made for these devices upfront in MET.

Analysis of the Financial Factor

Figure 5.11 shows the importance of the financial aspect of a business influencing MET. There are six factors included in this section: applications supporting mobile usage (e.g., bill payments), financial transactions using mobile gadgets, service and support for mobile usage, transparency in mobile charges (call costs), support for lost/stolen mobile gadgets, and costs of developing mobile applications factors in the process dimension of MET.

The result of the survey regarding the importance of the costs of developing mobile applications factors in the process dimension, which appears at the top of Figure 5.11, indicates that 44 percent of the participants in the survey think that

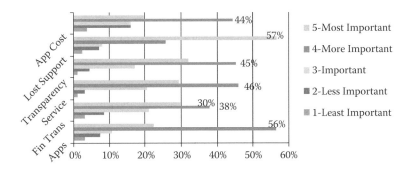

Figure 5.11   Analysis of the financial factors in the process dimension of MET.

the cost factor is more important, and 20 percent think it is most important. A total of 64 percent of participants think this factor is most to more important. Compared to that, 4 percent of participants think that it is least important. Thus, the costs of mobile application and development are significant in the minds of the participants and need to be considered by MET.

Regarding the importance of support for lost/stolen mobile gadget factors in the process dimension, which appears at the second from the top of Figure 5.11, indicates that 57 percent of the participants in the survey think that the support factor is most important, and 26 percent consider this more important, leading to a total of 83 percent thinking that it is crucial to the success of MET. Only 2 percent think it is the least important factor.

Regarding the importance of transparency in mobile charges (call costs) factors in the process dimension, which appears third from the top of Figure 5.11, indicates that 45 percent of the participants in the survey think that the factor is more important, and 32 percent think it is most important. A total of 77 percent think it is more to most important. Compared to that, only 1 percent think it is the least important factor.

Regarding the importance of service and support for mobile usage factors in the process dimension, which appears fourth from the top of Figure 5.11, indicates that 46 percent of the participants in the survey think it is more important, and 29 percent think it is most important. A total of 75 percent think this factor is more to most important. Compared to that, only 1 percent think it is the least important factor.

Regarding the importance of financial transactions using mobile gadgets factors in the process dimension, which appears second from the bottom of Figure 5.11, 30 percent of the participants think it is most important, and 38 percent think it is more important. A total of 68 percent think it is the more to most important in process dimension of MET. Only 3 percent think it is the least important factor.

Finally, the result of the survey regarding the importance of applications supporting mobile usage factor in the process dimension, which appears at the bottom of Figure 5.11, indicates that 56 percent of the participants think it is more important, and 22 percent think it is most important. A total is 78 percent think it is more to most important. Only 3 percent think it is the least important factor.

Analysis of the Sequencing of Drivers in the Process Dimension

Figure 5.12 shows the relative importance, of sequencing the process drivers in the MET framework. A total of 20.4 percent of the respondents indicated that creation of mobile business processes should be the primary driver within the overall technical drivers of MET, whereas 19.1 percent said that it is reengineering for mobile processes that need to be considered first. They are the first and second important factors, respectively, in the process dimension of MET by the result of the survey. Additionally, 17.6 percent of the participants think the cost is the most important factor to be considered first, and 16.3 percent think they will consider QoS first. There are 15.8 percent of the participants thinking that the mobile collaboration factor needs to be considered first. However, only 10.8 percent think that modeling "m" process specifications should be the most important factor to influence MET, which is the least percentage of people.

Figure 5.13 describes the overall MET framework from a process dimension viewpoint. The sequences of the process drivers in this figure are based on the previous analysis of these factors. The first of these as shown in Figure 5.13—the identification of mobile business processes and their modeling—are the most immediate factors that influence the process dimension in MET. Business managers as well as customers are involved in this effort. Reengineering of mobile processes is a logical extension of the modeling of processes. However, when it comes to modeling mobile collaborations, the exercise deals with processes that transcend multiple organizational boundaries. This activity is thus concerned with the important issues in providing QoS to mobile users. Governments and other regulatory bodies can be involved in ensuring that QoS is successfully provided to the transitioning business.

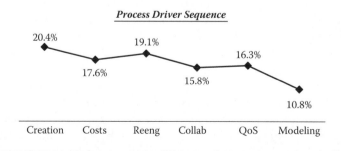

Figure 5.12 Analysis of the sequencing of drivers in the process dimension of MET.

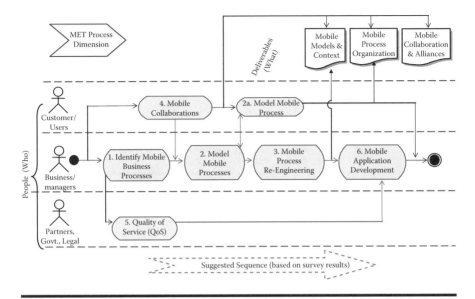

Figure 5.13   Mobile transition framework (process dimension).

Business Process Transitions

The increasingly complex nature of mobile business processes is reflected in the m-informative, m-transactive, m-operative, and m-collaborative usage of mobility by business. This step-wise transition of mobile processes reduces the transition risks. Informative usage of mobility is the least risky adoption of mobility in business processes. Collaborative usage is the most complex usage as it enables collaborations between businesses as well as between users. Collaborative usage of mobility employs mobile web services (MWSs).

The transition of mobile business processes evolve from informative to transactive to operative, and finally collaborative, processes. As mentioned earlier, process modeling can make use of the activity diagram of the UML or BPMN. Such modeling can handle the increasingly complex nature of the mobile business, as shown in Figure 5.14.

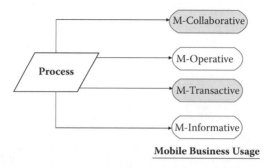

Figure 5.14 Mapping process dimension to mobile business usage.

Process–Informative

Informative mobile processes make greater use of "push" rather than "pull" technologies. The activities in informative process models are usually simple and sequential. However, care should be taken to ensure that the process to provide information to users should be modeled in such as way as to be least intrusive to them. This push model implies that the process is mostly "unidirectional," that is, going from the business to the customer or user. The informative processes are modeled to provide the most effective information to the user with minimum security requirements. Therefore, the advertisement processes are a prime example of such informative processes.

Process–Transactive

The transactive aspect of mobile processes deals with the external aspect of the business. These external processes that transverse organizational boundaries particularly need careful modeling. The modeling of mobile business processes becomes challenging and interesting as mobile business transactions depend on the context or location of mobile users. Security (multiparty authentication) also needs to come into the process. Business rules need to be incorporated in these transactive processes, which are usually the mobile commerce transactions conducted across the organizational boundary.

The external mobile business processes model the communication channels between the business and external entities such as customers, suppliers, and competitors. Incorporation of these external communication channels in the mobile transition strategy enables the business to widen its scope and, at the same time, has an effect on the structure of the organization.

Process–Operative

Mobile applications operating through customer portals provide customers with an instantaneous and unified view of the progress of their orders and services. This timely level of informative service results in higher customer satisfaction levels and, in turn, improves the organization's ability to attract and retain customers. Furthermore, the ability to capture customer transactions and preferences online provides the organization with the opportunity to track customer behavior, and thereby to customize products and services to cater to that behavior.

Operational usage of mobility also needs to be modeled as a workflow. This is so because workflow automation and inventory statistics are enhanced by the application of mobility to them. Mobility within operational business processes enables organizations to provide accurate estimates on customer orders right at the time of ordering. This capability of the organization to promise its customers what can be delivered to them in turn allows customers to plan their own orders and inventories more effectively (Gledhill 2002). Thus, mobile supply chain systems can improve turnover by reducing the need for safety stocks and the risk of retailer out-of-stocks. Inventory items need to be numbered consistently to facilitate measurement and tracking. RFID enabled mobile applications to reduce the overhead required to store high inventory levels.

Mobile supply-chain management systems are heavily employed in the operational aspect of mobile usage by businesses, resulting in graphical observation of the inventories, demand for the product, and existing schedules of production. Mobile systems enable the organization to have accurate demand planning with improved precision, reduced planning and production cycles, and facilitates the real-time update of content through a single and central data repository. Most importantly, though, mobile supply chain applications provide managers with the ability to respond to dynamically changing situations that may arise so as to minimize their impact on production.

Operational usage of mobility also deals with the processes related to human resources and employee management. These processes, influenced by mobility, include ones such as job analysis, position classification, employee training, employee selection, employee auditing and promotion, employee welfare, employee relations, work safety and sanitation, and documentation and filing. Each of these important HR tasks benefit from the availability of mobility as it makes the tasks real-time ones and enables instantaneous feedback to users through their personalized mobile devices. Numerous additional functions such as employee compensation and benefits, internal communications, and employees' amenities are also positively influenced by the use of mobility.

Process–operative usage employs the location data on workers to locate, manage, and communicate with them. Mobile services incorporated in operational business processes enable managers to determine the locations of their workers and determine the best located person to respond to a particular situation. Operational processes provide managers with alerts on movements of workers as they arrive at a given location, or enter or leave a specific location.

Operational processes of the organization are the internal processes that, in addition to careful process modeling, also need modeling of content internal to

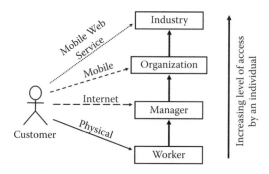

Figure 5.15 Increasing level of access by a customer due to mobility and mobile Web services.

the organization. These processes depend on a combination of wired and wireless networks, as the wired networks are the ones that have been carrying the bulk of operative processes in the past.

Process–Collaborative

Collaborative business processes have been studied in detail by Ghanbary (2006, 2007). Mobile business processes across multiple organizations have increased challenges due to involvement of the interests of many organizations that are interacting through a combination of wired and wireless networks. The technical discussion on collaboration in the previous chapter mentioned MWS. Although there is relatively easy technical availability of MWS, the mobility of service providers and customers need to be modeled formally to provide business value. Collaborations among businesses and among users need to be considered and modeled. Users (customers and employees) can be excellent contributors to the content of the business; therefore, collaborative mobile business processes should model interactions among customers that enable them to initiate discussions, identify advantages, and suggest limitations of products and services.

Figure 5.15 shows the way in which MWS come into play when a customer interacts with the business. Initially, the customer, without a technical means of interaction, used to physically meet up with the worker of an organization in order to get a service. This process then moved from a physical process to an electronic process, enabling the customer direct access to the management of the organization. However, in addition to Internet access, with the help of mobility, the customer can now get the service he or she wants without necessarily interacting with the worker or the manager. For example, many banking, ticketing, insurance, and hospital applications enable a mobile customer to get information, make bookings, schedule appointments, and purchase tickets without any interaction with anyone in the organization. MWS, however, enables collaboration among businesses as well as users, leading to an opportunity for the customer to access not only one

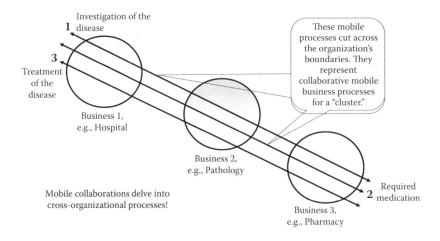

Figure 5.16 Mobile collaborations (using mobile Web services). (Based on Ghanbary, A. 2006. Effects of Mobile Web Services on Business Process Reengineering of a cluster. A Doctoral Consortium. *Proceedings of IMB International Conference,* IMB 2006. Sydney, Australia, 13–16 February; Health Domain Example.)

or two businesses but an entire range of related industries through a single point of contact via his or her mobile device. Figure 5.16 reflects this interaction of a mobile user making use of a mobile process that cuts across organizational boundaries. The hospital, pathology, and pharmacy are all separate organizations, but the example mobile processes (there are three of them: (1) investigation of the disease, (2) required medication, and (3) treatment of the disease) are making the organizations collaborate with each other to provide service.

Discussion Points

1. What is the significance of the process dimension of MET as compared with the economic and technical dimensions of MET discussed in the previous two chapters?
2. Discuss the context of the mobile user, the factors that create this context, and how this context affects the way in which a mobile business offers its services to its users.
3. How is a mobile-enabled process faster and more accurate than a corresponding land-based electronic process? Discuss the pros and cons of a mobile process from a quality angle.
4. How does mobility enable collaborations among various business partners and customers? What are the challenges in modeling such collaborative mobile business processes?

5. How can techniques such as the UML and BPMN help in handling the challenges of modeling mobile business processes?

6. Discuss the increasing complexities of modeling processes that provide information versus those that provide transaction and collaboration capabilities to the mobile business.

References

Booch, G., Rumbaugh, J., and Jacobson, I. 2003. *The Unified Modeling Language 2.0 User Guide.* Boston: Addison-Wesley Longman.

Ghanbary, A. 2006. Effects of Mobile Web Services on Business Process Reengineering of a cluster. A Doctoral Consortium. *Proceedings of IMB International Conference*, IMB 2006. Sydney, Australia, February 13–16.

Ghanbary, A. 2007. Collaborative Business Process Engineering (CBPE) Across Multiple Organisations, Ph.D. thesis, School of Computing and Mathematics, University of Western Sydney, Australia.

Gledhill, J. 2002. Create values with IT investment: How to generate a healthy ROI across the enterprise. *Food Processing*, September 63(9): 76–80.

Gupta, P. and Moitra, D. 2004. Evolving a pervasive IT infrastructure: A technology integration approach. *Personal and Ubiquitous Computing*, 8(1): 31–41.

Kalakota, R., Robinson, M., and Gundepudi, P. 2003. Mobile applications for adaptive supply chains: A landscape analysis, in *Advances in Mobile Commerce Technologies*, eds. K. Siau and E.-P. Lim. Hershey, PA: IGI Global.

Lan, Y., and Unhelkar, B. 2005. *Global Integrated Supply Chain Systems.* Hershey, PA: IGI Global.

Moses, A. 2008. Reporting in technology section of the *Sydney Morning Herald*, January 31, 2008; www.smh.com.au; ANZ will be first with the mobile banking functionality on February 11, while NAB will launch in April.

Pan, S. L. and Lee, J. 2003. Using a e-CRM for a unified view of the customer, *Communications of the ACM*, 46(4): 95–99.

Paypal, an online payment-processing company founded in 1999, https://www.paypal.com/.

Pedrasa et al. 2009. Context aware mobility management, chapter 4 in *Handbook of Research in Mobile Business II: Technical, Methodological, and Social Perspectives*, ed. B. Unhelkar. Hershey, PA: IGI Global.

Raisinghani, M., and Taylor, D. 2006. Going global: A technology review, chapter 2 in *Global Integrated Supply Chain Systems*, eds. Y. Lan and B. Unhelkar. Hershey, PA: IGI Global.

Ruhi, U. and Turel, O. 2005. Enabling the glass pipeline: The infusion of mobile technology applications in supply chain management, in *Global Integrated Supply Chain Systems*, eds. B. Unhelker and Y. lan. Hershey, PA: IGI Global.

Unhelkar, B. 2003. *Process Quality Assurance for UML-Based Projects.* Boston: Addison-Wesley.

Unhelkar, B. 2005a. *Practical Object Oriented Analysis.* Cengage, Melbourn, Australia: Thomson Publishing.

Unhelkar, B. 2005b. *Practical Object Oriented Design.* Cengage, Melbourn, Australia: Thomson Publishing.

Vyas, A. and Yoon, V. 2005. Information management in mobile environments using location-aware intelligent agent system (Lia), chapter in *Handbook of Research in Mobile Business: Technical, Methodological and Social Perspectives,* ed. B., Unhelka. Hershey, PA: IGI Global.

Wu, M., and Unhelkar, B. 2007. Extending Enterprise Architecture with Mobility to Create Mobile Enterprise Architecture (M-EA), Australian Conference on Information Systems (ACIS) 2007, Doctoral Consortium, December 4.

Wu, M., and Unhelkar, B. 2008. Extending Enterprise Architecture with Mobility, *Proceedings of IEEE VTC,* Singapore, May 12–15.

Wu, M., and Unhelkar, B. 2009. Extending enterprise architecture with mobility, chapter 47 in *Handbook of Research in Mobile Business: Technical, Methodological and Social Perspectives,* 2nd ed., ed. B. Unhelker. Hershey, PA: IGI Global.

Chapter 6

Mobile Enterprise Transitions: Social Dimension

Nothing in life is to be feared. It is only to be understood.

Marie Curie (1867–1934)

Chapter Key Points

- Discusses the social drivers in Mobile Enterprise Transition (MET)
- Discusses the social aspect of adaptation of mobile devices by mobile users
- Presents the issues of privacy in the use of personalized mobile devices
- Discusses the effect of mobile usage on the organizational team structures
- Discusses the principles and practices of usability in mobile applications
- Analyzes each of the social factors in MET for their perceived importance by the users
- Analyzes the social drivers in MET from the point of view of sequencing them within the social dimension of MET

Introduction

This chapter focuses on the social dimension of Mobile Enterprise Transition (MET). This social dimension transitioning using mobile technology is vital for the success of MET. This is so because this social dimension handles the *subjective* nature of MET as it focuses on the players involved in MET and how they are influenced by the process. Typically, these players are the users of the business (e.g., customers and employees) as well as the decision makers who are involved in undertaking the MET exercise. The discussion in this social dimension thus deals with the effect of mobility on the sociocultural aspects of people's lives. Examples of these sociocultural issues include rising user expectations from mobility; adaptability and usability of mobile devices and applications; attitude to privacy and trust of information; changing working formats and work ethics; changes to organizational and team structures; emergency help and support for the individuals; convenience and ease of usage; and health issues related to use of mobility—to name but a few. These personal and social challenges of mobility stem from the fact that it is one of the most pervasive emerging technologies of today. Mobility continues to fascinate and socially attract various categories and types of users. As discussed earlier, in Chapter 1, people's dependence on mobile technology is not only increasing, but the rate at which this dependence is increasing is also very high. Today's society is almost unimaginable without mobile technologies, covering all ranges of uses in all geographical regions and with all financial backgrounds. The social fabric affected by mobility covers, for example, employment, education, homes, and governance as well as relationships with family and friends.

Understandably, not all influences of mobility on society and the individual are positive. For example, the personal and individual nature of mobile phones has the potential for alienating people from one another. Family members and friends in this mobile era tend to spend less time together face to face than before the advent of mobile phones. Mobility also creates additional pressures in the daily working lives of people. For example, employees who are carrying a mobile gadget provided by the organization feel obliged to answer the calls to their phones even after working hours. Mobility, for many people, leads to the feeling of loss of privacy and erosion of the division between personal and working lives. People who are resistant to changes, especially the elderly, find the entire mobile transition of organizations that otherwise would provide them with face-to-face services, quite disconcerting.

Mobility leads to perpetual contact between people, especially the organization and the employee; the result is absolutely no "time off" for that employee. Mobile users communicate with each other while walking on the street, driving (risky and illegal), or resting in a hospital bed. Mobile etiquette also comes into play in this social dimension of MET, with the behavior of people who engage in a mobile phone conversation while another person is face to face with them being questioned. Bizarre, personalized, and loud ringtones and conversations that disrupt the quietness of a resting area, prayer halls, library, or hospital are daily occurrences in the modern mobile society. New policies, procedures, norms, rules, and regulations are continuously being framed in response to these situations. The quality of life of individuals in a mobile society is an important issue to be considered by businesses undergoing MET.

The main goal of this chapter is to arrive at an understanding of how all of these aforementioned issues in the social dimension of MET affect the enterprise, individuals, and the society. Unless this social dimension is studied carefully and incorporated formally into MET, the transitions to mobile business may not succeed. The social factors driving and influencing MET are surveyed, analyzed, and studied in this chapter. This chapter also analyzes and uses the survey data (the questionnaire is listed in Appendix A) on the sequencing of these MET factors from a social angle.

Social Dimension of MET (Who)

The social dimension of MET focuses on "who" are the players in MET, and how they influence and are influenced by the MET framework. These players in MET include the customers, employees, contractors, managers, and other "users" of the business. The issues that face these users when they interface with a mobile business include, as shown in Figure 6.1, those of usability, privacy, attitude to adoption, security, customer relationship management, changes to traditional organizational structure, changes to the social environment, and complications in the legal factors. These social factors, in addition to changing the team structure within the organization, also change the relationship of the users with the transitioning organization. The changes to work formats that result from telecommuting,

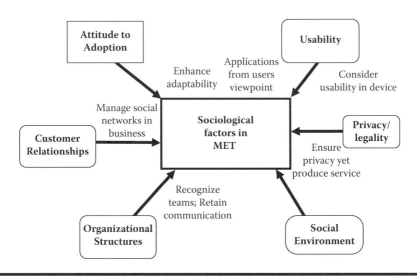

Figure 6.1   Social drivers of MET and the associated transition issues.

or "mobile-commuting," are also considered in this social dimension of MET. Furthermore, this social dimension also incorporates discussions on the nature of wireless connectivity and mobile gadgets (based on discussions such as Unhelkar 2005, 2008), which are highly "personalized" and location aware. The subsequent challenges to the security and privacy of individuals (Adam and Katos 2005; Elliott and Phillips 2004) need to be addressed socially (and technically; Chapter 4) for MET success. A formal study of these social factors is carried out in the research project associated with this book. The factors related to the social aspect of MET are listed in Table 6.1. The survey instrument that is used in this study is as discussed in Chapter 2 (see Appendix A for full survey questionnaire). Table 6.1 also highlights the specific mobile transition issues associated with these social factors of MET.

Mobile Social Landscape

Mobility, specifically its location independence, creates tremendous opportunities for new and unique social networks. Examples of these mobile social networks are the ones facilitated by mobile portals such as Twitter and Dopplr. The underlying mobile infrastructure of these portals, however, has to deal with issues of interoperability and privacy.

The discussion here on the mobile social landscape provides the backdrop for the discussion and analysis of the social factors in MET listed in Table 6.1 and carried out later in the chapter. The mobile social landscape consists of interesting topics such as mobile social networking, mobile shopping, privacy and security, legality of mobile usage, and mobile entertainment.

Social Networking and Mobility

Mobility has a huge impact on the way people interact and socialize with one another. Therefore, mobility influences wide-ranging aspects of human interaction, including one-on-one communication, formation and movement of dynamic social groups, new ethics and value systems, and operation of the government. Wireless social networks not only create new business opportunities but also create innovative social structures. Consider, for example, the customer electronic social networking sites such as MySpace (myspace.com) and Facebook (facebook.com), which create new and innovative ways for people with common interests to get

Table 6.1 Social drivers of MET

Social drivers for MET (Who?)	Transition issues
Attitude to adoption Age of the user (e.g., child, teen, adult, elderly) Perceived usefulness of the device Ease of use of the device Peer pressure for buying/using the device Upgrading to newer device Facilitating environment (e.g., government policy)	Enhance and ease the adaptability of mobility for these users by studying their attitude; this will vary widely depending on the sociology of the user.
Usability Size and weight Screen space (screen real estate) Keypad size (including buttons) Dictionary feature in SMS text typing Audio (sound) facilities Wallpapers and ringtones Battery (duration and recharging) Ruggedness of device (durability) Language support (e.g., English, Chinese)	Consider usability of the device, especially from a mobile application viewpoint. Improve ease of use to facilitate mobile adoption.
Privacy and safety Preventing others from knowing your location Using auto location information to seek assistance Transmitting instantaneous photographs Carrying mobile phones in public facilities (toilets, swimming pools, playgrounds, etc.)	Ensure privacy during mobile transition, but balance it with service.
Team structures Changes to employee reporting structures Changes to senior management Changes to consulting/training needs	Apply the principles of change management; recognize team for its effort. Ensure internal team communications.
Customer relationship structures Relationship between customer and employees Relationship between customer and business Relationship among customers	Create and manage social networks that also facilitate business activities.

together and chat, poll, and debate issues. These social sites store, share, and generate information for millions of its subscribers and members. Similarly, the mobile components in these social networking sites release their potential through location independence. Professional networking sites such as LinkedIn (linkedin.com) also provide electronic and mobile footprints of the individual, creating opportunities for the users of these sites to network with one another professionally. However, at the same time, these mobile footprints of the users may be creating traces of the user, perhaps without his or her knowledge. Needless to say, with increasing use of mobile devices, specific location data can be correlated with other social information already available on portals such as those mentioned earlier, with the result that substantial private knowledge about the individual is made available to anyone who peeps into these sites.

There are also other portals such as Twitter (http://twitter.com/), Dopplr (http://www.dopplr.com/), YouTube (youtube.com), and Orkut (orkut.com) that create advanced social networking opportunities that were not possible before the use of mobile technology. Twitter is a free social networking portal that accepts updation of personalized data stored on its portal. These personal updates that are received by the portal are then automatically forwarded to the subscriber to the Twitter portal. The sender of the information has the choice to restrict the transmission of the subscribed data to a few select users or group of users. Twitter-map also can display recent Twitter messages on Google Maps.

The other very interesting social networking portal is called Dopplr. Dopplr is a mobile social network for travelers. Dopplr synchronizes the travel schedules of a person with those of others. This synchronization provides people with information that enables them to meet friends and socialize while they are on the move. Social networking demonstrates one of the core principles of Mobile Web 2.0 (Harmon and Diam 2009), wherein mobile operators attempt to package the contents that are available on these social portals together with their own "value-adds" and offer them to the consumers. The increasing social importance of these mobile portals also means that the need for standards and interoperability among these various social portals has never been felt more strongly. For example, Google, which owns YouTube (for video sharing) and Orkut (socializing Web sites), finds it is necessary to technically interface with MySpace and Facebook to provide greater value to their subscribers. Thus, there is a need for greater collaboration rather than competition between mobile businesses in this social aspect of MET.

Social collaboration also needs to proceed hand in hand with the collaborations among mobile application developers. These various electronic and mobile social networks create a demand for development of mobile software applications and mobile agents that can operate on these sites irrespective of their operative environments. Although some service providers join in this standardization and collaborative effort, there are many others that don't subscribe to the standards, perhaps because of their desire to compete, or perhaps due to disagreement regarding standards.

Shopping and Mobility

Mobility has changed the social landscape dramatically. Godbole (2006) discusses this dramatic impact of "transactive" use of mobile devices on shopping. Shopping in most modern societies has gone beyond need-based shopping and moved into the realm of lifestyle. Mobility is able to support both types of shopping needs. However, there are a plethora of technical issues faced by these socially influential mobile devices. These issues include the challenges of interoperability among the applications and devices, and also significant issues related to security, service providers, and content generators. There are instantaneous authentication and legal enforceability of mobile shopping. Mobility includes some types of transactions that are more amendable to mobile commerce activities than others. Example of these mobile-friendly commercial transactions include instantaneous purchases, purchase of consumables (i.e., coffee, soda), and purchases based on "need of the time" (i.e., movie tickets). However, compare these simple two-way transactions with, say, the purchase of product with a longer purchase cycle and a bulky exchange of goods, such as a car or an air conditioner. Large purchases with a long purchase life cycle can't be entirely completed using mobility; however, mobility can add value to these large-scale transactions in some parts of their life cycle. Mobile devices and applications also provide excellent shopping value in terms of identifying sales and providing on-the-spot comparison for a purchase. For example, a mobile shopper in a shopping mall is able to immediately compare prices of a product offered by multiple vendors within the mall "at *that time* and in *that place.*" The mobile shopper does not have to go from shop to shop or visit a physical Internet connection to obtain the relevant information on a particular product of interest.

The shopping experience of mobile users can be further enhanced by the opening up of interfaces between the social networking sites. The interoperability between sites is both a challenge and an opportunity in mobile context. The resultant collaboration between various social sites can be very useful for determining the buying patterns of an individual. For example, vendors have an opportunity to offer products and services to potential clients if the client is in the vicinity. Google, which is pushing for these open interfaces between social networking sites, finds it beneficial to open up the mobile Web to its free services, advertising-based business model.

> Mobile shopping is a big influence on the society. Shopping ranges from "need" to "lifestyle." Mobility supports both kinds of shopping. Transitioning mobile businesses need to consider the way in which mobile shoppers search for products and sources, compare the offers, and conduct the actual purchases in a secured way. Interoperability creates new options and opportunities. Timing and location are both vital keys to enhance the mobile shopping experience.

Privacy and Mobility

The context of the mobile user needs to be determined to provide relevant service to him or her. However, this context also provides much knowledge about the mobile user, including the timing and location of his movements, the kinds of choices he makes in terms of his purchases, his entertainment choices, and his selections of traveling social and leisure activities. There is a great need to protect this context-based information of the user, ensure it is securely stored, properly encrypted during its transmission, and also formally cleaned up and deleted after it is no longer relevant. Mobile businesses need to ensure the privacy of information, especially in sensitive areas such as patient records, child tracking, shopping habits, and credit ratings. The mobile and telecom industry isn't viewed in a positive light by many in terms of protecting consumer privacy (Telecoms industry's worst 2007). The mobile industry is plagued by collection of excessive amounts of personal data that is then further used in ongoing marketing campaigns, advertisements, and unsolicited offers by mobile businesses. Mobile businesses need to realize that personal data is even more important than searching for more customers and selling more services to them as it helps build trust even before enforcement of legislation. The provision of location-specific services can no longer be based on trust alone between the parties involved. There is a need for regulations to monitor and manage the privacy of the information. Perusco and Michael (2007) have explored the impact of mobile technology on control, trust, privacy, and security of mobile users. These four interrelated issues need to be considered by the transitioning business to ensure mobile success.

Marketers need to recognize the fine balance that exists between personalization of services and addressing the privacy concerns of the users. Truly personalized context-specific location-based services require customer data from several sources. Marketers could potentially access a customer's financial and offline-shopping data, which is then used for tailoring messages and services to that consumer. When the use of personal offline data along with location information by the business becomes apparent to the consumer, serious privacy concerns can arise (Subramanian et al. 2002). Established retailers and marketers may have an advantage over unknown or fledgling providers of services. However, they could quickly fritter away this advantage if they mishandle privacy concerns of their customers.

Acceptance of location-based services would depend to a great degree on how well operators (and service providers) allay privacy concerns of consumers and build trust with their customers. For example, it is widely agreed that unsolicited mobile advertising is viewed as intrusive and unwelcomed; and being located on a tracking service by the business raises security and privacy concerns. Therefore, operators should carefully evaluate the option of making these services optional and based on preregistered permissions of the users. In fact, a core set of privacy, security, and safety factors needs to be carefully integrated with mobile business strategies and mobile applications that enable maintenance of the balance between total security and locking up of services versus providing loose access to those services. Highly secured, locked-up services usually increase the cost of the services and may turn away impatient users (e.g., if users are prompted too many times for password validation). Levels of security and authentication should depend on the type of the provided services. For example, transactions that only involve one interaction between user and business require less security, as also interactions between family members and other trustworthy individuals.

> The social dimension of MET is concerned with privacy, security, and integrity factors. These factors need to be finely balanced for the business to succeed in a mobile society. Too much privacy will turn away users as it will be inconvenient and cumbersome to use the system. Too little privacy, and the users are open to abuse based on their location-specific data.

Advertisement and Mobility

Mobility enables advertisers with a wide range of options to reach a selective audience based on their characteristics of purchases, voice calls, messages (SMS, MMS), and dynamically created offers from the part of mobile advertisement. For example, the advertising departments can forward a message to a selected group of people who are present in a mall, school, or hospital at a point in time to achieve maximum penetration with their audience. Advertisers also need to focus on both the technological and business aspects of their consumers' behavior to ensure that their advertisements are aligned with the potential needs of the users and the capabilities of the mobile gadgets.

Legal Issues in Mobility

This transcendence of mobile agents beyond geographical boundaries causes legal challenges in enforcing the deals executed by mobile agents. Neely and Unhelkar (2005) have also discussed these legal aspects in mobile business, particularly when mobile agents are used in a mobile collaborative environment. Mobile agents transport themselves on mobile devices, taking their code, data, and state with them and execute beyond geographical boundaries. The wireless communication ability of mobile devices creates legal challenges when there is a need to enforce transactions conducted using those devices. Potential entities for legal attentions are: network provider, programmer of the agent's code, owner of the mobile agent, owner of the server, etc. The legality of a piece of information in one geographical region does not mean it is legal in another region—where the mobile agent may be executing on an unsuspecting user's mobile device. When do the actions based on this usage constitute an offense? That is the primary legal challenge in mobile agent usage.

Mobile electronic signature and logs are helpful, but then they have the challenge of location-specific enforcement. For example, although there may be legal requirements for service provides and network operators to track user information, that tracking information may not be helpful if the enforcement authority is geographically in a different region. Furthermore, creating and maintaining extensive logs of all mobile activities and transactions become an extremely expensive and difficult task, especially as the mobile agent can be executing anywhere in the world.

Mobile Entertainment

Mobile TV and video play an important role in mobile entertainment business. Live streaming and downloading on demand of videos and news clips is particularly popular due to the faster 3G networks that enable smoother watching for the subscribers. Content generators and network operators both play a creative role in enabling this entertainment being made available to the mobile users. The popularity of mobile watching is growing equally rapidly in both developing and developed nations. As Kamdar (2007) correctly states "No one in television can afford to ignore mobile communications, especially not in India, where the latest television trend is interactive TV using cell phones." Similarly, IDC research reported by Baig (2006) indicates that by 2010, about 24 million U.S. cellular subscribers will be watching television and videos using mobile gadgets resulting in a sharp increase in mobile business revenues. Transitioning mobile businesses need to make strategic use of the mobile entertainment in promoting their offerings on mobile devices. For example, mobile advertisements need to be judiciously coupled with the mobile entertainment.

Technology versus Sociology

As mentioned earlier, the technical dimension continues to interplay regularly with the social dimension of mobile technologies. Technical issues such as standards of the applications, application platforms, and ability of these platforms to interoperate with one another and the quality of contents eventually translate and correlate to the issues in social dimension in terms of providing ease of use, timeliness and quality of services, support for emergencies, social networking, and improvements in lifestyle. For example, quality of a mobile user's location data is vital in coordinating and providing response to an emergency situation faced by the user. The specific location data and information of a mobile user in an emergency situation needs to be mapped to the various other elements of information such as maps, traffic, and weather details to enable a coordinated response to the situation. An integrated system brings together these bits of information in real-time (e.g., not only driving directions but also current traffic density and queues in the emergency departments of the nearby hospitals). The location of a person in need of emergency help by the roadside could be made available to a police or ambulance crew. Network standards, short- and long-range communications, interoperability, contents, and applications are examples of technical factors that affect and correlate to the aforementioned social scenarios. The mobile services are "pulled" from the mobile device of a user by the roadside and "pushed" on to the mobile devices of the emergency service providers. That mobile information also needs to be continuously authenticated and updated to be of value to users. Thus, there is a need for a balancing act between the technical and social dimensions of MET. The discussion thus far has laid out the mobile social landscape. The subsequent discussion deals the social factors listed in Table 6.1.

Attitude to Mobile Adoption

The user's attitude to adopting mobility in his or her daily life provide an important social context in the adoption and diffusion of mobile devices during MET (Ciganek and Ramamurthy 2006). These attitude factors are usually difficult to quantify because they are highly subjective and depend on the "moods" of the users. There are a number of factors that make up this "attitude to adaptation" of the mobile users, and these factors need to be studied and analyzed. These adaptation factors, summarized in Figure 6.2, are age of the user, perceived usefulness of the device, ease of use of the device, and peer pressure.

Age of the User

MET needs to consider the age and gender of the user as an important user demographic having major influence in a successful mobile transition. The user of a mobile service in the teenage bracket needs a different suite of service offerings from the service provider than, say, an elderly user. For example, a New Year celebration party will be most likely uppermost in the mind of a teenager inquiring about public transport in late December. The mobile service provider, therefore, needs to "collaborate" with other service providers to provide additional information to this user on a rock concert or a movie available in the city. However, an elderly person inquiring about train timetables in late December may be planning to make a celebratory visit to his family living in the country. Whether the user is a child,

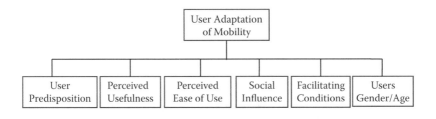

Figure 6.2 Subjectivity in user adaptation of mobility by users.

teenager, adolescent, adult, or elder, and whether the user is a male or female influence their attitude to adopting mobility. Mobile business decisions need to be based on the user attitude to mobility.

Perceived Usefulness of the Device

Usefulness and value of the mobile device on its own is not enough to ensure successful transition to a mobile business. There is also a corresponding need to consider the *perceived* usefulness by the users of the mobile devices and the services available on them. Successful MET needs to ensure that not only is good value offered to the client, but it is also perceived by the client to be of value. Perceptions of clients can change depending on the past history of their experiences with the company, the urgency of their needs, and their ability to use the devices and applications. For example, a farmer who has retired long ago will not perceive the usefulness of a mobile application on a PDA—which provides him with agricultural or weather information—although it may be of actual use to him in a speech he is about to deliver. An elderly patient in a nursing home may perceive the usefulness of a mobile entertainment but may not have the inclination of the skill to use the device with ease. A child may perceive the value of mobile different from her parent.

Ease of Use of the Device

The ease of use of a mobile device varies greatly depending on the individual user, and ergonomics can be vital in considering this factor of ease of use of mobile devices. Ergonomics is the study of scientific application and information concerning objects, systems, and environment for human use. Ergonomics has particularly come into play with the advent of miniaturized mobile phones and PDAs. Repetitive strain injury (RSI) through use of an uncomfortable mobile device in many office works can be a hindrance to MET. Therefore, the ease with which a mobile device can be used by an individual is an important social consideration in MET. The device manufacturer as well as the service providers needs to ensure that the user is able to operate the mobile device with ease. The miniaturization of the mobile device is attractive only up to a certain level—beyond which, the small size of the device can be a hindrance to the user. Smaller-sized mobile devices cannot be easily operated with finger-touch input mechanisms and may require the use of a stylus. Thus, the size of the keypad, keys, screen size, audio, and video control all play a part in this social factor.

Peer Pressure and Mobile Devices

Gala and Unhelkar (2009) discuss the interesting topic of mobility and adolescents. For example, mobile devices and networks provide adolescents with the opportunities to develop intimate relationships with secrecy and privacy. Thus, mobility enables this young age group to satisfy its intrinsic needs of "contact," and at the same time be free from physical proximity and spatial immobility associated with land-based communications. Mobile devices are known to function as stress busters in adolescents owing to the multifunctionalities these devices provide to their users. As a result of such growing social importance of mobile gadgets to adolescents and teenage users, gadgets assume a greater importance than their utility value. Mobile devices are becoming a status symbol among certain types of users. This status symbol is due to the status resulting from possessing a fashionable or "cool" gadget that is laden with features not required in daily phone use. Peer pressure also results in unnecessary device upgrades.

Upgrading to Newer Device

New and sophisticated mobile devices are continuously flooding the markets. As mentioned in the opening chapter of this book, the rate of change of mobile technology is higher than that of any other technology. Therefore, the features, costs, and availability of mobile devices change extremely rapidly. Users are keen to upgrade their mobile devices for multiple reasons. At the iPhone launch by Apple, many users bought the devices irrespective of their needs, merely because the device was available! However, businesses need to consider, cater to, and be responsible for this insatiable need of users to upgrade devices. The manufacturers of devices need to ensure that functionalities offered on the new devices be backward compatible with the old devices. Valuable personal data such as phone and other contact details, messages, ringtones, pictures, and personalized keypads all need to be transferred to the upgraded device.

> The users' predilection to adopt mobility plays a tremendous part in MET. Age, gender, perception, usability, and peer pressure play a role in this attitude creation. Successful mobile transitions require attention to, as well nurturing of, these highly subjective social factors.

Analysis of Attitude to Mobile Adoption

Figure 6.3 shows the importance of adoption attitude of users in influencing MET. There are six factors included in this section: age of the potential mobile user (e.g., child, teen, adult, or elderly), perceived usefulness of the mobile device, ease of use of the mobile device, peer pressure to buy/use the mobile device, upgrading to a new mobile device, and the facilitating mobile social environment (e.g., government policies). These factors in the social dimension of MET will now be studied with the help of data generated in the research survey.

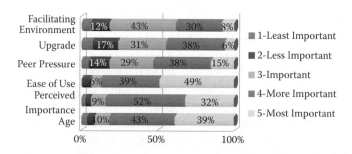

Figure 6.3   Analysis of attitude to mobile adoption driver in social dimension of MET.

The result of the survey shows the importance of facilitating environmental (e.g., government policy) factors in the social dimension, which appears at the top of Figure 6.3, and indicates that 8 percent of the participants in the survey think that the facilitating environment factor is most important, and 30 percent think it is more important. A total of 38 percent think the facilitating environment factor is most to more important in the social dimension of MET. A mere 6 percent of participants think that the facilitating environment factor is least important.

The result of the survey in regard to the importance of upgrading to a newer device in the social dimension, appearing just below the top of Figure 6.3, indicates that 6 percent of the participants in survey think that upgrading is the most important factor, and 38 percent think it is more important. A total of 44 percent think the upgrading to a new device factor is most to more important in the social dimension of MET. A mere 7 percent of participants think that upgrading to a newer device is least important.

The result of the survey in regard to the importance of peer pressure for buying/using the device in the social dimension, appearing third from the top of Figure 6.3, indicates that 15 percent of the participants in the survey think that peer pressure is the most important factor, and 38 percent think it is more important. A total of 53 percent think this factor is most to more important in the social dimension of MET. A mere 5 percent of participants think that the importance of peer pressure for buying/using the device is least important.

The result of the survey in regard to the importance of ease of use of the device in the social dimension, appearing at the fourth position from the top of Figure 6.3, indicates that 49 percent of the participants in the survey think that the ease of use factor is most important, and 39 percent think it is more important. A total of 88 percent think the ease of use of the device factor is more to most important in the social dimension of MET. A mere 1 percent of participants think that ease of use of the device is least important.

The result of the survey in regard to the importance of perceived usefulness of the device in the social dimension, appearing second from the bottom in Figure 6.3, indicates that 32 percent of the participants in the survey think that perceived usefulness is the most important factor, and 52 percent think it is more important. A total of 84 percent think perceived usefulness of the device factor is more to most important in the social dimension of MET. A mere 3 percent of participants think it is least important.

The result of the survey in regard to the importance of age of the user (e.g., child, teen, adult, or elderly) in the social dimension, appearing at the bottom of Figure 6.3, indicates that 39 percent of the participants in the survey think that the age of the user is most important, and 43 percent think it is more important. A total of 82 percent think age of the user is more to most important in social dimension of MET. However, note that only about 4 percent of the participants think it is least important.

Usability in Mobile Applications and Devices

Usability of mobile applications and corresponding mobile devices plays an important role in making mobility acceptable to customers. Usability of mobile applications and devices encompasses a range of factors, including size, screen space, keypad size, dictionary features, audio, ringtones, battery, ruggedness, and language. Additionally, the features that influence the usability of a mobile device include its mechanism for input and output (screen, keypad, and voice activation), its storage capacity (for the data), its processing capacity (with its memory and processing unit), its batteries, and the operating system for the device. These factors can be improved and enhanced by applying the principles and practice of usability to them.

Principles of Usability

Constantine and Lockwood (1999) present the principles and practices of usability for software applications, which also apply easily to mobile applications. The primary law of usability, according to Constantine and Lockwood (1999), is that "the system should be usable by a user with knowledge and experience in the application domain but no experience with the system—without help or instruction." This law indicates that it is important for the mobile device as well as the mobile application on the device to be "instinctively" usable. This instinctive usability includes being able to figure out the basic functionalities of the device as well as the application without having to undergo formal instruction and training. However, there are different categories of mobile users, and some of them will indeed need initial training and support to be able to use mobile applications successfully. The second law of usability states that "the system should not interfere with or impede efficient use by a skilled user having substantial experience with the system." This second law recognizes the need for the system to "grow" with the user. For example, a mobile user may need all the help and tool tips as she uses the mobile device or application initially. However, later, as she grows in her expertise, this extra help will no longer be required. Providing help when it is not required by an expert user becomes a hindrance, which needs to be recognized by the designers and developers of mobile devices and applications. These laws of usability are also supported by the principles of usability, support, structure, simplicity, visibility, reusability, feedback, and tolerance. Each of these principles provides a comprehensive quality angle to the mobile application being designed and produced.

The device should also be simple enough for developers to write applications for it. The device should be compatible with various accessories to be used with it. The memory and storage must be large enough for most mobile commerce applications.

Size and Weight

As mentioned earlier, the size and weight of mobile devices play an important role in their usability. Personalized mobile devices need to be able to fit comfortably in the hands of the users and single-handed functionalities also need to be considered when deciding upon the size and weight factor of the device. Smallness in size is not necessarily adding value to the usability of the device.

Mobile users like to carry a mobile device that is small enough to be held in one hand. Therefore, the device designers need to consider the input methods that are easy enough to use and learn with the use of one hand. The weight, size, color, and shape all add value to the desired characteristic of mobile gadgets. The following subsections describe the most attractive gadgets that mobile users prefer.

Screen Space (Screen Real Estate)

Mobile screens have limited screen space. Therefore, it is vital that screen space be fully utilized. The various functions available in a mobile application need to be organized in a logical and cohesive manner, depending on the needs of the users. This navigation becomes all the more important in a short-screen-spaced mobile application, in which the logical grouping, dependency, and performance of each mobile page is vital for the usability of the application. The screen must be large enough for mobile users to read the content effortlessly and use the stylus without difficulty. The large size of the screen is particularly helpful for elderly users.

Innovative ways of improving utilization of screen space have been tried out by mobile device designers. Use of a stylus, use of audio signals wherever possible, and even three-dimensional virtual display of the screen have been considered and used by mobile device designers. The challenge of small-sized display screens on mobile gadgets is resolved by the use of hologram projection (http://www.lightblueoptics.com/index.html). The cost of holographic projection and the consumption of battery power by these projections is still a challenge to their adoption, and consequently, the role they can play in usability.

Keypad Size (Including Buttons)

Mobile device manufacturers produce a variety of models of mobile gadgets in different shapes and sizes for convenience and to attract customers. The customer expects to have a small and lightweight gadget that enables him to watch TV, listen to music, type a message with ease, and also be mobile. The size of the keypad of the mobile device, the multiple use of the same keys (such as numbers and alpha characters), and audio cues corresponding to key press and virtual keypad are all options used by device manufacturers to enhance the usability of mobile devices.

Dictionary Feature in SMS Text Typing

Dictionary support is an important usability feature of mobile gadgets as users type messages with increasing frequency and speed. The limited size of the overall phone and the combination of numbers and text characters (usually three on a button) can be very daunting for new users of the mobile phone. However, younger users are quite comfortable at using the keypads, especially when they are supported by the dictionary feature that allows rapid typing of words to create a message. This dictionary support needs to be extended to languages other than English, and be easily configurable to various industrial domains such as airlines, hotels, and sports.

Audio (Sound) Features

Personalized audio features that enable a user to, say, activate her phone by simply using spoken word commands can go a long way in improving the usability of mobile devices. Similarly, audio volume of the device, speaker features, ability to connect to earphones, and car speakers (while driving) are audio features of mobile devices that are important in MET.

Wallpapers and Ringtones

Personalized ringtones enhance the usability of the mobile device by the user by assigning different ringtones to different callers. This feature enables the user to recognize the caller just by the ringtone. Additional features are auto pickup, the use of different wallpapers, screensavers, and startup screen and shutdown screen, all customized and personalized by the user.

Battery (Duration and Recharging)

Mobile devices are powered by batteries that have relatively short life—both in their daily usage (changing and recharging) as well as the overall operational life of the batteries. This battery limitation is primarily driven by the smaller size of the mobile device. Handheld devices in general have less memory, limited processing power, and restricted battery life as compared with corresponding nonmobile devices. Advances in battery and chip technologies are rapidly resolving these limitations. Furthermore, new and improved methods of operating these devices are also coming into play. The processors on the devices should be powerful enough to consume as little power as possible to produce extended battery life. Most mobile gadgets have batteries that last from two to seven days and beyond, depending on usage. Advances in battery technology means recharging of phones has become convenient and easy. Many public places such as airports and hotels have recharging booths provided, with the compliments of the manufacturers. Solar researching needs to be considered.

Ruggedness of Device (Durability)

The mobile device should have the durability and ruggedness to function in any kind of physical environment. The mobile device must work despite high temperatures, freezing temperatures, moisture, and impact, and yet provide a clear voice in these conditions. Furthermore, mobile devices, by their very personalized nature, are dropped far more often than a corresponding desk-based device. It is not uncommon to have a mobile device drop out of the hand onto the floor, or be left outdoors.

Language Support (e.g., English, Chinese)

Conversion from one language or culture to another is a feature that the device can support. However, this conversion and language support is still at the physical level. The users would want this conversion to be automatic and sufficient across different language, time zones, and regions of the world.

> Mobile devices play a significant role through their features in MET. Although ruggedness of devices and features such as longer battery life are important, even more important are features such as language conversion, which enable the mobile user to roam across the globe with ease. The global network connectivity and the capabilities on the mobile device itself can be brought together to provide these cross-language, cross-cultural features on mobile devices that were hitherto unthinkable without mobility.

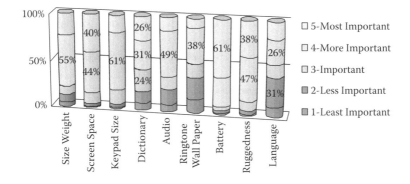

Figure 6.4   Analysis of the importance of usability factor in the social dimension of MET.

Analysis of the Importance of Usability Factor

Figure 6.4 shows the importance of the usability of gadgets in driving MET. These nine factors are included in the earlier discussions. These factors are size and weight, screen space (screen real estate), keypad size (including buttons), dictionary feature in SMS text typing, audio (sound) features, wallpapers and ringtones, battery (duration and recharging), ruggedness of device (durability), and language support (e.g., English, Chinese) in the social dimension of MET.

The result of the survey in regard to the importance of size and weight in the social dimension, appearing at the left of Figure 6.4, indicates that 23 percent of the participants in the survey think it is most important, and 55 percent think it is more important. A total of 78 percent think size and weight is more to most important in the social dimension of MET. Only 4 percent think it is least important.

The result of the survey in regard to the importance of screen space (screen real estate) in the social dimension, appearing second from left in Figure 6.4, indicates that 40 percent of the participants in the survey think it is most important, and 44 percent think it is more important. A total of 84 percent think it is more to most important in the social dimension of MET. A mere 1 percent participants think it is least important.

The result of the survey in regard to the importance of keypad size (including buttons) in the social dimension, appearing third from the left of Figure 6.4, indicates that 18 percent of the participants in the survey think it is most important, and 61 percent of the participants think it is more important. A total of 79 percent think it is more to most important in the social dimension of MET. A mere 2 percent participants think it is least important.

The result of the survey in regard to the importance of the dictionary feature in SMS text typing in the social dimension, appearing fourth from the left of Figure 6.4, indicates that 26 percent of the participants in the survey think it is most important, and 31 percent think it is more important. Thus, a total of 57 percent think it is more to most important in the social dimension of MET. Only 7 percent of participants think it is least important.

The result of the survey in regard to the importance of audio (sound) features in the social dimension, appearing in the middle of Figure 6.4, indicates that 14 percent of the participants in the survey think it is most important, and 49 percent think it is more important. Thus, a total of 63 percent think it is more to most important in the social dimension of MET. Only 7 percent of participants think it is least important.

The result of the survey in regard to the importance of wallpapers and ringtones in the social dimension, appearing fourth from the right of Figure 6.4, indicates that 50 percent of the participants in the survey think it is most important, and 38 percent think it is more important. Thus, a total of 88 percent think it is more to most important in the social dimension of MET. Only 14 percent of participants think it is least important.

The result of the survey in regard to the importance of battery (duration and recharging) in the social dimension, appearing third from the right side of Figure 6.4, indicates that 61 percent of the participants in the survey think it is most important, and 31 percent think it is more important. Thus, a total of 92 percent think it is more to most important in the social dimension of MET. Only 2 percent of participants think it is least important.

The result of the survey in regard to the importance of ruggedness of device (durability) in the social dimension, appearing second from the right side of Figure 6.4, indicates that 38 percent of the participants in the survey think it is most important, and 47 percent think it is more important. A total of 85 percent think it is more to most important in the social dimension of MET. Only 2 percent of the participants think it is least important.

The result of the survey in regard to the importance of language support (e.g., English, Chinese) factors in the social dimension, appearing at the right of Figure 6.4, indicates that 19 percent of the participants in the survey think it is most important, 26 percent think it is more important, 14 percent think it is important, 31 percent think it is less important, and 10 percent think it is least important in the social dimension.

Overall, high percentages for many of these factors seem to indicate (and confirm the assumption) that people are quite passionate about the usability aspects of mobile phones. Except for one factor, all factors were ranging three-fourths in importance, indicating that the transitioning mobile businesses must pay attention to these factors upfront in their attempt to become mature mobile businesses.

Privacy and Security Considerations

Privacy and security considerations in MET are important social factors that heavily influence MET. One of the many important social characteristics of mobility is that it enables businesses to create opportunities to provide services that are based on the specific location of the user. These location-based services, however, require the business to know the location of the user in the first place. There are increasing privacy-related issues to this location knowledge of the user by the business. At the same time, it is also increasingly being accepted that such location knowledge also has immense potential for businesses to provide a range of services—particularly emergency services, as noted by Unni and Harmon (2005). Providing complete privacy and security implies no access by the business to the user and vice versa; that is, no value to either party. Mobile devices are able to capture and transfer people-specific information to the business. Rules and regulations are required to protect people's information on mobile devices.

The social importance of mobility has resulted in safety and privacy being one of the primary value drivers in MET. The mobile business has knowledge of the user, his or her mobile gadgets, and the type and intensity of the use of mobile applications by the user. Although this information is necessary for the business to provide ongoing enhancements to its mobile services, the users need to be assuaged that the business will safeguard their personal data, including their location, time, and usage. Users require assurance that the aforementioned confidential information will not be divulged to their employers, friends, spouse, partners, or any other parties who may potentially want to misuse it. Today, users are not confident of the ability of businesses to secure their private data and related information. Overcoming this perception and ensuring that the users do feel confident that their privacy will not be violated is a vital social key to successful MET. However, providing unrestricted and open access between the user and the business can create major challenges as well. Thus, in undergoing MET, business undertakes a fine balancing act between the excellence of mobile devices to keep their users in constant contact with related parties and the loss of corresponding privacy owing to the usage of such devices. For example, primary schools undertaking MET are in a good position to offer better security to school-going kids who may be carrying mobile devices. However, at the same time, these schools need responsible and implementable policies and practices to ensure limited use of such information by sharing it only with the parents or caregivers of the child. Modern society abounds in examples of challenging and, at times, life-threatening situations wherein availability of location-specific information even at the cost of privacy is considered worthwhile for the user. For example, auto accidents, getting locked out of the car in an uncomfortable neighborhood, toddlers getting locked in the car when the outside temperatures are soaring, elders suffering from a medical emergency (e.g., heart attack), and so on.

According to Ghanbary (2006), the security of online payment, user behavior, rules and hassles, mobile virus protection, file encryption, access control, and authentication are some of the most important security factors in a mobile environment. This is so because mobile devices are very personal, and in case of their loss or theft, the personal data is likely to be lost and the corporate data exposed to misuse. Thus, security and integrity of these devices includes the data held and transmitted by them. The authenticity of the data, the owner of the data and the device, all needs to be validated against a corporate database. This, of course, brings about the challenge of security against privacy mentioned earlier in this chapter.

Health and safety are being studied along with security of mobile usage. Safety concerns, especially for use of mobile phones by individuals from different age groups are also being studied with interest. For example, according to an article in the *Sydney Morning Herald* by Louis Hall (January 27, 2008), Australian scientists are investigating if children are more vulnerable than adults to the effects of radiation from mobile phones. A study of 110 adults at the Australian Centre for Radiofrequency Bioeffects Research, partly funded by the federal government, confirmed that mobile phones cause a change in brain function by altering brainwaves known as alpha waves. Although the direct impact of mobile radiation on health is uncertain, there are still regular claims that frequent use of mobile phones can cause headaches, nausea, and problems with concentration.

Privacy of Location

Privacy of users is one of the most important factors in MET. Users are concerned, if not paranoid, about loss of privacy due to use of mobile devices. The challenges to privacy are, however, made more complicated by the fact that the same users would be more than happy to have their location identified in terms of their needs, such as when facing an emergency situation. Maintaining the privacy of users is a fine balancing act that all transitioning businesses have to undertake to succeed in providing services to their mobile users. At times, there are legal requirements for network operators to pinpoint the location of users, which adds further complications to the privacy needs and concerns of mobile users.

As discussed earlier, the advancement of mobile technology, particularly global positioning systems (GPSs), has created numerous opportunities for businesses and individuals to interact with one another utilizing knowledge of specific locations. Examples of these interactions include shopping, hospitals, ambulances, police, military, emergency situations, and others. Shopping malls are also able to track and transmit advertisements to mobile devices as soon as the device is within range. Thus, this information is invariably giving away the location information of the user. The challenges are to maintain the privacy of this location information. The only way to hide the presence of the user in that physical location is to turn the gadget off.

There is evidence, however, that mobile businesses and network operators are cognizant of these privacy issues and have taken appropriate steps to put in place sophisticated authentication and authorization frameworks (Spinney 2004). For example, Bell Mobility's MyFinder, TeliaSonera's Friend Finder, and AT&T's Find Friends indicate that they are keen to self-regulate to not only avoid legislative enforcement but also to gain the goodwill of their users. Regulations, however, do have their role to play, and stringent privacy regulations have to be complied with in some regions, especially in Europe (Camponovo and Cerutti 2004).

Auto Location Information Usage

Location information based on the personalized mobile device carried by the user is crucial when he or she seeks assistance. For example, a new bus driver on the first trip on a very complicated route suddenly realizes that he is lost. The reaction of this mobile user is to call the radio room and inform them of his predicament. However, the bus driver has no knowledge about his current location. Auto location information through a mobile gadget carried by the user or, as would be appropriate in this example, attached to the vehicle can be of great value to the user. *Tom Toms* and other route guides that are based on auto location information of the user are now affordable. Location information can be used to help people seeking assistance. The disadvantage is the loss of privacy of location information.

Although the E911 emergency response standard mandates an infrastructure that provides fairly precise location data, operators need to take into consideration the level of precision required in offering a service. This level of precision is provided by means of a business agreement between network operators, content providers, and mobile marketers. These business agreements ensure that the precise location data that is shared by these partners is not abused by the parties that are privy to that data. Trade-offs among these partners also ensure that the data and information on customer location is shared among them to provide value to the customer. Services related to emergencies would require precise location data, but services that provide a list of restaurants in a neighborhood may require less precise data. Marketers would be satisfied with access to less precise location data.

However, to provide the specific services required by the user, precise auto location of the user is required. This auto location information has potential for abuse, so the person who receives the message and comes to the rescue needs to be carefully selected. There are further social issues with auto location information usage, such as risks with presumption of miscommunication of emergencies, reliability by the users, and so on.

Instantaneous Data Transmission

Modern mobile gadgets have the capability of instantly transmitting voice, video, music, and pictures, and can execute various applications remotely. The transmitted information can provide opportunities for bringing together dispersed families or creation of virtual social groups. Information may take varied transmission paths; need encryption or decryption; and may perhaps need language translation if the data or information is going across borders. Instantaneous data transmission involves the challenge of detecting and not transmitting information that is illegal and antisocial in nature, especially when it is transmitted across borders.

Carrying Mobile Phones in Public Facilities

The rapid advances in and convergence of various technologies on mobile devices (with PDA functionality) allow users to send and receive voice, SMSs, e-mails, Web pages, music, games, and photographs. According to Abood (2006), this convergence in technology, although providing many benefits, also raises issues dealing with privacy and surveillance/spying. Most modern mobile phones are equipped with high-resolution cameras that can take photos and videos. Furthermore, people tend to carry their mobile phones with them everywhere. These mobile phone cameras also obviate the need to return to a desk machine and transfer the images from a digital camera. Instead, images can be directly transferred to the desired locations (including an e-mail address, another phone, or to a computer server) directly from the mobile phones. Thus, these mobile devices enable individuals to intrude into people's privacy or spy on them. Also, it is relatively easy to walk into a competitor's premises, take photos of a sensitive industrial nature, and transmit them instantaneously.

Individual privacy and industrial espionage are becoming two major concerns with mobile camera phones. Governments and organizations are grappling with how to deal with the growing misuse of these devices, and there does not seem to be a clear answer. Protecting an individual's and an organization's privacy while still allowing people to enjoy the benefits that mobile camera phones provide is a difficult juggling act.

Analysis of the Importance of Privacy Factor

Figure 6.5 shows the importance of privacy for mobile users in driving MET. There are four factors related to privacy in the social dimension of MET included in this section: preventing others from knowing your location, using auto location information to seek assistance, transmitting instantaneous photographs, and carrying mobile phones in public facilities (toilets, swimming pools, playgrounds, etc.).

The result of the survey in regard to the importance of the factor "preventing others from knowing location" in the social dimension, as appearing at the extreme left of Figure 6.5, indicates that 18 percent of the participants in the survey think that this factor is most important, and 47 percent of participants think this factor is more important. A total of 65 percent think this factor is more to most important in the social dimension. A mere 2 percent think that this factor is least important.

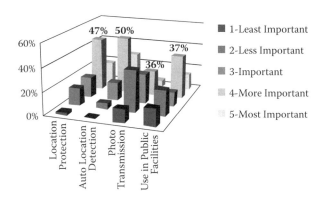

■ 1-Least Important
■ 2-Less Important
■ 3-Important
▨ 4-More Important
▨ 5-Most Important

Figure 6.5   Analysis of the importance of privacy factor in social dimension of MET.

The result of the survey in regard to the importance of the factor "using auto location information to seek assistance" in the social dimension, appearing second from the left position of Figure 6.5, indicates that 29 percent of the participants in the survey think that this factor is most important, and 50 percent of the participants think that this factor is more important. A total of 79 percent think that this factor is more to most important in the social dimension. Only 1 percent of participants think this factor is least important.

The result of the survey in regard to the importance of the factor "transmitting instantaneous photographs factors" in the social dimension, appearing second from the right in Figure 6.5, indicates that 36 percent (the highest percentage) of the participants in the survey think that this factor is less important. Eleven percent of participants think this factor is least important. Only 5 percent of the participants in the survey think it is most important, and 21 percent think this factor is more important. A total of 26 percent think this factor is more to most important in the social dimension.

The result of the survey in regard to the importance of the factor "carrying mobile phones in public facilities (toilets, swimming pools, playgrounds, etc.)" in the social dimension, appearing at the right in Figure 6.5, indicates that 14 percent of the participants in the survey think that this factor is most important, and 37 percent think this factor is more important. A total of 51 percent think this factor is more to most important in the social dimension. Fifteen percent of participants think it is least important.

Once again, similar to the earlier usability factors, these privacy factors elicit consistently high percentage responses. This confirms the growing importance of privacy and security in the minds of the users. Transitioning mobile organizations need to pay attention to these high percentages in undertaking MET.

Changing Organizational Structures for Mobile Business

Mobility influences business in radical ways, including changing its organizational structure. When an organization undergoes formal MET, its organizational structure is affected. Reengineering forced organizations to be process based, thereby flattening the hierarchy. Mobile processes take that reengineering further, and we have a loose, dynamically changing matrix-based flattened hierarchy.

Mobility enhances direct contact between employees and customers. Mobility also changes the nature of, and enhances, the communications between employees at all levels. This communication impacts the reporting structures within teams and organizations, resulting in an increase in the quality of output.

Organizing and managing people and their roles in a transitioning business are crucial to the success of MET. The organizational aspect of quality can be described as a *quality environment*. Creation and management of a quality environment is the responsibility of the MET project manager. The primary areas of influence of mobility with respect to the organization are planning and organizing people, changes to their supporting structures, and changes to the way the senior management handles responsibility and the way in which consulting and training needs of the teams are controlled. These factors are now discussed, followed by analysis of the statistics on their relative importance.

> Mobility provides direct contact between employees and customers of the business. This direct and personalized contact has an immediate effect on the organizational structure. The traditional hierarchical structures of teams and organizations are made redundant by the application of mobility in business processes.

Changes to Employee Reporting Structures

Employees equipped with mobile gadgets work outside the physical boundaries of organizations in different ways. For example, employees working from home or a branch office generally remain at a single location, but are remote to the central organization. Other types of employees and workers remain in multiple areas of their work environment such as the warehouse, shop floor, and meeting rooms.

Mobility restructures the employee reporting structure. This is because staff members equipped with mobile devices have a much better and timely line of communication with their supervisors. The use of mobility allows the employees to bypass the hierarchy of the organization. Similarly, the supervisor has improved and timely communication with his team. Mobility disrupts the traditional hierarchical organizational structure of the teams and overall business.

The discussion by Cigna and Ramamurthy (2006) on the vital issues of trust in the working environment takes on a special significance in the context of a mobile work environment. Trust refers to the extent to which employees within the organization can openly communicate with their superiors, seek their guidance and expertise, and be confident that the integrity of their personal and sensitive information will not be compromised. The sensitivity of personal information in mobility is crucial from the employees' point of view. The relationship between employees' perceptions (of usefulness and ease of use of the technology) and their intentions to adopt/use mobile computing devices for B2B transactions will be stronger in organizational contexts that promote and reinforce trust between employees and the organization.

Changes to Senior Management's Responsibilities

Mobility enables senior managers to monitor the staff even when they are away from the office. Mobility also facilitates decision making in real-time rather than waiting for a face-to-face or electronic meeting. Mobility allows the group to initiate an instantaneous group discussion without waiting for physical access. The senior management's responsibilities become more demanding in the mobile age, but management is also well supported by this mobile access.

Management's attitude toward the introduction of mobile technology innovation and extent to which it supports the adoption is crucial for the success of MET. The potentially disruptive features typically associated with the adoption of mobile innovations requires managers to encourage individual team members of the organization to take prudent risks, support adoption of technology innovations, and be supportive of the organization.

Changes to Consulting and Training Needs

Enhancement of the technology transforms organizations' needs and requirements related to consulting and training. Hence, consulting and training need to be modified to satisfy these new requirements of organizations with respect to mobility. Mobile technology enables consultants to engineer or reengineer new mobile processes and provide new methods to deliver training. Care should be taken by the transitioning business not to introduce mobility in the office or work environment without proper training, because it has the potential to create stress, and perhaps, hasty decision making. However, a properly monitored, gently stressed environment can lead to creatively employing mobile technology to provide innovative solutions. This creativity eases the challenges faced at work. Tasks that do not depend on geographic location (e.g., assembly line work in automotive manufacturing and patrons serviced in a restaurant or a bank) are ideally suited for the application of mobility to relieve time pressure in the work context. Informative use of mobile technology in a social context is the least stressful way of introducing mobility and associating training. Later, this informative usage can evolve to "testing" of the training provided through a two-way transactive usage of mobility.

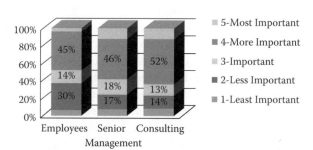

Figure 6.6 Analysis of the importance of organizational/team structure changes in the social dimension of MET.

Analysis of the Importance of Organizational and Team Structure Changes

Figure 6.6 shows the importance of changes to team structures resulting from MET. There are three factors included in this section: changes to employee reporting structures, changes to senior management, and changes to consulting/training needs in the social dimension of MET.

The result of the survey in regard to the importance of the factor "changes to employee reporting structures" in the social dimension, appearing at the left-hand side of Figure 6.6, indicates that 4 percent of the participants in the survey think that this factor is most important, 45 percent think this factor is more important, 14 percent think it is important, 30 percent think it is less important, and 7 percent think it is least important.

The result of the survey in regard to the importance of the factor "changes to senior management" in the social dimension, appearing at the middle of Figure 6.6, indicates that 12 percent of the participants in the survey think that this factor is most important, 46 percent think this factor is more important, 18 percent think it is important, 17 percent think it is less important, and 7 percent think it is least important.

The result of the survey in regard to the importance of changes to consulting/training factors in the social dimension, appearing at the right-hand side of Figure 6.6, indicates that 12 percent of the participants in the survey think that this factor is most important, 52 percent think this factor is more important, 13 percent think it is important, 14 percent think it is less important, and 8 percent think it is least important.

These percentage figures form a bell curve, indicating "normal" importance of these factors in the minds of the participants. These figures indicate that the end users are perhaps less concerned with organizational factors when it comes to mobility. Additional research is required to correlate the category of users with the foregoing results. For example, it is possible that the participants in the senior management category would be more concerned with organizational changes and training needs than the consulting categories.

Changing Customer Relationship Structures

The disruptive effect of mobility is felt in the way the relationship structures between customers and employees change. With mobility, there is also an enhanced and direct contact between the customers and the business itself as an entity, independent of human response. These contacts between customers, employees, and the business change depending on the various types of users. For example, some customers are merely looking for basic information and mobile phone contact with their business. This usage brings about only minimal changes to the customer relationship and service structures. However, there are also the ultimate mobile users who are on the road all the time, hardly spending any time in the office but require regular access to data and collaborative functionality while on the move. Examples of these types of workers include salespersons, doctors, ambulance crew, roadside motor vehicle assistants, and so on—they change customer relationships substantially. Application of mobility results in an *extended enterprise* that creates a mobile infrastructure, including communication and collaboration with e-mail, calendaring/scheduling, contact management, discussion forums, virtualized meetings, and so on. In a mobile-enabled extended enterprise, customer relationships undergo change. These changes are anticipated between the customers and the employees, and among the customers and the way in which the customers interact with the business as an entity. The ability of the customer to interact with the business as an entity, however, requires the transitioning business to be sensitive to the privacy and security aspects of the customer. Individual customers are particularly susceptible to advertisements and promotions on mobile devices.

Relationship between Customer and Employees

Mobility changes the relationship between customers and employees by enabling direct contact between them in real-time. The customer finds that he or she can reach the employees independent of location and time. For example, when a household customer calls and informs the water board about a pipe burst, the officer in charge of that area can be accessed irrespective of his location. Furthermore, through collaborative mobile strategies, that same water board officer can locate the plumber nearest to the area and send him to the needed location. The relationship between the customer and the employee becomes direct, and the response from the employees instantaneous with the use of mobility—should the business so desire.

Relationship between Customer and Business

Automated mobile processes enable the customer to submit a request and receive a response to the demand quickly. These requests to the business need not be made to an employee, but directly to the organization's mobile systems. As a result, a real-time and better customer relationship management (CRM) is achieved. Anywhere and anytime accessibility of the business and advances in providing services are due to this direct contact between the customer and the business. Mobile business processes, for example, enable a customer to customize and order a pizza directly from the system. Customers can similarly access information on sports scores or train timings by sending an SMS to the system (as against calling and speaking with an employee). This direct accessibility and the services provided by the mobile business systems help improve the relationship between the customer and business.

Advertisement and Mobility

Mobile network operators have information on the user's location. Mobile gadgets are also personalized gadgets carried by the user. Thus, there are opportunities to create mobile advertisements. The users' location and type of mobile phone usage can be used to personalize the messages that are sent out to these prospective customers. However, such advertisements and promotions need to be undertaken very carefully as there is a risk of customer backlash if the privacy and lifestyle of the customer are disturbed.

Mobile businesses need to realize that advertising and other solicitations cannot be pushed on the mobile device in the same way as they are pushed to the typical desktop-based Web application. This is because of the personalized nature of the mobile device. Unwanted messages increase the overall download time for the information the user wants, slows the progress of the transactions, and possibly increases costs (such as when the user is using a cell phone in an international roaming mode where she has to pay for advertising messages received). Nonetheless, there are some value-added types of advertising that are likely to become popular with mobile handheld users. Location awareness, temporal awareness, and preference awareness need to be incorporated in mobile advertisements to provide value. These opportunities in mobile advertisements with these types of awareness include opportunities to reach willing subscribers with consumer information that may be related to their physical location (e.g., near the mall) or the current time together with promotional materials (e.g., lunchtime or a spouse's birthday).

Mobile content providers use different ways to post advertisements and charge the owners of the advertisements. A wide variety of advertisement formats are available for mobile businesses that enable them to target options for potential customers. These formats include the ability of mobile businesses to display their advertisements, target specific advertisements against mobile messages and mobile searches by users, and provide location-specific promotions (such as sending a coupon through an SMS message). The costs of advertisements and promotions need to be factored in, as it may not be sufficiently cost-effective to broadcast wireless messages to a large number of potential customers.

Further challenges in mobile advertisements include the privacy concerns mentioned earlier. Unsolicited message and advertisements on mobile devices can result in customers switching off their device or switching to different service providers. Annoyance can also turn to anger and may lead to legal action, notably by customer groups. Therefore, there is a possibility that businesses may switch to request-based advertisements, such as the advertisement or promotion for the nearest gas station or restaurants requested by the user. There may also be a need to "add value" to the advertisement by providing the user information about the weather or sports scores along with the promotional material.

Relationship among Customers

Customer-to-customer interaction on the Internet is based on common topics of interest such as purchase, value, or satisfaction of the product. Similarly, mobile networks allow customers to communicate with one another when they are buying the product, or even later when they are trying to use the product. Mobile technology provides a much broader opportunity for customers to find and relate with other customers through their mobile gadgets as compared to land-based interactions.

Analysis of the Importance of Customer Relationships

Figure 6.7 shows the importance of changes to customer relationship (CR) structures resulting from MET. There are three factors in the social dimension of MET included in this section: relationship between customers and employees, relationship between customers and businesses, and relationship among customers.

The result of the survey in regard to the importance of the factor "relationship between customer and employees" in the social dimension, appearing to the left in Figure 6.7, indicates that 15 percent of the participants in the survey think that it is most important, and 50 percent think it is more important. A total of 65 percent think this factor is more to most important in the social dimension of MET. Only 2 percent of the participants think it is least important. These results demonstrate the growing importance of mobility in bringing together the customers and employees socially.

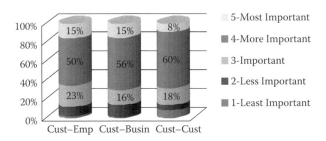

Figure 6.7   Analysis of the importance of customer relationship structure changes factor in the social dimension of MET.

The result of the survey in regard to the importance of the factor "relationship between customer and business" in the social dimension, appearing in the middle of Figure 6.7, indicates that 15 percent of the participants in the survey think that it is most important, and 56 percent think it is more important. A total of 71 percent think this factor is most to more important in the social dimension of MET. A mere 1 percent of participants think this factor is least important. These results indicate that the relationship between an individual customer and the business is even more important than that between the customer and the employee. This is so because, perhaps, the customer relates to the employee only in terms of getting a service from the business. If a part of that service can be obtained without personal interference, then perhaps users would prefer that as compared to obtaining that service from an employee.

The result of the survey in regard to the importance of the factor "relationship among customers" in the social dimension, appearing at the right-hand side of Figure 6.7, indicates that 8 percent of the participants in the survey think that it is most important, and 60 percent think it is more important. A total of 68 percent think this factor is most to more important in the social dimension of MET. Eight percent of the participants think this factor is least important. This result is slightly different from the previous two results—a very large number, 60 percent, think that interactions among customers is more important. Although this factor is not considered most important by many who considered the previous two factors most important up to 15 percent, still, a large number of participants think it is more important. This implies that customers would want mobile businesses to provide suitable opportunities for interactions among them, discussions on products and services, sharing of customer experiences, and perhaps even indicating to the decisions makers of the organization their choices and wish lists.

Mobile Transition Framework (Social Dimension)

Figure 6.8 shows the relative importance, in terms of sequencing, of the social drivers in the MET framework. The analysis shows that 24.8 percent of the respondents indicated that usability of devices should be the primary driver within the overall technical drivers of MET, whereas 19.4 percent said that it is privacy considerations that need to be considered first. They are the primary and secondary important factors in the social dimension of MET according to the results of the survey. Additionally, 17 percent of the participants think that attitude is the most important factor to be considered at first in a transition, whereas 13.8 percent consider organizational structure as a factor to be considered at the very beginning in a MET. However, 12.8 percent of the respondents consider social influence in the most important in the social dimension and 12.2 percent (the least percentage) think changes to customer relationships should be the most important to influence MET. On the basis of these statistics, a suggested sequence of factors that need to

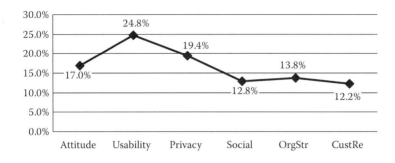

Figure 6.8   Analysis of sequencing of drivers in the social dimension of MET.

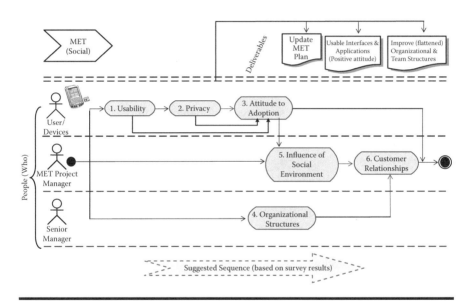

Figure 6.9   MET framework (social dimension).

be considered in a MET emerge. These factors for the social dimension in MET are used in constructing the transition framework sequence, as shown in Figure 6.9.

Figure 6.9 shows the social dimension of the MET framework. This framework is constructed taking into account the sequencing of the factors that influence the mobile business in the social dimension. Thus, the figure shows that usability of mobile devices and application is considered the most urgent of all factors that drive MET socially. A transitioning mobile organization should, therefore, focus its attention first and foremost on ensuring that the mobile devices through which it is providing information and services to its customers is user-friendly. The audio, video, screen, and numerous other features of mobile devices and their applications, as discussed in this chapter, come into play in ensuring that usability is handled properly during mobile transitions. However, immediately following usability is the issue of privacy, as shown in Figure 6.9. Privacy is uppermost in the minds of the users, and therefore, a transitioning organization must consider all aspects of privacy as it deploys mobile applications and services to its customers. The dynamics of privacy, when related to the employees, is also important as it affects the working methods and lifestyle of the employees. Therefore, in its operational use of mobility, the organization must ensure that the privacy of employees is maintained through consensus regarding the use of mobile devices among employees and management. Once the usability and privacy issues are handled to the satisfaction of users, there is a need to focus on the attitude to mobile adoption by these users. Here, the earlier discussions on the various factors that affect the attitude of users need to be considered from the point of view of the demographics of the organization's users. For example, if the organization is a university, then the users are likely to be students in a certain (e.g., adolescent) age group. However, if the organization is a travel agency, the age group of users is likely to vary widely depending on the products being offered by the organization. There is a need to understand the attitude to mobile devices and applications by these various user groups by the transitioning organization at this stage of its transition to a mobile business. Attitude needs to be nurtured, changed, or merely respected in deploying applications and services on mobile gadgets. Once the attitude to adoption has been duly considered, the changes to the organizational structures and team structures resulting from mobile adoption need to be considered. Herein, there are challenges to be handled owing to flattening of team hierarchies and expectations from users due to direct access to employees of the organization. Subsequently, the MET project manager also needs to work out the effects of mobility on both the internal and external social environment of the business. Internally, the workers will find the changes to the working lifestyle to be either positive or negative; externally, the relationships with the society and the environment will change. Eventually, there will be changes to the customer relationships and the systems that manage and analyze those relationships. Note, however, that the execution of this social dimension of the MET framework does not occur in isolation, but is intertwined with the other dimensions. A complete and comprehensive framework in practice will result in a project plan for MET that is shown and discussed in Chapter 7.

Social Dimension of MET Transition

Social–Informative

What is the value of the mobile information to the mobile client? Mostly, informative usage revolves around providing information to preregistered users (Figure 6.10). Furthermore, social-informative usage also revolves around promotions and

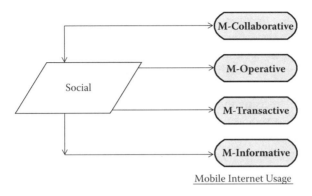

Figure 6.10 Mapping social dimension to mobile Internet usage.

advertisements that appear on the user's mobile device. However, as discussed earlier, mobile advertisement can be socially intrusive. Unless value is provided to the user, through informative figures, advertisements can be counterproductive for the business.

Spot-based information, such as traffic density in the peak hours on a specific road, has positive social connotations. Informative broadcasts within a targeted area can also help shape crowd or group behaviors through their mobile devices—and that may come in handy in large-scale emergency situations (such as floods, fires, or threatening situations).

The most significant aspect of this social-informative usage is that, similar to the informative usage in all other MET dimensions, it is the easiest usage to implement and therefore the business finds it most attractive and least risky to start its mobile usage through provision of information.

Social–Transactive

The impact of transactive use of mobility on the social dimension deals with the social willingness and need for two or more parties to transact or deal with one another. Thus, for willing parties, mobile transactions can lead to opportunities for further interesting social interactions, exchange of information and knowledge, or even simple and cheerful exchange of greetings.

Social–Operative

The operative use of mobility by business affects the employees, the quality of their time at work, and the issues of access to them during their personal or "off-duty" times. Changes to the operational procedures of the business due to mobility change the reporting structures and influences the personal growth of the employees. The operational nature of mobility also changes the internal business processes, and therefore, it is much more involved than the informative and transactive usage of mobility. Socially, the operative usage of mobility will impact team organization, as mobility enables different and direct reporting structures within the teams and the organization. Socially, the operative usage also enables workers to socialize using mobility, and thereby influences their union's decision-making process, as well as providing inputs to the management decision-making process. Thus, mobility in business operations has the potential to change the face of the organization as it works out the best way to change and manage its internal business processes.

Social–Collaborative

Socially, the collaborative nature of mobility allows the formation of groups particularly among teenagers, businesses, and various types of customers. Expertise and knowledge residing in these types of user groups can come together quickly, common interest being the glue, with the aid of mobile technology. Mobility also opens up opportunities for the formation of professional work-related clusters and groups both within and outside organizational boundaries. Thus, the social effect of mobility tends to transcend a single organization and moves toward multiple organizations in many groups with common interests or common needs to provide services to users.

Discussion Points

1. Which of the various social factors discussed in this social dimension of MET is the most important factor according to you? Discuss with reasons and examples.
2. Why is the social aspect of mobility extremely important for transitioning mobile businesses? Discuss from the point of view of context as well as personalized mobile devices.
3. What should be the approach of transitioning mobile businesses when they are faced with concerns of users in terms of potential loss of privacy due to their mobile devices?
4. Why should a mobile business process affect the hierarchy of a team structure? Explain whether the effect of that change is positive or negative from a customer's viewpoint? Also discuss the possible concerns employees might have with regard to such an adoption of mobility by business.
5. What are the principles of usability that apply to mobile application development and deployment? Discuss with examples.

References

Abood, C. 2006. Mobile camera phones—dealing with privacy, harassment and spying/surveillance concerns, chapter in *Handbook Resources of Mobile Business*, ed. B. Unhelkar. Hershey, PA: IDEAS Group Publication.

Adam, C. and Katos, V. 2005. The ubiquitous mobile and location-awareness time bomb, *Cutter IT Journal* 18(6): 20–26.

Baig, E. C. 2006. Where in the World Am I? Your Phone Might Know; More Consumer Call on Location-Based Services, *USA Today.*

Camponovo, G. and Cerutti, D. 2004. The spam issue in mobile business: A comparative regulatory review, *Proceedings of the International Conference on Mobile Business,* July 12–13, New York.

Ciganek, A. P. and Ramamurthy, K. 2006. Social context for mobile computing device adoption and diffusion: A proposed research model and key research issues, chapter in *Handbook Resources of Mobile Business*, ed. B. Unhelkar. Hershey, PA: IDEAS Group Publication.

Constantine, L. and Lockwood, L. 1999. *Software for Use: A Practical Guide to Models and Methods of Usage-Centered Design.* New York: Addison-Wesley, 1999. Also see www.foruse.com.

Elliott, G. and Phillips, N. 2004. *Mobile Commerce and Wireless Computing Systems.* Harlow, England: Pearson/Addison-Wesley.

Gala, J. and Unhelkar, B. 2009. Impact of mobile technologies and gadgets on adolescent's interpersonal relationships, chapter in *Handbook of Research in Mobile Business: Technical, Methodological and Social Perspectives*, 2nd ed., ed. B. Unhelkar. Hershey, PA: IGI Global.

Ghanbary, A. 2006. Evaluation of mobile technologies in the context of their application, limitation and transformation, chapter in *Handbook Resources of Mobile Business*, ed. B. Unhelkar. Hershey, PA: IDEAS Group Publication.

Godbole, N. 2006. Relating mobile computing to mobile commerce, chapter in *Handbook Resources of Mobile Business*, ed. B. Unhelkar. Hershey, PA: IDEAS Group Publication.

Harmon, R. and Diam, T. 2009. Assessing the future of location-based services: Technologies, applications, and strategies, chapter in *Handbook of Research in Mobile Business: Technical, Methodological and Social Perspectives,* 2nd ed., ed. B. Unhelkar. Hershey, PA: IGI Global.

Kamdar, M. 2007. *Planet India*, 72–also refs 32–35 in chapter "India imagines the future."

Louis Hall. January 27, 2008. *The Sydney Morning Herald,* www.smh.com.au.

Neely, M. and Unhelkar, B. 2005. The role of a collaborative commerce legal framework in IT-related litigation. *Cutter IT Journal,* 18(11): 11–17.

Perusco, L. and Michael, K. 2007. Control, trust, privacy, and security: Evaluating location-based services, *IEEE Technology and Society Magazine* 26(1): 4–16.

Spinney, J. 2004. Location-Based Services and the Proverbial Privacy Issue, *Directions Magazine*, March 1.

Subramanian, S., Peterson, R. A., and Jarvenpaa, S. L. 2002. Exploring the implications of M-Commerce for markets and marketing, *Journal of the Academy of Marketing Science* 30(4): 348–361.

Telecoms industry "worst for consumer privacy," 2007. March 6th, telecoms.com, from http://telecoms.com/itmgcontent/tcoms/news/articles/20017409490.html.

Unhelkar, B. 2005. Transitioning to a mobile enterprise: A three-dimensional framework. *Cutter IT Journal* (August) 18(8): 5–11.

Unhelkar, B. 2008. Mobile Enterprise Architecture: Model and Application, *Cutter Executive Report* (April) 1(3), www.cutter.com.

Unni, R. and Harmon, R. 2006. Location-based services—opportunities and challenges, chapter in *Handbook Resources of Mobile Business,* ed. B. Unhelkar. Hershey, PA: IDEAS Group Publication.

Chapter 7

Enacting and Managing Mobile Enterprise Transitions

> Each problem that I solved became a rule which served afterwards to solve other problems.
>
> **Rene Descartes (1596–1650)**

Chapter Key Points

- Describes the practical enactment of the Mobile Enterprise Transition (MET) framework, starting with identification of goals, demographics, and mobile maturity state of the organization
- Identifies the challenges and risks associated with the management of the MET project in practice
- Presents a practical implementation plan for the MET framework that encompasses the four dimensions (economic, technical, process, and social) of MET
- Highlights the important integration and training issues in mobile business when MET is enacted

Introduction

This chapter describes the practical enactment of the MET framework, which along with its management, form the dynamic aspect of the MET framework. The discussion thus far in this book outlines the framework and provides details of its four dimensions. The "enactment of MET" implies its practical implementation and brings together the theory of transition and the lessons learned from earlier transitions. Availability of the MET framework and its configuration for enactment are significant considerations in mobile transition. An equally important challenge is the practical aspect of carrying out the steps of the MET framework. Enactment synergizes the elements within MET's four dimensions (discussed in Chapters 3, 4, 5, and 6) as they are executed step by step to bring about the mobile transition. Thus, MET enactment is a project in itself, which not only uses the fundamentals of mobility and its transition discussed thus far but also draws upon the principles and practices of project management, its activities, and its deliverables already available in the project management literature (such as www.pmbok.org, www.pmi.org) for MET.

MET Project Mapping and Enactment

Figure 7.1 shows the overall positioning of MET as a project and what constitutes its enactment. It also shows a mapping between typical project management activities and the major phases within the MET project. Initially, the management contemplates MET in terms of various external and internal influences, which is an activity that is part of identifying the goals and visions of an organization as discussed in Chapter 2.

Once the organization commits to undertaking MET, it wants to ensure that its goals and visions are in line with the MET approach. For example, if the goals of a hospital are to improve patient flow, the MET approach will have to reflect that goal. The demographics of the organization, such as its size and location, play a role in influencing the MET deliberations by the management. The demographics and the goals of the organization thus influence the scope of the MET project. As mapped in Figure 7.1, planning and documenting of the MET project plan is an activity that results from the arguments for and approach to a project. The process framework of a project maps to the specific MET project plan. MET project plans are based on the scope (small, medium, or large) of the transition project. It includes activities and tasks from the economic, technical, process, and social dimensions. This planning and documenting of the project plan is followed by its launch, the core enactment of the MET framework, which needs to be actively supported by process, project management, and related CASE (computer-aided software engineering) tools.

Quality metrics also play an important role in the MET project. For example, in the technical dimension, the number of errors and enhancements to mobile software application development can be measured. Another example of quality metrics is the measurement of efficiency gained by providing service to a customer using a

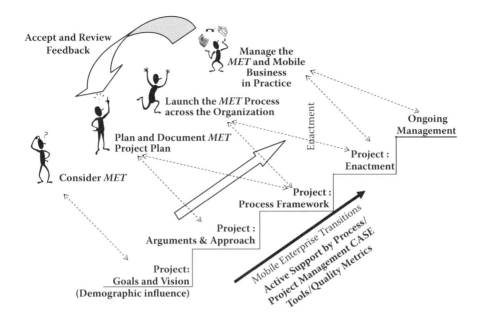

Figure 7.1 MET project enactment and mapping to process/project management.

mobile business process. Once the MET project is launched, it needs to be managed on an ongoing basis. Feedback on the progress of the project needs to be formally provided, accepted, and serviced. Process metrics tools again play an important role in facilitating feedback. Such feedback, shown in Figure 7.1, also enables fine-tuning of the MET project as it is enacted. Changes to the actual MET framework and project plans can be expected in a dynamically changing project, more so when it is accepting feedback from the implementers and potential users during its execution. The practical enactment of MET leads to a mobile business that matures in all the four dimensions through which it has transitioned. This maturity, in practice, is a stepwise evolution of the mobile business that results from enactment of MET.

The enactment of Mobile Enterprise Transitions (METs) is a project in itself that brings the discussions on the economic, technical, process, and social dimensions to fruition by practically implementing the MET framework. The MET enactment project thus needs to make use of the known principles and practices of project management, together with its own nuances of mobile technology adoption and implementation that come from the four dimensions.

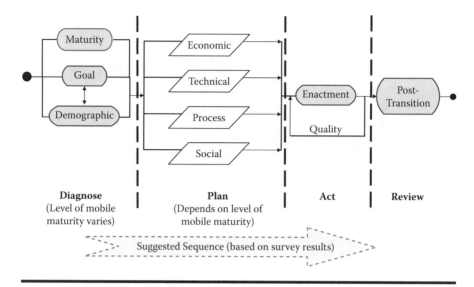

Figure 7.2   Core elements of METM framework in practice.

Practical Outline of METM Framework

Figure 7.2 shows the core elements of the MET and management (METM) framework and the way in which they are distributed among the phases associated with this framework in practice. These phases are diagnose, plan, act, and review.

The *diagnose* phase starts by identifying the goals of the organization in undertaking MET. The demographics of the organization (such as its size and location) and its maturity in terms of mobile usage influence the goals of the organization in undertaking MET. The activities undertaken in the diagnose phase are described in detail later in this chapter.

The next phase is the *planning* of MET enactment. The plans for the project make use of the factors discussed in the four dimensions of MET. The considerations of the four dimensions of MET in the planning phase are depicted in Figure 7.2. The economic dimension investigates the financial aspects of the transition, and thus, a cost–benefit analysis is undertaken. The result influences the goals of the transition. The demographics of the organization influence the activities within the economic dimension, also they dictate the nature and intensity of competition the organization faces in terms of mobile adoption.

The technical dimension includes creation of a technical prototype for the proposed transition path, which encompasses the mobile network transition, transition of contents, and mobile applications.

The process dimension enforces creation of the models of the mobile business processes, typically using a modeling technique such as Business Process Modeling Notation (BPMN) of Unified Modeling Language (UML). The process dimension also provides activities that deal with the measure of the quality of service (QoS).

Finally, in the planning phase, the social dimension also comes into play with the need to consider attitude to adoption, usability, legal and ethical issues, opportunities to create social network groups, and changes to the organizational structure. The need to incorporate formal change management in the MET project plan spans across the process and social dimensions.

In the *act* phase, the project plans for MET created in the planning phase that encompass activities from the four dimensions as well as the diagnose phase, are put into practice. The arguments throughout this enactment are to implement the transition plan for mobile business that will provide it with many of the strategic benefits discussed in Chapter 1.

There is always a need to undertake formal reviews after transition to ensure that the benefits have been derived. There are also a number of variations in the practical implementation of these plans due to differences in organizational goals, demographics, and maturity levels of the organization. These variations in the project plans need to be kept in mind during enactment, which involves the following:

- Accepting the formal MET approach to become a mobile business
- Diagnosing the organization to determine its current mobile maturity
- Identifying the goals and demographics of the organization and correlating them with mobile maturity
- Considering the pressing economic factors, particularly costs and competition, in formulating the MET project plan
- Creating the technical model for MET in the project plan, including mobile applications, mobile architecture, content, security, and networks
- Modeling the requirements for the new mobile business processes by bringing together user needs, UML/BPML (Business Process Modeling Language)
- Giving due credence to the sociocultural issues in both external and internal transitions
- Validating and verifying the entire MET by means of quality assurance activities, including thorough testing
- Getting postproject reviews and incorporating them in the MET project plan

Mobile Business Maturity

The practical application of the MET framework varies depending on how well the organization has already progressed in terms of the use of mobility. Thus, the enactment of the MET framework needs an understanding of the current level of maturity of the mobile business to ascertain the starting point for its implementation. Mobile business maturity can be understood as being made up of four states: ad hoc, preliminary, advanced, and managed. Figure 7.3 depicts these four states

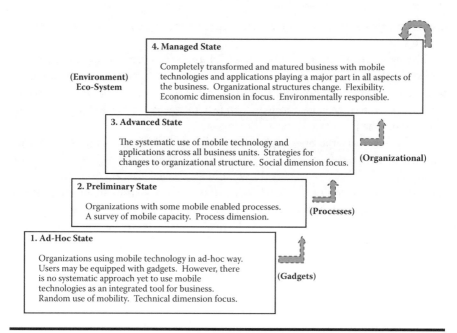

Figure 7.3   The four states of mobile business maturity. (Based on Arunatileka [2006], and Lan and Unhelkar [2005], who have extended the original concept of Kalakota and Robinson [2002].)

existing currently in an organization in terms of its overall mobile business maturity as it undergoes MET. The identification of the state of an organization with respect to its mobile maturity is an important practical step in deciding the approach to the application of MET. The organization matures to a mobile organization as it proceeds through these steps of mobile maturity.

> Businesses can be in any of the four mobile states: ad hoc, preliminary, advanced, and managed. Accurately diagnosing the current state of maturity of the organization during MET enactment plays a vital role in creating a practical and useful transition project plan. This is so because good diagnosis provides mobile maturity, which in turn ascertains the accurate starting point of enactment.

Ad Hoc State

This state is marked by a very casual and hazy idea of how to use mobile technology in conducting business. In the ad hoc state, customers, employees, and partners of the business may all be carrying and using mobile devices for their interactions with the business. Such unmanaged use of the phones reflects no particular effort yet being made by the organization to strategize and change its work practices and business processes with the help of mobile technology. It is one step above no use of mobility, just after mobile devices are procured and distributed among the various stakeholders of the business. Connecting people with each other through mobile phones only provides a very basic, although fundamental, advantage to business today. This ad hoc state of mobile maturity of a business relates to the technical dimension of MET.

However, this ad hoc state should impel the organization to start considering ways and means of using mobility in a more strategic manner in its business. A study and diagnosis of the existing business and its processes should be undertaken to ascertain the extent to which mobility is being used. A collation of existing technologies within the business, including its mobile software applications, content management and databases, and security and related mobile software assets, is made from the point of view of mobile usage. The type of network (e.g., cellular, Wi-Fi) can also be part of the study. In this ad hoc state of maturity, the organization can reduce the risks of mobile usage by restricting it to providing information only. Furthermore, a survey of mobile usage and applications by competitors and business partners can also be carried out now. The urgency for a more strategic use of mobility can come from the pressure of competition if the competing businesses are beyond the ad hoc state. Requests for changes to technology and processes in the business, and aspirations of mobile usage by the business stakeholders, are considered and documented in the ad hoc state. Such documentation provides the impetus for the MET project plan to enact the transition.

Preliminary State

The preliminary state of an organization implies a slightly more strategic approach to mobility than the ad hoc state. In this state, mobile technology starts getting used as a tool in many business processes of the organization. Mobile technologies, in the preliminary state, also influence customers, employees, and business partners. However, the overall use of mobility is still preliminary, as it is not sufficiently strategic and not mindful of the long-term sustainability of the organization. Its use in this state involves adaptation of mobile devices in the business processes of the organization. Mobile technology is not considered across all the dimensions by the organization, and thus there is considerable room for improvement in its existing usage by the business. Individuals (employees or customers) use handheld gadgets to accomplish their business processes in this state. The preliminary state requires the business to further identify, list, and prioritize business processes that are potential candidates for mobile transition. New mobile processes are also considered and modeled. The processes that may be obsolete as a result of the introduction of new technology are identified, and provision is made to drop these processes without affecting the service provided to the users of these processes. The preliminary state signifies the use of mobile technologies in various business processes of the organization, but without formal planning. It will involve both informative and transactive use of mobility. Therefore, the technical and process dimensions of the MET framework are active in this state of a mobile organization; however, the economic and social dimensions may be dormant.

Advanced State

When an organization is in the advanced state of mobile usage, it employs mobile technology in a substantial way in technical, process, and social dimensions. This includes informative, transactive, and operative use of mobility. Most departments and business units in an advanced mobile organization that use mobile technology include processes that influence organizational and team structures also. Thus, intrabusiness process communications are transitioned to incorporate mobile technology in them. However, further improvement is achieved by transitioning the interbusiness processes as well. For instance, the selling of a product employing mobile technology would incorporate a search by the customer, placing the order, making payment, and delivery of goods. Not all of these processes use mobile technology. Payment for the product may be undertaken electronically, and goods may be delivered physically. An organization in the advanced state has to refine its transitioned business processes to incorporate internal and external aspects. The important activities of the organization rely heavily on the use of mobile technology and the fine-tuning of business processes based on mobility. Thus, there is an enhancement of interdepartment and interbusiness processes in this advanced state of mobile maturity of the organization.

Managed State

This is the most desirable and stable state of an organization in terms of its usage of mobile technologies. It garners benefits from all the four dimensions of mobile transition. Thus, managed state is the one in which mobile technology is used by the business to

- Maintain its economic growth and prosperity
- Capitalize on the features and facilities provided by the technology
- Fine-tune change and optimize its mobile processes (such as its networks and devices) with ease
- Have a socially acceptable and creative use of mobility

Managed state is also able to make use of mobility for informative, transactive, operative, and, most important, collaborative purposes. All the significant processes in the business are fully transitioned to mobility, as also the day-to-day running of the business. For example, the purchase of a product, paying for it, and receiving delivery are all undertaken by the use of mobile technology in a managed state. Time and cost savings are achieved through the extensive and systematic use of mobile technology; meanwhile customers are offered a new and fully integrated technology for carrying out business transactions. Forward and backward integrations with suppliers and value-added service providers are facilitated. Mobile applications in the fully managed state for mobile business are flexible enough to accommodate the changes required by the business. This expected flexibility can be achieved by a transitioning organization by planning for it earlier in MET enactment. Flexibility incurs cost, but it is an asset in the ongoing management of mobile business. Finally, the managed state of a mobile business has also the opportunity to consider the environmental impacts of the business activities. This is so because, in this state, the business transcends the preliminary struggle associated with the adoption of mobile technology and also the related sociocultural issues. The subsequent two chapters (Chapters 8 and 9) are dedicated to discussing the expansion, growth, and management of mobile enterprises and their sustainability and environment, respectively.

MET Factors, States, and Timings

Figure 7.4 shows the current mobile maturity state of a typical transitioning organization. It also shows a typical one-year transition plan in action. Note that although

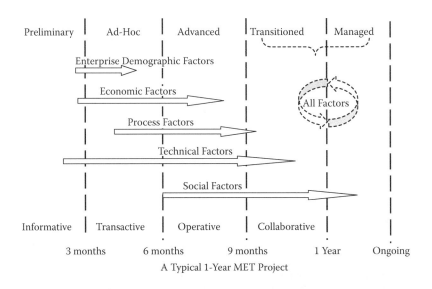

Figure 7.4 MET factors, states, and timings.

Figure 7.4 shows the four states of maturity of a mobile organization, it is also mapped to the four transition dimensions. An organization follows a unique path in transition, depending on its current state of mobile maturity. For example, an organization in the ad hoc state is most likely to focus on the technical and economic factors, whereas a preliminary organization focuses on the economic and process factors. The advanced-state organization is likely to have the economic, process, and technical dimensions in control but may have to focus on the social dimension. Finally, the fully transitioned and managed mobile business will have all factors iteratively influencing it and being influenced by it. This circular or iterative influence is shown in Figure 7.4. In a typical MET enactment, the first three months can be used in getting the organization to make full use of the mobile technologies. The next three months can focus on process as well as technical factors. This will transition the business to a preliminary business. The use of process, technical, and social factors together makes the organization advanced and, finally, the organization is in a managed state.

MET Enactment Risks

> The MET project, similar to any other project, has risks to face during its enactment. Disruptive mobile technologies and uncertainties of expectations are major risks. Creation of a pilot project and scoping the MET project goes a long way in ameliorating enactment risks.

There is a need to contain the exposure to risks associated with MET to the business. These risks were discussed in Chapter 1. The manner in which they can be mitigated in MET enactment are as follows:

■ Diagnosing the mobile maturity of the business to ascertain the optimum transition path—Lack of knowledge about the current state of mobile maturity of a business can lead to a failed MET.
■ Ensuring a proper match between the goals and demographics of the organization—If the goals of an organization do not make sense to the physical location of the organization or cannot be supported by the location or size of the organization, then we have a conflict in the project, which is a risk.
■ Creation of a pilot MET project and the initial selection of appropriate business processes for it—The business processes for mobility need not be very complex, but they should be important enough to have an impact on the organization.

- Planning the pilot over a complete business process and not just a part of it—A pilot business process in transition will encounter the economic, technical, and social aspects of MET only when it is modeled and transitioned from start to finish.
- Creating the scope of the transition—This depends on the size and maturity of the organization with respect to mobile maturity. A large organization, for example, will need the MET project to be large in scope; however, if the same organization is in a managed mobile state, the transition scope may be medium or small.
- Planning the measurement of the MET through a suite of metrics—These metrics can help evaluate the success of MET. Although the concept of metrics is not discussed in detail here, it is recommended that some project management and business metrics be applied to the transition process.
- Management of stakeholders and their expectations—This can be done by ensuring proper starting and completion of the pilot and mapping the MET goals to those provided in the business announcement and in the information for stakeholders.
- Properly timing the transition to derive maximum benefit and cause minimum disruption to the normal functioning of the business—For example, timing the start of the transition process during periods of low business activities will reduce disruptions to the customer, at the same time, ensuring the availability of staff.
- Eliciting feedback—This is done using process management tools and even by face-to-face interactions, to fine tune and optimize the transition process.
- Using the available consulting and training expertise or extending it—This enables the organization to capitalize on the transition experience of others.

Diagnose

There will be very few organizations that will start from scratch as mobile enterprises. Most will have ongoing business activities they have to deal with even when considering formal mobile transition. In fact, many enterprises will be already using mobile devices in their business processes. Therefore, launching MET requires a thorough assessment of the current state of an enterprise in terms of its readiness for mobile transition.

Demographics

The demographics of an organization provide a major impetus to its goals in transitions. Chapter 2 discussed the research survey (the questionnaire is presented in Appendix A), which starts with the demographic indicators of the organization. The organization can be small or medium or large. Its size plays a role in deciding the scope of the transition. Similarly, its location influences the scope of the transition.

Goal

The goals of MET must be streamlined with the goals of the business. MET goals may vary depending on the demographics and mobile maturity of the transiting organization. The known goals include dynamic customization of products and services, cost reduction, profit enhancement, flexibility in organizational structure, value added, personalized customer services, and timeliness of services. MET enactment can also help in the sustainability of the business and the development of an environmentally intelligent business system.

Mobile Maturity State

The organization's current mobile state needs to be identified through diagnosis, which provides an understanding of its mobile maturity. It could be undertaken organization-, department- or business-unit-wide, as per the particular requirements of the organization. The diagnosis requires a check on how well the organization is using mobility and investigation of its four dimensions—economic, technical, process, and social—to examine how they use mobility.

The more mature an organization, the more pervasive the use of mobility in the four dimensions. The organization has to be continuously sensitive to new technology breakthroughs and be ready to further improve the transitioned processes in terms of better mobile devices, higher bandwidths, and increased cost savings.

Plan

After diagnosing the organization for its goals, demographics, and mobile maturity, the MET project in enactment moves toward creation of a project plan as shown in Figure 7.5. However, the project plan itself (shown in Table 7.1) has diagnostic activities at its start.

Economic

The economic aspect of transition is reflected in the earlier part of the project plan. The economic investigations include study of the competitive pressures (perhaps through strength–weakness–opportunity–threat [SWOT] or political–economic–sociocultural–technical [PEST] analysis), calculations of the net present value (NPV) of the MET project, and the need to balance that with the economic growth and expansion of the business. The economic aspect of the project plan for MET includes, apart from the goals, the demographics of the business, its technology approach, and its maturity in terms of both quality and mobile usage. Such economic planning becomes an important upfront activity for MET because budget planning influences time and human resource planning of the project. Therefore, it is acceptable for some part of the cost–benefit analysis to take place even before project planning.

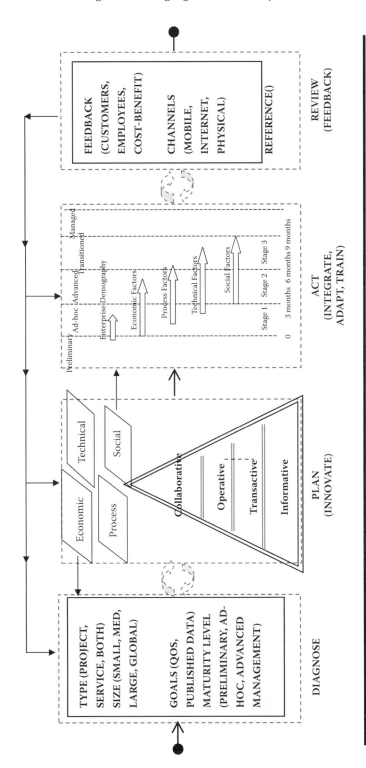

Figure 7.5   METM detailed framework during enactment.

Table 7.1 A typical MET project plan for a medium-sized organization with preliminary maturity

Activity no.	Activity name	Resource name
1	Identify the type of organization	Management
2	Identify and document the goals	Management
3	Identify the mobile maturity level	Management
4	Create MET budgets and plans	Management
5	Identify the cost and time	Management
6	Undertake SWOT for competition	Business partner (supplier)
7	Investigate and prototype gadget capabilities	User/gadget
8	Identify and document mobile business process	Technical designer
9	Apply usability and privacy concepts	User/gadget
10	Consider network coverage and bandwidth	Technical designer
11	Study the impact of transition customers/employees	User/gadget
12	Consider mobile network, device, and interoperability standards	User/gadget
13	Consider convenience/connectivity	Management
14	Discuss the attitude to mobile adoption, depending on user categories	User/gadget
15	Study mobile processes for reengineering	Management
16	Develop new mobile processes on the mobile application	User/gadget
17	Improve business control by the use of mobile application	Management
18	Consider various types of mobile usage by the user	User/gadget
19	Model mobile application and finance issues	Management
20	Model the changes to organizational structures	Management

Table 7.1 *(continued)* **A typical MET project plan for a medium-sized organization with preliminary maturity**

Activity no.	Activity name	Resource name
21	Mobile infrastructure consideration	Technical designer
22	Update and manage mobile content including the design of a content management system	Technical designer
23	Model engineer mobile business processes	Management
24	Prototype and improve the quality of service (QoS)	Management
25	Create and manage mobile collaborations among various stakeholders (incorporate mobile Web services [MWSs])	Business partner (supplier)
26	Manage customer relationships and expectations in using MET	Management
27	Consider social and environmental issues through mobility	Management
28	Apply quality techniques to all models	All
29	Provide review and feedback on the process	Management

As mentioned in Chapter 3, there are several approaches that could be used for planning the economic parts of the project. A typical planning approach starts with a SWOT analysis of the business. Alternatively, a PEST analysis may also be undertaken by the business in the context of MET. A third alternative is to use a balanced scorecard, although such a management tool is slightly further down the track in the economic dimension. These economic activities are shown in the typical MET project plan in Table 7.1. It should be noted that, although cost benefits are the upfront discussion topics in the project from the economic dimension, there are many other economic activities that may happen later in the project.

Technical

The technical dimension of the MET project plan primarily considers mobile networks and mobile devices in terms of their current and future use within the organization. These activities occasionally precede the activities in the economic dimension. The selection of the mobile infrastructure plays an important role in the MET project. This mobile infrastructure is made up of network coverage and bandwidth, mobile standards, and mobile content management. The enactment of

MET forces the organization to create technical prototypes of various parts of the mobile infrastructure to ascertain its relevance to the mobile organization.

Process

The process aspect of MET enactment deals with modeling and reengineering mobile processes. Some of the activities in this dimension appear later in tasks 15, 16, and 17 in Table 7.1. Mobile process reengineering, as discussed in Chapter 5, plays an important role in a mobile business by enabling real-time responses to user requests from multiple businesses. The process architecture ensures that updates and sourcing of content happen through a single and central data repository. Formulation of the business process plan includes planning the project schedule, reengineering the business processes, ensuring better business controls, maintaining the QoS, business modeling, and maintaining organizational structures. CASE tools that support process modeling, such as IBM's System Modeler (www.rational.com), Microsoft's Visio, and even open source CASE tools, such as StarUML come in handy in this part of the MET project.

Social

The social aspect of the MET project plan is shown in the tasks, such as 18, 19, 27, and 28 given in Table 7.1. The primary aim of the MET project in this dimension is to focus on planning and organizing people, managing changes to the supporting structures, enabling formal change management for the people, and enabling senior management to handle the consulting and training needs of the teams involved in MET. The MET project manager also needs to work out the effects of mobility on the internal and external social environments of the business. Internally, the workers will find changes to their working lifestyle as either positive or negative; externally, the relationships of the business with the society and the environment will change. The social factors related to mobility discussed in Chapter 6 come into play here.

Iterations in MET Project

The MET project benefits from an iterative and incremental approach. Such iterations and increments have been applied successfully in software projects. A MET project can apply these principles in creating and executing an iterative project plan. There are typically three iterations in such a plan: initial, major, and final. Creation of such a project plan is an important and core activity of MET project management. An iterative project plan provides valuable input to the early budgeting activity of MET. Thus, in a way, creation of the project plan in this case amounts to putting the scope of the project in a project management grid. The aim of the plan is not only to indicate how the activities and tasks from the four dimensions of MET are sequenced but also to show how they will be performed in an iterative way. Dynamic project and process management tools and techniques come into play during the creation and management of an iterative and incremental MET project plan.

Scoping the MET Project

Creating and understanding the scope of the MET project is important because it helps in setting the expectations of the entire project and also its resources and timings. Some factors that influence the scope of MET enactment are as follows:

- Level of mobile maturity of the organization—The more mobile mature the organization, the smaller is the scope of the transition project and vice versa.
- Demographics of the organization—The larger the organization, the larger is the scope.
- Pressure on the organization due to competition—The greater the urgency, the larger is the scope.
- Use of in-house resources or third party/external resources for MET—The more experienced the resources for undertaking MET, the less is the risk.
- Extent of the use of CRM and SCM packages within the organization, and the acceptability of these packages by customers.

During scoping, project management is working out the answer to the question "How extensive should the MET enactment be?" The scope of the enactment affects the creation of the project plan. The extensiveness of the MET project plan, in turn, determines the number of activities and tasks performed, the number of times an activity gets repeated, the number of people performing a particular activity, the amount of work involved in testing, and the manner in which the mobile system is deployed.

Small Scope

The scope of MET enactment is small when the organization is small in size and when it has already moved to a preliminary or advanced stage of mobile maturity. The latter indicates that the extent of the transition will not be from scratch as the organization already has some formal activities happening in the mobile space. The small scope is usually involved primarily with the extensive use of one or two dimensions of MET, with the other dimensions supporting it. A small scope also indicates that the organization does not need all of the activities described in the MET framework.

Medium Scope

The medium scope of MET enactment is most likely when the organization is medium to large in size and when its mobile maturity is ad hoc to preliminary. For medium scope, the organization will require all the MET dimensions. Therefore, it will need to plan for a majority of the transition activities given in Table 7.1. However, a medium-scope transition may not go through all three iterations (initial, major, and final), as the intensity of these iterations may not be as high as in the large scope one.

Large Scope

Large-scope transition enactment includes all dimensions and every aspect of the MET framework. The number of times the activities within the framework are repeated, and the intensity with which they are repeated, are also high in this scope. For example, the number of people or resources performing the same activities outlined in the MET framework will be higher in the large-scope project than in small- or medium-scope projects.

MET Project Plan

Table 7.1 shows a typical MET project plan. The four dimensions of MET do not occur as separate and isolated aspects. Also, the four layers of business usage of mobility, as discussed in Chapter 1 and depicted in Figure 1.3, are not sequential. This is because, in practice, we expect the business usage factors to be playing out simultaneously. The level of maturity of organizations with respect to mobility also plays a part in enacting MET, and the plan is accordingly different for each transitioning organization.

The roles mentioned in Table 7.1 are the generic roles in an organization undertaking MET: the management, user, technical designer, and the business partner. In practice, there will be many variations in these roles. Management is primarily involved in the planning, budgeting, and execution of the project; users and the gadgets used by them provide input to the process modeling aspect of MET; the technical designer provides the architecture and design for the solution; and the business partner indicates all external stakeholders such as suppliers and corporate customers.

The scope of the project shown in Table 7.1 is medium. This enables us to discuss the example plan without going into the situations of a large-scope transition. As mentioned earlier, the major difference between the medium and large scopes is that, in a large-scope project, the number of times an activity is carried out will increase, and so will the overall weighting of activities and tasks.

This project plan exhibits only a small part of the iterative nature of the project. There are tools that are able to place the activities and tasks of the process within the context of an iterative framework. Thus, the project management within the MET project will have to consider both types of tools: linear project planning tools such as Microsoft Project, as well as the tools that enable creation and management of dynamic iterations within the project.

Act

The action phase of MET is the step-by-step following of the project plan. The sequence and timings of a typical project plan come into play, and good estimations of timings become invaluable.

The action phase of transition involves actually following the plan given in Table 7.1. In Figure 7.5, the act phase is depicted in the third box within the overall enactment.

Typical Sequence and Timing of Enactment

The enactment of MET depends on many factors including the maturity state of the business, the timing of the start of the process, and the understanding and support of senior management. A discussion on the sequence and timing of events involved in MET enactment provides a rough idea of the actual days or dates that may be followed by many organizations.

The MET enactment process begins with the discussion on goals and visions that are in turn based on the demographics of the organization. The organization is required to have a sufficient budget to carry out the MET exercise.

The event timings and the resources available for MET enactment are functions of pressure due to competition, the mobile maturity level of the organization, etc. The level of preparedness or mobile maturity of the organization influences the extent of work or scope of MET transition.

After understanding the mobile maturity of the organization, activities from within the four dimensions (economic, technical, process, and social) of the MET framework are enacted, although not necessarily in sequence. They may overlap each other during enactment. The activity and task list is created by the transitioning organization depending on its needs. The respective dimensions of the MET framework concentrate on the following activities during enactment:

- The economic activities deal with goals and visions, interplaying with the demographics.
- The technical activities handle the core device, network, and database issues.
- The process activities bring together the business applications, context, and organizational behavior.
- The technical and process activities are coupled with social activities, which handle the people issues within the organization, organizational structure, confidence of the clients and suppliers outside the organization, and usability.

Table 7.2 Sequence and timings of MET (typical one-year project) activities for an organization at preliminary state

Sequence of events	Probable timings
Senior management considers MET. Convinced of Return on Investment (ROI) + budget (partly economic; ad hoc state)	January 2010
Organization-specific diagnosis of MET and creation of project plan (ad hoc state)	February–March 2010
Economic/technical (initial; ad hoc to preliminary state)	April–May 2010
Technical/process (preliminary state)	March–April 2010
Technical/process/social (initial)	June 2010
Process/social/enactment (toward advanced state)	August 2010
Organizational structure (perhaps trade unions), employee morale (advanced state)	August–September 2010
System, tests, QoS	October 2010
Managed state	November–December 2010
Postproject reviews	Ongoing

The activities taking place during enactment will influence the business partners of the organization. For example, the chain of suppliers will have to change the way they interact with the organization when MET takes place. There may be new legal agreements required. Training of staff may also be required. The end result of the overall enactment is an organization that is process oriented, flexible, and customer oriented—essentially a reengineered one that offers more and gains more than earlier.

The probable timings for a MET enactment can be summarized as shown in Table 7.2. These are typical timings for a small- to medium-sized firm undertaking MET from a preliminary state of mobile maturity.

MET and Project Management

Mobility radically changes both internal and external processes. Changes to internal processes also include changes to the organization's project management approach. Astute project management adopts mobility for creative solutions, uses project management tools, and moves to a flatter hierarchical structure.

Champy (1995) in *Reengineering Management* discusses the need to reengineer not just the work the organization does but also the management of this work. "It's about us, about changing our managerial work, the way we think about, organize, inspire, deploy, enable, measure, and reward the value-adding operational work," he states. A formal MET exercise provides the management with the opportunity to streamline its activities and reengineer itself. This section discusses the specific impact of mobility on project management within a transitioning organization.

Concentration on Essential Tasks

Project management within an organization changes as a result of MET enactment (also discussed very well by Brans 2003). Routine project management tasks need to be isolated from those related to transition project management. Project managers must concentrate on the essential tasks, and all mundane tasks, which also occupy considerable time, need to be handled separately so as to not distract the management in its transition effort. This is so because staff burdened with the routine management and IT issues (such as systems' uptime, project management, and program maintenance) will have little or no time to spend on exploiting the strategic opportunities possible through mobile technologies and systems. Technical and business staff will require training in the use of mobile technologies and architecture, in modeling mobile processes, and quality assurance to capitalize on the opportunities in this field.

Opportunities for Creative Solutions

MET enactment provides ample opportunities to design creative solutions for the business. Project management needs to be aware of these opportunities, and this enables the organization to make use of them. Managing an iterative and incremental MET project that ends in a reengineered organization is a process in itself. This MET project, as discussed in Chapter 5, allows management to create processes that provide time and cost advantages and also provides opportunities for new and unique solutions in the process dimension.

Using Project Management Tools

Project managers occasionally tend to manage by the seat of their pants. Such management starts with the use of mental models, and progresses, at the most, to tools such as spreadsheets and Microsoft Project. Although these tools have an important role to play in project management, the dynamic aspect of MET enactment provides opportunities to the project manager to use corresponding dynamic project management tools. Examples of such tools include the unified process, (Rational) Quality Software Process (method science), and so on.

"Flatter" Management Structure

Project management during the MET enactment effort (and the management structure as a result) should be a "flatter" structure when compared to the earlier (possibly) hierarchical management structure. This flat management structure within the MET project is an important advantage to the organization, as it can harness the creativity of the individuals involved in the technical and process activities of the project.

MET Project and People

> People issues are important in all projects—more so in MET enactment. The advantages of mobile transition need to be highlighted to all parties concerned. The MET project manager also needs to handle change management, risk management, and political hot spots during enactment. There is a need to iron out issues emerging out of the implementation of a disruptive technology such as mobile technology.

This section discusses the specific people issues in the MET project. The discussion here is different from the one on social dimension in Chapter 6, as it focuses on the project management issues that occur during the enactment. The known issues related to change management and people aspects in any project are important in MET projects also. The aim is to identify and iron out as many political issues as possible before the transition challenges commence.

Shortlist Strategic Advantages

The MET advantages discussed in Chapter 2 do not apply to all organizations at all times. The diagnose phase brings out the worthwhile advantages of MET in the context of a specific organization and its demographics. For example, the advantage of moving away from legacy systems may not mean much for a small PC-based software development shop. The advantage of MET for a small shop may be in terms of use of newer technologies or even a "soft factor" such as heightened employee morale and awareness. It is essential to shortlist the business and technical advantages of MET that are relevant to the organization and then highlight them to the employees who are involved in the project and who will be the users of the new mobile processes. Once people understand how MET can help them, there is an automatic "buy in" from those who are enlisted to work on the transition project.

Discuss Advantages with Senior Managers

Senior managers, including the project manager and the quality assurance manager, play a significant role in the overall MET. Therefore, it is essential to enlist their support during the transition project. Advantages such as reengineering of management and smart sourcing of business engineering are likely to be of utmost interest to the senior management. These need to be highlighted during MET enactment.

Highlight Advantages to the Technical Team

It is also important to highlight the strategic advantages of the transition to the technical team that works on the applications and programs in MET enactment. It is important to train them and inform them of the importance of their work to the business. The technical team will be interested in advantages that place its members in a personal and professional growth situation. Extensions to systems and databases, opportunity to provide a robust mobile system architecture, use of mobile agents and object-oriented technology, and incorporation of security in the systems are the types of professional advantages that the technical team members look for in MET enactment.

Transition Atmosphere

The MET project needs a transition atmosphere. This is particularly true in the mobile software development and business process modeling aspects of the transition. The atmosphere requires the MET project manager to create and manage the change, including technical and social change, that will affect the project and the business.

Physical Communication

Mobile technology provides ease of communication; however, the transition to mobility is a project that also requires ongoing communication. Therefore, all aspects of MET need to be communicated to the parties concerned, especially at the technical and social level. The MET project manager has the task of organizing and grouping the people participating in the transition. This effort also requires continuous communication with the employees on how mobility is being used to reengineer the organization and not to reduce or eliminate jobs.

Political Hot Spots

All changes are fraught with corresponding political issues. The MET transition project is no exception, and one would expect many people to have vested interests in the success (or otherwise) of the transition effort. Therefore, one of the important responsibilities of the MET project manager is to identify the political hot spots, internal conflicts, and vested interests of people involved in the project. There is a need to monitor the political will of the senior management and to create an atmosphere where the organizational objectives and those of the individual worker are brought together.

Ironing Out Issues

Once the hot spots within the transitioning project of the organization are identified, it is essential to sort out these political issues as quickly and effectively as possible. There are various ways in which political issues could be settled. Although some of these issues do form part of the social dimension of MET, they are important from a pure project management perspective also. The people and the issues that are likely to create friction within the organization and the transition project need to be sorted out. Ironing out the issues involves highlighting the strategic advantages of the project again and communicating them to the people involved. Retraining personnel and stressing that mobile application developers and business people need to come together are important in ironing out issues in the MET project.

Monitoring the MET Enactment

All four dimensions of MET are intertwined with each other, and they need continuous monitoring during enactment. Figure 7.6 shows how the factors from the four dimensions converge together in a project. There are three major types of elements in this diagram: the primary actors who are responsible for or affected by the MET framework, the actual activities of the framework carried out during the enactment, and the deliverables produced as a result of the enactment. This figure is a convergence of the earlier four figures appearing in Chapters 3 to 6 (Figure 3.12, Figure 4.19, Figure 5.13, and Figure 6.9) that depict the individual dimensions of the MET framework. Figure 7.6 shows all the activities together. The project, based on this figure, can start with the consideration of cost and time as important factors that mandate MET; or alternatively, the competition forces the business to undertake MET. The management takes the primary responsibility for developing the mobile business processes, reengineering them, modeling them, and developing mobile applications that handle these processes. The management is keen to improve business control and QoS. However, there are changes to the organizational and team structures that the management needs to handle, changes to customer relationships, and changes to the social environment in which the business exists and which the business influences.

The user is the primary influence on the business in terms of usability and privacy issues, as well as the way in which the convenience and connectivity of the network affects mobile usage. The capabilities of gadgets also influence mobile usage for both customers and employees. The attitude toward adoption of technology

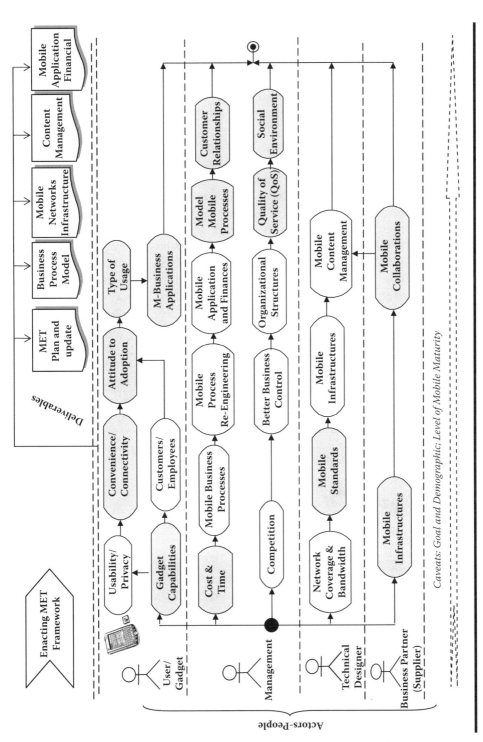

Figure 7.6   Enacting MET in practice.

needs to be studied keeping the users in mind, but that attitude is affected by the type of usage desired by the users. Finally, mobile business applications serve users on their devices as well as enable an organization to process information and provide services to the users.

The technical teams, especially designers and architects within the transitioning organization, are keen to work on network coverage and available wireless bandwidth for the organization. The existing and available mobile standards and infrastructures are also investigated by them. Most transitioning mobile businesses are likely to hire available infrastructure, but very large businesses may have the opportunity to create parts of the mobile infrastructure (e.g., using WiMax) to propagate their mobile content and services. These technical teams within the organization or who work in an advisory capacity also work on modeling the content management systems and sourcing and uploading the content. Mobile collaborations deal with existing and new business partners as well as suppliers who come together to provide unified services to customers. Business partners may also provide partnership opportunities for mobile infrastructures if they are infrastructure partners, such as network operators.

Balancing MET Plan with Practice

One of the important aspects of MET project management is the need to balance the project plan created during the planning phase with what happens in the action phase during practical enactment. Figure 7.7 shows a typical MET project in a balancing act. In the case of MET enactment, it is essential to balance the planned time and budgets with the actual. The MET framework during enactment has to continuously balance itself; if the project line is closer to the Y-axis, it implies the actual values are less than the planned ones, and vice versa.

Skewing Factor in MET Projects

Although the sequence and timings of events are discussed here with precise dates, in reality the project is not likely to follow them. The purpose of describing the timings here is to provide a benchmark of how a MET project for a preliminary organization with medium scope can proceed. There are a number of factors in practice, however, that can and does influence these timings. These factors can be called the *skewing factors*. They skew the timings shown in Table 7.2 from a few days to a few months. The MET project must incorporate this skewing factor in the ongoing/live project plan and modify the plan accordingly.

Managing Changes to the Mobile Transition Process

Feedback during the enactment is a valuable input to the MET project plan. The project plan outlined in Table 7.1 and the typical timings of MET enactment given

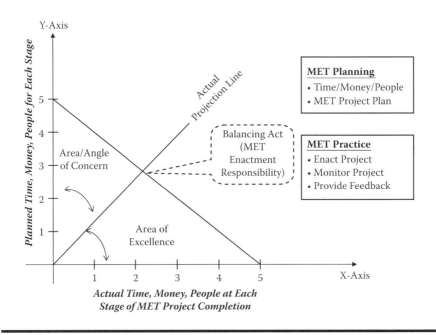

Figure 7.7   Balancing the MET plan with practice.

in Table 7.2 are both likely to undergo changes based on the feedback received. For example, if a certain partnership with a network operator is not going to work for the transitioning organization, the elements of the framework dealing with choice of networks will have to change. Commencement of MET enactment can reveal a different mobile maturity for an organization than that originally ascertained, which will again imply a change to the process. Thus, the changes during MET are not only related to the mobile business itself but also to the process of transitioning.

Organization of Training

An important part of MET enactment is ensuring that customers, suppliers, employees, and senior management are all trained in the use of mobile business processes. There are different types of users of mobile businesses, as seen in the discussion on demographics. Many of these users, who are beneficiaries of mobility, may not be in a position to use the devices themselves. For example, mobile processes related to nursing homes or hospitals, wherein the beneficiaries of the processes can be the elderly or infants who are unable to use mobile devices themselves. There is a need, during enactment, to consider the training of all kinds of users and their supporting users.

Such training can also be vital in ensuring the success of MET, particularly when it comes to employees. Businesses have been keen on using call centers (particularly outsourced) to enhance their ability to provide services to mobile users. In MET from the employees' viewpoint, for call centers and other related supporting entities, training needs to be factored in. Individual customers, however, are unlikely to participate in any formal training. It must be ensured that the cost of such training, should it be undertaken, does not blow the organization's budget. Client-side mobile software development has to provide sufficient help and guidance tutorials for such training.

MET Review and Feedback

The MET project must make provisions for continuous and ongoing feedback. This can be provided manually, electronically, and even using mobile devices themselves. Electronic bulletin boards can be considered as a mechanism to glean feedback from the users, and so can mobile SMSs. Anonymous feedback from clients, employees, and users can come in handy in updating and modifying the transition process. Feedback is also required after transition to evaluate and assess the quality of the transition process. Each MET provides valuable information on what went right and what can be improved. This information can be obtained from organizations where the process for transitioning has been applied. Such feedback—particularly posttransitional—needs to be incorporated in the process.

Discussion Points

1. Identify the demographics of the organization you are associated with, and then evaluate the mobile maturity of the transitioning organization.
2. What are the challenges and risks faced by a transitioning organization during the diagnose, plan, act, and review phases?
3. What is meant by the scope of transition? How does it help MET?
4. What is the role of a pilot project in MET? Discuss which factors (from each of the four MET dimensions) are important for your organization and how they can help in identifying a pilot project.
5. Discuss the importance of training in successful transitions.
6. What changes do MET bring about in the management of an organization?
7. How would you go about obtaining feedback before, during, and after the MET process has been enacted?

References

Arunatileka, D. 2006. Applying mobile technologies to banking business processes, in *Handbook of Research in Mobile Business: Technological, Methodological and Social Perspectives,* ed. B. Unhelkar. New York: Ideas Group.

Brans, P. 2003. *Mobilize Your Enterprise: Achieving Competitive Advantage through Wireless Technology.* Upper Saddle River, NJ: Pearson Education.

Champy, J. 1995. *Reengineering Management: Managing the Change to the Reengineered Corporation.* New York: HarperCollins.

Kalakota, R. and Robinson, M. 2002. *M-Business: The Race to Mobility.* New York: McGraw Hill.

Lan, Y. and Unhelkar, B. 2005. *Global Enterprise Transitions.* Hershey, PA: IDEAS Group.

Chapter 8

Mobile Enterprises: Expansion, Growth, and Management

In fact, when everything is too systematic you are imprisoned, freedom is crushed.

Freedom needs chaos.

Osho, in *Einstein the Buddha-II*, p. 129

Chapter Key Points

- Discusses the ongoing management of mobile business after transition
- Presents the posttransition growth and expansion strategies for mobile business as well as user value creation through mobility
- Focuses on the importance of "value creation" by mobile businesses
- Highlights the responsibilities of a mobile business beyond profit and the use of mobile business processes to provide that value to users, including customers and employees
- Outlines some of the new horizons, such as mass customization, made possible owing to maturity of mobile businesses; outlines the need for innovations and risk taking in mobile business

Introduction

The enactment of the Mobile Enterprise Transition (MET) framework as outlined in the previous chapter results in a mobile enterprise. Depending on the state of mobile maturity achieved, this mobile enterprise will have opportunities to expand and grow in many directions. This chapter discusses the growth, expansion, and management of such a mobile enterprise after its successful transition. This growth and ongoing management of mobile enterprises requires a synergy between the existing principles and practices of management and the upcoming challenges of managing a business that is based on mobility. The challenges of managing a mobile business stem primarily from the fact that such a business is part of a business ecosystem that is continuously changing. A dynamic business ecosystem forms clusters of collaborating businesses that come together to serve a particular customer need and then disperse posthaste. Mobile businesses pose further challenges to electronic collaborations (Unhelkar et al. 2009) because of mobile Web services, which, as discussed throughout this book, are location and time independent. However, in addition to the challenges of transitioning the enterprise, this chapter discusses issues related to ongoing growth and management of the enterprise based on the concepts of mobility.

Expansion and growth of a mobile enterprise depends on paying tremendous attention to the customer. David Siegel (1999) in his book *Futurize Your Enterprise* talks not only about the importance of paying attention to the needs of the customers but also getting them actively involved in business strategies and decision making. Growing mobile businesses have the opportunity to take this concept of a collaborative customer-centric decision-making process by involving the customer at every step of his or her needs. Mobility enables a continuous, seamless, and dynamic process of collaboration between the business, its partners, customers, suppliers, employees, and all other stakeholders who are mobile. This results in a unique customer-driven and sustainable enterprise that dynamically changes its responses to external changes. For example, the customer's demand for a particular service (such as tickets to a sports event, or bookings for a hotel room) can be ascertained by a mobile business instantaneously and utilized for providing higher levels of services or catering to the higher demand through mobile collaborations.

The concept of value creation for both the customers and the enterprises, due to strategic incorporation of mobility in business, is another important aspect of mobile business growth and management. This value creation is not necessarily immediate growth and expansion of the business; however, creating and providing value to customers, business partners, and employees is part of ongoing management of mobile business that is a direct result of the aforementioned collaborative organizational ecosystem that is made up of multiple enterprises. Together, these collaborative enterprises can withstand rapid changes to their external and internal organizational structures and behavior, challenges resulting from upcoming disruptive technologies and the ever-rising customer expectations.

Mobile Business Management

Economic Mobility Management

The economic aspect of managing an advanced to fully mature mobile business deals with the ongoing management of internal costs, external pricing models, and business partner relationships. These three factors—costs, pricing, and relationships—come into play from an economic viewpoint when a mobile content is generated, encapsulated as a service, transmitted over a mobile network, and consumed by a user. The manner in which this content is sourced, packaged, and distributed forms part of a portfolio of products and services offered by a mobile enterprise. Maintenance of that portfolio of offerings is a crucial aspect of the economic management of a mobile enterprise. The cost of generating and maintaining the contents includes the cost of sourcing them from business partners who are in the business of offering that content. Sourcing of content is typically undertaken using Web services from multiple partners in different geographical regions (countries). Thus, economic mobility management is an ongoing exercise undertaken by the business managers of the enterprise together with input from the technical managers in listing the sources of mobile content, and the manner in which it is packaged and then offered to the customers. The ongoing challenge results from the fact that both the consumers and the providers of contents and services change dynamically, providing a much reduced window of time to create and implement mobile product strategies. Advertisement and marketing of mobile products and services is often in catch-up mode compared to the launching of the actual product. Therefore, ongoing modeling of different economic and marketing scenarios is a must for management of mobile businesses. However, cost savings due to application of mobility internally by businesses are more feasible as the internal environment is under better control of the management than the external mobile environment.

Technical Mobility Management

The advance toward a mature and managed mobile business needs continuous attention to its various technical aspects such as mobile devices, applications, networks, contents, and security. Such aspects of mobility, discussed earlier in Chapter 4, need to be put together in a Mobile Enterprise Architecture (MEA) for the organization.

MEA enables the architects to make use of the published reference architectural frameworks (such as TOGAF; www.togaf.org) in developing their new mobile business architectures. An MEA deals with integrity and sourcing of content, networks, middleware, and presentation aspects of mobile technologies. It provides consistency and quality of communication so that users are able to enjoy predictable performance at an acceptable level in the face of dynamically changing networks and user locations. Thus, having an MEA and keeping it up to date is a vital ingredient of good technical mobile management.

Mobile communications is susceptible to greater disruptions than land-based communication. Good technology management requires plans and strategies to handle situations where communication is unexpectedly disrupted. For example, upon a break in mobile links, software applications, or services, applications should be able to gracefully disconnect from the network instead of abruptly terminating the connection. Such careful stepwise disconnection ensures that when service is restored, the application can restart from where it left off. On resumption of the network, connectivity has to be reported, and the user or application should be able to reestablish the session automatically. These are some of the ongoing technical issues required to be managed in a mobile business.

Finally, similar to economic mobility management, in technology management there also is a need to create a list or a repository of technology assets of the organization. This repository is made up of all the technology assets of the organizations, including hardware, software, and operating systems as well as the intellectual property of the organization resulting from sourcing of contents and services. The management of mobile-contents-sourcing contracts, mentioned earlier in the economic mobile management, also requires considerable technical inputs, and is a part of technology management.

Process Mobility Management

Management of mobile processes deals with managing "how" the contents is created and "how" the services are provided by the mobile business. The processes of creation and collation of content from these varied sources need to be modeled using the modeling standards discussed earlier in Chapter 5. Without the creation of standardized models of processes (preferably with a modeling tool), it is extremely difficult, if not impossible, to manage mobile business processes. Ongoing management of mature mobile business processes requires their modeling and fine-tuning from both the provider's and consumer's viewpoints. For example, a well-modeled mobile process that provides transactive capabilities to a customer for purchasing a ticket to a game can be improved upon quickly to provide multiple tickets to the same game, provided that information is gleaned from the mobile devices of the consumers. The process of providing these services can be made agile if the process is formally modeled and managed. Unhelkar et al. (2009) provide a detailed description of these dynamic collaborative processes, their modeling, and their ongoing management. Providing a unified service view of a number of collaborating businesses is the responsibility of process mobility management, and technology support through a "collaborative business model engine" in the background (such as that created by Ghanbary 2006) and the aforementioned economic mobile management portfolios need to work together for process success.

Mobile Software Applications in Management

The discussion on economic, technical, and process management of mobile business thus far needs to also consider the importance of mobile software applications to all these dimensions. When it comes to growth and management of mobile businesses, mobile software support is an essential ingredient. Thus, there is a need to modify and seamlessly extend the company's enterprise resource planning (ERP) and customer relationship management (CRM) systems to handle the mobile business processes. These mobile business processes need corresponding content and policies that change dynamically if required—and the supporting software needs to have sufficient flexibility to enable the users to change and reconfigure the software swiftly. These changes to mobile software applications help not only the customers but also the managers and decision makers of the organization. For example, through the customization of internal inventory processes using mobile inputs, an ERP system can quickly locate and provide information to the senior management on its capacity to serve a potential upcoming deal. The changing parameters that are required to be inputted in such an ERP system can be successfully set only if the software application is built in a flexible and configurable manner. Mobile software applications serve an important aspect of value generation by providing for optimum utilization of the organization's resources. These organizational resources are not just the inventory or mobile content, but also the people (such as the decision makers) who, without support of a mobile-enabled software application, would not be easily available to make a timely decision. For example, consider mobile applications such as Spectrax (discussed in Unhelkar 2008) that empower mobile workers by facilitating accurate, bidirectional information. These mobile applications, operating across a combination of mobile wireless and landline-based networks, generate value for the workers and the business.

Similar to mobile ERP applications, mobile CRM software applications also need to be modeled, modified, and extended on an ongoing basis to provide support to mobile management. Mobile CRM can be configured to function on the concept of value rather than profit by identifying the most appropriate locations, timings, needs, and quality factors relevant to the customer. Ongoing management of a mobile business involves mobile software applications that are able to equip the customers themselves to create and manage their own business needs through online and mobile access to the organization's CRM system.

CASE Tools for Modeling Processes and Applications

Although the importance of software applications in providing management support has been underscored earlier, the need for modeling tools in the aforementioned dimensions cannot be overstated. These modeling tools, typically called computer-aided software engineering (CASE) tools, have already played a major positive role in mobile applications development and management.

Modeling tools facilitate design and documentation of the various process and system models. These tools further interface, technically, with Object-Oriented (OO) languages such as C++ and Java, development environments (such as dotNet), and content management databases (such as Oracle or SQL Server). Tool vendors provide these technical interfaces by modifying, configuring, and deploying their tools in the environment of their users. CASE tools can be further extended and expanded to automate other technical and process functions such as testing and metrics related to mobile software applications and mobile business processes.

Successful use of CASE tools in management of software projects within mobile organizations requires that such tools be owned by a tool champion within the project. The training and experience in using these tools and their associated interfaces with development environments, programming languages, databases, and networks can provide immense benefits in terms of providing higher-quality software products, improved development and maintenance times, better estimation of effort, and easier training for users (typically employees and call center support staff) when processes change. Examples of some CASE tools used by the author are provided in Appendix C.

Social Mobility Management

Mature mobile businesses keep the sociocultural context of their services and processes in mind when they create and offer new services to their customers and users. An ongoing understanding of the demographics of the users, such as their location and age, is vital to managing the social dimension of the mobile business. Social mobility management deals with facilitating user interactions both electronically and socially—to help the users deal with issues and topics of common interest. Although some of these social facilitations may not be directly of economic consequence to the business, the role played by the organization in social network creation and management adds its own positive value to the organization. In addition to the customers, employees of the organization are also provided opportunities to create and manage their working groups and social networks using mobility.

Mobile socialization is an extension of the Internet-based social networking that includes locating people with common interests, common issues, and past histories (such as school groups). Mobile social applications include location-relevant features that help find friends and generate location-specific contents that can be shared by others (such as mobile video clips). Location-assisted collaborative mobile gaming leverages the trends of personalization, social networking, and entertainment as well as leads to a new social order (based on Kapko 2007). Managed mobile business has a need to create this networking opportunity, tap into it for business expansion, and at the same time be socially responsible in its business expansion.

Finally, social mobility management also includes keeping the organization abreast of legal changes in the mobile domain, and ensuring that its services are both legally binding and socially acceptable in the area of its operation.

Value Creation by Mobile Business

> Managing a mature mobile business requires a balance between economic, technical, process, and social dimensions of the business. Each of these needs to be introduced in the right mix to create value for the user. The user can be the customer, the business partner, or the employee. In each case, value differs depending on who the user is; therefore, the economic, technical, process, and social aspects of mobile business also differ for each one. Overall, however, it is important to note that the concept of value subsumes the concept of profit for a successful and mature mobile business.

Managing the four dimensions of a mobile business and keeping them in balance has a vital purpose to serve in its ongoing management. The vital purpose of a mobile business is to create and maintain values. The growth and expansion of a business is due to its focus on the value provided by it to its customer (primarily), but also to its partners and employees. The four dimensions of MET contribute toward providing this value. The following are some of the significant and specific mobile technology considerations in generating value for growth and management of mobile business:

1. Recognizing and understanding mobile technology, strengths and limitations within the context of the organization during the diagnostic stage of METM. Modeling of processes as well as mobile technology architecture plays an important role in helping an organization understand this value.
2. Recognizing that the concept of time and location independence is critical in value creation. Mobile gadgets and communication networks help in providing value; however, the business processes and social aspects of MET are the core means by which users find tremendous value in practice.
3. Reorganization and optimization of the organizational structure of an enterprise as it grows in terms of mobile maturity. Understanding and applying new technologies and concepts create the need for, as well as potential opportunities for, organizational changes. These optimizations of the organizational structure become meaningful and productive when the goal of "value creation and value maximization" is kept in mind.

4. Perception by users results in far more value than the actual value offered by the organization to its mobile customers. Therefore, studying and analyzing the perceived value of dynamic customer behavior is vital in creating value for the customer.
5. Recognizing the significance of the time factor in value creation. The longer a mobile business stays mature, the greater is the accrued value perceived by the user. The impact of time on business, and the particular significance of long-term strategies in sustenance are important for mobile business value creation, and were discussed as such in earlier chapters, particularly Chapter 3.

These observations are likely to be true of any disruptive technology, and they are especially true of mobile technology. This is so because of the personalized nature of the technology from the user's viewpoint and the vital importance of location independence from the business process viewpoint. A long-term, well-balanced, strategic view of mobile technology adoption ensures that the business undertakes ongoing optimization of its structure and puts flexible processes in place that continue to provide value to its customers and users well after it has formally adopted mobile business.

Understanding Value in Business

As mentioned earlier, the concept of providing value to the customer is not new in business. However, in this discussion, we specifically focus on the approach to value creation, value provision, and value maximization from a mobile business viewpoint. Younessi (2008) argues that creation of value in any dimension of business is paramount to its success. Therefore, each of the four dimensions of MET discussed in this book thus far can be approached from the value viewpoint to ensure sustainability and growth of the enterprise. Value creation is not mere profit making; however, it is also not against profit. In a way, value subsumes the concept of profit. A mobile business provides and enhances value to a customer by capitalizing on its unique capability to personalize and groom the relationship established between them. The growing mobile access to current and future customers results in opportunities to create new products and services that can scale up to match the expanding demands placed on them. Management of mobile business requires anticipation in the growth of mobile products and services, and then providing for those increased demands. By applying the concept of value rather than profit to the new mobile products and services, the organization is able to succeed in terms of both value and profit.

Customer Relevance in Value

One of the significant differences in the new mobile business era, as compared with the earlier electronic and paper era, is the need for collaboration among many businesses to provide for customer needs. Mobile business content and services need to be sourced from a variety of providers. These content and service providers include, in many instances, the customers themselves who upload or push timely content that may be of value to other customers and users of the business. For example, users accessing mobile updates and reports on current road conditions can also provide input and update their existing road conditions for the benefit of other users. This creation and uploading of location-specific content by the users of the content is unique to the mobile business, and needs to be nurtured by mature mobile businesses. Thus, the concept of dynamic collaboration with other mobile service providers gets extended to collaboration among all parties involved in a business transaction—both service providers and users get together to provide and consume content and services in a mobile environment.

Consider, for example, the availability of a certain pharmaceutical drug offered by a pharmaceutical company. That particular drug is easily and cheaply available across the counter. The company is focused on improving its production capabilities, cutting down its costs, and ensuring that sufficient quantities of the drug are available at pharmacy outlets. However, when incorporating mobility into its business processes, the company can consider, model, and implement mobile business processes that enable provision of the drug dynamically when and where it is needed most. The company grows as a result of making the drugs available through outlets it may not own, or even mobile outlets. The mobility of both consumers and suppliers of the drugs needs to be considered so as to provide value to customers. The urgent need of a consumer for a particular drug can be satisfied by potentially multiple pharmacies if they are working under the mobile collaboration umbrella. The collaborative business model will bring together the various services available from the different business partners and stakeholders in the pharmaceutical company. Furthermore, in a long-term strategic relationship between collaborators, there is potential to offer services in the areas of chemical, sourcing, research studies, packaging, and distribution. These services need to exist synergistically in a mobile business to provide value to the customer. Mobile businesses in a mature state are ideally poised to provide this synergy.

Management of mobile business continuously considers creation and maximization of value, which depends on the timing and location of the sale of the product or provision of the service. Values can be maximized by determining the optimum way of sourcing the ingredients that make up a product, or configuring the service, and providing or selling the service to the user. The dynamic aspect of mobility facilitates creation of opportunities to determine the product and the time and location of its sale, thereby maximizing its value to the customer. Value is also considered from the supplier's viewpoint because mobility plays an important part in the supply-chain process that provides materials and services to the organization. The pharmaceutical company mentioned earlier can apply mobility to its supply-chain process, specifying its own needs, timings, and locations for provision of supplies to its production, research, packaging, and warehousing facilities. These specific aspects of value creation in the pharmaceutical example are further expanded in the case study discussed in Chapter 10.

Managing User Values

The value that a mobile business can provide to its users depends on a number of factors that are themselves dependent on the user. Thus, the role of the user in the context of the business is very important. Similarly, the needs of the user, timing, location, amount of service required, and readiness of the user to pay for the service are all factors that contribute to the value of business. Furthermore, value is also made up of intangibles that are based on user perceptions, which are hard to measure but still need to be considered in understanding the overall significance of mobility to business.

We have described thus far the meaning of value in business and the relevance of the customer in expecting as well as generating that value. The ongoing management of a mature mobile business heavily relies on formally creating and maximizing these values. Harmon and Diam (2009) offer numerous examples of how this value can be created and provided to a mobile customer. Value creation requires a formal attempt at understanding what the customer wants, when he or she wants it, how much of the product or service he or she wants, what price the customer is prepared to pay for it, and how such requirements are managed by the business. Thus, managing user values requires a formal management approach that needs to consider all four mobile dimensions, posttransition, from the user's viewpoint. The cost–benefit considerations of the service, its technical quality, time and location relevance, and social context all come into play in managing user value.

Consider, for example, an insurance company that offers a location-based insurance quotation and premium (such as Safeco's "Teensurance" for parents of teenagers; Safeco 2007). This company can create and manage value in its service by capitalizing on the global positioning system (GPS)-enabled feature within a vehicle to enable real-time tracking and monitoring of the vehicle's location and speed. This data can provide "value" to the parents of the insured teenagers because they become aware of the movements of their children. Needless to say, this data also provides "value" to the insurance company. This is mobile value creation that is not entirely based on the aim of profit maximization or cost reduction. The customers derive value from a combination of high-quality wireless networks that are technically reliable, carefully modeled mobile business processes that are also carefully implemented, and a business ethic that is based on the importance of looking after the insurance customers. The value-based approach facilitates growth and expansion of mobile businesses because, by their very nature, they have a greater opportunity to provide these values to their users through personalization of the services. The value-based approach also helps mobile businesses mature fast, as they are required to use all their internal resources from all four dimensions to achieve the value goal.

Yet another example is Norwich Union, which aims to offer value to customers in the United Kingdom. This bank makes innovative use of GPS services available in mobile devices in vehicles, to ascertain monthly insurance premiums for its customers on the basis of distance driven, time of day, and type of road on which the vehicle moves (Reed 2007). This unique "value proposition" is dramatically different from the current approach of fixed-priced insurance for motoring. Value for the mobile user also arises out of initiatives that create and utilize roadside infrastructure such as driving directions, road conditions, parking, prevention of accidents, location of stolen vehicles, and so on.

Hospitals provide value to their patients through a wide range of services including scheduling of appointments, reminders for medications, and creation of postevent support groups outside of hospitals (Lan and Unhelkar 2005). Restaurants provide value to patrons through mobile menus that give choices and their selections in real-time by communicating wirelessly to the kitchen. Thus, navigation, personalized family tracking and monitoring, patient flow, motoring, and emergency services are some areas where mobile businesses are capitalizing on their great opportunity to provide value to the customers. Such areas for value creation for various domains served by mobile applications that are possible in an advanced and managed state of mobile business are summarized in Table 8.1.

Self-Value Creation by Users

Once the customers become familiar with the value that is coming their way through the services offered on their mobile devices, they themselves start making creative and effective use of these services. For example, personal navigation services provided by handheld mobile gadgets such as TomTom and Garmin (Hesseldahl 2007) are put to creative use by the consumers in finding directions and updating friends and family about their own locations. The highly popular "missed calls" services provided by all network operators is another example of creative uses of mobility by users; when a user wishes to inform the receiver of his presence or a similar preagreed bit of information, he or she merely makes a missed call to the receiving party who has, say, come to pick him or her up from a railway station or airport. The desire of sophisticated mobile users wanting to create and configure services on their devices is also an important self-generated value factor important in mobile business.

Table 8.1 Mobile business value creation in various domains

Mobile domain and application	Mobile business value proposition
Insurance	Providing dynamic insurance premiums corresponding to changing risk coverage in time and place, utilizing the transactive and collaborative capabilities of mobility. Such dynamic insurance strategies are quite different from the current flat systems of charging insurance. The dynamic calculation of insurance premiums is the value that is derived from mobility.
Hospitals	Providing patient care by the bedside, in the waiting rooms, or outside the hospital by ensuring timely information to patients, assuaging them, and enabling creation of collaborative support groups for postoperative patients. Furthermore, interacting dynamically to collaborate with pharmacies, investigative laboratories, and health insurance companies using mobility.
Transport	Providing vehicle navigation and routing capability that is based on dynamic road conditions such as traffic intensity, weather situation, history of peak and off-peak traffic, opportunities to combine public transport with private setting of variable speed limits, and negotiating speed humps. Providing value through a network of dynamic roadside assistance for breakdowns (e.g., flat tire, dead battery) and accidents.
Travel and tourism	Hotels, airlines, car rental, trains, and other public and private infrastructure information is collaborated and provided to the traveler by the mobile business. Points of visitor's interest, driving directions, supporting public transport schedules, opening hours of facilities, gas and restaurant services, and entertainment sites are also combined together and provided as a unified service to the user on his or her mobile gadget while the user is on the move.
Time management	Time and work management using mobile applications provides value to both the business and the employee by making use of personalization and location independence. Mobile operational management of employee/worker time, provision of support and security to field workers (e.g., sales representatives, door-to-door salesmen, or visiting doctors), and dynamically scheduling working times are some of the values derived by mobile businesses.

Table 8.1 *(continued)*   **Mobile business value creation in various domains**

Mobile domain and application	Mobile business value proposition
Courier services	Tracking of packages/courier items online and in real-time mode by utilizing a combination of RFID, cellular, and Wi-Fi networks. This is useful to the customer who is keen to know the location of her package. It is also helpful in dynamically scheduling courier delivery routes based on mobile information such as road and weather conditions, changes to drop and pickup points, and availability of other fellow couriers.
Social networking	Creation of discussion groups of people with common interests; dating through mobile gadgets; and sharing of medical, entertainment, or adventure experiences (such as discussed in Chapter 6).
Emergency services	Police, fire, and medical emergencies through the E911 and E112 standards that provide value to the user that is incomparable to its cost.
Law enforcement	Monitoring and tracking of prisoners or people on special bail conditions. Monitoring of traffic through speed cameras and ensuring security of the nation by preventing the use of the devices in terrorism-type activities.
Advertisement	Value is provided through informative use of mobility; however, as discussed earlier in Chapter 5, advertisements and other promotional material should be done with sensitivity; adding to the user's needs through hot spots based on local Wi-Fi networks as well as global cellular networks.
Gaming	Provides entertainment and, potentially, educational time value through games. These games can be local (restricted to the device) or interactive (spanning multiple users). RFID, Bluetooth, and Wi-Fi networks can be used to connect users locally. Music, video, and games can all be combined together for creating user experiences.

Employee-Value Management

The management and growth of a mobile organization through the concept of value creation is also based on continuous and responsible support from its employees. Without proper understanding of value, employees may feel weighed down by the technology. Mature mobile organizations create a proper understanding of value in their employees, which spans across the four transition dimensions. Overwhelming the company's working force with mobility or focusing only on cost savings by the business may result in lack of confidence and decrease in productivity.

The potential for the elimination of physical connectivity between communicating devices results in profound changes in the nature of the relationship between employees and business. For example, the impact of mobility on the organization of the business and its relationship with employees can be managed in a virtual manner. The independence accorded by mobility in terms of time and location brings about a social and behavioral revolution in employee management, trade unions, workplace ethics, etc. There is sufficient evidence, anecdotal and otherwise, pointing to the profound social and organizational changes that are inevitable consequences of the mobile revolution.

Thus, the concept of value for employees, already mentioned earlier, is as important as that for the customer. However, the way in which this value translates for employees is different from that of the customer. Therefore, in discussing the value addition by mobile business, it is important to focus separately on the specifics of employee value creation and management. The creation of value for employees of a mature mobile business is primarily from the operational use of mobility. The employee is looking at improving the quality of time at work, ensuring a balance between work and home, enhancing the service provided to the customers and, thereby, aspiring to improve his or her career growth prospects. The enhanced ability of an employee to serve the customer is a significant value addition to the employee's job. Mobile business may not immediately provide financial prosperity to the employee, but the use of mobility to enable employees to improve their ability to provide service leads to higher growth opportunity and job satisfaction. The time management and operational management issues presented in the previous section and listed in Table 8.1 are important in this value addition for the employee.

Measuring Value

> Measurement of the value of mobility in business is a combination of tangible and intangible benefits. Utility value is the routine value required from mobility, primarily by making available information independent of location. Exchange value is provided through mobile transactions. Essential value is realized through enhancing the potential for longevity or sustainability of the mobile business.

Value creation, as discussed earlier, subsumes the concept of profit, as value provides sufficiency as against the necessity of profit in terms of business growth. Therefore, measurement of value is always a combination of objective measurement of tangible benefits and the subjective measurement intangible value, so as to understand and measure value from different perspectives. Younessi (2008) has distinguished between *utility value, exchange value,* and *essential value.* Mobile business expansion and growth need to consider these values in terms of the use of mobility by business.

The utility value of mobility comes from the availability of certain information at a point in time and space. Therefore, it is usually available through the informative use of mobility by business. Utility value is also available to the employees of the business as mobility improves the internal business processes, that is, the operative usage of mobility by business.

The exchange value of mobility is derived from providing excellence in transactive usage of mobility by business. It is provided by the business when a mobile user can easily transact with it without any particular focus on cost saving or profit maximization. Thus, a bank might enable its customer to carry out inquiries or transfer amounts from one account to another using mobile units free of charge. The exchange value derived from such a transaction far outweighs the cost of such transaction to the bank.

The essential value of the mobile business accrues over a long period of time over which the customer or user realizes the benefits of mobility as an essential part of his or her daily life. Therefore, long-term sustainability becomes a vital strategy for a mature mobile business.

Measuring the aforementioned values is always very difficult and challenging. This is so because the very idea of value is subjective. In the case of mobile business, this depends on the needs of each individual user and the unique location and time when the user is asking for a particular product or service. The concept of *elasticity of demand* plays an important role in determining the value resulting from the mobile business initiative. This concept implies the degree of change in a product given the changes in the economic environment. These can be, for example, changes in interest rate or price. The value at any given time is going to result from a combination of timeliness, relevance of the service to the user, quality, and also costs. Knowing the changes to demand and price beforehand, storing and analyzing those pieces of information, and using them to "dynamically change the offerings" by the business are some of the significant aspects of mobile business growth and expansion strategy.

Traditional demands, price estimations, and forecasting approaches are also helpful in formulating mobile business strategies to indicate the required levels of production. Information on prices, competing products, incomes and wealth, and many other factors must be gathered to come up with the correct policy that can be embedded in a software system.

Resistance to Change

Ongoing use of mobile technology in business requires a shift in the mindset of the business, changes to its working style, and a flexible organizational structure. The change in mindset requires answers to questions such as "what does the process do?" and "what is its purpose?" and "how can the system be modeled dynamically using mobile objects or agents and their behavior?" This change is not always easy, as there is considerable difference between thinking in a wired way compared to thinking in a mobile or wireless way about the business. Mobile businesses resulting from mobile transitions are geared to thinking in these different terms right from their preliminary mobile usage stages.

Maturity of mobile business requires managing this resistance to the change from the traditional way of thinking about both technologies and processes. The shift of mindset required for mobile business also requires managing interactions with the external environment, which is also continuously changing.

Training

Managing a mobile business requires continuous focus on training of its users, particularly its employees. The dynamic aspect of mobile business processes requires effort for their acceptance by users. The end of a successful MET is actually the beginning of a formal and ongoing training program that helps the users to configure and manage their business processes. Software development staff, if onsite, also need formal training about maintaining mobile applications, databases, and networks. Training of customers is always tricky and challenging. This is because the individual customers do not have the time or inclination to undertake user training. In such cases, comprehensive help mechanisms need to be provided. Corporate customers can be made to realize the importance of training, which in turn provides value to the mature mobile business because it reduces errors and misunderstandings and helps in customization of services specific to the needs of a corporate customer.

Mobile Enterprise Platform

Management of a mobile business from a technical viewpoint requires a mobile enterprise platform. As discussed in Chapter 4, technically, mobile transition results in an opportunity to create a robust MEA. This advantage of being able to create a sound mobile architecture in a transitioned mobile business arises as the building blocks or components of the mobile systems and applications become available for customization and reuse. This new mobile architecture needs to incorporate available components and services and, at the same time, be forward-looking. A mobile architecture is not limited by the legacy past and can be the basis for a "platform" from which new mobile applications and services can be quickly configured and launched.

The modules or building blocks of the mobile enterprise platform are based on the concepts of *modularization* and *encapsulation*. Therefore, the new mobile designs can be made up of tightly encapsulated software modules. This results in a pluggable architectural platform, wherein software building blocks can be put together (plugged) in various ways to satisfy ongoing changes in user requirements.

Such modularized building blocks for the new mobile architecture also make use of the concept of architectural patterns. The discussion on middleware and components, undertaken in Chapter 4, is of relevance in creating a robust MEA. Middleware mobile technologies can be implemented in a managed enterprise easily, provided they utilize the experience of previous implementations. These previous experiences and implementations are made available as patterns. Thus, mobile architectural patterns are a significant part of the mobile enterprise platform.

User Literacy and Participation

In contrast with the era in which software systems had hardly any architecture or documentation and the user was at the end of the software life cycle, the new mobile business will see major involvement from the users of the system at all levels of the system development and maintenance life cycle. In addition to its obvious advantages during acceptance testing and deployment, user involvement in the development of mobile systems is likely to provide significant benefits at the architectural level also. This is so because user involvement affects the creation of the mobile enterprise platform, reflecting both current and future user needs. Users can influence not only in-house development but also procurement of third-party building blocks that can be incorporated in the current system or made part of the mobile enterprise platform.

Adhering to Quality

Mature mobile businesses have a tremendous opportunity to incorporate quality consciousness in all dimensions of their business activities. There is an atmosphere of change within the business as a result of MET; new mobile business processes and software systems are likely to be in place, and people within the organization will have overcome their resistance to change. This is the right environment to inculcate quality throughout the mobile business. The opportunity to introduce quality of service in both business as well as technical processes, including the processes of developing and maintaining software, needs to be capitalized on.

The various aspects of quality that need to be considered by a well-managed mobile business include quality of products, quality of service, quality of processes and models, and the overall quality of user experience. The software industry has approached quality from various angles, including testing, documentation, metrics, and measurements. The major emphasis of quality in the mobile software development area is on improving the processes of software application development. The ISO 9000 series of quality standards, applied by businesses to improve business and software processes, are also applied in mobile software development using the mobile enterprise platform.

Capability Maturity Model (CMM)

Measurement of the maturity of software development needs to be mentioned here in the context of mobile software application development. The Software Engineering Institute's (SEI) Capability Maturity Model (CMM) has been applied to measure the maturity of software processes. The five levels of CMM are as follows: initial, repeatable, defined, managed, and optimized. A quick look at these levels indicates that, for an organization to position itself at any of these levels, it should have processes that are properly defined as well as the ability to repeat such processes. Stable and mature mobile business requires processes in place that the organization can use and maintain in its application development and deployment activities.

Although the MET framework provides the starting point for a new business, it usually extends to the series of requirements for a number of applications that are a combination of wired and mobile. As well as providing quality within the mobile organization, repeatable quality processes can also provide advantages in dealing with other organizations. The ability of the organization in following and adopting mobility furthers its forward-looking approach. The maturity of processes at the development level is thus of immense importance to the overall mobile maturity of organizations.

Quality Management Made Easy due to Transition

It is easier to incorporate quality within processes during MET as compared to a normal business. This is because the transition effort results in new processes that can ensure quality consciousness right from the beginning through proper modeling and application of quality practices such as walkthroughs and inspections. Thus, MET provides all the advantages of implementing a new process and checking quality throughout the new processes.

Important Documentation

A mature mobile business with a mature mobile enterprise development platform will have good and quality documentation of processes, models, programs, databases, and content. Such documentation is a great asset to the mobile business, especially to the software project management aspect of the business. MET provides the opportunity for a culture change in documentation. The effort for quality control and documentation in MET is supported by the availability and ease of use of modeling tools and techniques that result in easier documentation and cross-referencing of a process, resulting in higher overall quality. Metrics and measurements are part of this electronic documentation approach, and also play a role in measuring and optimizing quality.

Mobile Business: New Horizons

> Mobility in a mature mobile business provides the unique opportunity for a synergy between mass production and customization. The ability of mobility to access and update the organization's production systems implies that the organization can customize its production to suit user needs and yet derive the advantage of mass production. The ability of mobility to provide the business with personalized access to the needs of the customer results in customization of the product or service to suit the specific needs of that customer.

Having discussed the growth and management of mobile businesses, we consider here what are the new horizons mobile businesses can look forward to. The ability of mobility to provide personalization comes into play when we consider the opportunities for customization of products and services en masse. Furthermore, the ability of electronic and mobile collaborations to break down the organizational boundaries leads to the concept of *open* mobile business. The ongoing needs for innovation and risk taking are also part and parcel of mobile maturity. These are some of the mobility-related new horizons for businesses resulting from mobility that we discuss in this last section of this chapter.

Mass Customization

Mass production was the direct result of the industrial age, when businesses measured their success through profit margins correlated to the prices and the cost of production. Traditional thinking was that if a business could lower costs—all other things being the same—we can make a higher profit which, in turn, would provide value to the shareholders. At the simple level, costs are best managed when the organization makes a lot of the same product, does not waste resources in making it, and the product is good enough to be sold at the best obtainable price. This resulted in a need for mass production. The need for mass production is met by improving the efficiency of the process of production, ensuring its quality, and, most importantly, producing goods in large numbers. The use of technology in industrial process and innovation are major factors in achieving these aims. The assembly line in the industrial age and lean systems in the contemporary electronic age are examples. Knowing how much to produce and how to produce high-quality products requires acquisition, retention, processing, and dissemination of a lot of information provided electronically.

However, with increasing demand for specific products and services from customers who could pay for them, there came a need to specifically customize the products to individual customer needs. Mass production, however, has been, traditionally, the opposite of customization. This is so because customization requires the business to change its production processes to meet the individual user's requirements.

Mobility provides an opportunity to bring together the two opposing requirements of mass production and customization. Mature mobile businesses are able to innovate and change their external as well as internal business processes that allow them to undertake "mass customization." Although production techniques of modern organizations are becoming increasingly flexible, mobility enables end users to specify in real-time their requirements. For example, a mature mobile business that is making take-out pizzas in large numbers is able to continue its mass production and, at the same time, link its production to the mobile inputs provided by customers.

A mobile business process also results in complete, accurate, and real-time information transfer between the ERP system and the field staff. Other benefits realized by mobile processes are the speeding up of customized orders as well as significant reduction in associated overhead costs.

Unless there is a logically more compelling reason, successful organizations are usually keen to remain in the same business. The length of stay in a business is related to business sustainability. Potential reasons for changing the business line are obvious better opportunities to make more profit or the risks involved in staying in the same business. All businesses entail risks, but there may come a time when the reward that ensues would not justify the risk. British Petroleum and Siemens spend a lot of money (that otherwise would be turned to profit) on environmental and ecological programs. In other words, they consciously *trade exchange value for essential value*. It may be from an enlightened self-interest than from an altruistic standpoint. They are the investments of organizations in their own futures, in the future of their resources and customers. They realize that unless they do so, their businesses would not be sustainable.

It is fundamentally important to avail ourselves of the relevant information accessible to determine how long one can continue the business in which one is engaged *and when to stop or change approach*—before it is too late. The information requirements of business sustainability constitute one of the central tenets of prudent mobile business management.

The more wisely firms use their available resources for production, the greater is their capacity to produce, all else being the same. Or, they can produce a set quantity for less cost. By production we do not simply mean making or fabricating a good. Although this is a common interpretation of the word, production in economic terms means not only the development of a good such as an automobile but also the provision of services such as fire insurance, catering services, or stock-brokerage. In addition, production includes production costs, that is, the cost of making the product available in the market. So, inventory, transportation, marketing, and sales costs are parts of production expenses. "Production" is not just "making" but an overall "offering" of goods and services. Mature mobile businesses are never static; they are continuously trying ways to utilize their materials, energy, space, and labor with the help of mobility to provide enhanced value to users and to themselves.

Open Mobile Business

Traditional businesses have been "closed" to the external world beyond organizational boundaries. For example, consider ERP and CRM systems, which are the core components of an organization's IT environment. These systems are available to the internal users of the organization, and only a thin highly secured level of these systems is available to external users. Thus, despite the benefits delivered by such systems, access is typically only available to individuals within the boundaries of the physical premises (usually less than 20 percent of workers have access). Field workers and customers beyond this perimeter have to transact via intermediary processes. These require access to a physical terminal or, in the worst case, methods such as handwritten forms that require subsequent manual data capture and collation. Mobility overcomes these problems by eliminating duplication of effort, capturing data at source, and providing various users direct access to its internal and external systems. The new mobile business is thus an "open" business that provides real-time output to its users on their handheld devices.

The extension or mobilization of m-ERP and m-CRM systems seamlessly extends beyond the boundaries of the organization. Such extension of business systems and their opening up is a key business innovation that is facilitated by mature mobile businesses. Service providers and knowledgeable customers are able to create interfaces and software applications on their mobile devices that are later synchronized with ERP and CRM systems.

The openness of systems due to mobility reduces the "distance" between the organization and its customers. Openness in a mobile business also empowers field staff with real-time access to current information when it is most required. Workers enjoy increased job satisfaction, and the customer's experience is also improved.

Innovation and Risk Taking

Apart from mass customization and open business structures, mature mobile businesses are also accustomed to taking risks and succeeding in them. A formal transition framework such as MET brings about a managed change and an awareness of the four dimensions of business. Further, calculated risks can be taken in any or all of these dimensions.

Murugesan and Unhelkar (2004) discuss how innovations reflect an organizational context in which employees believe in and understand the creation of value for themselves and their customers. Management's attitude toward change, often triggered by the introduction of mobile technologies, impacts the way in which innovations are nurtured and adopted. Senior management teams may have conservative attitudes toward innovation and associated risk. However, as the organization matures to a mobile business, they may take calculated risks and actually encourage and actively support the use of innovative mobile techniques for advancement. Such organizations usually try to obtain a competitive advantage by making dramatic changes and taking the inherent and associated risks. The potentially disruptive features typically associated with the adoption of (radical technology) innovations require an organizational context in which managers encourage individual members of the organization to take prudent levels of risk, back the adoption of technological innovations, and are supportive of changes within the organization. A mature mobile business has precisely the opportunity to do so.

Discussion Points

1. What, according to you, are the differences in the activities of an organization when it is undertaking MET and the activities after the mobile transition is complete?
2. Are your organizational processes available in a process model? If not, consider creating detailed mobile business process models. Use one of the CASE tools suggested in Appendix C for this purpose.
3. What is the concept of value? And how is it similar to and different from profit? Discuss the concept of user value from a mobile business perspective.
4. What is the relevance of customer perception in generating value for the customer? How is perception influenced in mobile business? Discuss the uniqueness of self-value creation that results from mobile business.
5. Which domains, apart from the ones listed in Table 8.1, are likely to derive value through mobile business?
6. A mobile enterprise platform needs to consider quality. Discuss how this quality can be brought about through mature development processes for mobile applications and services.
7. Why is mass production opposed to customization? How can mobility bring about a synergy between mass production and customization to result in mass customization?
8. Discuss why mobility is instrumental in creating an open business environment?
9. Why is it important for mature mobile businesses to be innovative? What plans can you formulate and put in action, on the basis of discussions in this chapter, to foster a culture of innovation in your mobile business?

References

Ghanbary, A. 2006. Evaluation of mobile technologies in the context of their application, limitation and transformation, chapter in *Handbook of Research in Mobile Business: Technical, Methodological and Social Perspectives,* ed. B. Unhelkar. Hershey, PA: IGI Global.

Harmon, R. and Diam, T. 2009. Assessing the future of location-based services: Technologies, applications, and strategies, chapter in *Handbook of Research in Mobile Business: Technical, Methodological and Social Perspectives,* 2nd ed., ed. B. Unhelkar. Hershey, PA: IGI Global.

Hesseldahl, A. 2007. Garmin and Tom Tom vie for TeleAtlas, *Businessweek.com*, http://businessweek.com/technology/content/nov2007/.

Kapko, M. 2007. Based on many articles on http://resources.bnet.com/topic/matt+kapko.html?tag=content;col1.

Lan, Y. and Unhelkar, B. 2005. *Global Enterprise Transitions.* Hershey, PA: IDEAS Group Publication (IGI Global).

Murugesan S., and Unhelkar, B. 2004. A road map for successful ICT innovations—Turning great ideas into successful implementations, *Cutter IT Journal,* 17(11): 5–12.

Reed, J. 2007. Rewards for Lack of Drive, *Financial Times.*

Safeco. 2007, Safeco Insurance launches Teensurance program, http://www.finacetech.com/.

Siegel, D. 1999. *Futurize Your Enterprise: Business Strategy in the Age of the E-customer,* 1st ed. New York: John Wiley & Sons.

Unhelkar, B. 2008. *Australasian Software Excellence-II.* Sydney, Australia: MethodScience Publications.

Unhelkar, B., Ghanbary, A., and Younessi, H. 2009. *Electronic Collaborations and Organizational Synergy.* Hershey, PA: IGI Global.

Younessi, H. 2009. Strategic view on creating business value through mobile technologies, chapter 1 in *Handbook of Research in Mobile Business: Technical, Methodological and Social Perspectives,* 2nd ed., ed. B. Unhelkar, Hershey, PA: IGI Global.

Chapter 9

Mobile Enterprises: Sustainability and the Environment

Some experiences are so intense while they are happening that time seems to stop altogether.

Al Gore, *An Inconvenient Truth*

Chapter Key Points

- Discusses the impact of sustainability and the environment on the transition to a mobile business
- Presents how people and processes of a mobile business can be organized to optimize their impact on the environment
- Considers the importance and relevance of mobile software applications in managing environmental issues in a business
- Considers the issues related to increasing environmental awareness with mobility
- Proposes dynamic environmental intelligence (EI) incorporating mobile Web services and mobile content

Introduction

This chapter discusses the impact of mobility on business sustenance and the physical environment in which the business exists. It also discusses the responsibility of mobility toward people and society from an environmental perspective. Rising energy prices, concerns about energy security, and increasing pressure from society to reduce greenhouse gas (GHG) emissions related to fossil fuels have heightened the demand for energy efficiency and renewable energy sources. Users are increasingly concerned with the cost of energy and the energy consumption of mobile and information and communication technology (ICT) equipment. Hence, improving energy efficiency in the use of mobility by businesses can help address legitimate concerns of their users by reducing the environmental impact associated with mobile usage. Mobile business enhances its short-term and long-term competitiveness, and also demonstrates environmental leadership by improving the energy efficiency of its products, processes, and operations.

The introduction of mobility in business and society through MET requires the transition process to demonstrate the importance of the environment as essential to any technical revolution. In fact, the environmental aspect of any technological transformation is vital, but more so with mobile computing. This is because mobile technologies, through their permeation into the fabric of our society, influence the physical environment as never before. The mobile technology itself and its rapid acceptance around the world have made mobility a unique environmental challenge.

This chapter considers mobility from a "green mobile" perspective. Green mobile can be considered as the adoption of mobility by business that considers its environmental impact in all its dimensions. Thus, economic viability, social responsibility, and technological capabilities are all considered together in identifying the effect of mobility on the environment.

The ubiquitous mobile phones, their batteries, the mobile networks, the RFID tags, the mobile transmission towers and the myriad mobile devices such as the PDAs and tablet PCs all form part of the growing environmentally challenging issue that mobile businesses need to address. For example, due to rapid obsolescence of mobile phones, there is a need to recycle these devices and the potentially hazardous batteries that power them. Another example of environmental considerations is the potential effect of radiation through the mobile gadgets on the brain cells, which continues to generate numerous inconclusive debates. MET approaches these environmental issues in a holistic and responsible manner. The MET framework is revisited and extended here to consider all four dimensions of transition from an environmental viewpoint. Thus, for example, MET aims to do more for the environmental issues than handling, say, the recycling of mobile phones. This responsible approach toward mobility is in sync with the thoughts on sustainability by business experts working in this area. For example, Cartland (2005) writes about the significance of studying and optimizing supply chains with regard to sustainability in business. Unhelkar and Dickens (2008) and Unhelkar and Trivedi (2009) have also argued in favor of green ICT and environmentally responsible business strategies (ERBSs). This chapter synergizes these thoughts on sustainability with those on mobility and explores the various ways in which mobility can help the environment and business sustain the business.

Mobility can play a vital role in the sustainability of a business, and sustainable businesses provide impetus for economic growth as well. Thus, mobility has a role to play in environmentally responsible business strategies that make an organization sustainable, which, in turn, makes it a long-lasting and profitable organization. Mobility can be said to help the business be environmentally intelligent.

Business Sustainability

One of the most significant modern management insights into business sustainability is presented by Younessi (2009) and was discussed in this book in earlier chapters on the economic dimension of mobility (Chapter 3) and mobile business expansion and growth (Chapter 8). Younessi dissuades managements from thinking only in terms of profits, and instead focuses their attention on the *need* for a business "to exist" for a long time. A business that focuses on only one single dimension, that of "making money," is likely to lose sight of the bigger picture in terms of sustainability. Mobility provides an excellent opportunity for businesses to use technology for the common good through sustainable business policies. The unique, wireless nature of mobility has immense potential to reduce the movement of people and material and radically optimize business processes from an environmental viewpoint. Thus, the MET framework is discussed and expanded in this chapter as a framework that not only delivers business change for profitability but also has a positive influence on sustainability and on the environment. Needless to say, contributions of mobile technology toward sustainability and environmental responsibility are increasingly going to be the criteria by which any new technology and innovation will be judged.

A simple interpretation of "sustainability" states that the longer a business stays "in business," the better are its chances of success, including economic success. Therefore, a correlation between the sustainability and economics (through time) can be established, as has been alluded to in the Stern report (Stern 2007). The Stern report has argued, and correctly so, that the issue of the environment is a formal business responsibility with economic impacts. This correlation between success and time has the potential for driving business advantage depending on the understanding and emancipation of the business leaders driving that particular business. This discussion aims to attract the attention of the senior management (leadership) of mobile businesses toward the opportunities of sustainability offered by mobility. Therefore, sustainability and environmental responsibility are considered as increasingly important goals of MET. The way to achieve sustainability through mobility is to approach and extend the four dimensions of MET in a balanced manner. Incorporation of environmental consciousness in each of the dimensions—economic, technical, process, and social—and keeping them in balance is part of the discussion in this chapter.

Environmental Responsibility

Environmental responsibility and sustainability go hand in hand. The need for sustainability is correlated with its existence and growth (and, eventually, economic performance); and by undertaking environmental responsibilities, mobile businesses move toward sustainability. Thus, sustainability of an enterprise can almost be considered as a benchmark of its wisdom. The wiser the enterprise, the greater are the chances that it will use its available resources in the most optimum way possible. Mobile technologies can be put to great use in improving the capacity of organizations to produce goods or enhance services. However, the purpose of such enhancements should be, besides profit, the maximization of environmental value as well. Thus, improving production capacity and making it efficient not only reduces costs but also has a positive impact on the environment. For example, using mobility to enhance the supply-chain management system of a pharmaceutical company results not only in time and cost savings but also benefits the environment. This is so because mobile supply-chain management (m-SCM), with its mobile-enabled business processes, can reduce packaging material wastages and greenhouse gas emissions that result from storage and distribution. Similarly, in a distributed service business, a mobile enterprise resource planning (m-ERP) solution can enable optimum routing of field service engineers or sales support staff; this not only reduces costs and enhances value to the customer but also provides a positive value to the environment by reducing unnecessary movement of people. These various environmental advantages need to be kept in mind in all activities relating to production, distribution, recycling, design, process, and services in an organization undertaking mobile transition.

Mobility and the Environment

As summarized in Figure 9.1, there is an ever-expanding influence of mobility on business and society (discussed earlier in Chapter 1), and also on the environment. For example, mobility influences the way people use mobile devices, which in turn influences the environment: a small wireless handheld device may require batteries; but this device has a much lesser need for energy than a larger desktop one. Also, processes are influenced by optimization of supply chains, customer relationships,

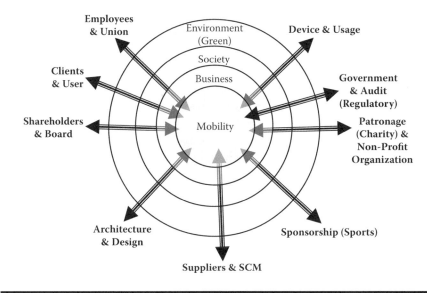

Figure 9.1 Mobility, business, society, and the environment.

and financial systems; changes to the social networking styles of employees and their unions; technical changes to the architecture; and design of software and enterprise systems that reflect environmental responsibility or the way corporate sponsorships change to the suit environmental considerations. These influences, summarized in Figure 9.1, are incorporated by Mobile Enterprise Transition and Management (METM), resulting in resulting in what Unhelkar and Dickens (2008) have called an environmentally responsible business strategy (ERBS). An ERBS that employs mobile technologies helps organizations achieve their social goals of reducing greenhouse emissions through redesign and recycling of products and optimization of processes. This reduction can be attributed to the strategic use of mobility in the organization. Examples of such use of mobility are incorporation of mobile processes that reduce transportation of men and materials, collaborative use of mobility in recycling of products (including their design), and making the wired networks within the organization redundant. Further, both the technical and process dimensions of MET encourage consolidation of mobile data centers as well as the use of virtualization through mobility, wherever possible. The resulting environmentally responsible businesses have less need for physical activities, which leads to reduced power consumption, lower carbon emissions, and savings in time and space.

Despite its seemingly obvious advantages, mobility faces some interesting and unique environmental challenges. Consider, for example, how mobility enables virtual collaborations between businesses and individuals. These collaborations, especially between businesses, can be challenging to manage for organizations implementing environmentally responsible strategies. This is so because in collaboration of businesses, all work together to provide services to individual customers.

This makes it difficult to precisely identify individual (in those collaborations) greenhouse gas emitters and polluters. Mobile users also present challenges from an environmental viewpoint. They are difficult to track due to their location independence, which makes it challenging to track their environmental activities and quantify the pollution that may have been generated.

Furthermore, networks, computers, and other IT infrastructure consume significant amounts of electrical energy, and their use continues to increase day by day. This increasing use places a heavy burden on the electric grid, which also contributes to greenhouse gas emissions, resulting in an imbalance in the environmental equilibrium. This imbalance can be further exacerbated with larger numbers of mobile networks and servers. Therefore, it is vital in MET to keep a balanced view of the transition and its environmental impact in mind all the time. Use of metrics to measure the environmental impact (such as, say, carbon emissions per unit of use of a mobile device or a mobile network) can be made more popular by incorporating those measures in the EI systems of the organization.

In addition to the technological balance, there is also a need for careful "engineering" of business processes of an organization from an ecofriendly viewpoint. This careful engineering of business processes can be achieved through excellence in modeling the way in which its people and technologies are employed to achieve the process goals. Modeling of mobile business processes can be based on the goals to be achieved by the users with minimal impact on the environment, reduced waste, and increased productivity. Process modeling can play a very creative role in the environmental performance of the organization by simply helping the users of the organization to do things differently. However, experience suggests that creation of such ecofriendly business processes can succeed only when they are part of the overall environmentally responsible business strategy.

> Mobility enables virtual collaboration between business and individuals. Reengineering business processes with mobility provides enormous opportunities for virtualization. The more virtual a business is, the less physical resources it will consume; therefore, well-modeled mobile processes greatly assist in the creation of ecofriendly business.

Green Mobile and the ICT

There are four specific reasons why an organization should consider environmentally responsible business strategies when undertaking MET. These reasons, which are summarized and depicted in Figure 9.2, are not isolated from one another; they

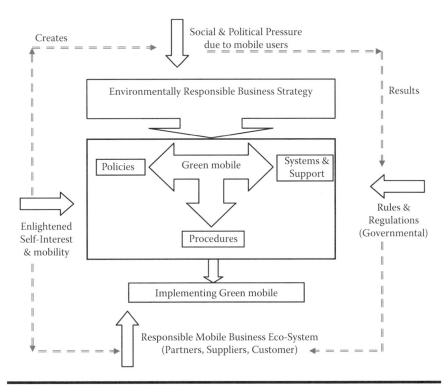

Figure 9.2   Green mobile ICT factors.

influence one another both directly as well as subtly. These reasons are (1) enlightened self-interest and mobility, which creates (2) social and political pressure from and on the users, resulting in (3) rules and regulations that are mobile specific and that result in (4) responsible mobile business ecosystems. These four interrelated environmental reasons in mobile business are discussed next.

Enlightened Self-Interest

This is an ideal reason why a mobile business should focus on the green aspect of mobility. Mobility helps the business grow and expand, resulting in greater value to its customers. This potential goodwill resulting from MET needs to be capitalized on by the organization; users and business partners can be gently nudged toward becoming environmentally responsible. The acknowledgement of environmental responsibility and initiatives toward green mobile by the transitioned business is an expression of its enlightened self-interest. The greater is this self-interest in pushing for green mobile, the greater will be its effect on the political and regulatory bodies. And a mobile organization that is promoting these changes is well placed to reap the rewards of creating and implementing green mobile policies and procedures with its ERBS.

Social and Political Pressure

When there is pressure on an organization from the society in which it exists and from the corresponding political entities, the organization is forced to consider mobility from an environmental perspective. This social pressure can come in various directions. For example, marketing departments that intend to differentiate their products or services from competitors may demand environmentally responsible mobile deployment. The education system can enforce green values in the upcoming generation of users for making the transitioning businesses environmentally responsible. There can also be political pressure from an electorate through public awareness campaigns mandating changes to rules and regulations governing mobile use. These changes are required for mere awareness; issues are not enough or legally binding. Collective opinion is required to bring about legal changes and to enforce good corporate citizenship.

Rules and Regulations of Mobility

As previously mentioned, legally binding environmental legislation plays an important role in promoting sustainability and a green environment. These legislations will make it mandatory for a company to implement environmental measures that should be incorporated as it transitions to mobility. For example, business operations may have to ensure that the mobile gadgets it produces meet the environmentally responsible standards set by legislations. These standards can include radiation levels, battery and gadget recycling, and environmentally friendly designs.

A transitioning organization exhibits enlightened self-interest and mobility on its own accord when it realizes the need to be environmentally responsible and creates or adopts a green mobile strategy. This factor can be subsequently used by the company for its brand recognition; or it may be driven by the need for business continuity and sustainability (Cartland 2005).

Responsible Business Ecosystem and Mobility

As shown in Figure 9.2, all the other factors and reasons are unified in a responsible business ecosystem. The ecosystem of the mobile business includes the industry it is a part of and the environment in which it operates, including its business partners, suppliers, and customers. This entire business ecosystem can be made to create and implement green mobile initiatives through METM-based mobile business initiatives. Being part of such a business ecosystem, an organization is forced to follow suit and create as well as participate in green mobile strategies. Notice how, for example, a consortium of IT enterprises have got together under the umbrella of Green Grid (www.thegreengrid.org) to form such an "ecosystem." These enterprises include Advanced Micro Devices (AMD), Dell, HP, IBM, Intel, Microsoft, Sun, and VMware; many of them are actually competing against each other when it comes to their mainstream business, but they have got together to form this grid from an environmental viewpoint. This growing consortium of industrial organizations is focused on the best-of-breed energy-efficient practices in data center operation, construction, and product design. The Green Grid's charter drives new user-centric metrics, technology standards, and best practices for curbing and managing power consumption for long-term sustainability. By working together, these companies expect to develop ways to hook their respective green technologies into one another and increase their overall effectiveness. Opportunities provided by mobility need to be considered to enable full utilization of their green initiatives.

An environmentally responsible business strategy (ERBS) is influenced by a number of factors such as social and political pressures; rules and regulations; demands from customers, suppliers, and business partners; and enlightened self-interest. Furthermore, an ERBS needs to be embraced by not just individual organizations but a group or consortium of similar-thinking organizations. Such a consortium-based approach to environmental responsibility creates an "ecosystem" of a group of companies that can propel ERBS throughout the industry.

Figure 9.2 further shows how the green mobile initiative within an organization is affected by three major aspects of the ERBS: the policies implemented through services, procedures and processes modeled on the concept of green mobile, and the systems and support from software applications. The interplay between mobile businesses and their corresponding environmental responsibility is discussed next.

Achieving Green Mobile Business

Green mobile businesses can be achieved by going through the four dimensions of MET—economic, technical, process, and social—from the viewpoint of their environmental responsibility. These four dimensions, however, need to be a part of an ERBS (Unhelkar and Dickens 2008). An ERBS itself, as shown in Figure 9.3, needs to be incorporated in the overall "mobile business strategy" of the organization. Thus, the four dimensions of MET become part of the ERBS through business strategies. They are thus an integral part of the environmental approach and not a separate and isolated addition to the business.

The working of ERBS is based on the increasing complexities of the informative, transactive, operative, and collaborative use of mobile businesses. This increasing

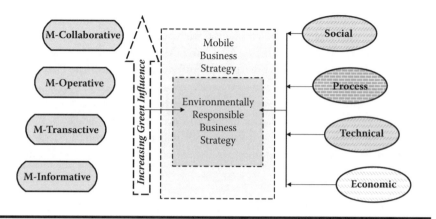

Figure 9.3   MET framework and the environmentally responsible business strategy (ERBS).

complexity, however, also has its rewards in that there is increasing opportunity to have a substantial effect on the environmental consciousness of the organization.

> Although the use of mobility becomes increasingly complex as the businesses move through informative, transactive, operative, and collaborative use, there are also corresponding advantages for the environment that are derived from such use.

The informative use of mobility enables the organization to provide environment-related information to various stakeholders within the business. It is possible to collect data on carbon emissions, temperature levels, etc., from the organization's activities and disburse them using mobile gadgets. Such informative use of mobility can also include an update by stakeholders of the terms of standards and benchmarks set by governments and various regulatory bodies on the acceptable levels of carbon emissions for specific industries.

Transactive mobile usage includes the collection, collation, and reporting of environmental data using handheld mobile as well as stationary but wireless devices. For example, the measurement of the temperature of a furnace or an engine can be conducted using wireless devices. This information is then further analyzed and used to manage, monitor, and control corresponding systems. The transactive capabilities of mobile or wireless devices can thus be put to good use to measure and monitor carbon emissions and report them to internal management and external regulatory bodies. Thus, the transactive use of mobility has a greater opportunity to influence the environment positively than its informative use.

Operative mobile use provides opportunities for the organization to model and optimize its internal processes to produce environmentally friendly results. Examples of such initiatives include the management of people to reduce their unnecessary movement, virtualization of teams to enable dispersed team members to get together without travel, and internal inventory management processes that reduce the burden on the environment, as well as reporting and optimization of these internal processes. Mobile telecommuting is a serious consideration for operative use by business, wherein workers need not be physically present at the premises of the company. Employees will have access to environmentally intelligent systems that help them carry out their day-to-day activities in an ecofriendly way.

In collaborative mobile use, organizations are influenced by the policies and strategies of their business partners toward the green environment. This results in a cluster or group of companies having environmentally responsible policies that are not limited to the boundaries of a single organization. Instead, the mobile collaboration influences the entire ecosystem of companies that are using mobility together.

Having thus discussed the gradually increasing complexity and influence of mobility on the environment, we now discuss the four dimensions of MET in this context.

Environmental–Economic Mobile Use

The economic influence of mobility needs to be considered here in terms of its relevance to the environment. For example, the economic reasons for transitioning to mobile business can be extended and discussed in terms of the economic reasons for transitioning to and managing a sustainable mobile business. The important economic factors of costs and competition for mobile transitions are correlated with the environmental issues as well. Focusing on the environmental issues in the short term tends to occasionally give an impression that additional costs will be incurred (such as costs of recycling gadgets or costs associated with modifying the mobile business processes). However, in the sustainable and long-term time frame, these costs translates to goodwill and, hence, customer retention and growth. At an individual level too, economic attitude translates into environmental attitude (such as, for example, not throwing away old and out-of-date, or out-of-fashion mobile devices but reusing such mobile devices or their parts).

Apart from the mobile gadgets, there are also costs associated with creating and implementing environmental strategies and costs associated with maintaining them through environmental programs within the organization. Furthermore, economic considerations need to be brought in with collaborating mobile businesses who need to be made aware of environmental considerations—in terms of their own budgets and willingness to spend money on environmental issues. Organizations are keen to promote their green awareness by providing part of their proceeds toward green activities. For example, the *Green broadband* from iPrimus is a green initiative that, based on less than a dollar per month extra, encourages the customers and the service providers companies to participate in tree-planting activities that can compensate for the greenhouse emissions (www.iprimus.com.au).

Environmental–Technical Mobile Use

Millions of new mobile phones are bought each year worldwide for various reasons including the socially driven reasons for the adolescent market, as discussed in Chapter 6. Mobile gadgets are environmental challenges during both manufacture and at disposal (Unhelkar and Dickens 2008). Mobile gadget manufacturers can play a major role in reducing the environmental impact of their products by ensuring that these products do not use hazardous materials such as brominated flame retardants (BFRs), PVCs, and heavy metals such as lead, cadmium, and mercury. Greenpeace has appealed to the electronics industry to design products that are free from hazardous substances, and the mobile industry needs to pay particular attention to this situation owing to the inundation of mobile gadgets worldwide. Beginning with their design, manufacturers need to improve reuse and recycling of their mobile products. Mobile phones that can be recycled at the end of their life are more environmental friendly than the ones that cannot be recycled. Manufacturers can offer an effective and responsible take-back and recycling program that can be put to good use by users. Regulatory approaches to product reuse and recycling also help in enforcing reuse and recycling.

Recycling mobile devices is not enough, though. Environmentally responsible mobile businesses apply the concept of reuse to the design and distribution of mobile gadgets as well. Technical designers seek to create mobile gadgets that will have minimum impact on the environment. This environmentally responsible design of mobile phones can reduce the amount of materials used, thereby reducing the impact of those materials and increasing the efficiency of use of mobile phones by customers. Some recent innovations in mobile product designs are worth noting, such as the "Sunflower Phone" introduced by Green Mobiles in the United Kingdom. This phone is claimed to be biodegradable as it has a built-in plant seed that will grow once the phone is planted in the ground. Nokia has released a model called 3110 Evolve that is claimed to use a bio-cover: the casing of the phone is composed of 50 percent recycled material and packaging made from 60 perent recycled material (http://www.compareindia.com). Furthermore, according to the specifications of the phone, this Nokia phone model also has a high-efficiency charger, as well as an ecofriendly user interface.

In addition to design of mobile devices, there is also a need to take environmental impact into account through optimized use of other mobile hardware such as base stations, transmitters, and computer servers that support mobile applications. For example, an environmentally responsible mobile infrastructure will include appropriate location of mobile transmission towers to ensure minimal environmental impact on people and forests. The inherently complex issues of mobile infrastructure planning need to take the environment into consideration. Thus, mobility infrastructure planning becomes a crucial technical aspect of environmental planning for a mobile organization. Such infrastructure planning goes beyond a single organization and becomes an important part of governmental initiatives, or that of the regulatory bodies. A major challenge in the setting up of systems and architectures is to take into account the impacts of the mobility system on environmental and social quality (Borri et al. 2005).

Environmental–Process Mobile Use

The way in which businesses operate can have a tremendous impact on the environment. Thus, all business processes need to be modeled, studied, and optimized from an environmental perspective as an organization undertakes MET. The potential of mobile devices to reduce people movement is obvious; this potential needs to be woven into the mobile business processes of an organization. A mobile worker who can access the information he needs at the location he is reduces physical and vehicle movement, making the business processes progress one successful step in going green.

Business intelligence processes can also make use of wireless capabilities to implement, maintain, and sustain environmentally intelligent business systems. IT has been thrust into the limelight as a key element in advancing strategic business objectives, and certainly mobile business intelligence (BI) plays a major role in achieving these objectives. Therefore, IT must have its own set of mobile BI capabilities to maintain and sustain the overall environment (Imhoff 2005).

Enterprises are looking to mobility for extending BI solutions to coordinate their office, field, and home decision-making processes. Mobility equips users with real-time access to critical business and analytical applications, decision-making systems, queries on performances, and customer data. These improvements enable organizations to gain environmental advantage by optimizing the mobile field and workforce.

BI users (executives, analysts, financial planners, strategists, and the field workforce) equipped with mobility are able to utilize their time and location-free connectivity to reduce movements. Companies with a high number of mobile sales and service personnel in industries such as retail, financial institutions such as banks, healthcare, and manufacturing are using mobile technologies and EI to improve their workers' access to data and information.

Environmental–Social Mobile Use

The social dimension of MET is related to the environment in many ways. For example, the ability of personalized transmission of messages can be utilized to raise environmental awareness among specific users. Mobile businesses can also take on additional social responsibilities by investing in communities that can be helped to learn, work, and thrive in a green environment. Mobile businesses can also facilitate mobile networking among interested groups of users on issues of the environment. For example, all transitioning organizations can setup green blogs, which could play an important role in the green initiatives of an organization. Blogs, wikis, and discussion groups can be an attractive way of creating and spreading social awareness of environmental issues. The free exchange of information among participants and between the readers can become an important part of public dialog on environmental matters (Dicum 2006). According to Alex Steffen, founder of one of the most widely read green blogs, "Climate change has become a big issue. A lot of people are interested in green building, green fashion and green product design." Mobile businesses need to encourage and support these social networking opportunities, enabling users and customers to express their views and share innovative ways to go green.

Mobile networks and devices can themselves be used in green networking, discussions, and blogging. Participants can exchange their views on climate and action, mobilize timely groups of people, and carry out substantial environmental activities.

Environmental Intelligence (EI)

Environmental intelligence can be understood as the use of business tools and technologies to understand and coordinate a response to environmental challenges. It results from the increasing analysis and correlation between silos of information, as shown in Figure 9.4. This figure shows how, starting with subjective observations and recording them on mobile gadgets, organizations can move up in environment-related knowledge and wisdom.

Mobility is a significant factor in the quality of life of individuals and society as a whole (Unhelkar 2005). Application of mobile business intelligence (BI) results in mobile EI applications that combine enterprise information access with mobile devices such as mobile phones, PDAs, smart phones, the BlackBerry, and other handheld wireless devices (based on Turban et al. 2006). Such a combination can enable the production of BI reports, key performance indicators (KPI), graphical dashboards, and business analytics with handheld mobile and wireless devices.

Mobility, through its innate ability of location independence, has a role to play in EI. Mobile data and information on potentially wasteful use of materials, energy, space, and labor can be taken advantage of by EI and converted into intelligence. Information on labor usage, physical work space, process flow, setup time, and management concepts such as lean systems and "Kaizan" can benefit in real-time by using mobile technologies. Kaizan can be considered a frame of

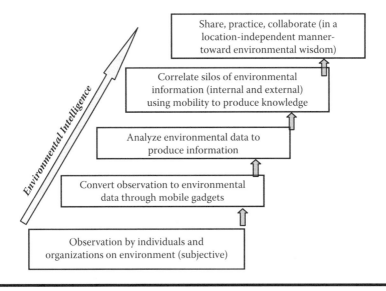

Figure 9.4 Path to environmental intelligence with mobility.

mind or a mindset within an organization, which aims to improve the efficiency of any organization by primarily discouraging any idle inventory. It aims to meet the demands of customers to have deliveries on time, shorten development cycle time, and be able to forecast the demand for products and services with minimum margin of error (www.tradescalm.com). These operational business processes of an organization can be optimized substantially by the real-time mobile usage.

Mobility can improve decision-making processes of the organization, which can result in environmental advantages to the enterprise and, in turn, society. For example, producing higher-quality products and services has a positive correlation with the environment. A high-quality product that lasts a year extra is an environmentally good product. This correlation is created, maintained, and utilized by bringing together data and information (that may otherwise have been unrelated) using mobility. The correlation of environment-related information and utilization of that information in a knowledge management system can lead to environmental intelligence systems (EISs). Mobility is a key player in EISs.

Enterprises are looking at the effects and uses of mobility to extend EI solutions. EI systems involve and employ mobility solutions to coordinate decision-making processes in the office, field, and home. Managers, business executives, and analysts can now access important business information through wireless devices such as mobile phones and PDAs (based on Turban et al. 2008).

The same mechanism for access and decision making that is used by business can be made specific to environmental issues, resulting in EI. EI can interface with many existing enterprise systems such as decision support systems (DSSs), executive information systems, and knowledge management systems (KMSs) to support decision making, as discussed by Clark et al. (2007) and Watson and Wixom (2007). Mobile EI is the successful collection, evaluation, and application of information by business leaders and users employing mobile gadgets, networks, and processes. According to a Gartner survey of CIOs, EI projects were the most important technology priority for companies in 2007. EI has been defined in many different ways in the literature with different contexts and meanings. It can be considered an umbrella term that encompasses tools, architecture, databases, data warehouses, performance management, methodologies, and so on that are unified and integrated into a mobile applications suite to support faster and better decision making for environmentally responsible strategies. EI systems consist of the tools, technologies, and processes involved in turning environmental data into information and environmental information into knowledge in order to optimize decision making. EI processes refine analysis and disseminate environmental business information to ensure effective and efficient use of green enterprise resources as well as compliance with green policies and procedures.

EIS collaborates information, knowledge, and intelligence related to all business activities with other members (organization/business) of the value chain. Also, companies can utilize Web services and mobile technologies for collaborative environmental intelligence on the mobile Internet. EIS allows companies to benefit from the well-coordinated efforts of mobile devices, wireless networks, mobile Internet, and mobile Web services.

Environmental intelligence (EI) combines tools, architecture, databases, data warehouses, business performance methodologies, and quality initiatives to produce environmentally responsible decisions and action. It is further enhanced by the availability and application of mobility that improves decision support systems (DSSs), executive information systems, and knowledge management systems (KMSs).

EI includes the basic activities of collecting and providing environmental data. Collection or sourcing of mobile data results in mobile data warehousing, online analytical processing (OLAP), and data mining, which are the most significant technologies in business intelligence (Zeng et al. 2006) applied to environmental intelligence. A mobile data warehouse is a large repository of data collected from operational sources that deal with environmental information. OLAP techniques are complex analyses of stored data in data warehouses. Data mining is used to identify and interpret patterns from organizational data for some specific business issue. In EI systems, OLAP and data mining techniques query data warehouses or other data sources to collect information and report the results to BI users (Sixto 2002).

BI consists of business users and applications accessing data from warehouses for reporting, OLAP, querying, and predictive analysis. Typical features of EI software tools include reporting and visualization, historical and emerging trend analysis, and predictive modeling. Visualization is the process of representing data as visual images. According to Azvine et al. (2006), EI comprises technologies such as data warehouses, analytical tools, and reporting tools, whereas visualization is used to create dashboards that summarize large amounts of data on a single screen.

Mobile environmental systems (MESs) can be divided into four major architectural components: EI data warehouse, mobility in business analytics, mobile business performance management, and a user interface. The EI data warehouse is a single repository populated by data from systems such as ERP, CRM (where mobility is the main considered factor), etc., to support decision making in organizations. The data will have some additional dimensions compared to traditional data warehouse constructions. This environmental data will be collected, classified, scrutinized, integrated, and transformed into a data warehouse. Such a data warehouse will be ecofriendly as it will reduce the access time and thereby the energy required by servers. The operational sources of business data are referred to as operational data stores (ODSs), from which data is extracted, transformed, and loaded (ETL) into a data mart. for the data mart is then subject to OLAP, in which data is drilled down and rolled up for analysis (based on Kimball et al. 1998). Mobile and handheld wireless devices can enter data and communicate with data warehouses and operational entry points such as ERP and CRM. Similarly, online and real-time data entry from PDA and other mobile devices using radio frequency (RF) signals can be used by field workers to provide real-time data to organizations for decision making. Also, when virtualization of systems—that is, one hardware operating two or more machines—are used with mobile devices, the whole system will become more ecofriendly as less energy will be consumed and location independence will enable operations from anywhere (in the possible range of a mobile gadget). We may therefore say that mobility added to a business system in an intelligent manner will always result in an ecofriendly system. Thus, EIS is a roadmap that incorporates environmental focus into the overall information architecture of an organization.

Advantages of Environmental Intelligence Systems (EISs)

An environmental intelligence system (EIS) undertakes to create and maintain a clean and green environment within and outside a business. An EIS is thus a technical- and systems-level support for ERBS.

The business office, in particular, is one of the major generators of green house gases with its great number of electronic gadgets such as computers, servers, phones, air conditioners, lights, kitchen equipment, paper, printer inks, and cartridges, and so on. As discussed by Unhelkar and Dickens (2008), business intelligence needs to capitalize on the intelligence aspect to facilitate optimum energy consumption and work practices. By enhancing and equipping business systems with mobility, we move toward the aforementioned EIS. An EIS can play a significant role in enhancing this ability of a business to coordinate its environmentally responsible approaches. The specific advantages of an EIS incorporated in business processes are as follows:

▪ Collecting environmental related data in real-time. Although EIS is geared to collect data such as number of devices in use and on standby, mobility further enhances this data capture and enables the EIS to then relate this data to other business applications.

▪ Providing querying tools, key performance indicators (KPIs), and business analytics to field workers and decision makers in the area of EI. Availability of querying mechanisms can provide information that enables closing down of unused servers, desk tops and other equipment.

▪ Enhancing the decision-making capabilities of senior management by collating and computing up-to-date information from varied external sources such as government regulatory bodies and weather information and feeding it into EIS. This service-oriented approach in EIS and the resultant real-time analytics goes a long way in enhancing the mobile organization's green credentials.

▪ EIS can also substantiate the green effort of the organization, thereby providing positive feedback to employees and increasing their sense of job satisfaction.

▪ EIS can continuously identify and upgrade business processes and business practices in manufacturing, sales, and field support operations in order to make them environmentally responsible. Mobile business processes (as discussed later in the Chapter 12 case study) can become environmentally responsible through the application of EIS.

▪ EIS also provides feedback to customers and other external users of the business on its environmental performance, potentially resulting in increased customer service and satisfaction, especially for the environmentally sensitive and responsible customers.

▪ Aligning office and home activities through EIS can tremendously boost the organizational effort in improving its green credentials. This is so because EIS can identify the areas of work that are overlapping with one another because of their location-specific nature and make them location-independent as far as possible.

▪ EIS extends the tools and techniques of business management (such as KPIs, business analytics, and reporting) and applies them to the environmental aspect of business. Mobility further enhances the application of these management tools and techniques. A transitioning mobile business can bring together good management and good environmental approaches through the use of EIS.

▪ EIS enables the business with the ability to sustain itself over the long term. An environmentally responsible business and a sustainable business are complementary. EIS, extended with mobility, offers an opportunity for the mobile business to come up with technologies and processes that promote sustainability.

- EIS enables collaboration among businesses for the purpose of achieving environmental responsibilities. This collaboration is achieved through service orientation of the EIS applications.

Future of Environmental Intelligence and Sustainability

Incorporation of mobile and communication technologies in the collaborative business ecosystem can add EI to the current business intelligence. Increasing awareness of adverse effects of current business activities on the environment will force the corporate sector to add EI to mobility to help our earth go green.

The future of EI is in the collaboration of the many "similar-thinking" businesses that can form part of a mobile business ecosystem. There is a need for both lateral as well as vertical integration of suppliers, manufacturers, distributors, and other business partners through mobility to enable environmental collaboration. Thus, the strategic approach to bringing about such a collaboration was discussed earlier in this chapter as an environmentally responsible business strategy. A good ERBS focuses on utilizing the m-SCM and m-CRM to make the flow of goods and services as highly optimized as possible for the benefit of the environment. The collaborative mobile business models for delivery of products and services are more complex than for single organizations. This is so because such models need to model and integrate mobile processes laterally and dynamically. Integration of such lateral processes across heterogeneous enterprises and geographical boundaries implies challenges in terms of identifying and pinning environmental responsibilities on collaborating organizations. Additional challenges from the environmental viewpoints stem from the dynamic aspect of mobile processes, which include users, nodes, and networks on the fly, making it challenging to identify the specific polluting nodes.

With the passage of time, one can expect more aggressive initiatives by businesses toward this paradigm shift of collaborative environmental responsibility. This will throw up multiple business and research opportunities in a completely new direction on mobility and the environment. Such opportunities will be created in the domains of various business ecosystems and industries as well as the mobile information and communication technology. Given the wide scope of environmental intelligence and mobility, there are opportunities in areas of international exchange of thought and collaborative research. Some of these are as follows:

- Creation of globally acceptable standards related to operations, transactions, workflow, and information flow in various industries, with respect to environmental intelligence with mobility.
- Fostering of an EI economy that capitalizes on the knowledge economy through use of mobile communications and applications.
- Creation of software components, frameworks, and libraries that can facilitate the implementation of an environmentally responsible management and decision support system.
- Innovating new concepts in sourcing, storing, and analyzing environmental data, and its management and sharing at a global level.
- Conceptualization of social networking management and models for ownership and control of environmentally responsible virtual communities.
- Creation of a legal framework that would govern the collaborations in the area of mobility and environment sustainability.

Discussion Points

1. What are the specific ways in which a MET can render an organization environmentally friendly? Base your discussion on the four dimensions of the MET framework.
2. Discuss with your own examples the effect of mobility on business, society, and the environment (Hint: Figure 9.1).
3. How can an environmentally responsible business strategy be made part of a mobile business strategy?
4. What, according to you, comprises EI? How is collaboration able to facilitate EI?

References

Azvine, B., Cui, Z., Nauck, D. D., and Majeed, B. 2006. Real Time Business Intelligence for the Adaptive Enterprise, paper presented at the E-Commerce Technology, 2006, *The 8th IEEE International Conference on Enterprise Computing, E-Commerce, and E-Services*, San Francisco, CA.

Borri D., Camarda D., and De Liddo, A. 2005. Mobility in Environmental ICT Gets Its Green House in Order, *Information Age,* December 2005, Publication of the Australian Computer Society.

Cartland, S. 2005. Business continuity challenges in global supply chains, chapter 19 in *Global Integrated Supply Chain Systems*, eds. Y. Lan and B. Unhelkar. Hershey, PA: IGI Global.

Clark, T. D. J., Jones, M. C., and Armstrong, C. P. 2007. The Dynamic Structure of Management Support Systems: Theory Development, Research Focus, and Direction, *MIS Quarterly* 31(3): 579–615.

Dicum, G. 2006. Green Blogs: The Green Revolution moves online, available at http://www.sfgate.com/cgi-bin/article.cgi?f=/g/a/2006/03/22/gree.DTL.

Imhoff, C. 2005. Business Intelligence Environments: The Need for Mobility, retrieved December 14, 2007, from http://www.b-eye-network.com/view/1128.

Kimball, R., Reeves, L., Thornthwaite, W., and Ross, M. 1998. *The Data Warehouse Lifecycle Toolkit: Expert Methods for Designing, Developing and Deploying Data.* New York: John Wiley.

Sixto, O. J. 2002. Is business intelligence a smart move? *Computer* 35(7): 11–14.

Stern, N. 2007. *Stern Review on the Economics of Climate Change*, Cambridge University Press, Cambridge, 2007 (www.hm-treasury. gov.uk/independent_reviews/ stern_review_economics_climate_change/stern_review_report.cfm).

Turban, E., Lee, J., King, D., and Chung, H. M. 2006. *Electronic Commerce 2006: A Managerial Perspective.* Upper Saddle River, NJ: Prentice Hall.

Turban, E., Sharda, R., Aronson, J. E., and King, D. 2008. *Business Intelligence: A Managerial Approach.* Upper Saddle River, NJ: Prentice Hall.

Unhelkar, B. 2005. Transitioning to a Mobile Enterprise: A Three-Dimensional Framework, *Cutter IT Journal*, special issue on Mobile Computing, ed. S. Murugesan. 18(8).

Unhelkar, B. and Dickens, A. 2008. Lessons in Implementing "Green" Business Strategies with ICT, *Cutter IT Journal*, special issue on "Can IT Go Green?" 21(2): 32–39.

Unhelkar, B. and Trivedi, B. 2009. Role of mobile technologies in an environmentally responsible business strategy, chapter in *Handbook of Research in Mobile Business: Technical, Methodological and Social Perspectives*, 2nd ed., ed. B. Unhelkar. Hershey, PA: IGI Global.

Watson, H. J. and Wixom, B. H. 2007. The current state of business intelligence. *Computer* 40(9): 96–99.

Younessi, H. 2009. Strategic view on creating business value through mobile technologies, chapter 1 in *Handbook of Research in Mobile Business: Technical, Methodological and Social Perspectives,* 2nd ed., ed. B. Unhelkar. Hershey, PA: IGI Global.

Zeng, L., Xu, L., Shi, Z., Wang, M., and Wu, W. 2006. Techniques, Process, and Enterprise Solutions of Business Intelligence, paper presented at the *Systems, Man and Cybernetics Conference*, 2006, Taipei, Taiwan.

Chapter 10

Case Study: Applying METM to a Medium-Sized Pharmaceutical Enterprise

Adaptability is not imitation. It means power of resistance and assimilation.

Mahatma Gandhi

Chapter Key Points

- Outlines a practical case study in Mobile Enterprise Transition and Management (METM) in which the transition framework can be applied
- Discusses the practical application of METM framework to a medium-sized pharmaceutical enterprise called Pharma
- Demonstrates the practical implementation of the diagnosis phase of METM and provides an understanding of the goals, demographics, and mobile maturity of Pharma
- Presents how the concept of change management in MET is applied in practice
- Outlines the MET project plan that considers all the four dimensions—economic, process, technical, and social—in a cohesive sequence of activities that can be enacted in a transition project
- Suggests how the transitioning Pharma organization should evolve from informative to transactive, operative, and collaborative use of mobility
- Suggests the posttransition reviews and feedbacks

Background to METM Case Studies

Mobile Enterprise Transition and Management (METM) is the application of MET and the ensuing management of a mobile enterprise. It has been applied practically to a few enterprises. MET can be applied in many wide-ranging industries such as education, healthcare, pharmaceutical, tourism, hospitality, automotive, aviation, banking and financial, sports, and entertainment. Figure 10.1 shows its application in six such specific industries. Also shown in the figure are keywords that depict the major role played by mobility in these enterprises. This book contains three case studies (outlined in Chapters 10, 11, and 12, respectively) that are selected from the aforementioned industries to depict certain aspects of the practical application of the METM framework. This chapter describes the first one: METM based on a medium-sized enterprise in the pharmaceutical industry. The subsequent two case studies are in the areas of travel and tourism (Chapter 11) and education environment (Chapter 12). The travel and tourism case study is for a small business, whereas that in Chapter 12 approaches mobility from the environmental point of view and its impact on green society and sustainability.

This chapter starts with the case study problem statement for the pharmaceutical enterprise, followed by the enactment of the diagnose phase wherein the demographics, goals, and mobile maturity of the enterprise are ascertained. The four dimensions of MET are then applied to create the MET enactment project; this is followed by the execution of the MET framework. Finally, the transition project ends with a posttransitional review and feedback.

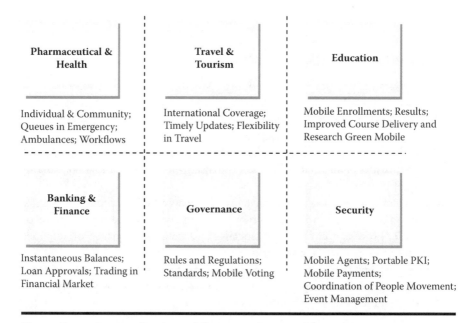

Figure 10.1   Case studies in Mobile Enterprise Transition (MET).

Pharma Problem Statement

Pharma is a medium-sized, family-owned, pharmaceutical manufacturing enterprise that specializes in a series of drugs that deal with control and management of diabetes and related disorders. It employs around 20 people who work in various capacities, such as managers, researchers, and workers within the enterprise. Pharma is located in one of the suburban regions of a major city within a developed country (say, Sydney, Australia). The region has a cluster of similar manufacturing units that deal with chemicals, drugs, and related products. The business has been owned by a family for two generations and is very successful. The owner, a pharmacist herself by profession, employs three specialist pharmacists to help her in her innovative research and experimentation in the niche market of diabetes-related drugs. The remaining staff deal with the process of manufacturing drugs and related specific pharmaceutical products.

This well-known business is linked to a large distribution chain and also to a couple of hospitals. Occasionally, the staff works in shifts to meet larger-than-usual orders for drugs. The manufacturing unit of Pharma also has a small shopfront where it is officially allowed to disburse prescription drugs. Furthermore, some cosmetics as well as products that do not require prescription are also sold over the counter. Pharma has recently set up some overseas alliances, especially in a developing country, to consider partial manufacturing overseas. Pharma has also sought and obtained licenses to source many cosmetics and related products from a developing country, and repackages and resells them over the counter.

The owner's son has recently completed a business degree. This young MBA is asked by his owner mother to help her expand and enrich the rudimentary Pharma *informative* Web site, which currently provides only basic information on the physical location of the business, contact details, specialization areas in diabetics drugs, and endorsements from some noted clients.

The owner is also concerned about a large pharmaceutical chain that is opening stores in her city as well as in a couple more cities from where she has been sourcing her business. She believes these changes are likely to pose a threat to her growth and, to an extent, even the survival of her business. However, being the leader of the national pharmaceutical union, she is also well connected with the industry and collaborates with many other business partners on an ongoing and regular basis. Pharma has now a job of not only taking advantage of the Internet or electronic world but also of capitalizing on the rapidly growing mobile world to expand its business and grow.

Diagnostics of Pharma

The diagnostic phase, as shown in Figure 10.2, is the initial phase of mobile transition. This phase includes the identification of the type and size of the organization, its goals with respect to mobile transitions, and its mobile maturity level.

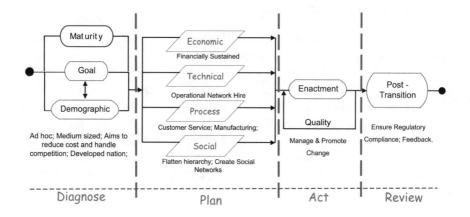

Figure 10.2 METM framework in practice for the medium-sized mobile-Pharma enterprise.

The activities in this early phase of METM also include budgeting, planning, and undertaking a strength–weakness–opportunity–threat (SWOT) analysis of the organization. These activities during the diagnostic phase also help in ascertaining the costs and time required to undertake the transition. This information feeds into the business case for METM. Although the economic dimension of MET is meant to deal with the financial aspects of the transition in greater detail, some of the activities are conducted early in the process. In practice, this diagnostic phase can be considered as a part of the business case preparation and, therefore, it contains the details of costs and benefits associated with MET.

The Pharma enterprise described in the case study problem statement is a medium-sized organization that deals with manufacturing medical drugs, primarily in the area of diabetes. This is an important piece of information obtained during diagnosis that can help shape the mobile transition project. Pharma also has a small shopfront that dispenses prescription drugs as well as cosmetics over the counter. This feature also needs to be factored in during MET. The level of maturity of Pharma in terms of mobile usage is ad hoc. This is ascertained by inspecting the current mobile processes within the organization, all of which revolve around the simple use of mobile phones for voice calls and sending text messages.

Goals

The main goal of the proposed mobile transition is to enhance the location-based customer service of Pharma externally and optimize its internal operational costs. Pharma aims to provide excellence in mobile online prescription drug services, mobile location-specific sale and distribution, personalized patient care and reminder services, and education anywhere at anytime through specialized mobile applications.

Furthermore, internal administration systems must be transitioned to mobile applications, and a system is required to facilitate global processes for management and control by the owner of the organization. The mobile-enabled Pharma will also be able to support the supply chain that deals with chemicals, base drugs, packaging, etc. These cross-functionalities between customers, owner, and pharmacist in charge of production are all important requirements of Pharma, which are ascertained by studying the business and conducting workshops with the stakeholders of the company. In addition, due to the sensitive nature of prescriptions and related patient details, the mobile solution is also expected to be completely secured with the help of encryption technologies and corresponding security processes. The specific business goals and ensuing advantages resulting from MET to Pharma can be listed as follows:

- Online and real-time prescription services that eliminate the time lag between the writing of the scripts and their arrival at the pharmacy
- Online offerings of associated healthcare services from the pharmacy to the customers
- The facility to provide 24/7 mobile access to customers in terms of availability and offering of medical drugs
- Reduction in the operational costs associated with drug manufacture through modeling and execution of internal processes
- Optimization of both internal and external business processes with mobility, which would lead to both tangible and intangible advantages
- Secured mobile portal to ensure privacy of patient and prescription information during transmission and storage
- Data integration and centralization, which will improve accuracy of prescriptions and reduce errors in dispensing medicines
- Creation of patient-related social networks that can help patients understand their medication better, including potential side effects
- Enhanced interaction with the pharmacy association and improved collaboration among pharmacists

User Types

As a part of the diagnostic phase, it is worth identifying the actors (or roles) involved in the mobile business. The mobile transition of Pharma will have to deal with the following specific user types that will influence devices, usability, supporting software applications, as well as training requirements.

Patients (Customers)

Mobile Pharma (m-Pharma) will enable patients and their caregivers to access the business 24/7 from anywhere using mobile devices. Patients require up-to-date information regarding the availability of diabetic drugs on mobile devices and the ability to correlate drug information with prescriptions. They can also benefit from brief educational updates on their preregistered mobile gadgets. Decision support for patients and a reminder service for dosages and timings can be some of the mobile business processes of value that Pharma will endeavor to deliver while undergoing MET.

Physicians and Healthcare Specialists

Pharma will change the way both physicians and specialists conduct their examinations and prescription service. It will help them in providing medical diagnosis, treatment, prescription, and education, which will all be incorporated in the mobile business processes of m-Pharma. The audio and video facilities available through high-speed broadband networks (e.g., the upcoming 3G networks) and the mobile Internet can be used for real-time information updates of prescriptions by physicians.

Pharma Staff

The Pharma staff includes the pharmacist receptionist, attendant, and technical production staff. They will benefit by MET as follows (typical examples):

Pharmacist: The proposed system should provide real-time updates on handheld devices.

Receptionist: The proposed system should create simple Web-based administrative management, featuring online booking of consultation times, billing statement, and the nurses working and on leave.

Attendant: The proposed system should support and allow easy access to any related nonmedical activities.

Technical production staff: The proposed system is required to be reliable, flexible, and secure. In addition, it should be easy to maintain, it should cause minimal technical problems, and immediate recovery must be possible.

Suppliers (e.g., Pharmaceutical and Chemical Providers)

The proposed mobile-Pharma can provide value to suppliers by helping them improve the management of their inventories of medical supplies. For example, Pharma can help a client hospital by linking its inventory management system with its own production and supply databases. Radio frequency identification (RFID) tags can be used to identify items at low levels, and that information can be directly linked to the Pharma database.

Pharmacist

Distribution of pharmaceutical goods to pharmacies can also be mobile enabled through the proposed mobile portal of Pharma. These partner pharmacies, once integrated with m-Pharma, can help in improving the service to patients, as they can have timely information regarding the availability of drugs as well as upcoming prescriptions.

Government Agencies

M-Pharma is monitored by government agencies in terms of its accuracy, privacy, and compliance with Medicare rules and regulations related to medical care. These monitoring and reporting processes are improved because of MET as the agencies are provided timely updates from the mobile Pharma portal on the basis of the latest data on production, batch numbers and distribution of drugs, as well as regulated cosmetic items.

Scope

The MET project for Pharma is based on a medium-scoped project plan (this was discussed in Chapter 7, Table 7.1). The initiation and implementation details of that project plan are discussed in this chapter as part of the overall MET framework. The medium scope of the project is ascertained based on the ad hoc mobile maturity of the organization. This is established by considering the way employees use mobile phones for voice calls, the location and size (demographics) of the organization, and its goals.

Pharma MET Plan

SWOT (strengths, weaknesses, opportunities, and threats) analysis has been discussed in Chapter 3. For Pharma (Figure 10.3), this is carried out to analyze its strengths and weaknesses and to study the opportunities and threats in the mobile business environment. The SWOT analysis is performed to understand the strengths and weaknesses of the organization, and also to identify the m-Pharma opportunities and threats. SWOT can also assist in risk identification by having project teams focus on the broad perspectives of potential risk for particular projects to prepare for risk and change management. The outcome of SWOT analysis for Pharma, as summarized in Figure 10.3, shows that its

Table 10.1 Set of hypothetical figures for revenues and expenses

	Projected cost		
	Year 1	Year 2	Year 3
Revenue			
Current + additional due to MET which will not occur in year 1	$1,350,000	$1,500,000	$2,010,000
Total Revenue	**$1,350,000**	**$1,500,000**	**$2,010,000**
Expenses			
MET transition including procuring PMS (software package) and creating mobile infrastructure	$230,000	$100,000	$70,000
Ongoing system maintenance	$200,000	$150,000	$105,000
Call center support	$20,000	$30,000	$30,000
Total cost	**$450,000**	**$280,000**	**$205,000**
Net profit	**$900,000**	**$1,220,000**	**$1,805,000**

Strength	Weakness
1. Reputed medical drug manufacturer 2. Well-known owner/researcher, who also leads the pharmaceutical network 3. Dedicated staff, who are all able to use mobile gadgets 4. Specialization in diabetic-related drugs, for varying age groups and different level of medical conditions	1. Not a technically savvy company, with minimal use of mobile technology for communication; paper-based processes 2. Hierarchical organizational structure 3. Inability to keep up with the speed of research and demand from patient/customers 4. Outsourcing management
Opportunities	**Threats**
1. New research resulting in creation of diabetic drugs 2. Staff is keen to adopt formal mobile technologies to enhance quality of work 3. Partner organizations keen to support mobility through extranets and collaborative processes	1. Competition from overseas pharmaceutical chains 2. Need to comply with privacy protection (especially due to prescription data) 3. Lack of experience in mobile technologies

Figure 10.3 SWOT analysis of Pharma.

strengths are in being a reputed medical drug manufacturer, being a leader in research, having dedicated staff who are able to use gadgets, and being specialized in diabetic-related drugs. The analysis also shows its weaknesses: minimal use of mobile technology, inability to keep up with the speed of research, challenges in managing outsourcing arrangements, and potentially rigid organizational structure. The results of SWOT analysis suggest that there are opportunities for new research, able staff to adopt new mobile technologies, and support of partners for collaborative processes. It also highlights that Pharma faces threats such as competition from pharmaceutical chains and privacy protection issues. The SWOT analysis provides input into the four dimensions of MET, and this is discussed next.

Economic Dimension in Pharma

The economic dimension considers the costs and benefits of MET to Pharma. Mobility gives it the potential to reduce its cost of operation as well as the advantage of providing better service to its customers. The estimated total cost of the proposed transition is made up of procurement costs of new hardware and software related to mobile technologies, modeling mobile processes, and change management. The revenue increases resulting from MET may not usually show a profit in the first year. Typically, a three-year forecast can be used to estimate profitability or losses that might be incurred during the course of the transition. It is usual to show a three-year projection for both revenues and expenses as the return on investment (ROI) is expected to occur in time, over a period of two–three years. A set of hypothetical figures for revenue and expenses is shown in Table 10.1. This is in line with the discussion on strategic benefits (as against routine operational benefits) of mobility discussed earlier in Chapter 3. Apart from external customer benefits such as growth in services and improved market position, there are also many internal process-related benefits that deal with, for example, leave, personnel policies, job postings, and payroll data. The economic benefits of using mobility and the resulting ROI need to consider both external and internal benefits. A growth rate of around 15 percent in the second and third years can be expected from formal MET (based on personal experiences).

Technical Dimension in Pharma

The technical dimension provides MET activities that deal with the study of the mobile gadgets used by Pharma employees and customers, and their suitable utilization by the business. The available mobile network bandwidths and best ways to provide mobile content to users also need to be studied in this dimension. Although the customers of Pharma have mobile devices, their employees need an upgrade from their current phones to PDAs. This is particularly true of managers who are in charge of production as there are substantial opportunities to reduce operating costs. The actual implementation of mobile software applications results in a pharmaceutical management system (PMS). This is a mobile-enabled third-party ERP software solution aimed primarily at pharmaceutical markets. The software solution is a mobile collaborative system that brings together customers, various businesses involved in global research and production of drugs, their distributors and disbursements (primarily pharmacists), and government/regulatory agencies. PMS is thus meant to be a comprehensive collaborative electronic and mobile business solution for pharmaceutical business that is a solution for m-Pharma.

The mobile enterprise architecture includes network topology, database design, hardware and software components, security issues, backup strategies, and modernization of Pharma that will enable it to interface with PMS. The architecture is flexible enough to allow easy update of the infrastructure.

This mobile application solution for Pharma also covers security and privacy issues. Technically, security is enhanced as all messaging traffic passing the firewall is filtered by a message proxy. The proxy then changes the IP address of the packet to deliver it to the appropriate site within the internal network. This mechanism protects the internal addresses from potential external abuse.

Security is further enhanced with the entire transaction traveling under the protection of public key encryption (PKI), and digital certificates verifying the customers as well as identities of the doctors writing the prescriptions. The prescriptions are authorized by means of digital signatures, which ensures that the originality of the document is not changed during the transmission process. The purpose of digital signatures in a document is not only to identify the sender, but also to ensure the authentic and originality of that document. An additional mobile-specific security feature that will be used by m-Pharma is the CLEW (closed-loop environment for wireless; www.alacritytech.com). This will send messages to the prescribing doctors requesting authentication of, say, repeat prescriptions. CLEW requires a sign-off with a password and, therefore, it is much more secure than SMS. This back-end CLEW-based system can also send out messages to a predetermined list of patients and doctors related to Pharma.

Process Dimension in Pharma

The process dimension includes identification and documentation of current processes related to Pharma as well as new mobile business processes. These will be modeled based on the "actors" of mobile applications (i.e., customers, doctors, and employees). The mobile business processes relate to prescription, ordering, production, inventory, sales, and distribution of, diabetes-related drugs.

The process dimension of Pharma also makes use of mobile-Telehealth by incorporating mobile processes in medical care. Customization of the PMS package with mobile-Telehealth brings patients, physicians, healthcare specialists, and pharmacists together under the m-Pharma portal, although they may all be in different locations; this is particularly relevant in rural areas. PMS, the proposed software solution, is able to capitalize on opportunities to take prescriptions and supply medicines using mobile communications. Mobile-Telehealth will enable pharmacists and physicians to network with one another using sophisticated PDAs and wireless laptops to consult, cross-check, and dispense drugs. Eventually, PMS can be integrated with digital images, x-rays, and other related information stored in the linked hospitals. After a careful review, the physician can prescribe drugs using mobile gadgets, which are then received and fulfilled by Pharma.

Mobility enables patients to receive medications from leading pharmacies at lower cost. Doctors in Pharma can create m-prescription files for particular patients and record them into the database for future reference. Patients may use the m-prescriptions to purchase medicines from Pharma's allied pharmacies. This service is available on the m-Pharma portal.

Specifically, Pharma will provide detailed information and support to customers/patients. For example, member customers of PMS will know their nearest pharmacies, their opening timings, information on new and alternative drugs, and information on their respective medications and alternative therapies. Visitors to the Pharma Web site will also find relevant information that is in the public domain. The system is also expected to be linked with those of participating doctors and hospitals, thereby enabling automatic and legal authorization of their medications and refills.

Operationally, marketing representatives of Pharma can reference company data and update their records while traveling. They can also synchronize their information with the database at the company's headquarters via wired or wireless connections. Further, they can complete their own sales reports and memos without returning to their offices. In particular, some compliance tasks such as tracking the distribution of drug samples to physicians is greatly facilitated by the ability to enter this data immediately into a corporate database.

The following section discusses a few specific business processes for Pharma based on mobility.

Business Process—Production of a Drug

The role of the project manager in the production process is supported and enhanced by the application of mobility. This process is initiated when a new drug is planned for production. Production can be of an existing formula, or it can be a long, drawn-out process for manufacturing a new stream of diabetes drugs. In any case, the approach is iterative and incremental, and it ensures sufficient quality assurance and process control. Initial iteration requires creation of a plan, to be reviewed by the management. The project manager ensures that the plan shows the relationships with suppliers of base drugs, chemicals, and packaging materials.

Mobility changes these processes immensely. First, the project manager is now able to check the ability of the potential supplier to supply the necessary chemical.

The mobile gadget, modeled and incorporated into the process, enables the project manager to be mobile in the different locations of the lab, identifying needed chemicals. In the next stage, the mobile gadget allows him to view the progress of the project while the project is in process. The mobile process also enables the project manager to select potential chemical suppliers, register project details, and assign the project to development. These activities within this mobile business take place while the project manager is moving and not stationary at his particular desk.

Mobile processes also enable the pharmacist, who is providing input into the drug production process, along with the project manager, to view the inventory. In case the required chemicals are not available in the inventory, it enables him or her to search for the manufacturer of the required drug. The pharmacist can also check the available projects to determine the chemicals required for progress of the projects. The mobile gadget also helps the pharmacist to check the details of the projects and organize them. The new proposed process thus enables the pharmacist to monitor projects while on site and personally viewing their progress.

Mobile-Enabled Drug Process (Government Regulations)

This process, now undergoing MET, shows the mobile-enabled drug process from the regulatory or government point of view. Mobile processes can help government regulators to check conformance to policies and regulations in the development of new drugs. The government officer or regulator uses the mobile gadget and requests details of specific drugs under development. The gadget receives the information, searches for the specific batch to be displayed, and displays the details, enabling the regulator to speed up the process. The mobile process also interacts with some physical processes. For example, the regulator can make personal visits to the factory premises as and when necessary.

Business Process—Checking Expiry Dates of Medicines

Pharmacists at the storefront shop of Pharma are responsible for checking medications and cosmetics on the shelves and removing those that are out of date. The existing process is a manual one. The pharmacist has to physically check every shelf and almost every package as a daily routine and remove all expired medications. Alternatively, the list of purchased medications can be printed out at the end of the month to certify that there are no expired medications in the store.

With m-Pharma, the medication packages placed on the shelves of the storefront shop are equipped with RFID chips, and a message is sent to the pharmacist's handheld mobile gadget a week before the expiry date of drugs for further action. The pharmacist can then check the shelves and inventory via his mobile device and validate the stock and available time before expiration; if necessary he can order fresh purchase via his mobile device.

Social Dimension in Pharma

Usability and privacy are the most important social issues in m-Pharma. Therefore, they will be given priority when deploying mobility throughout and outside the enterprise, particularly when customers are registering for mobile processes. The effect of incorporating mobility in the team structure and hierarchy internally also needs to be considered in this transition. For example, by providing PDAs or smart phones to employees, it will now be possible for government regulators to directly access data produced by them during a drug manufacturing process.

Pharma needs to maintain trust among their electronic and mobile business partners, clients, and subscribers. This is to ensure the integrity and security of prescription data and is vital for the purposes of risk management and potential dispute resolution should a situation arise. Legal issues can become more complex, especially as m-Pharma transactions are expected to take place in different countries.

Additional factors in the social dimension of MET are taxation and copyright conformance to production regulations.

Confidentiality and Privacy

The mobile transition of Pharma has heightened awareness of the need to protect the enormous quantities of information that get collected due to mobile prescription services. Confidentiality and privacy require their encryption; but there are other issues also related to access and control of information. These include information on patients' medication, diseases, and physical movements in addition to prescriptions and their fulfillment.

MET Project Plan

Table 10.2 shows a medium-sized MET project plan. Its tasks are based on the overall project plan discussed in Chapter 7. The selection of tasks can vary depending on the results of the diagnostic phase. Specific attention is drawn to the comments underneath each task that relate to m-Pharma.

Act

This is the third phase in MET enactment, as shown in Figure 10.2. The action phase will also apply change management. First, employ the informative use of mobility by providing relevant information to customers, pharmacists, and workers. Then, gradually move to the transactive, operative, and collaborative use of mobility by businesses. These four actions based on the increasingly complex use of mobility are described in greater detail next.

Table 10.2 A typical MET project plan for a medium-sized organization with ad hoc maturity resulting in medium scope for the transition

Task no.	Task name	Resource name
1	Discuss the attitude to adoption (of patients, prescribing doctors, employees)	Management
2	Mobile processes for reengineering (prescription, fulfillment, production)	Management
3	Develop m-business process (prescription, fulfillment, production)	Management
4	Improve business control (owner's or manager's accounting)	Management
5	Consider type of usage (work)	Management
6	Mobile application and finances (PMS; m-enabled package)	Supplier
7	Change organizational structures (flatter hierarchy of workers)	User/gadget
8	Mobile infrastructure (WLANS, mobile Internet)	Technical designer
9	Update and manage mobile contents (prescription and patient data)	User/gadget
10	Model mobile business processes (use BPMN)	Technical designer
11	Prototype and improve quality of service (QoS) (conduct sample QoS prototypes)	User/gadget
12	Create and manage mobile collaborations (pharmacist associations, chemical suppliers)	User/gadget
13	Manage customer relationships (MCRM)	Management
14	Consider social environment (patient networks)	User/gadget

M-Informative

M-Pharma starts by providing information to its users on their mobile devices. This can be on various diseases such as diabetes, blood pressure, and asthma; this can be of value not only to patients but also to researchers. Hence, this information needs to be updated by experts in the field, that is, medical doctors, with their own research. Pharma facilitates formal collaborations between the experts and other users of Pharma. Thus, it becomes a library resource for current and potential customers. The main purpose of these resources is to provide useful health information on mobile devices. Users can get a wide range of information on healthcare and research on matters such as diseases, drug guides, and medical tests, or can even search for any medical information from journals and articles, provided their mobile Web browsers can handle it. Pharma health science libraries are designed to deliver expert medical information to healthcare providers—and patients—at the care centers to help them take better care of patients, as well as to other users, including the contributors.

Pharma's PMS will carry out analyses of patient (customer) populations based on their age, past history of diseases, genetic issues, financial/insurance positions, geographical locations, and so on to generate valuable and relevant information on mobile devices. Patient and nonpatient users will visit m-Pharma mobile portals for a range of relative cross-functionalities (such as sports information). Furthermore, information about local activities may also keep the community aware of the existence of m-Pharma.

M-Transactive

The transactive use of mobility, or m-transactive, will be between Pharma and the distribution pharmacies, and also the users. This use includes the purchase of drugs by patients as well as a distributing pharmacist. (See Appendix B for example use cases that represent these transactive processes.) There are many other mobile transaction possibilities, such as mobile prescriptions, mobile order of repeat prescription, and mobile payments.

M-Pharma enables pharmacists to interact with their clients both electronically as well as through personal mobile devices of the clients. These transactions include providing alerts to customers on their dosages, alerts for possible timely refills, and also information on interactions and reactions of their drugs with other drugs; these need to be provided on a personalized basis to customers through mobile devices.

M-Operative

There are a number of operational areas of Pharma that are benefited by the application of mobility. These internal business processes include location of drugs, tracking of batches, ordering of supplies, transmission of warnings on expiry dates of drugs, and movement of people and goods.

M-Pharma information is sent to handheld devices of its sales representatives in real-time. This helps sales representatives to pitch their products (drugs, equipment, etc.) to doctors and administrators in large hospitals. This system collaborates with the publicly available (electronically) government data on drug usage per region. Pharma is also linked with collaborating pharmacies from where it can procure legally available prescription information (without parting with patient-identifying information).

Pharma uses its system for drug tracking and communication with field inventory via General Packet Radio Service (GPRS). PMS of m-Pharma also has a system to create a seamless interface among prescribing doctors, inventories, and couriers. When a Pharma customer calls with a drug order, a service representative uses the address region to match a relevant pharmacy to the order. The relevant requests are immediately sent wirelessly to the suppliers. Field representatives use tablet PCs equipped with GPRS modems and Bluetooth personal area network (PAN) technology to ensure unbroken two-way communications even if the stream is interrupted.

As inventories and scheduling uses mobility, operative processes undergo transition. This implies the use of mobile devices to schedule the most convenient shifts for workers and the use of RFID tags for highly mobile inventory items.

Also, to save costs and reduce the time taken for mundane tasks, a range of internal administrative systems such as booking for consultation, accounting of patients, or leave roster of nurses will be moved to Internet-based systems that can be accessed with mobile devices. The m-Pharma portal provides potential links of the hospitals' systems with those of the local or overseas drug suppliers to keep a tab on the inventories of medical supplies in partnering hospitals.

Employee rostering, especially for large-scale orders, is usually a time-consuming and frustrating, and error-prone task. The cost of maintaining a roster can be very high, and inaccurate roster shifts will lead to frustrated staff. Mobility, together with the Internet, provides software that enables virtual rostering. This software has been developed and designed to suit the most complicated roster. By using this mobile roster application, m-Pharma can reduce administration costs and increase productivity.

M-Collaborative

The collaborative nature of Pharma is seen in Figure 10.4. Pharma, through its Web service interface, can obtain prescription information (with patient information removed) from pharmaceutical databases that reveal (via data mining) the identities of physicians, their hospitals, and their prescriptions. Marketing efforts can then be targeted at relevant medical professionals, using mobile devices to educate them about the company's range of drugs, and to distribute samples and build relationships.

Pharma will allow pharmacists to directly collaborate with various drug manufacturers (Figure 10.4) across geographical regions using mobile networks and electronics. This will require pharmacists to tap software systems and databases of willing manufacturers through Web-services-based interfaces. Further, all these businesses should list their services through a directory service (such as UDDI—see www.uddi.org—as shown in Figure 10.4).

Pharma will use mobility to update its inventories and provide personalized services to its member customers. These businesses will also have access to the latest information on new drugs coming into the market, and the corresponding legal

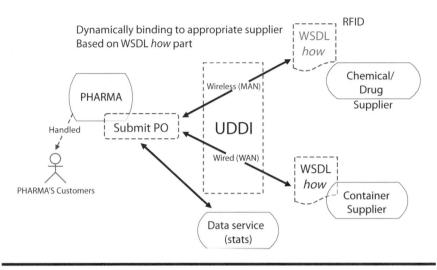

Figure 10.4 Mobile Web services and collaborative process for drug manufacturing.

and other regulatory information; besides, they will have the ability to interact with corresponding government (E-governance) departments and inquire about and prepare for new drugs coming out of laboratories. This will thus result in the various businesses and customers interacting with one another through the Pharma platform, which will facilitate genuine collaborative business.

This will require courier service providers to be part of this collaboration; it will enable member customers to not only receive their ordered medication officially and legally, but also get refills, alternatives, and related medications—all home delivered. However, the system has to ensure that at no point are the security and safety as well as the privacy of the customers compromised. Preauthorization for certain drugs and their quantities, strengths, and dosages needs to be obtained from physicians through the system. Further, the system has to ensure that the drugs are made available to the patient sufficiently in advance for administration, and that medical checks and balances are in place (e.g., certain injectable drugs require presence of a nurse, whereas oral drugs do not). The system should also ensure that a physician is contactable when highly sensitive drugs are administered in homes of patients.

Mobility can help owners streamline their business processes, both external and internal, in particularly drug manufacturing organizations. Owners aim to form alliances with other peripheral organizations to streamline their businesses. These alliances are typically with suppliers, hospitals, doctors, gift suppliers, naturopaths, accountants, and banks. Occasionally dietitians and even herbalists may be involved in providing collaborative business opportunities to Pharma. The ever-changing government rules and regulations, such as on-the-spot removal of some products from shelves, are crucial to pharmacists' businesses. These areas can benefit immensely with the application of mobile technologies, and the owners of Pharma will want its application along with sophisticated electronic Internet-based technologies.

Collaboration is further enhanced when pharmacists at m-Pharma have real-time wireless access to medical records of their patients on tablet PCs. They can also use PDAs to capture prescriptions and corresponding charges while working at production facilities. A typical implementation can be an effective mobile electronic medical records system based on Cisco Systems Wi-Fi network. Such a system can provide m-Pharma with preloaded potential prescriptions and charge applications on mobile gadgets that are integrated with its recording and accounting system. M-Pharma also provides a private Web portal connection to production facilities that the staff from partnering hospitals can access via tablet PCs, enabling physicians to obtain the latest information on both drug research and distribution.

Pharma Change Management

Change management at m-Pharma is shown in Figure 10.5. To take advantage of the transition, the management at Pharma needs to manage the change formally. This change management approach needs to go hand in hand with continuous seeking of new opportunities to improve its processes and offerings. Change management at m-Pharma includes planning for the change; architecting the communication system; and creating the transition change team, customer management team, and integration team. This is summarized in Figure 10.5.

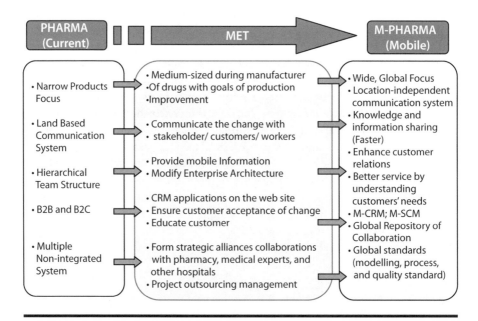

Figure 10.5   METM—Pharmaceutical goals and change management.

The potential risk of shortcomings in terms of knowledge transfer and training for m-Pharma is also identified in this process. During the transition to mobile business, many staff members may not be able to handle the complexity of the integrated systems owing to lack of training. This in turn would raise the cost of integration and personnel training. Therefore, there is a need to manage this change carefully, with provision for in-process training. This change management team may include support (help desk) on how to use the software, how to share information and knowledge, how to communicate effectively through the system, and so on. Furthermore, the team helps employees implement the new services to Pharma's customers such as mobile prescription, electronic and mobile registration, etc. It is imperative that during transitioning, Pharma has the insight to developing next-level strategies and the commitment to train staff members to perform their new roles. Hence, training and appropriate placement of people should be seen as an integral part of the transformation process. Change management also ensures smooth acceptance of the change by the customer and also provides help in training of the customer on how to use the new mobile system.

Outsourcing

Customization and implementation of PMS is outsourced to small, specialized IT organizations. Outsourcing provides significant savings and an opportunity for mobile Pharma to focus on its core competencies. Outsourcing of the PMS is preferred as Pharma does not have such departments to do the jobs. Setting up of these departments will increase costs dramatically. But by outsourcing, Pharma will not have to worry about hiring the right people or training employees for particular jobs. However, management of outsourcing vendors can be a challenging aspect of MET. For example, as competitors turn to the same vendors, the project development may become more homogeneous. This may erode the company's distinctiveness and lead to price competition.

Therefore, it is imperative for Pharma's management to have thoughtful planning of the transition process. Careful management of the vendor once that transition has taken place will help ensure that the E-business venture reaps the full benefits of outsourcing.

Posttransition Challenges

M-Pharma needs to handle posttransition changes, reviews, and feedback resulting from transitions. The importance of these posttransition reviews were discussed in Chapter 7. Typical results from a posttransition review of Pharma can be as follows:

- Acceptance by patients of changes to the mobile business processes, which provided them with the convenience of receiving prescription medicines from a network of Pharma and related stores, was easy. There was initially some concern about the privacy of the data, which was quickly dispelled by proper explanation of the robust security and privacy processes in place.

- Physicians and health care professionals were not easily convinced of the privacy and security issues in METM of Pharma. Therefore, example prototypes and detailed test cases had to be created to convince them. However, these system-level prototypes and testing provided excellent (and reusable) information to the users.
- Employees—both production staff and storefront staff—were happy with the transition. Initial training in the use of PMS was helpful. However, they were keen to highlight the importance of initial training that was provided to them in the use of PMS.
- The production process was made collaborative; however, enlisting the trust of some of the suppliers was initially challenging.
- Pharma was also able to provide value to the pharmacist association through mobile networking and thereby creating goodwill.
- Government regulatory compliance in terms of drug manufacturing was simplified. However, technical service-level interfaces between the regulatory systems and the m-Pharma's systems required ongoing validation as these interfaces kept changing from the regulatory authority's side.

Chapter 11

Case Study: Applying METM to a Small-Sized Travel and Tourism Enterprise

Everything comes to us that belongs to us if we create the capacity to receive it.

Rabindranath Tagore

Chapter Key Points

- Discusses the practical application of the Mobile Enterprise Transition and Management (METM) framework to a small-sized travel and tourism organization called Bluewaters travel
- Demonstrates the diagnose phase of METM by applying it to Bluewaters
- Outlines the MET project plan that considers all four dimensions (economic, technical, process, and social) in a cohesive sequence of activities to transition Bluewaters to a mobile business
- Suggests how the transitioning organization should evolve from informative to transactive, operative, and, finally, collaborative use of mobility
- Suggests how to conduct the posttransitional review and feedback

Introduction

This chapter describes the second of the three METM case studies discussed in this book. This case study is based on a small business in the travel and tourism industry. The chapter first describes the problem statement for the enterprise, followed by the enactment of METM to transition it to a mobile enterprise. This enactment contains creation of the MET project plan derived from the four dimensions of MET, acting out of the plan, review, and feedback.

Bluewaters Problem Statement

Bluewaters is a small travel agency in the middle of a large and bustling city (say, New York), employing around 10–12 people. Its owner is himself an avid traveler, a veteran of long and exciting journeys. He is aware of the significance of mobile technologies and the Internet in the modern-age travel business. The business has an informative Web site, which is hosted by another small company that hires out the infrastructure. This basic Web site provides the necessary information on the physical location of the company, contact details, and upcoming journeys and planned tour packages. Bluewaters's foray in the technology world is restricted to this basic informative Web site and a mobile phone with each of its employees.

However, now Bluewaters finds that there are increasing opportunities for it to expand globally, especially with the increasing access to global travelers and travel business through use of mobile technologies, applications, and networks. The company wants to create and provide content and services through mobile networks and increase its reach in providing packaged tours to Europe, America, and South Africa. It is now further offering packaged tours for sporting events such as the Olympics, soccer world cups, and cricket (held in the Commonwealth group of countries such as ones in the Indian subcontinent, Australia, and New Zealand). Furthermore, the owner of Bluewaters discovers that his current and future customers are increasingly becoming "smarter" in terms of their mobile usage and are looking for more choices and options available on and through their mobile devices. This increasing demand requires the travel agency to lift its game and provide mobile-specific content and services to its traveling customers. The owner realizes that such a technology-based approach is one unique way for Bluewaters to form alliances with associated businesses such as airlines and hotels and other larger travel agencies that may want to collaborate with it as the company itself does not have the know-how of the geographical regions where its business is likely to expand and grow.

As Bluewaters looks for immediate strategic use of mobility and the Internet to globalize its business, the owner is also aware of the need to be able to manage a large part of his business while being away from the physical office. This requires the mobile business software package to have operational support such as ability to track his employees, their work, time, and salaries. The employees also want to create and record their work, including promotional sales calls, travel schedules, and customer support using mobility. There is also need for the owner to have some basic accounting information on his mobile gadget, which requires the mobile application software package to be secure. He is personally keen to start using a wireless laptop connected to the mobile Internet for many of his managerial and administrative activities.

MET Approach

The MET framework, shown in Figure 11.1, provides the outline for the enactment of MET. The MET approach is divided into four phases that are specific to the case study presented in this chapter. Further description and discussion of the case study in greater detail is given the remaining pages.

Diagnose

Bluewaters is a small-sized company. This travel agency's demographic location is in a developed country. Therefore, it has access to the physical as well as IT infrastructure that supports the business. The organization is obviously ad hoc in its use and maturity of mobility. The ad hoc nature of the business, in terms of its mobile usage, is ascertained by investigating its business processes. The owner and employees are equipped with mobile phones, but these are not part of their formal business process.

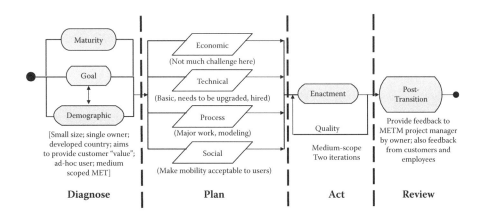

Figure 11.1 METM framework in practice for small-sized travel and tourism enterprise.

Goals

A primary goal of Bluewaters in adopting MET is to provide excellent service to its customers. The need to provide better value to the traveling customers than before is felt very strongly by the management. Furthermore, Bluewaters wants to capitalize on the opportunities provided by mobility to expand and reach newer and wider cross-sections of customers globally. Currently, in the company, there is relatively less concern in terms of cost and competition from a MET viewpoint and more concern with customer service—an area targeted for mobility.

Users

Travelers are the main users of this mobile business. They are made up of many age groups and are of different financial backgrounds. The employees of the organization, equipped with mobile gadgets, are also users of the potential mobile business. The employees who use the system include travel consultants or agents, administrative assistants, and the owner-manager. The owner is a special type of user who not only needs to promote the business and support the traveling customer but also needs better control of his business with the help of mobility. He is thus also seeking mobility for the purpose of accounting and management activities.

Scope

Bluewaters is a small company with ad hoc mobile use. Therefore, the MET project for such an organization will be of medium scope. This implies that not all of the activities from all the dimensions will come in to play when the transition project is put together and executed. Instead, all the relevant activities that are significant in achieving the goals of the organization are incorporated in the MET project plan. Note that if this were a large organization, the scope of the transition would also be large.

Plan

Economic Dimension in Bluewaters

The economic drivers for MET in the case of Bluewaters are based on enhanced service to its customers. The concept of value discussed in Chapter 8 is, in this case, not at the end of the transition but a part of the transition itself. The SWOT analysis for Bluewaters, shown in Figure 11.2, shows the various strengths, weaknesses, opportunities, and threats. The strength of this enterprise is that it is a well-controlled and well-managed single-owner small enterprise. Therefore, the company has sufficient funds to invest in this MET project. The direct involvement and interest of the owner-manager provides excellent motivation for the staff.

Strength	Weakness
1. Single-owner enterprise	1. Ad-hoc use of mobility
2. Well-controlled management due to single ownership	2. Lack of formal business processes
3. Motivated staff who wants to provide service	3. Minimal available mobile infrastructure within the enterprise
4. Good customer base who trust and enjoy the service	
Opportunities	**Threats**
1. Expand customer base, especially overseas	1. Change uncertainty by existing staff and some customers
2. Provide new and dynamics services	
3. Improve internal processes to save cost	2. Global rules and regulations related to travel
4. Improve collaboration with other travel business and service providers in these markets	3. Insecurity as potential collaboration are competition

Figure 11.2 SWOT analysis of Bluewaters.

The enterprise also has a good customer base. This provides it a good opportunity to expand and grow by expanding its customer base and providing new and dynamic services to its existing customers (travelers). However, mobility as an emerging technology is used in an ad hoc manner. There are no formal business processes in place. There is hardly any mobile infrastructure within the enterprise, which is not surprising given its small size. The lack of any existing infrastructure can prove to be challenging when changes are introduced, as it will mean significant changes to the working style of the current employees. The feeling of uncertainty internally and the challenges of collaborating with external (and potentially unknown) parties are threats to the transitioning Bluewaters business.

Technical Dimension in Bluewaters

As mentioned during the SWOT analysis, the current mobile technology at Bluewaters is made up of an assorted collection of mobile phones. The office has a LAN to provide connectivity, and the current client information is stored using a simple (e.g., Access or Excel) database. The employees are reliant on their own motivation and knowledge about the current travel environment, changes to schedules and fares, and their personal rapport with the customer.

Technically, an ideal way to incorporate mobility in Bluewaters is to procure a small mobile-enabled software package (m-CRM). This is so because the enterprise on its own has neither the interest nor the resources to get involved in any of the mobile software development aspects of the transition. The m-CRM that can be shortlisted in the MET enactment should be purchased "off the shelf." Such mobile business software, which is also Internet-enabled, provides opportunity to the employees of Bluewaters to tap into real-time information on fares and schedules, create tours and travels and related content, provide that content to the customers through a partnership with network operators, reach a wide range of new customers, and support the existing customers, while they travel.

Thus, technically, the transition strategy of Bluewaters aims to partner with known service providers such as Google and Yahoo and offer its services on various mobile networks such as Cingular, Sprint Nextel, and T-Mobile. Its client-side application is usable on any phone handset. Smart-phone travelers will need the Java programming language on their devices. However, some travelers using Verizon Blackberries and Palm devices may need to have a different technical environment. Google's application and service are free, but users of these services need to subscribe to a network operator—an interesting challenge for a small-time operator such as Bluewaters.

The technical dimension also handles issues such as how to architect the applications and how they are integrated, availability of networks used by mobile applications, security issues in the new organization (the mobile-transformed organization), and the devices that could be used to facilitate enhanced service delivery by employees.

A Service-Oriented Architecture (SOA) ensures that the customer (traveler) will get a unified view of his or her travel needs irrespective of internal collaborations among various service providers. The SOA is required to implement the m-CRM package, and is modeled using a deployment diagram of the UML as shown in Figure 11.3. The Bluewaters travel application interacts with the Web Server to offer and consume services, as well as provide security. The wireless application protocol (WAP) Proxy is able to convert the service requests and offerings through wireless markup language (WML) and present them to the traveler. The graphical user

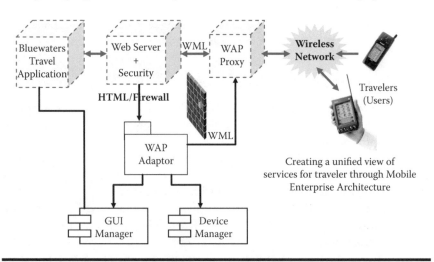

Figure 11.3   Mobile enterprise deployment diagram for Bluewaters.

interface (GUI) manager and the device manager components, through the WAP adaptor, are able to help the WAP proxy with the presentation of the requests and responses to the traveler. There GUI manager and device manager can be third-party components used together with the m-CRM software package.

Process Dimension in Bluewaters

The process dimension of the transition of Bluewaters to a mobile business deals with creation of process models that reflect both existing and new (mobile-enabled) processes. The modeling of the processes needs to firmly keep the mobile user (which, in the case of external processes, is the traveler) in focus. Therefore, models of the processes, which are based on use cases and activity diagrams, are created from the mobile traveler's view of the business.

The process dimension of MET considers mobile processes as vital to provide and enhance services that are currently being offered to travelers. Furthermore, the travel agency is paying extra attention to its corporate customers. If the service level for them can be enhanced through mobile business processes, the agency would be able to retain and grow its business substantially.

Social Dimension in Bluewaters

The social dimension of the transition deals with changes to the way in which travelers network socially with the travel agency and with one another. Bluewaters is keen to make use of its mobility to facilitate social networking among fellow travelers. This will not only enhance the social experience of the travelers, but it can also come in handy in case of need and in emergencies. For example, travelers that belong to Bluewaters can always know the location of the nearest fellow traveler, who may be able to advise and provide guidance to a potentially stranded traveler. This social dimension of MET requires Bluewaters to create new processes and procedures that need to be followed in facilitating such networks.

The changes to the organizational structure, which was itself pretty informal to start with, also require careful change management from the owner-manager. The owner himself needs to understand that with sophisticated mobile processes in place, travelers will not need to ring him for every need of theirs and, instead, the m-CRM application and the employees themselves will be able to handle most of the routine queries and needs. There is a need for training of employees in terms of not only the use of the m-CRM system, but also new devices, business processes, and new security measures. New activities in the travel process comprise downloading information, e-mails, and social networking information on mobile devices. However, throughout the transition, Bluewaters will have to show sensitivity to the need for privacy and security of the travelers. Global travelers will also need usability in their interfaces with mobile applications.

Issues such as management of the entire change process, along with any legal implications and privacy issues in the new organization, fall within the sociological perspective. Providing training to employees in these areas is also of utmost importance.

Finally, METM also needs to consider, along the lines of "themes" for each of the travel packages, a tour that is primarily aimed at getting younger folks together; another one that would be a "conference-cum-tour" enabling conferences to be held as tours and conferences; and yet another that would combine travel-associated medical procedures (such as visiting, say India, to get a surgery done at low cost and supported by the medical insurance company).

Act

Figure 11.4 shows that the current processes of Bluewaters on the left. These include the ad hoc use of mobile devices and manual management control. The METM enables these processes to be globally focused; provides dynamic information that is also shared among the owner, employees, and customers; and maintains ongoing collaboration by applying global standards. METM goals for Bluewaters are shown on the right in Figure 11.4, and the change management process (that would encompass all four MET dimensions) in the middle.

MET Project Plan

Table 11.1 shows the MET project plan for a medium-scope transition. The enactment of the project plan leads to a systematic transition of Bluewaters to a mobile business. The activities in the project plan have been discussed in Chapter 7 during the enactment. The diagnosis of Bluewaters leads to a variation in the project plan presented in Chapter 7. Eventually, the business evolves to a mobile business by providing information, then conducting transactions, followed by use of mobility in its operational procedures, and finally collaborating with other businesses to provide a wide variety of services to its customers. The use of mobility in all dimensions of the business also leads to it becoming a mature and managed mobile business. The transition through the various business usages of mobility is described here for Bluewaters.

Mobile Informative

The initial use of mobility by the transitioning business is to provide a range of information to its mobile customers. This information can be provided as messages that follow the unidirectional communication path on simple handheld devices. For example, PDAs and tablet PCs can be suggested as interacting with the m-CRM to provide a number of small messaging and attached services. These services provided to travelers alert them with changes to weather conditions in various regions as well

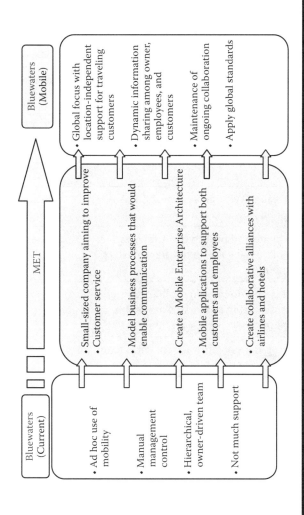

Figure 11.4 METM—Bluewaters Travel and Tourism (goals and change management).

Table 11.1   The MET project plan for Bluewaters (ad hoc maturity)

Activity no.	Activity name	Resource name
1	Identify the type of organization that Bluewaters is in terms of its size and location	Management
2	Identify and document the goals	Management
3	Identify the mobile maturity level of Bluewaters in the context of MET (in the case of Bluewaters it is ad hoc)	Management
4	Create MET budgets and project plans	Management
5	Identify the cost and time (estimated) for the project	Management
6	Undertake SWOT analysis from the competition viewpoint	Business partner (supplier)
7	Investigate and prototype mobile gadget capabilities—again from different users' viewpoints	User/gadget
8	Identify and document mobile business processes using a standard modeling technique	Technical designer
9	Apply usability and privacy concepts to models of mobile usage	User/gadget
10	Consider network coverage and bandwidth that is available to Bluewaters	Technical designer
11	Study impact of transition on customers/ employees from a change management viewpoint	User/gadget
12	Consider mobile network, device, and interoperability standards to ensure smooth transition	User/gadget
13	Discuss attitude to mobile adoption depending on user categories	User/gadget
14	Develop new processes on mobile application	User/gadget
15	Improve business control through use of mobile application	Management
16	Model mobile application and finance issues	Management

Table 11.1 *(continued)* **The MET project plan for Bluewaters (ad hoc maturity)**

Activity no.	Activity name	Resource name
17	Mobile infrastructure consideration	Technical designer
18	Update and manage mobile content including design of content management system	Technical designer
19	Create and manage mobile collaborations among various stakeholders (incorporate MWS)	Business partner (supplier)
20	Manage customer relationships and expectations due to MET	Management
21	Provide review and feedback on the mobile transition process to the management	Management

as other information that may be peripheral to the travelers but of importance— such as, say, changes to the financial markets or helping them participate in mobile online auctions. These gadgets need a middleware component that aggregates information from online sources, condenses and formats this information for its devices, and transmits that information (continuously) to the devices. Packaging the mobile informative services as part of the overall travel service offered by Bluewaters is a part of the economic dimension of the transition.

Mobile Transactive

The transactive use of mobility enables Bluewaters to start dealing with its customers through their mobile devices to conduct complete business transactions. The mobile applications that are implemented by Bluewaters enable provision of real-time mobile travel management services to business travelers. For example, assistance can be provided to customers by using the mobile channels to locate a desired hotel in the vicinity of the traveler's current location, purchase tickets for local travel or shows, make transportation arrangements such as car rentals or buses, and so on. These services also extend the reach of relationship-oriented companies beyond their current channels and helps mobile users identify, attract, serve, and retain valuable customers. Furthermore, through collaborative arrangements with travel service providers (e.g., Yahoo), Bluewaters is able to offer services such as *mobile travel guides* (which would allow mobile travelers to research hotels and guesthouses, locate places of interests in numerous cities worldwide, read travel reviews, view photos, and check maps that are dynamically updated by the partner). This service can help the mobile-equipped traveler to customize a trip and take advantage of good travel deals. *Trip planner* would allow mobile travelers to plan and schedule hotels, attractions, restaurants, and mark maps with customized travel dates and comments. Trip planner could be dynamically updated to enable travelers to find and compare flights and hotels that meet their budget and travel schedules. Web sites and mobile portals help travelers complete their purchases.

Bluewaters is also aware of the need to provide accurate and up-to-date weather reports for travelers who are likely to pack their bags or plan their trips based on the predicted weather at their destination. Most mobile service partners offer these weather reports that Bluewaters can plug into. For example, Google provides the following local weather information: (1) three-day weather forecasts, including lowest and highest temperatures; (2) current temperature; (3) humidity; (4) weather conditions with pictures; and (5) wind, including direction and speed.

The two travel processes discussed herein are the ones identified to be transformed to make them a fully mobile process. There are many such processes within Bluewaters that need the attention of MET sponsors. For example, after successful MET, the traveler goes all around the world using his or her mobile device and remains in contact with Bluewaters. Later, the traveler, who may be on a tour for weeks, may also want facilities on his or her mobile device that go beyond the core travel process. For example, the traveler may have a need for facilities such as insurance and health related to the travel. The two processes described here are the "travel agent consultation" and the actual "process of travel." Both are described before and after MET.

Business Process 1: Current Travel Agent Consultation

The current travel agent consultation processes deal with the potential traveler (customer) appearing physically to meet with the travel agent, who is usually one of the employees of Bluewaters. However, in the case of an important customer or a group customer trying to put together a packaged tour, the owner is usually present. The consultation process starts "ground up" and deals with a range of factors that the traveler would want to incorporate in the travel, such as class of travel, dates, local areas of interests, accommodations, and local travel. Group tours require the travel agent to manually document the myriad requirements related to the entire group, including its personal needs for food and accommodations in a "package." Once the consultation is complete, the travel agent "stores" the package. This package is then used in providing support for the tour. This package can also be refined based on the feedback from the tour. The agent also uses the details of the package as a reference for future tours. There is some electronic input to this process due to the existence of the basic Internet site for Bluewaters. However, currently, there is no element of mobility in this process other than the use of a mobile phone number by the traveler to call up the agency.

Business Process 1: METM-Enabled Travel Agent Consultation

Mobility can be introduced in the aforementioned travel agent consultation process at various levels. The increasingly complex use of mobility by business (i.e., going from m-informative through to m-collaborative) can be implemented in this transition. The introduction of mobility in business processes, as discussed in Chapter 5, requires formal modeling of the processes using either Unified Modeling Language (UML)-based activity diagrams or the Business Process Modeling Notation (BPMN)-based diagrams. The models of the processes are studied to see where and how mobility can be introduced in them. For example, enhancement to the consultation service takes place when the traveler is able to find out details of many tour packages on the Bluewaters Web site through his or her mobile gadget. This will better prepare the customer to ask questions, specify requirements, and clarify doubts regarding the tour he or she is trying to put together. The travel agent himself/herself can benefit by having access to a mobile Internet that can be used to get the latest information on traveling conditions, weather conditions, etc., which can be used in real-time in offering the service to the customer. Because the travel agent is not merely using his or her mobile phone for voice calls with the travelers but, rather, using it strategically to tap into the content of Bluewaters, the agent is potentially able to offer the complete service to a potential traveler outside the office (e.g., in a coffee shop) using a laptop connected to the wireless Internet. Preregistered customers may also be able to put together a basic structure of their tour package by visiting Bluewaters's m-CRM system. Special deals can be offered depending on the type of customer. The new mobile processes increase productivity for the travel agent, whereas customers would perceive a higher service level. There is considerable time saving in the delivery of proposals, etc. This also leads to greater accuracy as the data is entered at the Bluewaters's site and verified immediately. Thus, there are appreciable monetary savings due to this faster process, and also additional revenue as customers can be signed up earlier than in the current process. The travel agency can also be ahead of the competition by providing higher, varied, and timely service.

Business Process 2: Current Process of Travel

In the existing travel process, the traveler is mainly using paper-based or electronic tickets. Once the travel has commenced, there is very little contact with Bluewaters except through occasional e-mails. Therefore, the customer would be traveling for days and, depending on type of travel (such as a trekking tour), even weeks could pass with no access to the travel agent system. During this time the travel agency is unable to provide the support it would normally provide its clients. Any change to the travel plan leaves the traveler on his or her own. The feedback from the traveler to the agency also happens after the travel is completed.

Business Process 2: METM-Enabled Process of Travel

The mobile-enabled process is modeled to enable Bluewaters to provide all the support it can to its travelers while they are traveling. Consider, for example, the case of a traveler who has entered an airport and realized that his or her flight is canceled. The passenger has already booked a hotel for the same day, and the canceled flight means she is unlikely to use his or her hotel room either. The airline informs the traveler that the next available flight is in fact the next day. This requires the traveler to either switch the airline or change hotel booking. The traveler is connected through mobile PDA to Bluewaters's m-CRM system, which enables him or her to change the flight based on the conditions of ticket issue.

The desire of Bluewaters to go global and support its travelers worldwide requires the travel agent to be completely aware of what is happening all over the world. Therefore, the travel agent needs to be dynamically connected to the proper systems; that is, he or she must have the capability of accessing data at any time and from anywhere. Mobile CRM will allow the travel agents to have the operational capacity to service their current globally traveling clients.

Mobile processes also allow the travel agent to respond to the needs of the traveler while the agent may be out of the office. This is particularly true of group tours when the owner-manager takes personal interest to ensure that the trip is progressing smoothly.

Mobile Operative

The operative aspect of Bluewaters deals with the internal operation and management of the travel agency by the owner-manager. These internal operational processes primarily deal with providing optimized management control to the owner of Bluewaters through mobile processes. These management processes deal with real-time and automated update of data on employees' work, numbers of travel packages sold, and the accounting status of the organization.

Mobile Collaborative

Collaborative use of mobility by Bluewaters involves forming alliances with network operators and even popular service providers. Figure 11.5 shows a snapshot view of how collaborations among multiple service providers work to provide a unified service view for the mobile traveler. The hotel, plane, and car rental organizations are all getting together under the umbrella of Web services to collaborate and provide service to the mobile traveler. The change in itinerary is also reflected in this collaboration through the mobile networks.

Additional opportunities for collaboration include, for example, Google Maps, which can provide map services to the traveling customers of Bluewaters. These online map services are packaged by Bluewaters to provide useful information to

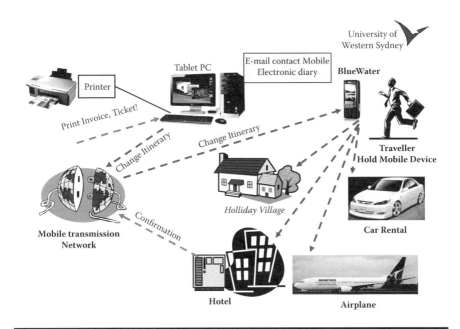

Figure 11.5 Mobile traveler—A unified view with underlying collaboration. *Source*: www.MethodScience.com.

its mobile customers. Some of the most useful map services that are combined by Bluewaters for its touring customers are providing driving/walking directions from the starting location to the destination, finding local hangouts and businesses across town or the country from their mobile phones, finding local points of interests for sightseeing, having a meal, and watching a movie. Furthermore, there are additional tools that Bluewaters has in its collaborative offerings that use the technology to turn a mobile phone into a full GPS navigation system. Travel routes are further optimized based on road conditions and speed as well as driving distances.

Thus, collaborations open up business opportunities to create newer markets, forming alliances with similar travel agencies from other countries, as well as connecting directly to government agencies to handle the numerous legal and visa requirements for travelers/customers.

Posttransitional Challenges for Bluewaters

Once the mobile transition is complete, Bluewaters moves to the "advanced stage" of mobile maturity, going beyond the preliminary stage where the formal use of mobility is limited to only some processes. The change in processes also implies a change in the way the company operates both externally and internally. There will be a need to ensure compliance with regulations on traveler support such as insurance, emergencies, and related help.

The adaptation and training of the travel agents to the mobile business process needs to be formally undertaken. The current feedback is that the training could have been handled better by providing the agents a formal presentation and trial runs of the m-CRM software. The new mobile processes need to be adapted gradually, and the organization needs to be ensured that the adoption is not too overwhelming for employees.

The owner-manager also needs to make policy changes in the operational procedures of the company, which would ensure that the mobile transition benefits are realized by all employees. These policy changes, for example, can deal with mandating mobile PDA use by all travel agents while providing consulting services to travelers.

Discussion Points

1. What are the additional economic reasons you can think of that would force Bluewaters to undertake MET? Consider this question in the context of the diagnostic phase of Bluewaters.
2. What are the reasons that can prevent Bluewaters from undertaking MET? These reasons can be based on the small size of the organization.
3. How can the MET framework be customized to handle Bluewaters's transition if the enterprise is in a developing nation? What could be done if the enterprise had no mobile maturity at all?
4. What is the significance of the collaboration and various partnerships and alliances that Bluewaters has to set up to attract customers and provide comprehensive services to existing customers?

Chapter 12

Case Study: Applying METM to a University for a Sustainable Environment

If you lose touch with nature you lose touch with humanity.

J. Krishnamurti (*Journals*, April 4, 1975)

Chapter Key Points

- Discusses the application of the Mobile Enterprise Transition (MET) framework to a large educational institution with a global presence
- Approaches the application of MET with the goal of using mobility toward becoming a green enterprise
- Outlines the application of the four dimensions of MET (economic, technical, process, and social) in the context of creating a sustainable and environmentally responsible approach for the organization
- Highlights the social importance of the use of mobility, which can result in a responsible organization

Introduction

This chapter discusses a practical case study wherein the principles and processes of mobile enterprise transitions that are discussed in the context of sustainability and the environment (in Chapter 9) are applied in practice. Thus, this chapter aims to apply the MET framework with a goal that is different from the goals of the previous two case studies, discussed in Chapters 10 and 11. The case study considered for the purpose of using the Mobile Enterprise Transition and Management (METM) framework in creating an environmentally responsible enterprise is based on a large higher-education institution (typically a university) that has global presence in the United States, Australia, India, and China. A hypothetical name for this institution is Global Polytechnic Institute (referred to as GPI throughout this case study). This chapter starts by creating an understanding of what GPI is, its brief business background, its available technical infrastructure, staff organization, and student numbers across continents. The current state of sophistication and mobile maturity of GPI is also outlined with respect to mobility. This discussion is followed by the specific challenges of sustainability and environment faced by GPI. The METM framework and the four specific dimensions within the framework (economic, technical, process, and social) are discussed from the environmental viewpoint. These factors (MET) within the four dimensions are then applied to GPI and discussed to bring about a successful application of METM in creating a sustainable and environmentally responsible educational institution.

Global Polytechnic Institute (GPI) Problem Statement

GPI is a well-established, large educational institution in the United States. It has an abundance of brilliance, knowledge, and skills, both in terms of its staff and students as well as technical infrastructure. The number of people ranges around 120 teaching staff and 20 administrative staff; the student numbers range in the thousands on the main campus. Proportionate numbers are found in the overseas campuses. GPI is a highly reputed institution that has been serving the country and society for more than a century. It has always been at the forefront of technical creation, application, and absorption throughout its history. Therefore, when it comes to making use of mobile technologies, GPI is able to incorporate them in aspects of its educational business processes, such as teaching, enrollment of students, evaluation, and assessment.

However, GPI is increasingly becoming more aware of the implications of the environment and sustainability and the role it plays in business. Environmental sustainability has a positive correlation with the longevity of the business; it literally enables a business (or an institute, in this case) to stay in business for a very long time. Such long-term sustainability has many advantages for GPI: it stays in business for the benefit of society, makes enough profit to sustain itself, provides a role model for environment responsibility, and dissipates that knowledge in society.

Thus, given the rapidly rising importance of environmental responsibility within the sociocultural context, GPI has decided to apply mobility to reduce its carbon emissions, improve its reuse and recycling, reduce its student and staff movements, and coordinate across the globe to influence its sites and premises in both developed and developing nations—by the use of mobile and wireless technologies—to improve its environmental or "green" performance.

Enacting Mobile Enterprise Transition for GPI

As noted earlier, GPI is an institute with global presence. Therefore, students enrolled in the institute are from different countries and continents. Students and teachers are also physically spread out on a large campus. Thus, the enactment of MET will first and foremost help students, teachers, and administrators to communicate with each other far more effectively than before.

The application of MET to an organization depends on the type and size of the enterprise to which it is being applied. Thus in the case of GPI, it will have to start by giving due credence to its large size and global location factor. As ascertained next, its size and maturity will be helpful in arriving at the scope of the MET project.

Diagnose

Goals, Demographics, and Maturity

The students and teachers of GPI are physically spread across its large campus. Furthermore, they are also located in different cities, countries, and continents. As an academic institute, the student population of GPI consists of adolescents and young adults. The academic staff, however, spans across multiple age groups. The delivery of education, management, and administration is currently coordinated by an enterprise resource planning (ERP) package configured for education. In addition to the currently functioning ERP system, GPI is well equipped with mobile gadgets and has an existing mobile infrastructure. This availability of mobility is reflected in the mobile maturity of GPI, which is ascertained at an advanced level. Therefore, the scope of the MET project will be small. This is so because GPI is not looking at making large-scale changes to its existing processes. Instead, it wants to introduce and reuse mobility for the environment.

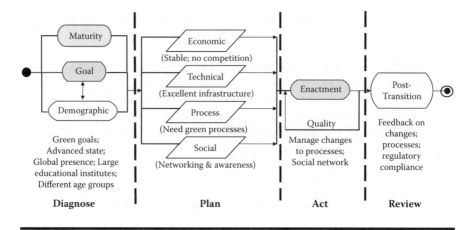

Figure 12.1 Applying the METM framework for mobile green education.

Plan

The MET project plan depends on goals and demographics; it also depends on the way in which the four dimensions of MET are applied to the organization. Therefore, we first discuss these four MET dimensions in the context of GPI, followed by the creation of the MET project plan.

Economic Dimension in GPI

Figure 12.2 provides a SWOT analysis for GPI. It reveals the particular and special responsibility that GPI has toward the environment. This is so because the environmental initiative at GPI is not limited to it; it has a "flow-on" effect on society. Besides, these initiatives are practical even from a business viewpoint in that they are likely to attract the young generation of students who are quite aware of environmental issues and the significance of a large institute committing to the green mobile. Thus, the environmentally responsible approach at GPI is in line with the strategic view toward sustainability and the environment discussed earlier in Chapters 8 and 9. Although there is no immediate economic pressure for GPI to adopt mobility, the thinkers and senior administrators of the institute are keen to make use of mobility toward enhancing the organization's social and environmental responsibility. The potential for the use of mobility to improve the social interaction between the various mobile users (students and teachers), administration, management, and other business organizations and workshop-organizing partners associated in the development and running of the GPI institute is enormous. Incorporation of mobility in the day-to-day operations and external transactions will transition the organization toward a wireless technical environment with positive connotations for

Strength	Weakness
1. Staff and students with multiple skills.	1. Limited usage of technology in communication.
2. Eager to become mobile and environmentally responsible.	2. Face-to-face teaching process.
3. Flexible organization structure.	3. Bureaucracy in decision making.
4. Excellent channel relationship between staff and other departments.	4. Physically widespread campus across counties; involve travelers.
5. Excellent infrastructure, Web site, and library.	
6. Financially stable.	
Opportunities	**Threats**
1. Mobile process re-engineering for teaching/learning.	1. International competition in educational domain.
2. Mobile methods of evaluation & marketing.	2. Government regulations on mobile and green.
3. Create process efficiencies to save time, money & carbon.	3. Potential turnover of erudite staff.
4. Create new teaching programs.	4. Nonacceptance of process changes by staff and students.
5. Ease of enrollment, marketing & results.	

Figure 12.2   SWOT analysis of GPI.

the physical environment. Mobile devices, mobile network connectivity, and changes to the content are some of the essential technical considerations in this green mobile initiative. However, the specific economic factors that are considered at GPI with respect to the use of mobility in its environmental responsibility are as follows:

- Introducing ecofriendly mobile gadgets to all users associated with GPI. This will require GPI to form alliances with device providers that will result in financial benefits and encouragement to mobile users who will be purchasing/upgrading their devices based on the green mobile initiative.
- Making use of existing mobile gadgets in an ecofriendly way. The economic benefits from reusing and recycling devices that are fully functional have been discussed in Chapter 9. GPI will consider such reuse seriously and will encourage users to reuse their devices provided the upcoming green functionalities are not sacrificed.
- Reduce the cost of the transaction with environmentally friendly mobile gadgets. This economic factor will require excellence in technical as well as process modeling, to ensure optimum transactions.
- Exploit the available mobile bandwidth fully from an economic viewpoint by ensuring that the processes that use this bandwidth are modeled and fully optimized.

■ Investigate mobile network devices and other accessories to ensure that they are ecofriendly.
■ Form alliances with network operators and create GPI-owned hot spots for cheap and ecofriendly disbursement of teaching materials as well as administrative processes such as marking.

Technical Dimension in GPI

The technical dimension of MET in GPI provides focus on the technology of networks, devices, content, and applications that will all be used in supporting the green mobile initiative. Thus, for example, the institute will use mobile devices and networks to enable sharing and transfer of knowledge from teachers to students and among students with the available and newly procured mobile gadgets and mobile technologies. Adopting such green IT practices requires consideration of both technologies and processes; however, such practices do provide a competitive edge to the organization adopting mobility (Murugesan 2008).

The technical dimension will promote use of green mobiles as well as the green broadband to carry out the education functions of GPI. The institute promotes an environmentally responsible business strategy (ERBS) by setting up additional hot spots, creation of local as well as global convenience, and optimum utilization of its own communication network. The transaction of data should be in an optimal manner to reduce its access time. GPI also creates and administers a new green policy on procurement of mobile devices used for the operations of the organization. This policy is based on ecofriendly designs, radiation amounts from mobile devices, as well as the opportunity for recycling. With the procurement of these new devices, the administration and the technical department also need to upgrade their systems and improve reusage of the devices. Wireless and mobile infrastructure uses fewer materials and is less intrusive than cabled networks (Ryan 2008). The students can get more information from their mobile devices, such as mobile videoconferencing. This usage will reduce physical movement and thus save carbon (or green gases) output.

Figure 12.3 shows a technical architecture for a mobile-enabled enrollment system. Whereas parts of this system did exist at GPI, the focus on creating this new technical architecture is to examine the areas in which the concept of green mobile, as discussed in Chapter 9, can be applied. The enrollment transactions that the students need to undertake has itself the potential for streamlining to make it more ecofriendly.

Further, although mobile transactions are capable of reducing greenhouse gas emissions, database administrators need to take some serious care to reduce the access time of the data. Innovative data management techniques such as data duplication will help to get more data from a local hub. Data standardization and integration should be done, and metadata management and virtualization of data with mobile business intelligence should be integrated to make METM more efficient.

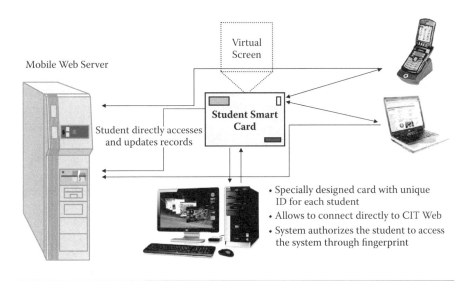

Figure 12.3   Mobile architecture of student enrollment system.

Process Dimension in GPI

The process dimension of MET at GPI deals with the various business processes of the institute. Examples of these processes are inquiry forms submission, entrance examination, fees submission, enrollment in the institution, teaching, disbursement of study material, examinations marking, results, and inquiries. These processes are modeled and studied so as to enable adoption of environment-friendly mobile gadgets. The primary purpose of using mobility here is to give the user the freedom to communicate and share the information and knowledge without physically changing the location to receive that information. Apart from the obvious environmental advantages in these mobile-enabled processes, there are also excellent opportunities for physically challenged students to receive the lecture material and associated advice and discussions without being physically present in the classroom. These process are thus likely to encourage a certain demographic of students to enroll and participate in the courses at GPI.

A judicious combination of mobile technology and mobile processes provides enormous opportunities for GPI to be creative in terms of use of its physical infrastructure. For example, mobile gadgets together with properly modeled processes can be used to manage the lights, air conditioners, and all other electronic equipment. Those not in current use can be switched off via the mobile gadget by the administrator even if he or she is physically away from the actual workplace. This "mobilization" of administrative functions saves energy and thus helps the environment by reducing emissions.

Figure 12.4 shows the existing student enrollment process, which is potentially wasting time, energy, and paper. This is so because, as shown in Figure 12.4, it is a manual process that requires students to fill out forms and wait for the response from GPI in terms of their enrollment status.

Figure 12.5 shows how a mobile reengineered enrollment process can save on all three—time, energy, and paper. This is so because the process makes use of mobility to bypass some of the bureaucratic steps in the previous process shown in Figure 12.4. Mobility, in this new process, also enhances the workability and delivery of decisions from officials to students in almost real-time. A location-independent technology platform also enhances the ability of GPI to put together new and creative processes that enable the organization of work, administration, and socialization with flexibility and improved efficiency.

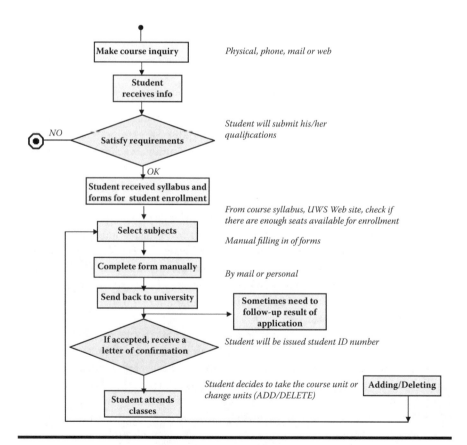

Figure 12.4   Existing student enrollment process flow.

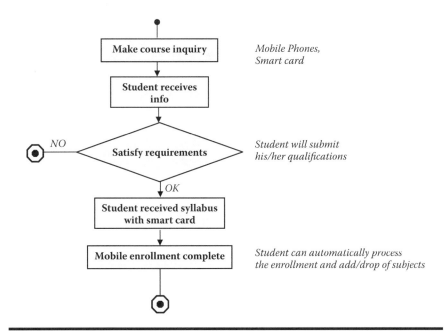

Figure 12.5   Mobile reengineered student enrollment process flow.

Social Dimension in GPI

GPI, as a well established polytechnic institute, has an existing wireless infrastructure. This existing infrastructure has already been used for some social activities. However, together with the upcoming changes due to the green mobile initiative, this wireless infrastructure can be used to enhance social networking and interaction among students of different demographic backgrounds. Further, the social responsibility of GPI encourages adoption of systems that are environment friendly. Through mobile gadgets, the institute is capable of facilitating networking of social groups. As mentioned in Chapter 9, the enlightened self-interest of the people and the organization creates a social and political momentum that encourages and demonstrates the approach to going green, making optimal use of mobility; thereafter, these pressures finally help to formulate the rules and the regulations that result in environmental awareness and changes.

Figure 12.6 demonstrates the mobile influence on the various social activities among the main roles within GPI. The interaction between students, lecturers, and administrators is streamlined and improved by mobility, and socialization within these user groups is also improved. Thus, the mobile influence on social networking can help in furthering green initiatives.

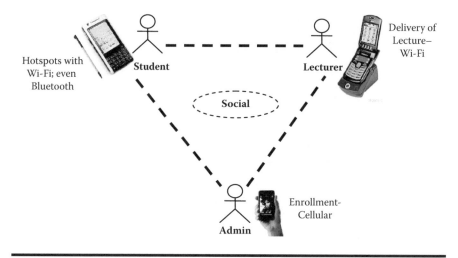

Figure 12.6   Mobile influence on social networking.

MET Project Plan

The enactment of MET in GPI is based on the project plan. A typical MET project plan that considers mobility and environmental factors for an educational institution such as GPI is shown in Table 12.1.

Act

The project plan in the Table 12.1, together with the concepts discussed in the four dimensions, are acted out in this phase. The MET project manager would carry out the steps in the detailed project plan at GPI to ensure its successful transition. Note that the focus of MET in this phase is not so much on mobile technical advances as utilization of mobile technology to change the processes at GPI and create a social approach to the environment. The following sections describe how, through the enactment of MET, the four increasingly complex mobile usages are implemented. The mobile business usage triangle transitions the organization from providing mobile information to using mobility for transactions, and then to mobile operations and mobile collaborations.

Mobile Informative Use by GPI

The informative use of mobility brings about changes to the one-way communication at GPI. These can include, for example, providing information on lecture rooms, changes to schedules, or even delivery of a lecture. To do the latter, some technical infrastructure changes will be required in the classrooms and labs

Table 12.1 A typical MET project plan for environment—mobile

Task no.	Task name	Resource name
1	Identify the type of institute, which in this case is a large education institute	GPI management
2	Identify the goals of the institute, which are to go green, and demonstrate its environmental responsibility	GPI management
3	Undertake SWOT for GPI, which indicates less competition but more environmental awareness and responsibility	GPI management
4	Identify the users (students, administrators, lecturers)	GPI management
5	Identify and document mobile business processes that undergo change (e.g., student enrollment) with due regard to environmental factors	Technical designer
6	Check usability and security factors (exam papers and account information)	GPI administration
7	Consider network coverage and bandwidth (green broadband and green blogs)	Technical designer
8	Study impact of transactions between students, teachers, and administration	User
9	Consider convenience and connectivity and impact on the environment	User/mobile gadget
10	Mobile infrastructure consideration	Technical designer
11	Interpersonal relationship between users and the management	GPI management
12	Review of mobile services with respect to green achievement, as well as confidentiality and timeliness	GPI administration

to enable them to broadcast wireless video and audio. To relieve the pressure on campus resources, wireless LANs are often used to hook PCs or mobile handheld devices to the Internet and other systems. As a result, students are able to access many of the required resources without taking up valuable lab space.

The educational innovation that is applied at GPI is the wireless-connected university with smaller and interactive computing devices and anywhere-anytime access to the campus infrastructure. Thus, GPI is deploying Palm™ handhelds to all its first-year students. Lecturers upload their teaching materials in the form of Web pages, office documents, and small video streams to a server. Students are able to download the material from that server on their mobile gadgets, potentially using Bluetooth or infrared ports if they are in the vicinity of the hot spot. Thus, in such virtual classes, they need not be present to attend lectures as almost all the content is available on their mobile devices. Previous lectures can also be accessed at the time, so this works for the green lectures where a student is not moving physically and is still able to learn through them. This approach to delivering study material means dispersal of information and knowledge in a way that has minimum impact on the environment.

Mobile Transactive Use by GPI

Mobile transactions also have enormous potential for going green. The principles of reengineering, discussed in Chapters 4 and 5, are enacted here. The transactions among GPI students and administration increase the service integrity. Mobile gadgets also reduce the operating cost of these transactions. Mobile Net-conferencing, Voice-over-IP (VOIP), and virtual project collaboration among students and teachers can provide flexibility to communicate without influencing the environment through the institute premise and travel. Interdepartmental transactions can become quick and handy. Using mobility for transactions ensures that the users do not have to wait for long to complete any of them, as may happen in traditional study centers. Transactions can be retrieved and some of the administrative work can happen through the virtual mobile office.

Mobile Operative Use by GPI

The areas of operations that can be changed with the help of mobility and that will benefit GPI from an environmental viewpoint are primarily the administrative operations. These deal with the way in which the staff is internally organized for lectures, rooms are allocated to subjects, and laboratory spaces are managed per student. Staff allocation is based on two categories of staff—the permanent professorial staff who come in to deliver lectures; and the visiting or casual faculty that is brought in on an as-needed basis or due to setting up of new research alliances with other academic and industrial institutions.

Staff movement across various campuses of GPI can be considered as a significant green gas contributor. Therefore, with the help of mobility, GPI puts together processes that reduce staff movement.

Mobile Collaborative Use by GPI

GPI has a need to deal with external business partners in terms of providing the infrastructure and administrative functions to students and staff. These infrastructure requirements deal with providing the necessary rooms, furniture, air-conditioning, canteen, library, and numerous other such facilities that are all supporting the main teaching activity of the organization. Although GPI is extremely well equipped to provide its teaching and research services throughout the country and even outside it, it can still benefit greatly by reducing the overhead activities in terms of providing the infrastructure and its administration. This is an area where it can collaborate using mobility to reduce its overall carbon emissions. For example, the administration and staff can communicate with each other location independently; for the overall performance of GPI, MET will work as a mobile ERP that can take care of the transactions of GPI considering the security and integration of the data. A good rapport will be there between the collaborative parties of GPI with less traveling. Electricity consumption and transportation expenses will be saved by implementing METM, and thus it will lead to reduction of CO_2 and other toxic gases. The people associated with GPI will switch on mobile gadgets whenever required so that unnecessary radiation through computers can be avoided.

Change Management in GPI

Implementation of MET will change the management of the institution for mobile green education. This change management is summarized in Figure 12.7. In the current system the administration first tries to find land for establishment of an institution and then starts with some limited courses targeting a limited number of students, but MET will give freedom to the institution or organization to operate location independently, and can work with a motto that knowledge does not have any boundaries. A student from any part of the world can be enrolled and can get

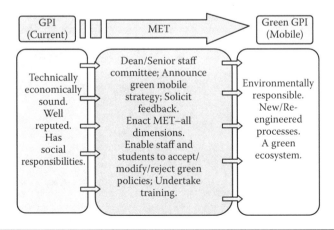

Figure 12.7   METM—Change management in GPI for green mobile education.

the best knowledge from the world's best experts in that field. The implementation of MET will make an institution more like a collaborative business system, so new rules for integration of data, communication, and security measures will help an institution grow as an organization that has a global presence.

Posttransitional Challenges and Review

Implementation of METM will surely enhance the economic and technical status of the organization (GPI). There will be an ease of communication and availability, but some factors should be considered to avoid overuse of devices:

- Proper training to use mobile gadgets for users, especially lecturers and the administration
- Availability of recyclable mobile gadgets and mobile devices across the continents
- Emphasis on optimal processes across the campus, and provision for optimization of these mobile-enabled processes
- Ensuring authenticity of the student on a regular basis

References

Ryan, E. 2008. Building sustainable IT, *Cutter IT Journal.*
Murugesan, S. 2008. *Cutter IT Journal.*
Unhelkar, B. and Dickens, A. 2008. Lessons in implementing "Green" business strategies with ICT.

Appendix A*:
Mobile Enterprise Transitions (METs)— Research Project

---

* The following questionnaire was used in eliciting survey responses for the MET data and analysis presented in this book.

MOBILE ENTERPRISE TRANSITIONS "MET": RESEARCH PROJECT

Greetings! Thank you in advance for providing 10 minutes of your precious time to answer this 'research' survey. The answers can be based on your company, your primary client, or your erudite opinions. The aim of this research project is to ascertain, validate and improve the effectiveness of the crucial elements in Mobile Enterprise Transitions (MET). The raw data collected through this survey will be analysed, processed and stored safely within University of Western Sydney for next five years. This survey respects the privacy of the individuals and the confidentiality of the organizations. As such, the answers you provide here will only be discussed collectively. The ensuing analysis will also be presented in seminars, published in journals and, eventually in a book titled *Mobile Enterprise Transitions and Management.* Your participation is voluntary, your answers remain confidential and your honesty in answering this survey is deeply appreciated.   Regards,   **Bhuvan Unhelkar,** PhD, FACS

About You: (Optional)			
Your Name: _____ Company Name:_____ Contact: _____			
Your Role:	[ ] Senior Management	[ ] Project Management	[ ] Sales & Support
	[ ] Consultant	[ ] Technical	[ ] Other _____
Company Size	[ ] Small (< 20 workers)	[ ] Medium (20-200 workers)	[ ] Large (> 200 workers);
Business Type	[ ] Selling Products	[ ] Selling Services	[ ] Other_____
Industry Category	[ ] Education & Training	[ ] Building & Construction	[ ] Professional Services
	[ ] Manufacturing	[ ] Banking & Finance	[ ] Information Technology
	[ ] Health & Community	[ ] Government;	[ ] Other _____
Primary Region:	[ ] Australia/NZ	[ ] Europe/UK	[ ] North America/Canada;
	[ ] Sub-continent (India, SriLanka)	[ ] Japan, Singapore, China	[ ] Other_____

Business Drivers for Mobile Enterprise Transitions (WHY?)   Least ←--------------→ Most
                                                                Important   Important

Please rate the following factors in terms of their importance in driving Mobile business

		Least Important ← → Most Important				
Costs:	Mobile Gadgets (Phones/PDA/Blackberry etc)	[]	[]	[]	[]	[]
	Costs per transaction (Calls, SMS)	[]	[]	[]	[]	[]
	Upfront Setup costs (networks, infrastructures)	[]	[]	[]	[]	[]
	Operational costs (regular, ongoing)	[]	[]	[]	[]	[]
Competition:	Sophisticated mobile services offered by Competitor	[]	[]	[]	[]	[]
	Excellence in mobile Contents offered by Competitor	[]	[]	[]	[]	[]
	Advertisement/Marketing of Mobility by Competitor	[]	[]	[]	[]	[]
Customers/Employees:	Customer's demands for mobile services	[]	[]	[]	[]	[]
	Business partner's demand for mobile processes	[]	[]	[]	[]	[]
	Employee's ability to provide better services to Customers	[]	[]	[]	[]	[]
Convenience:	Local connectivity (location independence)	[]	[]	[]	[]	[]
	Global connectivity (roaming)	[]	[]	[]	[]	[]

Please rate the following Mobile usage in terms of their importance to MET

Mobile Usage:	Leisure (e.g. Sports, Entertainment)	[]	[]	[]	[]	[]
	Work (e.g. keeping contact with employees)	[]	[]	[]	[]	[]
	Emergency services (e.g. Fire, Police, Ambulance)	[]	[]	[]	[]	[]

Any other Business drivers you can think of that will influence MET

Others:	(Specify) _____	[]	[]	[]	[]	[]

*Please rank the following six **business** factors in terms of their **sequence** of importance (1= consider first; 6= consider last) in influencing Mobile Enterprise Transitions*

[ ] Cost & time savings	[ ] Demands from competition	[ ] Demands from customers
[ ] Better control of business	[ ] Convenience of use	[ ] Type of usage

MOBILE ENTERPRISE TRANSITIONS "MET": RESEARCH PROJECT

Technological Drivers for Mobile Enterprise Transitions (WHAT?)		Least ←-----------------→ Most Important Important				
Importance of the following mobile gadgets in influencing Mobile Enterprise Transition (MET)						
Gadgets/Device:	Mobile Phones	[]	[]	[]	[]	[]
	PDA (Wireless enabled, Blackberry)	[]	[]	[]	[]	[]
	Wireless Laptop/Tablet PC	[]	[]	[]	[]	[]
	Wi-Fi Devices (Printers, Speakers, Phones)	[]	[]	[]	[]	[]
	Look & Feel (e.g. Color, Shape)	[]	[]	[]	[]	[]
Importance of the following mobile/wireless networks in Mobile Enterprise Transition (MET)						
Mobile Networking:	Wireless Broadband Network ("3G", Next G)	[]	[]	[]	[]	[]
	Wireless Local Area Network	[]	[]	[]	[]	[]
	Infrared	[]	[]	[]	[]	[]
	Bluetooth	[]	[]	[]	[]	[]
	Wi-Max	[]	[]	[]	[]	[]
	Radio Frequency Identification (RFID)/E-Tag	[]	[]	[]	[]	[]
	Mobile Satellite Networks	[]	[]	[]	[]	[]
Importance of standards and applications in Mobile Enterprise Transition (MET)						
Standards & Applications:	Standards (e.g. 802.11; .22 type standards)	[]	[]	[]	[]	[]
	Vendor's desire to comply with standards	[]	[]	[]	[]	[]
	Customer's desire to use applications	[]	[]	[]	[]	[]
	Availability of mobile applications	[]	[]	[]	[]	[]
Importance of mobile Infrastructures in Mobile Enterprise Transition (MET)						
Infrastructures:	Transmission Towers	[]	[]	[]	[]	[]
	Satellites	[]	[]	[]	[]	[]
	Power lines	[]	[]	[]	[]	[]
Importance of Content Management Systems in Mobile Enterprise Transition (MET)						
Contents:	Uploading vendor contents	[]	[]	[]	[]	[]
	Pushing contents to Customers	[]	[]	[]	[]	[]
	Enabling Customers to Pull contents	[]	[]	[]	[]	[]
	Multi-media aspect of contents	[]	[]	[]	[]	[]
Any other Technological factor you can think of that will influence MET						
Others:	(specify) _____	[]	[]	[]	[]	[]

*Please rank the following six **technological** factors in terms of their **sequence** of importance (1= consider first; 6= consider last) in influencing Mobile Enterprise Transitions*

[ ] Mobile Gadget capabilities   [ ] Networks Coverage & Bandwidth   [ ] Mobile Standards

[ ] Mobile Infrastructures   [ ] Mobile content management   [ ] Mobile business applications

Process Drivers for Mobile Enterprise Transitions (HOW?)		Least ←-----------------→ Most Important Important				
Importance of Business Processes in driving Mobile Enterprise Transitions (MET)						
Business Processes:	Business to Consumer (B 2 C)	[]	[]	[]	[]	[]
	Business to Business (B 2 B)	[]	[]	[]	[]	[]
	Government to Individual	[]	[]	[]	[]	[]
	Collaborative (many to many)	[]	[]	[]	[]	[]
Importance of merging Mobile processes with Electronic processes in MET						
Merging Mobile processes	Creating new mobile processes	[]	[]	[]	[]	[]

MOBILE ENTERPRISE TRANSITIONS "MET": RESEARCH PROJECT

Re-engineering existing "e" with mobile processes	[]	[]	[]	[]	[]
Removing redundant "e" processes	[]	[]	[]	[]	[]
Modeling of mobile business processes	[]	[]	[]	[]	[]

Importance of Quality of Service (QoS) in driving Mobile Enterprise Transitions (MET)

QoS:

Real time response when compared with Costs	[]	[]	[]	[]	[]
Coverage when compared with Costs	[]	[]	[]	[]	[]
Coverage when compared with Security	[]	[]	[]	[]	[]
Accuracy when compared with Costs	[]	[]	[]	[]	[]

Importance of Financial aspect of a business in influencing Mobile Enterprise Transitions

Financial:

Applications supporting mobile usage (e.g. bill payments)	[]	[]	[]	[]	[]
Financial transactions using mobile gadgets	[]	[]	[]	[]	[]
Service & support for mobile usage	[]	[]	[]	[]	[]
Transparency in mobile charges (call costs)	[]	[]	[]	[]	[]
Support for lost/stolen mobile gadgets	[]	[]	[]	[]	[]
Costs of developing mobile applications	[]	[]	[]	[]	[]

Any other Process factor you can think of that will influence MET

Others:

(specify) _____	[]	[]	[]	[]	[]

*Please rank the following six **Process** factors in terms of their **sequence** of importance (1= consider first; 6= consider last) in influencing Mobile Enterprise Transitions*

[ ] Creation of mobile business processes   [ ] Costs of application development   [ ] Re-engineering for mobile processes

[ ] Collaboration between businesses   [ ] Quality of Services   [ ] Modeling "m" process specifications

---

Sociological Drivers for Mobile Enterprise Transitions (WHO?)	Least ←------------------→ Most				
	Important				Important

Importance of Adoption Attitude of users in influencing Mobile Enterprise Transitions (MET)

Attitude to Adoption:

Age of the user (e.g. child, teen, adult, elderly)	[]	[]	[]	[]	[]
Perceived usefulness of the device	[]	[]	[]	[]	[]
Ease of use of the device	[]	[]	[]	[]	[]
Peer pressure for buying/using the device	[]	[]	[]	[]	[]
Upgrading to newer device	[]	[]	[]	[]	[]
Facilitating environment (e.g. government policy)	[]	[]	[]	[]	[]

*Importance of **usability** of gadgets in driving Mobile Enterprise Transitions (MET)*

Usability:

Size & weight	[]	[]	[]	[]	[]
Screen space (screen real estate)	[]	[]	[]	[]	[]
Keypad size (including buttons)	[]	[]	[]	[]	[]
Dictionary feature in SMS text typing	[]	[]	[]	[]	[]
Audio (sound) facilities	[]	[]	[]	[]	[]
Wallpapers & Ring tones	[]	[]	[]	[]	[]
Battery (duration and re-charging)	[]	[]	[]	[]	[]
Ruggedness of device (durability)	[]	[]	[]	[]	[]
Language support (e.g. English, Chinese)	[]	[]	[]	[]	[]

Importance of Privacy of users in driving Mobile Enterprise Transitions (MET)

Privacy:

Preventing others from knowing your location	[]	[]	[]	[]	[]
Using auto location information to seek assistance	[]	[]	[]	[]	[]
Transmitting instantaneous photographs	[]	[]	[]	[]	[]

MOBILE ENTERPRISE TRANSITIONS "MET": RESEARCH PROJECT

	Carrying mobile phones in public facilities (toilets, swimming pools, playgrounds)	[ ]	[ ]	[ ]	[ ]	[ ]

Importance of changes to Organizational structures resulting from MET

Team structures:	Changes to Employee reporting structures	[ ]	[ ]	[ ]	[ ]	[ ]
	Changes to senior management	[ ]	[ ]	[ ]	[ ]	[ ]
	Changes to Consulting/Training needs	[ ]	[ ]	[ ]	[ ]	[ ]
Customer Relationship structures:	Relationship between customer & employees	[ ]	[ ]	[ ]	[ ]	[ ]
	Relationship between customer & business	[ ]	[ ]	[ ]	[ ]	[ ]
	Relationship amongst customers	[ ]	[ ]	[ ]	[ ]	[ ]

Any other Sociological factor you can think of that will influence MET

Others:	(specify) _____	[ ]	[ ]	[ ]	[ ]	[ ]

*Please rank the following six **sociological** factors in terms of their **sequence** of importance (1= consider first; 6= consider last) in influencing Mobile Enterprise Transitions*

[ ] Attitude to adoption of mobility   [ ] Usability of devices   [ ] Privacy considerations

[ ] Influence of Social Environment   [ ] Changes to Organizational structure   [ ] Changes to Customer relationships

Your descriptive responses to the following questions in the context of Mobile Enterprise Transitions is highly appreciated

Question 1: What, according to you, are the two most crucial reasons for a business to transition to a Mobile business?

(a) _____

(b) _____

Question 2: What would you consider that two most factors that would *hinder* the adoption of mobility by business?

(a) _____

(b) _____

Question 3: What would you consider as the two highest risks associated with Mobile Enterprise Transitions? And how would you recommend they be overcome?

(a) _____

(b) _____

Question 4: What are the two most important issues in Mobile standards and applications that will influence Mobile Business?

(a) _____

(b) _____

Comment: Any other descriptive comment that will help Mobile Enterprise Transitions:

_____

_____

End of Survey: Thanks You for Your time! Postal Address:
Room - ECG 63, Parramatta Campus, School of Computing and Maths, University of Western Sydney
Locked Bag 1797, South Penrith DC; NSW, 1797. AUSTRALIA.

Appendix B: Mobile Enterprise Transitions (METs)—Example Use Cases from Various Case Studies

M-Pharma Use Cases

1. Inquiring about New Drug Availability

Use case 1:	Inquiring about New Drug Availability
Actors:	Staff
Description:	This use case describes the process of the Pharma staff making a request through a mobile device to the system to provide new information on drugs. This information is made available through a collaboration of various entities (such as government, laboratories, and manufacturers) that provide up-to-date information on medical ingredients and their suppliers.
Precondition:	Staff has secure mobile connection; staff has access to the system.
Postcondition:	New drug information is provided to the staff.
Type:	Simple
Normal course of events:	1. Staff makes the request for an on-the-spot inquiry on new drugs using his or her handheld device by logging into the system. 2. System asks for the type of information needed by the staff on the drugs (A1). 3. Staff makes a selection of the "type of drug" and the information required on the drug (detailed information on drug types available in the business requirements document). 4. System links to the relevant site (government, laboratories, etc.) to ascertain the information as a service. 5. System displays an integrated suite of information on the new drug to the staff.
Alternate course of events:	A1: These options would be information on government regulations, laboratories, drug manufacturers, etc.
References:	Abbass, G. and Wu, M.

2. Creating New Order for a Drug

Use case 2:	Creating New Order for a Drug
Actors:	Staff, supplier
Description:	This use case describes the process of placing a new order for a drug. After the new order is recorded, the supplier of that specific drug can use that information to supply the new drug.
Precondition:	Existence of the inventory level (stock take); supplier has a valid log-on to the system.
Postcondition:	N/A
Type:	Simple
Normal course of events:	1. The staff requests the system to display the drugs and the suppliers for a specific set of drugs on the PDA. 2. System gives the options of viewing the inventory level and new drug information to the staff (A1). 3. The staff selects a specific drug with the help of the PDA. 4. Staff specifies a new order for the drug selected (A2). 5. System provides draft of a new order on the screen (A3). 6. Staff confirms the draft specification of the order containing drug type, description, and amount. 7. System sends corresponding intimation to the supplier. 8. Supplier logs into the system and requests to view the new order. 9. System permits the supplier to view all orders for that specific supplier. 10. Supplier executes the relevant orders for the new drugs (A3). 11. System updates relevant inventory of the drugs.
Alternate course of events:	A1: Staff may need to know existing information on new drugs to decide on the new order. A2: This new order includes the inventory-level use case and its stock take to get information on shortage of drug and staff interaction to make a new order. A3: The order can be scheduled for future execution rather than immediately.
References:	Abbass, G. and Wu, M.

3. Delivering Drugs to Patients

Use case 3:	Delivering Drugs to Patients
Actors:	Courier, pharmacist, physician, patient
Description:	This use case describes how a patient makes a request for delivery of drugs from the nearest pharmacy. The pharmacist checks with the physician and then makes a dispatch to the customer by sending an e-mail to the courier to deliver the drugs to the customer. Courier gets all the detailed information related to the customer through the system and then delivers the drugs to the customer.
Precondition:	Patient has a prescription and is a registered member.
Postcondition:	Customer gets the medicine delivered at his or her door.
Type:	Simple
Normal course of events:	1. System gives the customer the option to select the type of drugs that he or she wants to order (these may be a combination of prescription and cosmetics or either one of them). 2. Customer selects a new drug that he or she wants to order. 3. System provides the customer with a list of nearby pharmacies that are linked to the system (these are the collaborating pharmacies). 4. Customer selects the pharmacy from where he or she would like to place the order. 5. System sends a message to the specific pharmacy with details of the customer and details of the drugs. 6. Pharmacy receives and records the message (A1). 7. Pharmacy packs the drugs and records them on the system. 8. Pharmacy interfaces with the courier to pick the drugs and deliver them to the customer. 9. Courier receives a message on his or her handheld device containing details such as the customer's address and delivery timings. 10. Courier delivers the medicines to the customer.
Alternate course of events:	A1: If a physician is required to further authorize the drugs, then the system would wait for the acceptance to come through.
References:	Abbass, G. and Wu, M.

4. Writing Prescription

Use case 4:	Writing Prescription
Actors:	Practitioner, patient
Description:	This use case describes the writing of a prescription by a practitioner on the basis of a patient's visits; the prescription is then electronically entered into the database.
Precondition:	Patient and practitioner should have valid user names and passwords for the pharmaceutical management system (PMS).
Postcondition:	Practitioner will enter the prescription for the patient into the database.
Type:	Simple
Normal course of events:	1. Patient visits the practitioner and explains his or her problem. (*Note*: See the procedures on visit bookings, protocols, and payments that are described separately in the business requirements document.) 2. Practitioner accesses the system to identify patient details (A1). 3. System provides details of the patient; practitioner accesses the system to ascertain the drugs he or she would like to order for the patient through the system. 4. System provides various options to the practitioner in terms of drugs and the prescriptions that can be electronically written for the drugs. 5. Practitioner makes the selection to enter the new prescription for the patient. 6. System provides the practitioner with a format for writing the prescription. 7. Practitioner fills out the prescription form. 8. Practitioner requests the system to save the new prescription to the database (A2). 9. System adds the patient's new prescription to the database.
Alternate course of events:	A1: Sufficient details of patient do not exist on the system to enable the writing of electronic prescriptions. A2: System generates appropriate error on the incorrect filling of the prescription.
References:	Abbass, G. and Wu, M.

5. Checking Expiry Date of Drugs

Use case 5:	Checking Expiry Date of Drugs
Actors:	System, pharmacist
Description:	This use case deals with checking the expiry date of available drugs. The medical drug packages are equipped with radio frequency identification (RFID) technology, and the pharmacist's mobile device is linked to RFID.
Precondition:	RFID transmission is checked. The expired medicines are still on the shelves.
Postcondition:	The pharmacist is informed about the expired medications. The expired medications are removed from the shelves.
Type:	Complex
Normal course of events:	1. RFID-enabled medical drug packages check their expiry dates electronically. 2. Medical drug packages send message to the system when they have expired. 3. Pharmacist's nominated mobile device receives the message from the medical drug package's RFID tag. 4. Pharmacist rechecks the inventory via the mobile device by searching the medical drug package number. 5. Pharmacist removes the expired medications from the shelves.
Alternate course of events:	None
References:	Abbass, G. and Wu, M.

6. Order Purchase

Use case 6:	Order Purchase
Actors:	System, pharmacist, closed-loop environment for wireless (CLEW) system, manager, supplier
Description:	This use case deals with the ordering of required medicines that are out of stock.
Precondition:	Medicines are out of stock and are required.
Postcondition:	The pharmacist is informed about the required medications. The system is ready to receive the next message.
Type:	Complex
Normal course of events:	1. RFID-enabled packages send message. 2. Pharmacist's mobile device receives the message. 3. Pharmacist checks the inventory via a mobile device. 4. Pharmacist submits the order via the mobile device. 5. CLEW technology receives the order. 6. CLEW technology validates the integrity of the order (A1). 7. CLEW technology sends the order to the manager. 8. Manager approves (A2). 9. CLEW technology receives the approval. 10. CLEW technology submits the order to the supplier.
Alternate course of events:	A1: If the order is not validated by CLEW technology, the pharmacist receives the information for reorder. A2: If the manager does not approve the purchase, the CLEW technology informs the pharmacist.
References:	The use case "Checking Expiry Date of Drugs" can also use this use case when ordering new packages.

Mobile Travel and Tourism Company Use Cases

1. Rebooking Trip

Use case 1:	Rebooking Trip
Actors:	Traveler, system, airline, hotel
Description:	This use case deals with rebooking for a trip by a traveler.
Precondition:	The traveler's initially booked trip has been cancelled. The mobile device has all the necessary information of the traveler.
Postcondition:	The system has booked the next available flight and corresponding room. The traveler has been informed.
Type:	Complex
Normal course of events:	1. Traveler requests updated information via a mobile device. 2. System loads the schedule update (A1). 3. Traveler selects the desired schedule. 4. System prioritizes the order and forwards the update to the relevant interfaces for airline and hotel. 5. Traveler's booking for airline and hotel is made through related interface. 6. Confirmation of the booking is forwarded to the system. 7. System collects all the required data. 8. System forwards the data to the traveler. 9. Traveler uses the new schedule for travel.
Alternate course of events:	A1: System does not have the specific schedule the traveler is looking for. The system then allows traveler to customize existing schedule according to his or her requirement.
References:	Abbass, G.

2. Rebooking Process via Travel Agent

Use case 2:	Rebooking Process via Travel Agent
Actors:	Travel agent, system, traveler, airline, hotel
Description:	This use case deals with the rebooking process through a travel agent. Traveler contacts the agent to rebook for the next available flight and corresponding hotel room.
Precondition:	The traveler's initially booked trip has been cancelled. The agent, airline, and hotel have all the necessary information of the traveler.
Postcondition:	The system has booked the next available flight and corresponding room. The traveler has been informed.
Type:	Complex
Normal course of events:	1. Agent submits an application to the system to download all the information of the customer on his or her mobile device. 2. System forms are preloaded to capture customer details. 3. Agent receives the details. 4. Agent submits an application to the airline and hotel. 5. System sends the updated schedule to the agent's device. 6. Agent forwards the updated schedule to the traveler. 7. Traveler receives the new schedule and selects the desired schedule (A1). 8. Agent receives the confirmation. 9. Agent submits the new schedule to airline and hotel interfaces through the system. 10. Agent receives the confirmation and forwards it to the traveler. 11. Traveler uses the new schedule for travel.
Alternate course of events:	A1: Traveler customizes the existing schedule if the schedule is not according to his or her requirement.
References:	—

Appendix C: Modeling CASE Tools*

StarUML

Information	http://staruml.sourceforge.net/en/download.php
Comments	The aforementioned download link is for this popular open source tool that can be used in modeling mobile business processes and mobile software applications. The open-source nature of this tool makes it popular but, at the same time, limited in an industrial setting (such as teamwork).

Visual Paradigm

Information	http://www.visual-paradigm.com/
Comments	This industrial-strength tool for modeling facilitates excellent teamwork; ideal for a group of business analysts and enterprise architects to use in Mobile Enterprise Transitions (METs) using Business Process Modeling Notation (BPMN). The neat and tidy visual interfaces and its ability to facilitate teamwork in outsourced projects are obvious when this tool is used. It can be used as a good reverse-engineering tool and also for the generation of integrated development interfaces (IDEs) as well as their integration. In addition, this tool provides a good repository and reporting infrastructure.

---

* Disclaimer: Please note that these are the Unified Modeling Language (UML)-based computer-aided software engineering (CASE) tools and process tools that the author is aware of and have occasionally used. No one tool is recommended over the other. The order of presentation of these tools is random.

ARIS by IDS Scheer

Information	http://www.ids-scheer.com/en/ARIS
Comments	IDS Scheer is a well-known modeling platform, used in various domains such as insurance, banking, and telecom. It is capable of UML-based modeling and business process modeling using BPMN. Aris is a good governance engine that regulates and automates—and therefore improves—tool and process management.

IBM's Telelogic System Architect

Information	http://www.telelogic.com/products/systemarchitect/index.cfm
Comments	Telelogic's System Architect, together with DOORS, is a valuable UML-based modeling tool that has the ability to handle third-party integrations in medium-to-large projects. Furthermore, because of its integration with DOORS (particularly for requirements management), this tool is excellent for requirements traceability.

Borland's Together (earlier Togethersoft)

Information	http://www.borland.com/us/products/together/index.html http://togethersoft.net/index.html
Comments	TogetherSoft control center is based on excellent architecture and has a sleek user interface. Aimed at the high end of the market, it does an excellent job in large projects with multiple teams. The availability of patterns within the tool helps with reuse and quality.

IBM's Rational Rose

Information	http://www-01.ibm.com/software/awdtools/developer/rose/
Comments	IBM's Rational Object Software Engineering (ROSE) still remains a popular tool for modeling processes and systems. There is a suite of tools that work with ROSE, configuration management, testing, and process.

ArgoUML 0.9 from Tigris

Information	http://argouml.tigris.org/
Comments	This tool has been used across many projects beyond the mobile business.

VisualUML from Visual Object Modelers

Information	www.visualuml.com
Comments	VisualUML is aimed at the medium to low end of the market. It is ideal for small to medium projects. However, the tool can scale up and relates to various development environments.

Magicdraw from NoMagic

Information	http://www.magicdraw.com/
Comments	MagicDraw UML is a product of NoMagic. NoMagic is not a tool vendor but more of a technology partner. MagicDraw also provides excellent support for UML-based modeling, particularly in the problem space (creation of metaobject protocols [MOPS]).

Visio 2007

Information	http://office.microsoft.com/en-us/visio/default.aspx
Comments	Occasionally, modelers have used Visio—but the general impression Visio gives is that it is more of a UML (and other) documentation tool rather than a design tool.

Following are some process tools that can come in handy in modeling the mobile business processes discussed in Chapter 5. Investigation and study of process tools helps to (1) customize the process to enable the best use of the tool or (2) customize the tool to ensure that it best fits the project requirements. Process tools can also provide additional help to the project manager in his or her measurement and estimation efforts for the project.

Rational Unified Process (RUP)

Information	http://www-01.ibm.com/software/awdtools/rup/
Comments	Rational's RUP is a process tool that is tightly integrated with ROSE. RUP also has the robust research background provided by Jacobson's earlier process work in objectory.

Object-Oriented Process, Environment, and Notation (OPEN)

Information	www.open.org.au
Comments	Original work on the OPEN process (the OPEN process specification, Addison-Wesley, 1997, Essex, UK) was done by Graham, Henderson-Sellers, and Younessi, followed by several other methodologists. However, OPEN needs to be configured within another tool of your choice, because OPEN itself is not a process tool but an extremely well-researched process framework.

Catalysis

Information	http://www.catalysis.org/ D'Souza, D. and Wills, A. (1999). *Objects, Components and Frameworks with UML: The Catalysis Approach*. Reading, MA: Addison-Wesley.
Comments	A comprehensive process, together with UML notations and diagrams.

ICONIX

Information	Rosenberg, D. with Scott, K. (1999). *Use Case Driven Object Modeling with UML: A Practical Approach*. Reading, MA: Addison-Wesley. http://www.iconixsw.com/
Comments	A UML-based process that, for the most part, I like and agree with.

ETrack

Information	www.eTrack.com.au
Comments	A uniquely architected process tool that allows one to create a genuine iterative and incremental process plan. Because of its integration with Microsoft Project, it is easier for project managers to create an IIP plan and then translate it into a linear project plan.

Author

Bhuvan Unhelkar (BE, MDBA, MSc, PhD; FACS) has 26 years of strategic as well as hands-on professional experience in information and communication technology, and its application to business and management. He is founder of MethodScience.com and has provided strategic leadership and guidance to organizations in capability enhancement (process and quality), software engineering (modeling with UML and BPMN), testing, information architecture (with SOA), enterprise globalization, outsourcing, and mobile business. He has been an executive consultant with global experience in providing focused facilitation in various domains including financial markets, telecom, banking, insurance, retail, and government. He is a master trainer to senior business executives and ICT professionals.

Unhelkar earned his doctorate in the field of object orientation from the University of Technology, Sydney. In his academic role at the University of Western Sydney, he has organized the Mobile Internet Research and Applications Group (MIRAG) and has had three successful PhD supervisions. He has authored and edited 14 books, and has extensively presented and published research papers and case studies. He is a sought-after speaker, a fellow of the Australian Computer Society, life member of the Computer Society of India, a Rotarian, and a previous TiE mentor.

Endorsements (In Praise of *METM*)

Warren Adkins, Services Manager, Dialog Information Technology, Sydney
As a company focused on customized software development, increasingly we are required to integrate mobile devices into the technology mix. While at a certain level mobile technology represents just another user interface mechanism, there are deeper issues surrounding this emerging trend beyond technology integration. In this book Dr. Unhelkar has achieved a significant milestone by bringing together four significant aspects that affect any business in mobile enterprise transitions. The framework described in this book is a balance of economic, technical, process, and social aspects. A must have on any consultant's desk!

Professor Akshai Aggrawal, Interim Director, School of Computer Science, University of Windsor, Canada
Mobile Enterprise Transition and Enterprise by Bhuvan Unhelkar presents the "best practices" that a business should use, if it is to benefit from mobility. The book contains a rigorously researched technical dimension, specifying Service Oriented Architecture and the issues of security, followed by processes and sociology issues. I recommend this book to all researchers as well as practitioners in the area of mobility for obtaining an enterprisewide perspective on introducing these handheld and increasingly miniaturized devices into enterprises.

Dave Curtis, Enterprise Architect, Sydney, Australia
Unhelkar provides an excellent practical insight into transitioning to formal mobile organizations. This book takes the reader step-by-step, particularly through the mobile technology space, and highlights architectural issues and solutions in a very practical usable manner. I had the opportunity to participate in some of the research that underwent in this book, but from a practitioner's viewpoint. The end-product, this book, is a great result for hands-on professionals like myself.

Julian Day, Managing Director, Consensus Pty. Ltd., and Chairman, QESP A/NZ (Quantitative Enterprise Software Performance), Australia
An exceptional encapsulation of current and future capability focused on the pragmatic application of mobility for practitioners, researchers, and organizations. An essential in-depth companion for those wishing to understand, embrace, and leverage the adoption of mobile technology.

Dr. Elaine Lawrence, Associate Professor and Head of Computer Systems Department, Faculty of Information Technology, University of Technology, Sydney, Australia
This book provides a robust research-intense framework for mobile enterprise transitions that is directly and practically applicable in the industry. Unhelkar's work not only deserves compliments but also needs to be heartily encouraged in many other areas of business transitions as the framework described here for mobile enterprise transitions has potential for a much wider application than just mobile transitions.

Professor San Murugesan, Professor of Information Systems and IT Management, Multimedia University, Malaysia
Mere deployment of mobile and wireless technologies would not automatically yield the anticipated benefits. To benefit from mobile technology, each enterprise must think afresh about how to take advantage of mobile technologies and comprehensively address the mobile transition along multiple dimensions technology, process, economy, and sociology. *Mobile Enterprise Transition and Management* by Bhuvan Unhelkar presents a practical framework that will help enterprises successfully transition into mobile enterprises. The book is unique in its coverage in addressing and managing the transition from several different perspectives and will be a very helpful resource to all those interested in enterprise mobility, be they executives, academics, or researchers.

Kumar Parakala, President, the Australian Computer Society
Mobile technologies are increasingly impacting our businesses and lives. It is important for business leaders and strategists to understand and embrace these technologies to achieve optimal benefit. The book addresses these aspects extremely well and is a compulsory reading for organizational leaders transitioning into digital business.

Christopher Payne, IT Development Manager, Fairfax Media Ltd., Judge, Consensus Software Awards. Sydney, Australia
This book demonstrates typical Unhelkar energy, enthusiasm, and depth of research in a subject that is changing our daily lives dramatically. This book will undoubtedly be a valuable resource for both academia and industry in understanding the mobile phenomenon and extracting commercial advantage from mobile technology.

Prabhat (S.D.) Pradhan, CEO, Argentum Engineering Design, Pune, India
Dr. Unhelkar has once again shown his holistic grasp of the enterprise and its continuing challenges and opportunities. Mobility is already well upon us; this book shows us the why, the how, and the how much, in a simple yet sophisticated way.

Keith Sherringham, Independent Business Consultant; Author of
Cookbook for Shareholder Value and Market Dominance. **Sydney, Australia**
The Internet wave that swept through business toward the end of the last decade will be seen as a ripple in a pond compared to those resulting from mobile computing. Strategically aligning business and ICT now for mobile computing is a business imperative. This book allows enterprises to realize the benefits of mobile computing without making the mistakes that occurred when the Internet was first adopted into business.

Adrian Tatham, CEO, Alacrity Technologies, Canberra, Australia
Mobility is proved to significantly improve organizational efficiencies. However, to achieve those efficiencies, understanding and implementing the process in transitioning to a mobile enterprise is critical. There are many factors that must be investigated in this process, and security is a crucial element of this strategy. This book delivers organizations with a powerful and comprehensive guide to managing the mobile transition that evolves them into a successful mobile enterprise. Alacrity is pleased to have used some of the early research output from these processes outlined by Dr. Unhelkar in this book.

Ketan Vanjara, Senior Vice President, SunGard Technology Services,
Pune, India
Mobile technologies and devices are becoming all-pervasive in business and our lives. The enterprise response to this mobile revolution, as well as the convergence of communication, internet, and information technologies, can no longer be restricted to just "m-enabling" some software/applications. A strategic approach is the need of the hour. METM provides a comprehensive, holistic, and structured framework to enterprises willing to leverage this transition for their future growth. The research-based framework is suitable for practitioners and academics alike.

Professor Houman Younessi, Professor of Science, Engineering, and
Management, Assistant Dean of Academic Programs, Rensselaer Polytechnic
Instituteñ Hartford Graduate Campus, Connecticut, United States
The enhanced ability in communication and mobility afforded us by the Internet, and the frameworks and services for which it forms a foundation, have underpinned the most recent of our socioeconomic revolutions, one which is just beginning. Dr. Unhelkarís *Mobile Enterprise Transition and Management* provides a much needed methodological and evidence-based approach to effectively moving enterprises into embracing this revolution and to maintaining, nurturing, and managing them once there. I congratulate Dr. Unhelkar, his collaborators, and Taylor & Francis Group on their efforts for bringing us this important work.

Index